THE SELECTED WORKS OF GORDON TULLOCK

VOLUME 6

Bureaucracy

THE SELECTED WORKS OF GORDON TULLOCK

VOLUME 1 *Virginia Political Economy*

VOLUME 2 *The Calculus of Consent: Logical Foundations of Constitutional Democracy* (with James M. Buchanan)

VOLUME 3 *The Organization of Inquiry*

VOLUME 4 *The Economics of Politics*

VOLUME 5 *The Rent-Seeking Society*

VOLUME 6 *Bureaucracy*

VOLUME 7 *The Economics and Politics of Wealth Redistribution*

VOLUME 8 *The Social Dilemma: Of Autocracy, Revolution, Coup d'Etat, and War*

VOLUME 9 *Law and Economics*

VOLUME 10 *Economics without Frontiers* (includes a cumulative index for the series)

Gordon Tullock

THE SELECTED WORKS OF GORDON TULLOCK

VOLUME 6

Bureaucracy

GORDON TULLOCK

Edited and with an Introduction by

CHARLES K. ROWLEY

Liberty Fund

This book is published by Liberty Fund, Inc., a foundation established to encourage study of the ideal of a society of free and responsible individuals.

The cuneiform inscription that serves as our logo and as the design motif for our endpapers is the earliest-known written appearance of the work "freedom" (*amagi*), or "liberty." It is taken from a clay document written about 2300 B.C. in the Sumerian city-state of Lagash.

Printed in the United States of America

Paperback cover photo courtesy of the
American Economic Review

Frontispiece courtesy of Center for Study of Public Choice,
George Mason University, Fairfax, Virginia

05 17 18 19 20 C 5 4 3 2 1
17 18 19 20 21 P 7 6 5 4 3

Library of Congress Cataloging-in-Publication Data
Tullock, Gordon.
Bureaucracy / Gordon Tullock ; edited and with an introduction by Charles K. Rowley.
p. cm.—(Selected works of Gordon Tullock ; v. 6)
Includes two previously published books by the author: The politics of bureaucracy (1965) and Economic hierarchies, organization and the structure of production (1992).
Includes bibliographical references and index.
ISBN 0-86597-525-6 (alk. paper)—ISBN 0-86597-536-1 (pbk. : alk. paper)
1. Bureaucracy. 2. Public administration. 3. Industrial organization (Economic theory). I. Tullock, Gordon. Politics of bureaucracy. II. Tullock, Gordon. Economic hierarchies, organization and the structure of production. III. Title.
JF1351.T79 2004
302.3′5—dc22 2004048629

LIBERTY FUND, INC.
11301 North Meridian Street
Carmel, Indiana 46032-4564

CONTENTS

INTRODUCTION

The sixth volume in this series, *Bureaucracy* brings together two books by Gordon Tullock, namely, *The Politics of Bureaucracy* and *Economic Hierarchies, Organization and the Structure of Production*. It is important to note that these contributions deal with economic relationships that extend beyond bureaucracy in its narrow definition.[1]

THE INTELLECTUAL ENVIRONMENT IN 1965

In 1965, when Gordon Tullock published *The Politics of Bureaucracy*, the intellectual climate in all western countries was extremely favorable to bureaucracy. Bureaucrats were widely viewed as impartial, even omniscient, servants of the public good, and they were accorded the respect that such an inference demanded, at least among members of the intellectual elite.

Following William Niskanen, bureaus are defined as organizations endowed with the following characteristics: (1) The owners and employees of these organizations do not appropriate any part of the difference between revenues and costs as personal income. (2) Some part of the recurring revenues of the organization derives from other than the sale of output as a per-unit rate.[2] In this sense, bureaus are nonprofit organizations that are financed, at least in part, by a periodic appropriation or grant. This includes most government agencies, most educational institutions, some hospitals, and many forms of social, charitable, and religious organizations. It extends to some component units in profit-seeking organizations, most especially staff units providing such services as advertising, public relations, and research.

The term *bureaucracy* comes with a pejorative flavor, defined as "government by a central administrative group, especially one not accountable to the public." In this sense, as Mancur Olson notes, the study of bureaucracy has to deal with an elemental paradox: the role of bureaucracy has increased dramatically throughout the western democracies in modern times but with-

1. Gordon Tullock, *The Politics of Bureaucracy* (Washington, D.C.: Public Affairs Press, 1965); Gordon Tullock, *Economic Hierarchies, Organization and the Structure of Production* (Boston/Dordrecht/London: Kluwer Academic Publishers, 1992).

2. William A. Niskanen, *Bureaucracy and Representative Government* (Chicago: Aldine-Atherton Press, 1971).

out any evident enthusiasm that ought to be associated with such a rapid expansion.[3]

This tension was very much evident during the early 1960s, when Tullock made his first contribution to the economics of bureaucracy. Tullock's thinking was strongly influenced by earlier contributions by Niccolò Machiavelli, Max Weber, and C. Northcote Parkinson. A brief summary of each of the relevant ideas advanced by these scholars helps us to understand Tullock's writings.

Machiavelli's famous treatise on statecraft, *The Prince*, uncompromisingly outlines the way a prince should govern if he is to maintain his own position and secure his principality from outside aggression.[4] So shocking was his advice to "men of goodwill" during the sixteenth century that Machiavelli was identified with Satan himself.

Machiavelli wanted a strong state, capable of imposing its authority on a badly divided Italy. *The Prince* frankly and amorally acknowledges that successful governments must always be prepared to act ruthlessly to attain their goals. In the final resort, in politics, whether an action is evil or not can be decided only in the light of what it is meant to achieve, and whether it successfully achieves it. For Machiavelli, the ends indisputably justify the means.

> A prince has of necessity to be so prudent that he knows how to escape the evil reputation attached to those vices which could lose him his state, and how to avoid those vices which are not so dangerous, if he possibly can; but, if he cannot, he need not worry much about the latter. And then, he must not flinch from being blamed for vices which are necessary for safeguarding the State. This is because, taking everything into account, he will find that some of the things that appear to be virtues will, if he practises them, ruin him, and some of the things that appear to be vices will bring him security and prosperity.[5]

Machiavelli is equally clear that the successful prince will rule more through the use of fear than of love: "on this question of being loved or feared, I conclude that since some men love as they please but fear when the prince

3. Mancur Olson, "Bureaucracy," in *The New Palgrave: A Dictionary of Economics*, ed. John Eatwell, Murray Milgate, and Peter Newman, vol. 1 (London and New York: Macmillan, 1987), 296–99.

4. Niccolò Machiavelli, *The Prince* (1514; London: Penguin Classics, 1981).

5. Ibid., 92.

pleases, a wise prince should rely on what he controls, not on what he cannot control. He must only endeavor, as I said, to escape being hated."[6] He stresses, also, that the successful prince must take great care to avoid flatterers, in order to ensure that he is well informed on matters of policy.

> The only way to safeguard yourself against flatterers is by letting people understand that you are not offended by the truth; but if everyone can speak the truth to you then you lose respect. So a shrewd prince should adopt a middle way, choosing wise men for his government and allowing only those the freedom to speak the truth to him, and then only concerning matters on which he asks their opinion, and nothing else. But he should also question them thoroughly and listen to what they say; then he should make up his own mind, by himself.[7]

As the reader of this volume will see, this hardheaded approach to statecraft powerfully influences Tullock's analyses of hierarchical relationships within any kind of bureaucracy.

Max Weber's book *Economy and Society*[8] blends ideas drawn from the German historical school of political economy with Weber's own ideas drawn from sociology to provide an original analysis of the strengths and weaknesses of bureaucracy. According to this analysis, a distinctive feature of capitalism is that, as firms grow in size, there is a change in their internal mode of organization, namely, the extension of a hierarchical structure of administration that increasingly resembles the bureaucracy already well established in the political sphere.[9]

In Weber's judgment, the bureaucratic model of administration was increasingly dominant because of its efficiency in performing complex organizational tasks. Associated with this advance was the emergence of a new middle class whose position depended neither on physical capital nor on physical labor, but, rather, on its possession of technical and organizational skills and on its authority position within the bureaucratic hierarchy. Weber had no doubt that members of the bureaucracy selflessly served the goals of their superiors, whether in the private or the public sector.

6. Ibid., 98.

7. Ibid., 126.

8. Max Weber, *Economy and Society* (1922; New York: Bedminster Press, 1968).

9. David Beetham, "Weber, Max (1864–1920)," in *The New Palgrave: A Dictionary of Economics*, vol. 4, 886–88.

Tullock's analyses of bureaucracy and hierarchical structures constitute a direct rational choice attack on Weber's views. In this sense, Weber provided Tullock with the fulcrum from which he would launch his devastating critique at an early stage in the public choice revolution.

"Work expands so as to fill the time available for its completion."[10] With these fateful words, C. Northcote Parkinson, in 1957, launched the modern theory of bureaucracy and challenged at its roots the earlier twentieth-century theory of bureaucracy dominated by Weberian notions of impartial, efficient service by government officials concerned exclusively to serve the public interest as interpreted by their governments.

Parkinson's Law, as it is known, is characterized as a scientific statement identified from detailed statistical analyses, first of British Admiralty data and subsequently of British Colonial Office data, each stretching over an extensive period of time.

The strength of the British navy in 1914 consisted of 146,000 officers and crew, 3,249 dockyard officials and clerks, and 57,000 dockyard workmen. By 1928 the number of warships was a mere fraction of its 1914 strength, with only twenty capital ships under commission compared with sixty-two in 1914. The navy had declined by one-third in men and two-thirds in ships. Its size was limited for the foreseeable future by the Washington Naval Agreement. Yet the number of Admiralty officials had grown at a compound rate of 5.6 percent per annum, providing a "magnificent navy on land."[11]

The administrative staff at the British Colonial Office grew from 372 in 1932 to 1,661 in 1954, despite the major shrinkage of the British Empire as colonies were granted self-government. The compound annual rate of growth throughout this period was remarkably similar to that of Admiralty staff previously analyzed. Parkinson generalized from these two empirical studies that the staff of any public administrative department would grow at an annual percentage rate (X), given by the formula

$$X = 100\ (2k^m + l/yn)$$

where ***k*** represents the number of staff seeking promotion through the appointment of subordinates, where l represents the difference between the ages at appointment and retirement, where ***m*** represents the number of man-hours devoted to answering minutes within the departments, where ***n*** repre-

10. C. Northcote Parkinson, *Parkinson's Law* (New York: Ballantine Books, 1957).

11. Ibid., 9.

sents the number of units being administered, and where y represents the number of original staff.

Fundamentally, Parkinson's Law predicts that staff will increase in any public bureau at an annual rate of between 5.17 and 6.56 percent, "irrespective of any variation in the amount of work (if any) to be done."[12]

The publication of *Parkinson's Law* coincided with a rising undercurrent of popular criticism of bureaucrats on the grounds of laziness and insensitivity to citizens' preferences ("busy loafers," as Nikita Krushchev contemptuously labeled them). Nevertheless, economists obsessed with remedying the alleged failures of private markets and political scientists still wedded to idealized Platonic notions of government simply continued to ignore the writing on the wall.

THE POLITICS OF BUREAUCRACY

Tullock's groundbreaking book, *The Politics of Bureaucracy*, combines the contributions of Machiavelli and Parkinson, together with his own original rational choice approach, into a full-scale attack on the then overwhelming complacency toward bureaucracy of economists, political scientists, and sociologists.

Part 1, consisting of two chapters, introduces key concepts and outlines the methodology of the study.

Tullock uses the term *politics* to describe situations in which the dominant or primary relations are those between superiors and subordinates in a hierarchy. This contrasts with *economic exchange*, in which the dominant or primary relations are between equals. Government employment is the field in which the superior-subordinate relationship is most characteristic. The typical government employee can hope for promotion only by pleasing his superiors. He cannot readily change employers without suffering a personal financial loss. This is the core insight on which Tullock develops his theory of the politics of bureaucracy.

Tullock notes that governmental systems in which a large number of officials are selected on hereditary grounds and hold their positions for life are historically rare. For the most part governmental systems are composed of individuals who may move up or down in the hierarchy depending on merit, broadly determined as performance that pleases their respective superiors. In such circumstances Tullock explains the nature of the bias against morality

12. Ibid., 14.

within hierarchical systems, echoing some of the arguments about how "the worst get on top," advanced earlier by Friedrich von Hayek.[13]

The methodological approach adopted by Tullock is that of "understanding." We understand how others feel or act because we know how we would feel or act under similar circumstances. While recognizing that this approach is not as scientifically prestigious as deploying mathematics and statistical analysis, Tullock makes a strong claim for its implementation within the social sciences.

As Tullock notes, the application of this methodology has a paradoxical consequence. Instead of presenting concrete evidence for his assertions, Tullock appeals to the intuition and experience of the reader. If the reader's intuition leads him to the same conclusion that Tullock reaches, then the reader should be able to accept Tullock's statements, at least in principle, as being true.

Part 2, consisting of eight chapters, introduces the reader to the politician's world.

Because hierarchies differ greatly in detail, although they are always pyramidical in structure, Tullock simplifies analysis by focusing attention on an individual politician as the reference base and classifying other individuals in terms of their relationship to that individual, that is, higher rank, equal rank, or lower rank.

Tullock separates all the individuals with whom the ambitious reference-base politician makes contact into either allies or spectators. Allies are those who are directly involved in struggle for advancement, whether favorable or hostile to his cause. Spectators are all those individuals, whether or not in his hierarchy, who are too removed to be directly involved. Tullock explains why the ambitious politician will cultivate a favorable general reputation among the spectators, and he explains why his relationship with allies will differ, with much more attention paid to those of higher, than to those of equal or lower, status.

The most important category in the politician's world is that of the sovereigns, defined as those individuals who are able to reward or to punish the reference politician, and thus those toward whom he must act in such a manner that they will reward him. Tullock devotes several chapters to analyzing the relationship between sovereign and reference politician and to showing

13. Friedrich von Hayek, *The Road to Serfdom* (Chicago: University of Chicago Press, 1944).

how this relationship changes as the hierarchy varies from the single sovereign to the group sovereign to the multiple sovereign situation. In each case, he analyzes the roles played by the peers of the reference politician. In all these several models, the influence of Machiavelli is clearly evident.

Part 3, consisting of the remaining fourteen short chapters, analyzes the behavior of the reference politician as he looks downward and attempts to ensure that his inferiors perform according to his wishes. I shall focus on three important insights offered in this section of the book.

The first arises in chapter 13, where Tullock critically analyzes Parkinson's Law. He acknowledges that bureaucratic imperialism of the kind outlined by Parkinson does exist in bureaucratic systems. In terms of the broad sweep of history, however, he rejects the notion that such imperialism is inevitable. He claims that the idea has been given more attention than is its due because of the concentration on recent American and European hierarchies where the phenomenon has been pervasive. Where it does exist, he argues that the condition is pathological. The ultimate sovereigns should reward their subordinates in terms of their accomplishments, not in terms of the number of subordinates that they have managed to acquire. Information deficiencies by the ultimate sovereigns is the real explanation of this pattern of bureaucratic imperialism.

This leads Tullock, in chapter 14, directly into a discussion of the nature of the information problem within a hierarchical system. He illustrates by reference to the game of "whispering down the lane," in which an initial message is passed along a chain of individuals and usually ends up with a completely distorted message. The problem is especially serious when the politician at the apex of the hierarchy makes all the final decisions on the basis of information that has moved up several tiers. Tullock's suggested reform is that the ultimate sovereign should structure his bureau along incentive-compatible lines so that decisions made at lower levels are in conformity with his grand design.

The third insight follows in chapter 20, where Tullock addresses the issue of enforcing compliance by subordinates with the instructions that they receive from above. As Tullock points out, if the ultimate sovereign monitors in detail, he will spend all his time on that activity. Tullock's suggested solution is a statistical method of control in which superiors at each level in the hierarchy review specific performances by inferiors, randomly and without prior warning, and in which the ultimate sovereign does the same with his immediate inferiors.

The Politics of Bureaucracy provided the first-ever rational-choice evaluation of the inner workings of a bureau, and it set the scene for the more ambitious modeling and the statistical evaluations that would shortly follow.

ECONOMIC HIERARCHIES, ORGANIZATION AND THE STRUCTURE OF PRODUCTION

In 1992 Tullock returned to the theme that he had left in 1965, basing his new book on a significantly different literature dealing with the theory of the firm, most of which had developed during the intervening period. This second book, in consequence, compares the politics of bureaucracy with the economics of industrial organization and offers new insights into the nature of hierarchical systems that operate under different institutional constraints.

The key insight of the industrial organization literature seized upon by Tullock in *Economic Hierarchies* is the importance of transaction costs for the emergence of firms, for their size, for their market reach, and for their internal organization. The point of departure for this literature is the seminal 1937 paper by Ronald Coase on the nature of the firm.[14]

Before Coase, the firm in economic theory was a shadowy concept, treated as a black box that transformed inputs into outputs and motivated by a desire to maximize profit. Coase made a determined attempt to rectify this weakness both by providing a rationale for the existence of the firm in a free market economy and by explaining the nature of the forces that determine the range of its activities.

Coase noted in his essay that production could conceivably be carried out in a completely decentralized way by means of contracts between individuals. Such transactions, however, are often costly. Firms will emerge to replace market transactions whenever their costs at the margin are less than the costs of carrying out such transactions through the market. The limit to the size and the range of the firm is set where its transaction costs are equal to those of the market. Though neglected for some thirty-five years, this notion of transaction costs would be harnessed during the 1970s and 1980s into a thoroughgoing revision of the theory of firms and markets.[15]

14. Ronald H. Coase, "The Nature of the Firm," *Economica*, n.s. 4 (November 1937): 386–405.

15. Armen Alchian and Harold Demsetz, "Production, Information Costs and Economic Organization," *American Economic Review* 62 (1972): 777–95; Eugene Fama, "Agency Problems and the Theory of the Firm," *Journal of Political Economy* 88 (1980): 288–307; Michael

Tullock draws upon these insights to demonstrate the superior economic efficiency of corporations over government bureaus. Even when corporations are organized as hierarchies, he notes, their efficiency is monitored externally through the capital market and the outside labor market. Takeovers, mergers, buyouts, and sellouts provide flexible mechanisms for the internal reorganization of the inefficient corporation. No such control mechanisms exist to monitor and to reorganize the inefficient bureau. The only mechanism available to the public bureau is that of internal incentives, and these are rarely deployed effectively in practice.

The Politics of Bureaucracy, the first-ever book devoted to the economic analysis of bureaucracy, opened a major field of research that challenged Max Weber's view that bureaucrats are impartial servants of the public good. *Economic Hierarchies, Organization and the Structure of Production* was an early attempt to deploy new insights from industrial organization theory to explain why public bureaus predictably are less efficient than their private corporate counterparts. In complementary fashion, the two books shed light on the complex economic relationships that exist in bureaucracies and the implications those relationships have on the workings of a free society.

CHARLES K. ROWLEY

Duncan Black Professor of Economics, George Mason University

Senior Fellow, James M. Buchanan Center for Political Economy, George Mason University

General Director, The Locke Institute

Jensen and William Meckling, "Theory of the Firm: Managerial Behavior, Agency Costs and Ownership Structure," *Journal of Financial Economics* 3 (1976): 305–60; Oliver Williamson, *Markets and Hierarchies: Analysis and Antitrust Implications* (New York: Free Press, 1975).

The Politics of Bureaucracy

FOREWORD

"It is not from the benevolence of the butcher, the brewer, or the baker, that we expect our dinner, but from their regard to their own interest." This statement is, perhaps, the most renowned in the classic book in political economy, Adam Smith's *Wealth of Nations*. From Smith onwards, the appropriate function of political economy, and political economists, has been that of demonstrating how the market system, as a perfectible social organization, can, and to an extent does, channel the private interests of individuals toward the satisfaction of desires other than their own. Insofar as this cruder instinct of man toward acquisitiveness, toward self-preservation, can be harnessed through the interactions of the market mechanism, the necessity for reliance on the nobler virtues, those of benevolence and self-sacrifice, is minimized. This fact, as Sir Dennis Robertson has so eloquently reminded us, gives the economist a reason for existing, and his "warning bark" must be heeded by those decision makers who fail to recognize the need for economizing on "love."

Despite such warning barks (and some of these have sounded strangely like shouts of praise), the politicians for many reasons have, over the past century, placed more and more burden of organized social activity on political, governmental processes. As governments have been called upon to do more and more important things, the degree of popular democratic control over separate public or governmental decisions has been gradually reduced. In a real sense, Western societies have attained universal suffrage only after popular democracy has disappeared. The electorate, the ultimate sovereign, must, to an extent not dreamed of by democracy's philosophers, be content to choose its leaders. The ordinary decisions of government emerge from a bureaucracy of ever-increasing dimensions. Non-governmental and quasi-governmental bureaucracies have accompanied the governmental in its growth. The administrative hierarchy of a modern corporate giant differs less from the federal bureaucracy than it does from the freely contracting tradesman envisaged by Adam Smith.

This set, this drift, of history toward bigness, both in "public" and in "private" government, has caused many a cowardly scholar to despair and to seek escape by migrating to a dreamworld that never was. It has caused other "downstream" scholars to snicker with glee at the apparent demise of man, the individual. In this book, by contrast, Tullock firmly grasps the nettle offered by the modern bureaucratic state. In effect, he says: "If we must have bureaucratic bigness, let us, at the least, open our eyes to its inner workings. Man does not simply cease to exist because he is submerged in an administrative hierarchy. He remains an individual, with individual motives, impulses, and desires." This seems a plausible view of things. But, and surprisingly, we find that few theorists of bureaucracy have started from this base. Much of administrative theory, ancient or modern, is based on the contrary view that man becomes as a machine when he is placed within a hierarchy, a machine that faithfully carries out the orders of its superiors who act for the whole organization in reaching policy decisions. Tullock returns us to Adam Smith's statement, and he rephrases it as follows: "It is not from the benevolence of the bureaucrat that we expect our research grant or our welfare check, but out of his regard to his own, not the public interest."

Adam Smith and the economists have been, and Tullock will be, accused of discussing a world peopled with evil and immoral men. Men "should not" be either "getting and spending" or "politicking." Such accusations, and they never cease, are almost wholly irrelevant. Some social critics simply do not like the world as it is, and they refuse to allow the social scientist, who may not like it either, to analyze reality. To the scientist, of course, analysis must precede prescription, and prescription must precede improvement. The road to Utopia must start from here, and this road cannot be transversed until here is located, regardless of the beautiful descriptions of yonder. Tullock's analysis is an attempt to locate the "here" in the real, existing world of modern bureaucracy. His assumptions about behavior in this world are empirical, not ethical. He is quite willing to leave the test of his model to the reader and to future scholars. If, in fact, men in modern bureaucracy do not seek "more" rather than "less," measured in terms of their own career advancement, when they are confronted with relevant choices, Tullock would readily admit the failure of his model to be explanatory in other than some purely tautological sense.

When it is admitted, as all honesty suggests, that some individuals remain individuals, even in a bureaucratic hierarchy, Tullock's analysis assumes meaning. It provides the basis for discussing seriously the prospects for improving the "efficiency" of these bureaucratic structures in accomplishing the tasks assigned to them. There are two stages in any assessment of the efficiency of organizational hierarchies, just as there are in the discussions of the efficiency of the market organization. First, there must be a description, an explanation, a theory, of the behavior of the individual units that make up the structure. This theory, as in the theory of markets, can serve two purposes, and, because of this, methodological confusion is compounded. Such an explanatory, descriptive theory of individual behavior can serve a normative purpose, can provide a guide to the behavior of an individual unit which accepts the objectives or goals postulated in the analytical model. In a wholly different sense, however, the theory can serve a descriptive, explanatory function in a positive manner, describing the behavior of the average or representative unit, without normative implications *for* behavior of any sort. This important distinction requires major stress here. It has never been fully clarified in economic theory, where the contrast is significantly sharper than in the nascent political theory that Tullock and a few others are currently attempting to develop.

The analogy with the theory of the firm is worth discussing in some detail here. This theory of the firm, an individual unit in the organized market economy, serves two purposes. It may, if properly employed, serve as a guide to a firm that seeks to further the objectives specified in the model. As such, the theory of the firm falls wholly outside economics, political economy, and, rather, falls within business administration or managerial science. Essentially the same analysis may, however, be employed, by the economist, as a descriptive theory that helps the student of market organization to understand the workings of this system which is necessarily composed of individual units.

Tullock's theory of the behavior of the individual "politician" in bureaucracy can be, and should be, similarly interpreted. Insofar as such units, the "politicians," accept the objectives postulated—in this case, advancement in this administrative hierarchy—Tullock's analysis can serve as a "guide" to the ambitious bureaucrat. To think primarily of the analysis in this light would, in my view, be grossly misleading. Instead the analysis of the behavior of the individual politician should be treated as descriptive and explanatory, and its validity should be sought in its ability to assist us in the understanding of the operation of bureaucratic systems generally.

Once this basic theory of the behavior of the individual unit is constructed, it becomes possible to begin the construction of a theory of the inclusive system, which is composed of a pattern of interactions among the individual units. By the nature of the systems with which he works, administrative hierarchies, Tullock's "theory of organization" here is less fully developed than is the analogous "theory of markets." A more sophisticated theory may be possible here, and, if so, Tullock's analysis can be an important helpmate to whoever chooses to elaborate it.

Finally, the important step can be taken from positive analysis to normative prescription, not for the improvement of the strategically-oriented behavior of the individual unit directly, but for the improvement in the set of working rules that describe the organization. This step, which must be the ultimate objective of all social science, can be taken only after the underlying theory has enabled the observer to make some comparisons among alternatives. The last half of this book is primarily devoted to the development of such norms for "improving" the functioning of organizational hierarchies.

Tullock's "politician" is, to be sure, an "economic" man of sorts. No claim is made, however, that this man, this politician, is wholly descriptive of the real world. More modestly, Tullock suggests (or should do so, if he does not) that the reference politician is an ideal type, one that we must recognize as being always a part of reality, although he does not, presumably, occupy existing bureaucratic structures to the exclusion of all other men. One of Tullock's primary contributions, or so it appears to me, lies in his ability to put flesh and blood on the bureaucratic man, to equip him with his own power to make decisions, to take action. Heretofore, theorists of bureaucracy, to my knowledge, have not really succeeded in peopling their hierarchies. What serves to motivate the bureaucrat in modern administrative theory? I suspect that one must search at some length to find an answer that is as explicit as that provided by Tullock. Because explicit motivation is introduced, a model containing predictive value can be built, and the predictions can be conceptually refuted by appeal to evidence. It is difficult to imagine how a "theory" of bureaucracy in any meaningful sense could be begun in any other way.

By implication, my comments to this point may be interpreted to mean that Tullock's approach to a theory of administration is an "economic" one, and that the most accurate shorthand description of this book would be to say that it represents an "economist's" approach to bureaucracy. This would be, in one sense, correct, but at the same time such a description would tend to cloud over and subordinate Tullock's second major contribution. This lies in his sharp dichotomization of the "economic" and the "political" relationships among men. Since this book is devoted almost exclusively to an examination of the "political" relationship, it has little that is "economic" in its content. It represents an economist's approach to the political relationship among individuals. This is a more adequate summary, but this, too, would not convey to the prospective reader who is unfamiliar with Tullock's usage of the particular words the proper scope of the analysis. I have, in the discussion above, tried to clarify the meaning of the economist's approach. There remains the important distinction between the "economic" and the "political" relationship.

This distinction is, in one sense, the central theme of the book. In a foreword, it is not proper to quarrel with an author's usage, but synonyms are sometimes helpful in clearing away ambiguities. Tullock distinguishes, basically, between the relationship of *exchange*, which he calls the economic, and the relationship of *slavery*, which he calls the political. I use bold words here, but I do so deliberately. In its pure or ideal form, the superior-inferior relationship is that of the master and the slave. If the inferior has no alternative means of improving his own well-being other than through pleasing his superior, he is, in fact, a "slave," pure and simple. This remains true quite independent of the particular institutional constraints that may or may not inhibit the behavior of the superior. It matters not whether the superior can capitalize the human personality of the inferior and market him as an asset. Interestingly enough, the common usage of the word "slavery" refers to an institutional structure in which exchange was a dominant relationship. In other words, to the social scientist at any rate, the mention of "slavery" calls to mind the exchange process, with the things exchanged being "slaves." The word itself does not particularize the relationship between master and slave at all. Thus, as with so many instances in Tullock's book, we find no words that describe adequately the relationships that he discusses. Examples, however, serve to clarify. Would I be less a "slave" if you, as my master, could not exchange me, provided only that I have no alternative source of income? My income may depend exclusively on my pleasing you, my master, despite the fact that you, too, may be locked into the relationship. "Serfdom," as distinct from "slavery," may be a more descriptive term, especially since Tullock finds many practical examples for his analysis in feudal systems.

The difficulty in explaining the "political" relationship in itself attests to the importance of Tullock's analysis, and, as he suggests, the whole book can be considered a definition of this relationship. The sources of the difficulty are apparent. First of all, the "political" relationship is not commonly encountered in its pure form, that of abject slavery as noted above. By contrast, its counterpart, the economic or exchange relationship, is, at least conceptually, visualized in its pure form, and, in certain instances, the relationship actually exists. This amounts to saying that, without quite realizing what we are doing, we think of ourselves as free men living in a free society. The economic relationship comes more or less naturally to us as the appropriate organizational arrangement through which cooperative endeavor among individuals is carried forward in a social system. Unconsciously, we rebel at the idea of ourselves in a slave or serf culture, and we refuse, again unconsciously, to face up to the reality that, in fact, many of our relationships with our fellows are "political" in the Tullockian sense. Only this blindness toward reality can explain the failure of modern scholars to have developed a more satisfactory theory of individual behavior in hierarchic structures. This also explains why Tullock has found it necessary to go to the Eastern literature and to the discussions in earlier historical epochs for comparative analysis.

Traditional economic analysis can be helpful in illustrating this fundamental distinction between the economic and the political relationship. A seller is in a purely economic relationship with his buyers when he confronts a number of them, any one of which is prepared to purchase his commodity or service at the established market price. He is a slave to no single buyer, and he need "please" no one, provided only that he performs the task for which he contracts, that he "delivers the goods." By contrast, consider the seller who confronts a single buyer with no alternative buyer existent. In this case, the relationship becomes wholly "political." The price becomes exclusively that which the economist calls "pure rent," since, by hypothesis, the seller has no alternative use to which he can put his commodity or service. He is, thus, at the absolute mercy of the single buyer. He is, in fact, a "slave" to this buyer, and he must "please" in order to secure favorable terms, in order to advance his own welfare. Note here that the domestic servant who contracts "to please" a buyer of his services may, in fact, remain in a predominantly economic relationship if a sufficient number of alternative buyers for his services exist, whereas the corporation executive who supervises a sizeable number of people may be in a predominantly political relationship with his own superior. To the economist, Tullock provides a discussion of the origins of economic rent, and a theory of the relationship between the recipient and the donor of economic rent.

Tullock's distinction here can also be useful in discussing an age-old philosophical dilemma. When is a man confronted with a free choice? The traveler's choice between giving up his purse and death, as offered to him by the highwayman, is, in reality, no choice at all. Yet philosophers have found it difficult to define explicitly the line that divides situations into categories of free and unfree or coerced choices. One approach to a possible classification here lies in the extent to which individual response to an apparent choice situation might be predicted by an external observer. If, in fact, the specific action of the individual, confronted with an apparent choice, is predictable within narrow limits, no effective choosing or deciding process could take place. By comparison, if the individual response is not predictable with a high degree of probability, choice can be defined as being effectively free. By implication, Tullock's analysis would suggest that individual action in a political relationship might be somewhat more predictable than individual action in the economic relationship because of the simple fact that, in the latter, there exist alternatives. If this implication is correctly drawn, the possibilities of developing a predictive "science" of "politics" would seem to be inherently greater than those of developing a science of economics. Yet we observe, of course, that economic theory has an established and legitimate claim to the position as being the only social science with genuine predictive value. The apparent paradox here is explained by the generality with which the economist can apply his criteria for measuring the results of individual choice. Through his ability to bring many results within the "measuring rod of money," the economist is able to make reasonably accurate predictions about the behavior of "average" or "representative" men; behavior that, in individual cases, stems from unconstrained, or free, choices. Only through this possibility of relying on representative individuals can economics be a predictive science; predictions about the behavior of individually identifiable human beings are clearly impossible except in rare instances. By contrast, because his choice is less free, the behavior of the individual politican in a bureaucratic hierarchy can be predicted with somewhat greater accuracy than the behavior of the individual in the marketplace. But there exist no general, quantitatively measurable criteria that will allow the external observer to test hypotheses about political behavior. There exists no measuring rod for bureaucratic advancement comparable to the economist's money scale. For these reasons, hypotheses about individual behavior are more important in Tullock's analysis, and the absence of external variables that are subject to quantification makes the refutation of positive hypotheses difficult in the extreme. For assistance here, Tullock introduces a simple, but neglected, method. He asks the reader whether or not his own experience leads him to accept or to reject the hypotheses concerning the behavior of the politician in bureaucracy.

Tullock makes no attempt to conceal from view his opinion that large hierarchical structures are, with certain explicit exceptions, unnecessary evils, that these are not appropriate parts of the good society. A unique value of the book lies, however, in the fact that this becomes more than mere opinion, more than mere expression of personal value judgments. The emphasis is properly placed on the need for greater scientific analysis. Far too often social scientists have, I fear, introduced explicit value judgments before analysis should have ceased. Ultimately, of course, discussion must reduce to values, but when it does so it is done. If the indolent scholar relies on an appeal to values at the outset, his role in genuine discussion is, almost by definition, eliminated.

The bureaucratic world that Tullock pictures for us is not an attractive one, even when its abstract character is recognized, and even if the reference politician of that world is not assigned the dominant role in real life. Those of us who accept the essential ethics of the free society find this world difficult to think about, much less to discuss critically and to evaluate. External events, however, force us to the realization that this is, to a large extent, the world in which we now live. The ideal society of freely contracting "equals," always a noble fiction, has, for all practical purposes, disappeared, even as a norm in this age of increasing collectivization: political, economic, and philosophical.

Faced with this reality, the libertarian need not despair. The technology of the twentieth century has made small organizations inefficient in many respects, and the Jeffersonion image of the free society can never be realized. However, just as the critics of the laissez-faire economic order were successful in their efforts to undermine the public faith in the functioning of the invisible hand, the new critics of the emerging bureaucratic order can be successful in undermining an equally naive faith in the benevolence of governmental bureaucracy. Tullock's analysis, above all else, arouses the reader to an awareness of the inefficiencies of large hierarchical structures, independent of the presumed purposes or objectives of these organizations. The benevolent despot image of government, that seems now to exist in the minds of so many men, is effectively shattered.

Genuine progress toward the reform of social institutions becomes possible when man learns that the ideal order of affairs is neither the laissez-faire dream of Herbert Spencer nor the benevolent despotism image of an "economy under law" espoused by Mr. W. H. Ferry of the Center for the Study of Democratic Institutions. Man in the West, as well as in the East, must learn that governments, even governments by the people, can do so many things poorly, and many things not at all. If this very simple fact could be more widely recognized by the public at large (the ultimate sovereign in any society over the long run), a genuinely free society of individuals and groups might again become a realizable goal for the organization of man's cooperative endeavors. We do not yet know the structure of this society, and we may have to grope our way along for decades. Surely and certainly, however, man must cling to that uniquely important discovery of modern history, the discovery of man, the individual human being. If we abandon or forget this discovery, and allow ourselves to be drawn along any one of the many roads to serfdom by false gods, we do not deserve to survive.

James M. Buchanan

PART I

INTRODUCTION

CHAPTER I

WHAT THIS BOOK IS ABOUT

The perfectly good word "politics" has an extremely broad range of meaning. We speak of "national politics," "bureaucratic politics," "army politics," and "corporation politics"; and we know that the word "politician" refers to an individual with particular characteristics in any one of these organizational settings. Any general theory about politics should have some relevance for each of these organizational structures. Traditionally, national politics—which includes the activities of the President, the Congress, and the Supreme Court—has commanded much wider interest than, say, army politics, or any one of the other types alluded to above. Surely political activity, as such, is quantitatively far more significant in almost any of the major hierarchial structures that characterize large organizations than it is among the strictly limited group of individuals assumed to be engaged in national politics at any one time. Traditional political theory seems to have neglected, in a relative sense, this extremely important "politics of bureaucracy," or "politics at the lower level." This book is designed to help redress this imbalance.

"Politics" is also used with reference to "policies" carried out in collective decision processes. This aspect will not be discussed at length in this book. Substantive matters of policy will be employed in illustrating various principles, but the primary concern here will be on the organizational and administrative aspects. In fact the only implications for policy, *per se*, that may be drawn from the analysis relate to the inherent limitations that administrative and organizational constraints place upon the choice of policies. No government should undertake action that is impossible of accomplishment, and we shall see that some conceivable policies are administratively impossible and, for this reason, must be avoided.

With this limitation, the usage of the word "politics" in these pages will be in general agreement with that of ordinary speech. It will not be absolutely identical with the usual meaning of the word, because we will follow a slightly different way of looking at the political relationship and at political behavior. Any writer who uses a word in a new or different way, even if the difference is slight, should give a full definition of the sense in which he uses the term. Unfortunately, I cannot follow this wholly desirable principle with my usage of the word "politics." In one sense, the book itself is my definition.

The general differentiating features of the relationships or the behavior covered by the term can, however, be briefly described. *Generally speaking, "politics" describes social situations in which the dominant or primary relations are those between superior and subordinate.*

POLITICS AND ECONOMICS

This general meaning can perhaps best be clarified by comparison and contrast with "economics." The latter, as a discipline, describes social situations in which persons deal with one another as freely contracting equals. Or, to put the statement more carefully, it describes situations in which such relations are primary or dominant. Pure cases may be difficult to locate, but they undoubtedly exist. The organized commodity and stock markets are examples. Most economic exchange takes place under conditions which more or less approximate the ideal, at least sufficiently so to insure the validity of models based on the analysis of pure types. To take an example which is perhaps more controversial than any other, the ordinary laborer in the United States, although he may receive much less than his more highly skilled fellow employees, is free to change his employment as he sees fit, and, under normal circumstances, his employer is equally free to dismiss him. Insofar as the alternatives for employment are limited, and the shifting of either jobs or employees involves costs, the secondary, or "political," relationship enters even here. But, so long as available alternatives remain open, the basic relationship must be described as economic not political.

In the higher reaches of management, by comparison, politics becomes considerably more important. The "market" for corporation executives is very poorly organized. A man who resigns a position in one company may spend a considerable period of time before he secures employment with another firm, and even then he may have to be content with a less satisfactory position. One need not feel particularly sorry for executives because of this fact, but it should be recognized that, vis-à-vis the market for their services, they are in a rather different position from that which confronts the ordinary laborer who is far below them in rank and income. The most obvious empirical verification of this difference is the degree of deference shown to superiors. The common laborer, contractually, is required to obey the orders of a foreman or supervisor. If we disregard the existence of labor unions (and the larger part of the American labor force is non-union), the foreman is strictly limited in the demands that he can make on his men, because he knows that the latter can always change employers. A company that desires to treat its laborers in an arbitrary way must expect to have to pay relatively higher wages than its competitors. As one moves up the managerial pyramid, however, this relative independence of the employee becomes less and less pronounced. Managerial politics vary tremendously, but many executives of large corporations make use of the fact that officers directly beneath them must look to them for promotion (or security against demotion) and that these officers would have difficulty in changing positions. As a result, one observes a degree of personal servility in these higher-paid executives that no foreman could ever expect to secure from an ordinary laborer.

Government employment is the field in which the superior-subordinate relationship is most characteristic. For some employees transfer to non-government employment is relatively easy, but for the bulk of government employees the making of such a shift would involve significant personal sacrifice. The typical government employee, in a strictly "political" relationship, can hope for promotion only by pleasing his superiors. If he displeases them, or if they simply come to dislike him, his career opportunities are severely restricted. He cannot readily change employers. A transfer to another department or bureau may be difficult to arrange. Most civil servants, especially at the higher levels, are, therefore, committed to a career of finding out what their superiors want (frequently not an easy task) and doing it in the hope that these superiors will then reward such behavior with promotions. In the United States civil service, the individual career employee is generally not expected to put up with quite so much "pushing around" by superiors as he might endure in the higher ranks of some large corporations. To balance this, he will also be receiving less salary, and he will probably find that the orders which he is expected to implement are less rational than those he could expect to receive in private industry.

Again we need not pity the individual in the bureaucratic hierarchy. He is frozen in his present employment only to the extent that he is unwilling to accept the personal financial sacrifice necessary to get out. There are parts of the government service, particularly the armed services, where it might be extremely difficult, and sometimes (in war) impossible, for the employee to quit. In such cases, economic considerations hardly enter at all. Alternatives are unimportant in influencing behavior.

For political relations of a pure or ideal type, unmixed with any economic considerations, we must leave the United States. The "plural society" is a historical oddity. Throughout most of history, the greater part of the world has been subject to "monolithic" regimes. Under such regimes,[1] instead of many more or less independent (although interacting) organizations, there exists only a single gigantic organizational structure which controls, or attempts to control, all aspects of social life. The unity of such a structure is more a matter of theory than of practice. It is as impossible for the Russian praesidium to control completely all aspects of Soviet life as it was for the Chinese emperor to do the same for the vast population of China. Nevertheless, these systems are completely unitary in theory, and, for some purposes, must be analyzed as such.[2]

In almost all real-world situations, there are some elements of both the economic and the political relationship. The art of salesmanship, so highly developed in twentieth-century America, is largely an effort to apply political methods to what is essentially the economic relationship of exchange. The salesman applies to his customer the same arts that are used by the courtier on his ruler. (The customer is always "sirred" in retail establishments.) In the ordinary economic transaction, however, despite the apparent inferiority of the seller to be inferred from his outward behavior, the relationship is one between equals. Conversely, even in imperial China a high-ranking civil servant who became sufficiently fed up with court life could usually escape, either by "retiring" or, in extreme cases, by committing suicide (many did). But the existence of such alternatives hardly served to make the system one in which free contractual relationships among individuals could be said to have existed.

Summarizing, we can say that economic theory is based on the assumption that the central behavioral relationship to be analyzed is that among

1. Karl Wittfogel's *Oriental Despotism*, Yale, 1956, is the most complete catalogue of the various types of monolithic regimes which have ruled the bulk of the world's population through most of history. It should be noted that feudalism, which immediately preceded the modern system in Europe, is, from the standpoint of world history, just as much of a deviation from the "norm" as is modern capitalistic democracy.

2. This theoretical unity can be illustrated by the fact that, in classical China, when the district magistrate visited a household, protocol required that he, rather than the head of the family, serve as host. For the individual who found himself in such a system, advancement, and indeed in some cases life itself, depended solely on the favor of his superiors. Due to administrative defects, he might have had, in practice, some choice as among superiors, but such freedom was severely restricted and declined progressively as the top of the system was approached. Obviously, in such systems, it would be absurd to speak of a contractual relationship between an individual and his "employer."

freely contracting individuals. This relationship is recognized to be an approximation of reality rather than an accurate description in all but a few limiting cases. Economic theory abstracts from the other aspects of the human relationship, and studies its own limited part of reality.

There are important areas for which the economist's assumptions are clearly inapplicable, notably the governmental bureaucracy. In the monolithic societies that have dominated much of the world throughout its history the analysis of markets has relatively little application. Here the dominant relationship is that between superior and inferior. It is this type of social relationship, this type of social situation, that this book will discuss. As with economic theory, the analysis here will abstract from other aspects of reality. In almost any real-world situation, the superior will realize that he does not possess complete dominance over the subordinate. Alternatives for the latter do exist, and if the superior overplays his role, the inferior may withdraw from the relationship. The penalties of withdrawing may, however, be large, so large that few human beings would be willing to incur them.

METHODOLOGY

In the field of social studies, it is the fashion to begin with a methodological discussion. I shall follow this fashion, but not because my methods are particularly complex. On the contrary, methodologically, this book is quite simple. I have tried to employ the method that seemed to me best suited to getting at the truth in each particular instance. This, unfortunately, leads to frequent use of a method that is frowned on by many modern social scientists. I shall, for this reason, explain briefly why I consider this particular method to be a respectable means of reaching the truth in appropriate situations.

We have, basically, three ways of finding things out. First there is mathematics, or pure abstract thought. In a sense this is an exploration of the logical categories of the human mind. A second method is observation of our environment, a category which includes the "highly scientific" processes of experiment and investigation carried on in laboratories. The third method of finding things out I should like to call, with Max Weber, "understanding." In a sense this is as introspective as mathematics. We understand how others feel or act, because we know how we would act or feel under similar circumstances. This method, used by practically everyone in everyday life, is not applicable to the physical sciences for obvious reasons. In investigating the properties of a chemical, little progress can be made by saying to yourself: "If I were sodium hydroxide, what would I do?" It can be applied, in a very limited way, in zoology, particularly in dealing with the animals more closely related to man, but its principal sphere of usefulness is obviously in the study of human beings. In recent years students of human phenomena have sometimes tried to avoid the use of this tool. This appears to spring from a misunderstanding of the situation. The physical scientists, and particularly the physicists, have established positions of great prestige in the present-day learned world. For the reasons given above, they make almost no use of "understanding" in their work. From this a number of "social scientists," anxious to establish their claim to be *real* scientists, have deduced that this method is "unscientific" and to be avoided.

Except for the questionable purpose of gaining social prestige within a university faculty, however, there seems to be no good reason for deliberately refusing to employ this method of investigating human behavior. The fact that the social scientist can use this tool which is unavailable to the physical scientist should be considered an advantage. This is not to suggest the abandonment of other methods. The problems are difficult, and the discarding of any tool that may assist in their solution would be unwise.

The use of this approach or method has, however, a strange, even paradoxical, consequence. For a number of the assertions that will be made in this book, the supporting evidence must be found in the mind of the reader. That is to say, instead of presenting concrete evidence, I shall simply try to convince the skeptical reader by appealing to his own intuition and experience. I shall offer examples of [selected] types of behavior, not to prove particular points, but simply to explain the points better to the reader so that he may judge whether human beings, in general, behave in the manner that I suggest. If his "understanding" leads him to the same conclusion that I have reached in a particular case, he can then accept my statement of the principle as being true.

CHAPTER 2

PRELIMINARIES

Broadly speaking, the term "social mobility" should be interpreted to include all changes of status by individuals in a social system. Normally, however, the term is used only with reference to vertical changes. An improvement or worsening of a person's position in the society by shifts up or down the vertical scale is the typical example of the concept. There is no known society in which this sort of change is completely prohibited, although mobility is severely restricted in several societies, Hindu India being perhaps the classic example. Even there, the restrictions merely imposed a ceiling and (less securely) a floor on the space within which a given person could move in the social structure. At the opposite extreme to such "closed" societies are "open" societies in which there is, theoretically, no limit to the extent to which an individual may rise or fall. Present-day United States is a good example, although, of course, there are real limits even here. No Negro is likely to be elected President in the very near future. Most societies fall somewhere in between these extremes, with the individual having less freedom to rise and fall within the social structure than in the United States and more freedom than in classical India.

Social mobility has been analyzed from many points of view by numerous writers. As might be expected, American students think that the "open" society is desirable, while some of those scholars accustomed to a more closed system feel that too much mobility may be undesirable. I shall not be concerned with this problem as such, but rather with some of the consequences which may be expected to emerge when vertical mobility is present in a large organization.

MERIT SYSTEMS

Governmental systems in which a large number of officials are selected on hereditary grounds and hold their posts for life are unusual historically. Normally governmental machines have been composed of people who may move up or down in the hierarchy. The higher officials are simply people who have been exceptionally successful. In most historical cases of bureaucratic systems in which mobility is normal, advancement is the result of conscious selection by somebody in terms of some characteristics which are thought desirable.

We shall call promotion by such a conscious choice "merit" selection. In our usage "merit" will have an extremely broad meaning. Democratic election of officials will be one example, since this is selection by someone, in terms of some characteristics thought desirable; so will ordinary promotion procedures in such a bureaucracy as the Department of State. As an extreme example, the degenerate king who selects his ministers in terms of their attractiveness as drinking companions is also exercising merit selection in our sense of the term. "Merit" then, in our sense, has no moral connotations. A merit selection system, however, will function in certain ways regardless of the criteria used for promotion or demotion.

As an analogy to the functioning of this system, let us consider what was until recently the largest single industrial installation in the world: the gaseous diffusion plant at Oak Ridge, Tennessee. This plant, erected to separate U 235 from U 237, makes use of the fact that if two gases of different weights are diffused through a porous barrier, the lighter will pass through faster. The mechanism consists of a series of chambers separated by such barriers. The uranium, in the form of uranium hexafluoride gas, is introduced into one of these chambers. Part of it passes through the porous barrier into the next chamber, and this part will be slightly richer in U 235 than was the original gas. Similarly the portion of the gas which did not pass the barrier will be slightly richer in U 237. Since the weights of U 235 and U 237 are close, and since the gas takes part of its weight from the fluorine, the change in concentration at each passage of a barrier is very small. The separating chambers are thus arranged into "cascades," a long series of such chambers in each of which the concentration of U 235 is slightly increased. At the end of the process practically pure U 235 (hexafluoride) is produced.

The process has a further complication. At each stage the concentration of U 235 is increased in the chamber into which the gas diffuses; it is also, obviously, reduced in the chamber from which the diffusion takes place. Since there is still some U 235 in the second chamber, an elaborate system was devised for this gas to be reintroduced into the cascade at an earlier point where its concentration of U 235 and the concentration in the main body of gas are identical. The system was then extended, backward so to speak, to deal with gas which, as a result of the diffusion process, had a considerably lower concentration of U 235 than is normally found in uranium. Thus, while the system produces practically pure U 235 at one end, it produces at the other a mixture of U 235 and U 237 which is much richer in U 237 than is natural uranium.

Any political hierarchy in which personnel are selected for promotion by the system we have designated "merit" will function in much the same way. People entering the system are either a random selection or the result of a preliminary selection process. Once they are in the system, they are confronted with a number of situations in which they may either rise, remain in the same position, or fall. These "test" situations do not necessarily refer to formal promotions in the bureaucratic hierarchy. There are usually numerous smaller steps which prepare the way for formal promotion or demotion. The obtaining of a good assignment, earning the confidence of your superiors, getting a "good name around the office," all may be equated to the porous barriers of the gaseous diffusion plant. As in the gaseous diffusion plant, failure to make a given advance is seldom final, and any advance simply puts the man in a position where he will once again be subject to a further separation process. A drop in rank, an unfortunate assignment, merely returns the man to a position where he, in company with others who are in that lower position, will have further opportunities to rise (or fall). He remains in the machine, except in extreme cases, and continues to be tested regularly with rises and falls in his position resulting from these tests.

Selection in a political hierarchy is seldom for anything as simple and unchanging as atomic weight. Usually the "barriers" will select for a large number of different characteristics, and these characteristics will vary from time to time and from place to place within the machine. As a result, the process is never as mechanical as in the gaseous diffusion plant. Partly this is the result of the problems inevitably raised by attempts to judge human beings, but partly it is the result of the fact that the political machine, unlike the gaseous diffusion plant, is normally not designed for the simple end of selection, but as an apparatus for doing something else.

"SUCCESS" CHARACTERISTICS

Although we are primarily interested in political structures, what we have to say about systems permitting social mobility is relevant to any such system, not only to hierarchies. It is true, for example, of any capitalistic economy which permits free rise and fall of individuals. It is true of the academic community, where an individual may rise and fall both in his position in a given university and in his reputation within the wider community. All of these systems, in effect, separate people according to various characteristics. Usually the characteristics affecting selection are complex and varying, but we can derive a few general statements on the type of characteristics which will lead to "success" in any such system.

The most obvious characteristic for which any system will select is a desire to rise or ambition. This should not be misunderstood; almost everyone wants to succeed. The degree of intensity of this desire, however, varies considerably. People are continually confronted with choices between various courses of action. Their action will frequently be affected by the intensity of their desire for various ends, each one of which may be separately desirable. An individual who really would like to make a million dollars may, nevertheless, decide to go fishing instead of working. This is an unduly simple illustration, but it will serve to indicate the effect of weak ambition. Going fishing once would have only a slight effect, but anyone who devotes the bulk of his time to this pastime will not rise very high in the business community. Any individual in any system will continually be confronted with choices between courses of action which will have at least some favorable effect on his chances and others which are less desirable from that point of view, but which have other advantages. Only the person who usually chooses in terms of his "career" will be likely to rise to the top.

There are some systems, particularly religious hierarchies, where humbleness and lack of ambition are considered to be desirable for the holders of high office. This undoubtedly provides some barrier to success for the man who very much wants to succeed. If it were possible to select in such terms, then the system using this principle of selection would be headed largely by men who had no great desire to be in their exalted positions. In most systems which purport to use such criteria, however, a more accurate statement would be that they select for high position in terms of outward signs of humbleness and lack of ambition. An ambitious and intelligent man, who finds himself in such a system, will normally be better able to convince bystanders of his humbleness and lack of ambition than would a genuinely humble man who would have no particular motive for display.

This brings us, naturally, to intelligence. Almost any system in which social mobility with merit selection is permitted will select for intelligence. The most intelligent members of the community, or at least those among them who are highly ambitious, will be better at figuring out what is necessary to rise in the system than will their less well endowed fellows. It should be noted that by "intelligence" I do not mean "what the intelligence test tests" (whatever that is), but the ability to make "correct" decisions. The ability to make up one's mind is as crucial as the ability to think accurately. Hamlet is the classic example of a man who was not lacking in mental acumen, but who could not make up his mind.

It is sometimes said that a high intelligence and a high level of information about any difficult problem are likely to lead to inaction; that decisions are usually made by people who are, intellectually, not quite top drawer. It seems to me that the ability to make decisions may well be combined with a highly perceptive intelligence. In any event, for our purposes, only the decisions a man makes are counted in deciding whether he is or is not intelligent. If he normally makes incorrect decisions, or if he frequently just can't make up his mind, he will lose out in competition with others who make correct decisions. The reasons for the man's failure to make up his mind may, in fact, be an "intelligence" which sees disadvantages in every course, but he will not rise as rapidly as another man who was quicker to make decisions.

It should be noted that intelligence, in this connection, differs in another way from what might be expected. The man who makes the most intelligent decisions and rises most rapidly in a military hierarchy will not necessarily be a brilliant tactician. Decisions, in our sense, are intelligent not because they conform to the ostensible objective of the particular organization, but because they will, in fact, advance the career of the person making them.

INDIVIDUAL AND ORGANIZATIONAL GOALS

There is no necessary conflict between action that will advance the "purposes" of an organization, and action that will advance the career of a single member of that organization. It is conceivable that an ambitious and intelligent man might never have to choose between two courses of action, one of which would promote the attainment of the objectives for which the organization is created, and the other of which would advance his own personal objectives. In most cases, however, there will arise situations in which the individual will be confronted with this choice. The frequency of occurrence of such situations will vary, both with the task that the individual is called upon to perform and the organizational efficiency of the hierarchical structure in which he is located.

An obvious requirement for efficient administration is that the opportunities to make such choices be minimized. When a member of a hierarchy takes a course of action that is best for his own career but that is not best for the achievement of the objectives of the organization, two major disadvantages are to be noted. First, at the very least, organizational goal achievement is not maximized. Second, the concentration of people near the top of the hierarchy who are not particularly interested in the "function" of the organization is increased. To return to the gaseous diffusion plant analogy, the barriers act so as to select by criteria that are not only irrelevant from the standpoint of the designers, but which will, in the future, result in even poorer performance and selection.

"EFFICIENCY" IN ORGANIZATION

Let us consider two hypothetical individuals. One of these, A, is interested solely in his own career; the other, B, is interested only in the objectives of the organization in which he finds himself. Both are highly intelligent in their judgments of the consequences of their decisions. In the ideal or perfect administrative structure, each individual would take the *same* course of action in equivalent situations. The reason for this identity would be A's realization that his chances for promotion were best if all of his decisions were those that furthered the goals of the organization. In other words, in this ideal structure, A would never be confronted with a real choice between two courses of action, one of which would benefit his career while the other would benefit the organization. The degree of efficiency that is required for this result is, however, most unusual. Normally, the best that might be hoped for is that the "realistic" A will have only a relatively small advantage over "idealistic" B. It seems highly doubtful whether most existing governmental organizations attain even this minimal level of efficiency. As a consequence it appears probable that the higher ranks of most governmental bureaus are made up of people who are less interested in the ostensible objectives of the organization than in their own personal well-being.

In the ideally efficient organization, then, the man dominated by ambition would find himself taking the same courses of action as an idealist simply because such procedure would be the most effective for him in achieving the personal goals that he seeks. At the other extreme, an organization may be so badly designed that an idealist may find it necessary to take an almost completely opportunistic position because only in this manner can his ideals be served. The idealist, in such cases, may find that only by taking the course of action that will advance his own career can he remain in the organization and advance to a position where he can hope to influence events. This is administrative organization at its worst.

In part, good or bad, efficient or inefficient, administration is beyond the control of the designer of the formal structure. Some types of activity lend themselves to good administration and others do not. A businessman, whose activity is such that a good accountant can more or less closely approximate the contribution of each employee to total profit, is in a much better position to insure that the best route to advancement for his employees lies in their high level of organizational performance than is, say, a colonial governor who really has no objective method of judging the organizational performance of his subordinates.

MORALS IN ORGANIZATION

It may be objected at this point that I am ignoring the part that morals play in directing human action, and it may be argued that morally "correct" persons will not take courses of action that are contrary to the purposes of the hierarchy even if it would benefit their own careers. This objection is relevant, although, as we shall see, it involves a serious oversimplification. The consequence to be pointed out here is that an organizational system, to the extent that the conflict discussed above is present, will select against moral rectitude. A man with no morals will possess a marked advantage over the moral man who is willing to sacrifice career objectives. From this it follows that the man who tends to ignore moral considerations and chooses courses of action designed to advance his own personal status will be the man likely to advance in the hierarchy. The general "moral level" of those bureaucrats who have reached the top layers in such a structure will tend to be relatively low.[1]

Thus, and apparently paradoxically, the more important that moral considerations are to a man trying to rise in a hierarchy, the more likely is that hierarchy to select for higher leadership people who have relatively little concern for moral matters. Moral systems vary tremendously from culture to culture. Further, the requirements for rapid advancement vary greatly from hierarchy to hierarchy. We have a system with two independent variables, but if the relationship of the moral system of a given culture and the conditions for advancement in a given hierarchy are such that a man not concerned with moral issues is likely to rise more rapidly than is a strictly moral man, then the higher levels of the hierarchy are likely to be largely composed of people who have little concern with moral issues. Conversely, if the moral system and the hierarchy are so related that strict morality is no handicap to the man who wants to rise rapidly, then the higher officials are likely to be a mixture of moral and immoral people similar to the general population.

1. See William Riker, *The Theory of Political Coalitions*, Yale, 1962, pp. 208–10, for a somewhat similar discussion.

It is impossible to design a system that will select against the man of relatively low morals. This is because the intelligent but unscrupulous man will always assume the morally proper course of action if, in fact, this should be the one that is the most likely to be successful. The immoral man may not be highly intelligent, and he may miscalculate; but here the difficulty lies in his lack of intelligence, not in his immorality. The difference between two men, both intelligent and both of whom want to rise in a given hierarchy, but one of whom conforms strictly to the prevailing moral codes while the other does not, is simply that the second has a wider range of choice. If, in terms of advancing his own personal interest, the "best" course of action lies within the morally acceptable set, the immoral man will not choose differently from the moral man. It is only if the "best" course should be barred by the standards of prevailing morality that the difference in moral orientation comes into play, and here it is evident that the man who is willing to transgress possesses an advantage.

THE BIAS AGAINST MORALITY

From this it follows that any organizational structure in which selection on a merit basis is employed is likely, at least to some extent, to select against morality. The degree of this bias against morality will, of course, vary greatly from organization to organization. The American business community, for example, represents a system that permits substantial social mobility and which uses merit for selection. Since success, to some extent, depends upon salesmanship—and personal salesmanship in particular—the system tends to select against the rigidly honest and truthful man. There are other relationships within the business system, however, which are almost wholly impersonal. Here success is simply a question of making correct decisions, without the necessity of "making a good impression" on anyone. In general, the moral standards of the persons engaged in economic activity which closely approximates to the model of perfect competition are probably considerably higher than are those of persons in governmental bureaucracy or in the higher reaches of corporate hierarchies. This is true simply because "dishonesty" is of less assistance in situations characterized by active competition.

It must be emphasized that, when I speak of "morality" here, I am applying objective, external criteria, and I am not examining the state of the politician's conscience. If my observations are correct, there are highly ambitious "careerists" who do not consciously violate any ethical or moral code. These men quite sincerely believe that the various decisions that they take in order to benefit their careers are also desirable for the attainment of organizational goals. As suggested above, sometimes the two objectives do not conflict. Even when the conflict is present and obvious to the external observer, the well-adjusted "politician" may not sense its presence, and he may take the action that benefits him personally without realizing that such action is improper for the attainment of organizational goals.

It is always difficult to distinguish between "what is good for me" and "what is good." The general good is never readily discernible. The "politician," the bureaucrat, who makes no especial effort to keep these two categories distinct can quite genuinely believe that a course of action which may appear cold-blooded and dishonest to the outsider falls legitimately within his range of duty.

Most people have what might be called a "low sales resistance" when confronted with projects that will advance their own fortunes. Either they may think that the action in question will also be for the general good, or they may simply never give this aspect of the matter a second thought. Such men may be subjectively honest while being objectively dishonest. It seems likely that most "politicians," at least occasionally, are dishonest in both of these senses.[2]

Recognizing the dilemma with which they are likely to be faced in this respect, many highly perceptive and moral persons deliberately avoid employment in such hierarchical systems. Such persons recognize that they cannot be, by their nature, sufficiently dull as to remain subjectively honest in genuine conflict situations while they are unwilling, on moral grounds, to adopt consciously dishonest positions. In any event, few people expect career civil servants to act contrary to their own interests.[3]

OFFSETTING THE BIAS AGAINST MORALITY

As we have seen, the head of any organization has strong motives for penalizing rather than rewarding the immoral subordinate who attempts to climb rapidly by various dishonest expedients. The usual reason for the

2. Based on my own experience, persons in the Department of State normally seem to take the side of any question (to which the consideration is relevant) that would benefit them personally. They do not, of course, argue specifically in such terms, but rather in terms of broader objectives. Nevertheless, an argument to the effect that a specific position would be beneficial to their interests seems much more likely to modify their views than an argument couched in terms of the ostensible purposes of the organization.

3. Footnote by JMB: A conflict similar to that discussed here has been effectively dramatized by Terence Rattigan in his play "Ross." Rattigan depicts T. E. Lawrence as a man torn between self-aggrandizement and self-knowledge, and, as the character is developed, he is shown in sharp contrast with the more simple-minded British career officers.

immorality of these methods is that they involve behavior which the head of the organization does not want but which the subordinate feels will, in fact, be profitable to himself. Further, the superior does not want a high concentration of untrustworthy people directly below him. There is no method, however, by which he can eliminate the fundamentally dishonest man who realizes that, in the given situation, acting as though he were honest is the best way to get ahead. Limiting the advantage of the dishonest man is the maximum achievement that is possible.

The method through which this may be accomplished is not difficult to outline, although it may frequently be very difficult to implement. Paradoxically, the appropriate rule is that of never trusting subordinates. These can deceive a superior only to the extent that he accepts their reports, does not investigate their activities, and believes what they tell him. This proposal perhaps sounds cold-blooded, but reflection will indicate that it does provide the only course of action that will effectively minimize the advantage that a dishonest man has over the honest man. If, through the continuous scrutiny of a superior, a dishonest subordinate is made to realize that he will never gain from an immoral action, he will have no advantage over the honest employee who may be barred from all such actions by his own conscience. In this way, through explicit distrust of subordinates the superior gives those who are trustworthy their best chance, and places restraints on those who might be untrustworthy.

This apparently simple solution immediately raises major problems. A feeling of mutual confidence among the members of an organization is usually considered to be desirable. Continuous checks on the actions of subordinates by superiors will not lead to such a feeling of mutual trust. Thus, there arise two directly conflicting objectives. In each case, the superior must balance off the desirability of maintaining a "happy ship" against the danger of being deceived into rewarding a man for actions which may be contrary to the objectives of the organization. The rapid rise of a man who is believed by most of the staff to be dishonest will not, of course, contribute to high morale, but this is unlikely to be a major consideration in any moderately well organized hierarchy. If a large number of members of the organization have "got the number" of an ambitious and unscrupulous individual, the chief of the organization will likely hear about it. In any but the worst organizational messes, the dishonest but intelligent man will have to conceal his machinations not only from his superiors, but from his equals and (most of) his subordinates.

A strictly analogous problem arises in another sphere of organizational activity. People who handle money fully expect that they will be subject to careful accounting and auditing controls. These controls are very largely inspired by the fear that employees will steal or embezzle funds. This simple fact is clear to anyone who thinks about the matter (which, presumably, most employees do). It is probably true that morale could be raised if the management should announce, one day, that they were prepared to trust their employees and that all such precautions were to be abolished. Nevertheless, even without this radical innovation, morale in financial organizations does not appear unduly low, and it seems likely that management distrust in other areas would have no greater effect once it came to be accepted as a routine order of affairs.

In fact, the method advocated here represents nothing new, except perhaps in terminology. Anyone who has served in a hierarchy recognizes that the superiors do not wholly trust their subordinates. They ask to see the original documents, they talk to other people about given incidents, and they cross-examine employees. They may, on occasion, go to great lengths to reduce their dependence on the honesty of their subordinates. What I am here suggesting is that this behavior of almost all successful executives be discussed and described in direct rather than in allusive terms.

THE POLITICIAN

Economists build upon the postulated behavior of men who try to maximize their utilities in an economic situation. In this book I intend to consider the behavior of a utility maximizer in a political situation. Among these utility maximizers, some will reach the top of the hierarchy. As we have seen, merit selection will reward with promotion persons who are both intelligent and highly ambitious. It will also have a tendency to select relatively unscrupulous persons, but the strength of this tendency will vary with the efficiency of the organization. The people who rise in hierarchy are the most important. *I propose, therefore, to give special emphasis to the behavior of an intelligent, ambitious, and somewhat unscrupulous man in an organizational hierarchy.* For purposes of this study, this man will be the typical “politician.” From the analysis of his behavior I shall attempt to develop general rules or principles on the functioning of organizations, to outline methods through which their efficiency might be improved, and to suggest limitations on the type of social tasks which hierarchical organizations may accomplish.

Certain objections may be raised to this procedure. My assumption of “intelligence” seems to imply “rationality,” and there are those who deny that man is rational. The assumption of self-interest may also be questioned, and my doubts about the complete moral probity of public servants may be criticized. From the standpoint of strict science such objections would be beside the point. The apparent realism of the premises of a theory is less important than its usefulness in helping us to deal with the real world. Nevertheless, it seems worthwhile to devote a few pages to the consideration of these problems.

RATIONALITY

People who argue that men are not rational are, in a sense, contradicting themselves. If men are not rational, there is no point, or possibility, of argument or discussion. It can be consistently argued that men are rational only sometimes, or that only some men (including, by necessity, both the man stating the argument and his auditors) are rational. If only certain people are rational, they would be the ones selected by a merit-type system of social mobility for high position. Similarly, if men are rational only sometimes, and if they, as seems likely, vary among themselves as to how much of the time they are rational, then the system would select people who had the highest proportion of rationality for high positions. Thus an assumption of universal rationality is not necessary. The people who rise in any merit-type hierarchy will be, at least, among the most rational of men.

There is no need, however, to confine ourselves to this highly cautious position. While men vary greatly in intelligence, they all seem to be more or less rational. The commonly held view that some peoples, particularly primitive peoples, do not think rationally seems to be based on a simple misunderstanding. The actions of people in a culture different from his own are often difficult for the individual to understand. This is not because other peoples are irrational, but rather because they aim at different objectives and base their operations on different "information" about the real world. The savage tribesman who blows on a conch horn and performs certain other ceremonies (almost always including the pouring out of water) in order to cause rain is behaving as rationally as a modern American who seeds clouds with silver iodide. The savage is less likely to be successful, but this is no reflection on his mental powers. He knows less about the real mechanism of rain, and his reasoning is less likely to lead to effective action, but, given his initial "information," his thought processes are as rational as those of his civilized counterpart.

Much of the feeling that man is irrational in his behavior stems from using the term in a wider sense than that which is intended here. To clarify my position, I shall borrow a distinction from economics. The motives for all human actions can be divided into two categories, instrumental and ultimate. When an action is taken for its own sake, then this action is the result of an ultimate motivation. I eat a candy bar because I like it. To such an action, the conception of rationality hardly applies. We assume that most people do, in fact, know what they like, that they do not eat candy bars which they find unattractive, but there is no means through which we can check this assumption. The individual alone can judge whether or not he likes some item of food, a movie, or a girl. Outsiders have no way of deciding whether choice of this sort is or is not rational.

By comparison, instrumental actions are taken for an ulterior purpose. A boy may carry newspapers, not because he likes it, but because he hopes by so doing to earn money which he may use to buy candy bars. Instrumental actions are embarked on, not for their own sake, but because they are expected to improve the position of the actor with respect to his ultimate desires. In particular cases, these two motives may be intertwined. A manufacturer may get a strong feeling of aesthetic pleasure from a new machine tool. Similarly, if he hires a beautiful blonde secretary he is likely to expect at least some work out of her.

Actions motivated by instrumental considerations are, almost by definition, rational. They are undertaken to obtain some end, and they must proceed out of a chain of reasoning, however elementary this may be. This reasoning may contain errors, but it seems a little strained to say that the schoolboy who multiplies 274 by 583 and gets 169,642 is behaving irrationally. Most statements that men are irrational depend on the observed fact that men frequently undertake courses of action which appear inappropriate to the outside observer. The difference between the course of action chosen and the one thought appropriate by the outsider probably arises not from any irrationality on the part of the acting man, but from simple error or the difference between his ultimate goals and those of the outside observer. A man may inform a social scientist that he is trying to achieve some goal by a given course of action although the course of action does not seem well chosen in view of the stated goal. An incautious social scientist may then conclude that the man is irrational. The real explanation may simply be that the goals aimed at are different from the stated goals. Almost all human beings have extremely complex aspirations, and any action is thought of as a method of reaching numerous ultimate ends. In explaining his actions a man is apt to simplify greatly his actual ultimate ends, with the consequence that his actions may seem inappropriate to his stated ends.

The propensity of human beings to make errors is of considerable importance. Everyone makes errors in computations. This fact is of some relevance for the theory that I shall develop. In the first place, those individuals who tend to make the largest number of errors will be excluded, while those who make the smallest number will be apt to rise to high ranks in an organizational structure. This is simply another way of stating that the merit system will tend to select for intelligence. Secondly, the fact of human error means that no organization can ever function perfectly. The tendency to error has, perhaps, been too much neglected by economists, largely because errors tend to cancel out in an economic situation. We shall discover that, in the typical organizational hierarchy, errors tend to compound each other. The imperfection of human beings is thus of more importance for the theory to be developed here than it is for economic theory.

SELF-INTEREST

Let us turn now to the subject of selfishness, or self-interest (which might arouse less opposition if I replaced these terms with "career-centered motivation"). The problem may be solved by definition. Presumably, each human being, when he takes a given action, chooses that alternative which he expects to disturb him least. A man who gives all of his food to the poor does so because the hunger of the poor disturbs him more than his own hunger. But such action is not what is normally meant by the term "selfishness." Within the context of an organizational hierarchy, the more normal meaning may be simply stated as the desire to get ahead, to move up, in the hierarchy. It is quite clear that not all bureaucrats feel strongly about career advancement. Most members of a hierarchy will, however, have at least some desire to rise, and among those who have successfully advanced to the higher scales, this desire is apt to be quite strong.

As noted previously, a given individual may try to work himself up the scale in a bureaucracy from highly altruistic motives, in the normal sense of these terms. It is conceivable that he may genuinely want to rise to the top solely in order that he may use the resulting power for "good." The extent that this actually happens seems an open question, but it is certainly true that there are people who enter upon their careers with this motivation, and who keep it in their minds during most of their careers. The very process of moving up, however, may serve to warp their judgment so that those who actually do attain superior positions may be rather uncertain as to what they conceive to be "good." Savonarola is the classic example of this type.

As we suggested earlier, many politicians rationalize their own actions in terms of the greater good, and there is no need to discuss here whether they believe their own rationalizations. The important feature, for the purpose of this analysis, is that the politicians act in ways that would advance their careers. Therefore, while behavior may be basically altruistic, or basically selfish, we can normally treat the individual politician *as if* he were behaving out of selfish motives.

Selfishness should not be interpreted or described entirely in terms of creature comforts or large bank accounts. There have existed political situations in which the man who wanted to rise found it necessary to limit severely his own standard of living. More normally, political power and physical comfort are closely correlated in any hierarchic structure. Even monastic religious orders, functioning with a vow of poverty, normally provide their higher officials with a few more of the conveniences of life than the ordinary members.

MORALITY

The "moral level" of the politicians has been discussed inferentially in the preceding section. It is now proper to discuss the subject in more detail. Before doing so, however, I shall explain why it is necessary for my analysis that I introduce the assumption that this moral level is relatively low, whereas the economist, whose methods are otherwise rather similar to my own, need make no parallel assumption. The reason for the difference is fairly simple. Under modern conditions, the morality or the immorality of the businessman is more or less irrelevant. There are situations, as we have mentioned, in which a lack of moral scruples is helpful in business, but the fundamental behavioral norms of economic life, reflected in the operations of ordinary markets, and summarized by the operations of buying in the cheapest market, selling in the most expensive, are themselves neutral under the present moral codes.[4] This was not always the case. In the Middle Ages, moral codes of Western peoples prohibited much behavior that now is accepted as ordinary trading. Even today, one of the reasons why important areas of the world remain economically underdeveloped is to be found in the prevailing moral codes. The change in the moral code that more or less coincided with the

4. Unfortunately, there seems to be some current effort to make such traditionally accepted practices "immoral." Modern American politicians seem to be continuously exhorting business firms to refrain from increasing prices, and labor unions to refrain from seeking wage increases. This movement, insofar as it is meaningful, surely represents a replacement of the economic relationship with the political one.

emergence of the modern era was, quite literally, indispensable for the development of modern economic life, and modern economics.

If we consider the situation which existed before this change in the moral climate, economic success required that the individual violate the prevailing standards of conduct. The code was, in this case, enforced by a non-economic organization, the State, powerfully aided by the church. The result was that immoral behavior was both difficult and dangerous. Wealthy merchants, who did exist in the Middle Ages, lived in small enclaves in which the moral system was not enforced or else owed their wealth, not to economic, but to political reasons.

The situation in a political hierarchy is different. Here the type of activity forbidden by the ruling moral code may be likely to lead to success within the political hierarchy. No external agency exists that can enforce moral standards upon members of the state bureaucracy. We have here a coincidence between a moral code that bans specific types of activity and a governmental hierarchical organization in which just these types of activity may lead to success. In such a situation, men who are not particularly bothered by moral scruples will surely possess an advantage over their more upright brethren. It becomes necessary, therefore, to consider the activity of a man who is intelligent and ambitious but who, in addition, has no morals. Through considering Mr. Holmes's "wicked man," we can learn how to frustrate him, and how to improve the general moral level of any hierarchical structure.

It is an interesting fact, and indirect supporting evidence for the validity of our approach, that most people, in most cultures, have felt that "politics" is a dirty game, and that its practitioners are rather immoral in some relative sense. This attitude can be found even in China, where the government official stands at the very pinnacle of the social system. The attitude is also to be found in most large corporations, where the higher officials are usually suspected of having attained their positions by bootlicking of one sort or another. In part, this general attitude may be put down to envy. No one likes to admit that the man who has risen higher has done so by reason of superior merit.[5] Still, there seems no reason to doubt that there remains considerable

5. This is the great attraction of caste systems. The bulk of the human race can never rise very high in any situation, because the room at the top is, by definition, limited. In a caste situation, a man's failure to rise reflects the accident of birth, not his own lack of "ability." If you are born and brought up as a peasant, and know from the time you are old enough to know anything that you will always be a peasant, this is easier to bear than being a peasant in a society in which every boy has an equal opportunity to be President.

objective truth in the common suspicion of the moral standards of the politician. The man who is a success in most political systems has had to cut corners, to lie, or at least distort the truth, and to engage in some backstabbing. The degree to which this is descriptive of the behavior of the ordinary politician varies, of course, from system to system. A high premium on immoral behavior is not a necessary part of any political hierarchy, and I hope that this book will be helpful in suggesting ways in which such a premium as exists may be reduced.

It is probable that some readers will, by this time, have become highly excited about this book itself on "moral" grounds. They may accuse me of being cynical about human nature, or not trusting my fellow man, and, probably also, of being a totalitarian. Since it is not my purpose to deceive anyone, I shall take space here to indicate what I do think on these various matters. The view that men are rational will not be contested on moral grounds, although it may be questioned for other reasons. That men differ in intelligence, in the degree of self-centeredness, and moral rectitude will not, also, be subject to much dispute. As to the accusation that I do not trust human beings, this seems to me to be completely irrelevant. I am trying, in this analysis, to understand human beings and to suggest effective means for arranging their cooperation in dealing with problems that require the activity of more than a few of them. If we first create an imaginary ideal man, and then judge real men in his image, we are likely to find that the real men fall far short of the ideal. By avoiding this first step, by taking men only as they are, we not only save ourselves unnecessary trouble, we also avoid the necessity of any judgment as to whether or not a man has particular defects. The engineer does not say that steel is untrustworthy because it will not stand strains five times its tensile limits. Similarly, we should not deduce that men are bad because they are not better than they are.

In many respects, my view of human nature is more "idealistic" than that which will be taken, I am sure, by some of my critics. Many people seem to think that man is a small machine. If given a task he will simply go ahead and perform it in a completely mechanical manner. By contrast, I think that every man is an individual with his own private ends and ambitions. He will carry out assigned tasks only if this proves to be the best way of attaining his own ends, and he will make every effort to change the tasks so as to make them more in keeping with these objectives. A machine will carry out instructions given to it. A man is not so confined.

PART 2

THE POLITICIAN'S WORLD

CHAPTER 3

THE GENERAL ATMOSPHERE

It will be useful to start with a description of the environment within which all politicians, in our sense of the term, function. If one considers Senator Hubert Humphrey of Minnesota, Major General Nabokov of the (former) MVD, and His Excellency Liu Ping-an, viceroy of the Great Tang emperor in Kiang-nan, the differences seem overwhelming. Numerous similarities are present, however, and this study will explore these similarities rather than the differences. Each of these men has risen in a system in which a certain type of merit selection has been applied. We can, as a result, be confident that each of them is both intelligent and ambitious. It seems also likely that, in each case, the advancement achieved has required at least some actions which more scrupulous men might have avoided. This last consideration provides a good illustration of the type of uniformity that this analysis emphasizes. Since the three men used here as illustrative examples come from three markedly different cultures, they owe allegiance to three different moral codes. The characteristic that they possess in common is some willingness to violate their own moral code if advancement is to be gained thereby.

By stressing these similarities I am not denying the importance of the great differences that separate the three political systems in which these men have risen. Each of the three politicians is, presumably, an expert in the particular functioning of the system in which he finds himself. In order to develop general theories, stress must be placed, however, on the factors that all systems have in common. In this and following chapters, I shall develop a generalized model of *any* administrative organization as this appears to the politician who finds himself within it. In one sense, Part 2 may be considered a guide to the "climber," and may suggest to him various ways of accelerating his progress. The purpose of the section is not, of course, directly normative in this way.

A general description of hierarchic systems in terms of structure is difficult because of the wide variation that is encountered from system to system. About all that can be said is that all systems are pyramidal in shape, with fewer people at the top than there are in the lower ranks. Any division of personnel into executive, supervisory, decision-making, etc., classes is almost completely arbitrary. Such divisions offer little assistance to the student who wishes to understand the problems involving administrative organization in general, no matter how valuable classes of this sort may be to the organization itself.

What I propose here is to give up all attempts at developing a classification system based on an external observer's view of the organization. I propose, instead, to use the individual politician within the organization as a base point. In this way, all of the other members in the organizational structure can be fitted readily into a few general categories. From the view of the external observer the variety among separate organizations appears almost infinite, but from the vantage point of a member of any single organization all structures have many elements of similarity. This fact probably accounts, in part, for the ease with which persons who have been highly successful in one organization normally adjust themselves to life in another.

In our procedure individual persons will be classified in terms of their relationship to the particular reference individual. Since people will have different relationships with different members of a hierarchy, the category in which we shall place any given individual will depend strictly upon the reference individual chosen. The disembodied observer has the ability to change the reference individual or base, but the individual politican must, by definition, be the base of his own organizational model. He will find all other persons with whom he comes into contact fitting into one or another of the categories. He will not be able to shift readily his own position so as to change these categories.

This method differs radically from that usually used in political science, which has been to accept the vantage point of the external observer. The approach differs from traditional political science in another important respect. This discipline has concentrated attention on the very top of the administrative hierarchy or pyramid. The ultimate sovereign, whether this be a dictator or the electorate, has been the normal subject of study, and the relationship of this ultimate sovereign to its immediate inferiors has been the traditional area of concentration. The central focus here, by contrast, is lower down in the administrative pyramid. The relationships at the top are analyzed simply as special cases of phenomena having much wider applicability. We shall, of course, give considerable attention to these special cases, since they are of great importance on any count. There is also a methodological reason for considering them at length. Generally speaking, the relations between, say, a dictator and his immediate inferiors are much simpler than are the relations between superiors and inferiors farther down in the administrative hierarchy. It is easier, therefore, to consider first the most simple arrangements and to discuss the problems arising in the lower ranks as complications of these fairly straightforward structural relationships.

From the standpoint of any given politician, everyone in his organization can be divided into three rough classes, those above, those below, and those more or less on his level. This classification can serve as the first step in the construction, and we shall consider it at some length. Offhand, it would appear that this division, graphically displayed, would look like this:

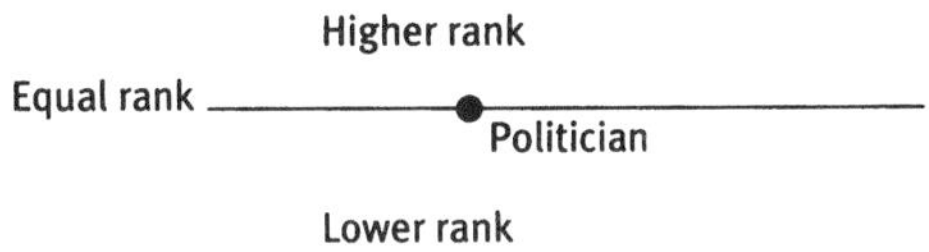

In fact, the situation should be diagrammed like this:

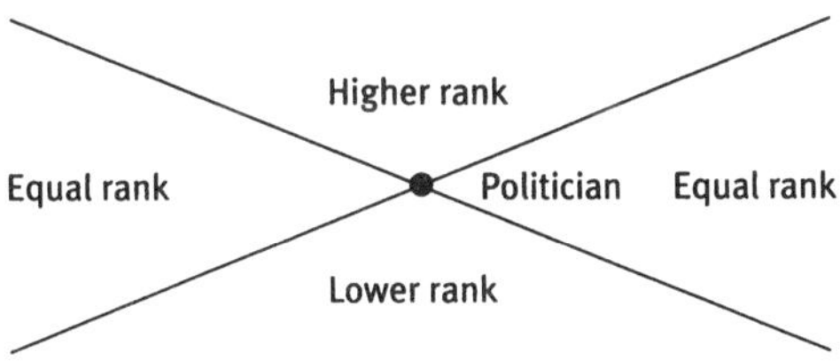

The equals are not people on an absolute dead level with our politician, but people in a zone which progressively widens as the horizontal distance from our politician increases. This widening is due to a number of factors. First, exact measurement of rank is extremely difficult, and becomes more so as the distance increases. More important, there is a natural tendency to classify people less and less exactly as the distance increases. The social importance of such classification is progressively reduced, and the classifying individual's interest also falls off.

The actual configuration will vary significantly from one situation to another. In our particular society, America in 1964, the assumption of equality is made unless there is some specific reason for the contrary one. The result is that, on a diagram such as the one above, the intersecting lines diverge from the horizontal more than in the average or normal case. In Tokugawa Japan, to take an opposite case, inequality was assumed, and the lines in the diagram probably would lie close to the horizontal. A hierarchic organization in which lines on a diagram would approach the vertical seems likely to be more pleasing than a system in which such lines approach the horizontal. In a very real sense as well as in a purely conceptual manner, the angle formed by the intersecting lines can be said to represent the range of choice open to the individual. In the "economic" relationship the lines would be vertical, since individuals treat each other as freely contracting equals.

GENERAL ATMOSPHERE

The environment within which a politician functions is essentially a human one, and his basic problems are those of dealing with other human beings. The term "general atmosphere" seems to suggest non-human elements in a situation, and, in a sense, it does so. Nevertheless, the general atmosphere within which he must operate is very much a reality to the politician. By this term, I shall refer to the set of ideas that are common to all members of the hierarchy with whom the reference politician must deal. It should be noted that most of the individuals within any given hierarchy will tend to share a set of attitudes, but that these sets will vary greatly from one organization to another. In fact, this is one of the areas where the variation among separate hierarchical structures is most radical. It will be useful to examine some of the elements of this general atmosphere.

CULTURE

Probably the most important determinant of the general atmosphere within which the politician must work is the culture of the community. Anthropologists have studied the differences in cultures exhaustively, but, to my knowledge, they have undertaken no serious analysis of those factors that would have to be taken into account by the successful politician in divergent cultural patterns. Differences among cultures in this respect should be expected to be large. For example, a United States politician will probably never even think of assassination as a method of eliminating a dangerous rival. In certain parts of the Middle East, by contrast, this method would surely be considered by the politician seeking to rise. There was, in fact, one powerful dynasty,[1] which depended on assassination as its primary "method of government," both in domestic and in foreign affairs.

There are less obvious areas where cultural differences are also very significant to the politician. The Chinese, for example, will normally deal only with persons with whom they have "connections" (*lien-lao*), a term

1. The "Old Man of the Mountains." Probably the best short description of this organization is to be found in *The History of the Arabs*, by Phillip K. Hitti, pages 446 and subsequent.

which means considerably more than its English equivalent. Each individual in a hierarchy, in addition to his official position, will also form a part of a vast chain of "connections" reaching to distant parts of the organization itself and outside. His loyalty to this chain will frequently be greater than his loyalty to anything else except his family, which may, in any case, form a part of the chain. Americans may have something analogous to this, but on a much smaller scale. Bureaucratic cliques seldom involve more than five or six persons in American practice, and groups of twenty or more are extremely rare. In China, by contrast, groups of less than twenty members would be equally rare.

Although any successful politician will be strongly influenced by his cultural environment, this influence is probably almost always completely unconscious. As a result of his indoctrination in a native cultural pattern, the individual simply will not realize that there might exist alternative ways of doing things.[2] This unconscious cultural indoctrination will tend to be reinforced by rational considerations. In order to be successful, the politician must be trusted by other persons, particularly by his superiors, and he will recognize that these people will, with rare exceptions, be members of his own cultural group. If he should develop a deviant personality, he would be unlikely to inspire much confidence in others. The rational politician will, therefore, make every effort to appear to conform to the image of the "proper" person that is held by the membership of the organization. He must become an "organization man."

The image will vary from one organization to another, even within the same culture, and also within the organization itself, depending upon rank and classification. These intracultural differences are, however, probably minor in comparison with the differences among separate cultures. Even between cultures certain similar features appear in the successful politician. It seems that almost all successful practitioners of the art are superb "personality salesmen." They will tend to exude an atmosphere of honesty, simplicity, intelligence, subtlety or whatever else might be expected of people in their particular group. It is interesting to recall that the various "bosses" who

2. Several years ago, I spent quite a period of time trying to convince an intelligent, English-speaking Korean that he could merely write to an American university and apply for admission without first establishing a "connection." Such a proposal seemed as unlikely to him as a suggestion that parading naked down Main Street would be a good means of securing a scholarship would seem to an American.

controlled corrupt city machines in the United States around the turn of the century frequently rejoiced in such names as "honest John." Presumably such titles were earned. In spite of what must surely have been questionable morals, these men were capable of giving an impression of honesty to their electorates.

ETHICS

The ethical system prevailing within a specific hierarchy is an important determinant of the general atmosphere surrounding the politician. As we have earlier suggested, this aspect of the environment need not be significant if the organization is designed so that the immoral man has little differential advantage. But in organizations in which an absence of genuine moral conviction represents a decided advantage (and these appear quite common), the general ethical problem becomes relevant. The successful politician is unlikely to adhere to the highest standards of ethics, but he must make a show of doing so. In order to accomplish this, he must be well versed in the particular ethical system of his culture or subculture.

The point here may be illustrated by reference to the scene in Shakespeare's *Richard III*, in which the people are brought to the palace to demand that Richard assume the throne. Both Richard's public position, apparently of the highest standard, and his private maneuvers to gain the crown are forcefully demonstrated. This play illustrates yet another feature of the internal ethical system that the politician must face. During his period of plotting to gain power, Richard makes a number of promises to various persons whom he hopes to convert to his cause. These promises, in and of themselves, are unethical in terms of the prevalent moral standards of the culture. Nevertheless, Shakespeare makes much of the fact that Richard later broke these promises. Certainly, Buckingham deserved everything he got, yet Shakespeare makes everyone who sees the play feel that Richard's conduct toward him was wicked.

This illustration suggests the fact that political systems normally have internal ethical systems that differ from the ethical system prevailing in the remainder of the society. "There is honor among thieves," a fact that is generally recognized. As in Richard's case, a violation of this internal code represents something of a more serious nature than the mere violation of what might be called the public standard of morality. These internal ethical systems, unlike ethical systems in general, are pragmatically based, at least to a large extent. For this reason, they tend to vary less from culture to culture than do the basic ethical systems of societies at large.

The principal features of internal ethical systems include the requirement that promises and agreements are to be binding, once made, and that members of cliques and groups are to be "loyal" to each other. For the politician who wants to rise in the hierarchy and desires to do so through the employment of intrigue, these clearly represent the minimal ethical requirements. The man who is not considered loyal, who is not known for keeping his promises, will find it impossible to use non-official alliances and agreements to promote his ambitions. The successful politician will need to organize alliances and to join cliques, and he will be able to do so because other parties trust him within the limits of the internal ethic. This may be true despite his recognized unscrupulous behavior in other, external, aspects of his actions. Consider, for example, *The Last Hurrah*.[3] All of the professional politicians portrayed are dishonest in their relations with the general public, yet they trust each other implicitly, and they feel confident that each will conform to the standards of the group.

The politician, in particular circumstances, may have to consider and balance off at least two moral codes when these come into conflict with each other. In the American bureaucracy, for example, he will be expected to be "loyal" to his immediate superior, whoever this may be. He will also be expected to take the part of his own subsection in the general organization. He must support his superior against those in the next rank above, that is, against his superior's superiors. On occasion, he may gain by "going behind his superior's back" in order to undermine his superior with the still-higher rank, but this is normally held to be in violation of the bureaucratic ethic. The more usual rule, for well-indoctrinated American bureaucrats, is that of maintaining loyalty to the immediate superior even should he be engaged in frustrating the desires of those higher up in the hierarchy. This behavior pattern can lead to odd results. If A, for example, should be head of a bureau, and if he finds that B, one of his section chiefs, is sabotaging his policies, and, in so doing, is vigorously assisted by C, one of B's subsection chiefs, then A is likely to remove B from his position, and to promote C to B's job. C then is expected to, and does, give A the same type of loyalty previously rendered to B, and A finds that his policies are effectively implemented.

All of this suggests that the moral or ethical decisions of a politician are likely to be exceedingly complex. He will frequently face situations in which the various moral systems within which he operates conflict with each other. Even the man without scruples—indeed especially this man—will realize that

3. Edwin O'Connor, Boston, Little, Brown, 1956.

he cannot openly flout the ethic of the general culture group. The internal code of his hierarchy is such that a reputation for violating it will surely end his opportunities for advancement through intrigue and maneuver. He will, by necessity, confront difficult choices. Frequently, however, he will be able to conceal his final action from those people who might be able to "enforce" one or the other code of behavior. Thus, the violation of the general ethic of the culture by an American civil servant is not likely to be known by anyone except his immediate associates in the organization. If this action conforms to the internal ethic of the system, these are not likely to take action against him. In still other situations, the politician may be able to represent the same action as springing from different sources to different sets of people. The President of the United States is observed to announce frequently that so-and-so has been appointed to high office because of his particular and outstanding qualifications, while at the same time he tells the prospective public servant that this is a reward for his assistance in winning the last election.

HIERARCHICAL PATRIOTISM

The general atmosphere of an organization will be determined by other forces of less obvious significance than the prevailing culture and the internal ethical system. There will almost certainly exist specific "in-group" feelings or attitudes that cannot be described as falling within either of the influences previously discussed. A politician, if he expects to succeed, must normally make it clear to others that he feels that his own organization is somehow superior to all others. Organizational patriotism may be as necessary to the politician working within a hierarchy as is national patriotism to a man seeking election to the United States Senate. For example, employees in the Department of State tend to feel that many things wrong with the world of today derive from the "military mind" of the Pentagon. The military, on the other hand, distrusts the "cookie pushers" and "striped pants boys" of the Department of State.

This deep distrust of rival organizations is not only of significance for national policy; it also can greatly affect individual careers, and it is this element that is stressed here. A man who desires to rise in the Department of State should not take the side of the military in internal discussion, and contrariwise at the Pentagon. Some people in each group are able to secure a reputation for "getting along" with the rival organization, but these are thought of in much the same terms as those formerly applied to an individual who possessed special talents for dealing with the Chinese. By and large, if an employee wishes to get ahead, he must make his basic loyalty to the organization clear to all beholders. In most cases, all members of a single hierarchic organization are united against outsiders, and each subgroup within the given hierarchy is united against other subgroups. The ambitious politician is normally well advised to cultivate an appearance of strong in-group exclusiveness. If he should be promoted out of a given in-group he should immediately drop his former in-group patriotism and adopt another more suitable to his newly attained position. Doenitz, as head of the German Submarine Forces, vigorously opposed diversion of resources to the surface fleet. When he was promoted to command of the whole navy, his "view widened," and he took steps to protect the battleships.

CONFORMITY TO TYPE

It is highly probable that the man anxious to succeed in a given hierarchical system will find it necessary to make a few changes in his personality, at least outwardly. There are, in fact, recognizable State Department types, army types, etc. Even within such large organizations, subdivisions may have distinct personality characteristics. Sir John Tilley, in his book, *The Foreign Office*, remarks: "The Eastern Department being my own, I have put it first, but we regarded it, and I believe it was generally regarded, as the most important; the rest of the Officers, indeed, thought that it gave itself airs and considered itself 'smart.' The African Department, by contrast, rather affected the character of rough country gentlemen, and smoked pipes" (page 131).

The man who hopes to rise must conform. He must be the type of man who seems "sound" to his co-workers, which means that he cannot seriously deviate from them. His superiors must be able to identify with him to a degree great enough to provide them with the necessary confidence. All of these elements require that the successful politician make a rather careful study of the personality type that is dominant in his organization and make an effort to "fit in." Since success in accomplishing this will be one of the criteria governing promotion, the "ideal type" will assume proportionately more dominance as higher brackets are attained.

It is not infrequently the case that the desired type for different ranks within a single hierarchy will be different. In *Melville Godwin, USA,* Marquand several times mentions the fact that Lieutenant Generals are expected to be brilliant, while Major Generals should not be. The Major General who wants to be promoted should try to convey the impression of "soundness," and only attempt to demonstrate "brilliance" after he has added his third star. Obviously a system of this sort requires considerable plasticity on the part of the man who wants to rise. The man of overly rigid characteristics will get stopped somewhere along the promotion ladder. The novel by Marquand may, in fact, be interpreted in this way. Godwin was the perfect type of the modern Major General, but his aversion to staff jobs reflects the feeling that he could not assume the role of the "brilliant" officer required by higher rank.

CHARACTERISTICS OF EMPLOYMENT AND CRITERIA FOR PROMOTION

Still another determinant of the general atmosphere of the politician will be the type of "work" which he is expected to perform and the manner in which this relates to the criteria for promotion. The type of activity that will lead to promotion is frequently not what the external observer might predict. For example, in the Department of State, the outsider might expect that some ability to speak foreign languages, to develop social relations with "foreigners," a knowledge of foreign cultures and political patterns, and an ability to influence foreigners in the direction of American goals would be the basic requirements for the diplomatic officer. Almost each one of these qualities, however, is distinctly minor in determining promotion. Less than one-half of all American diplomats have a speaking knowledge of even one foreign language. Since personnel administrators give little weight to language competency in any case, most of those diplomats who do speak a foreign language are, at any one time, assigned to posts where the language in question cannot be used. The important social contacts for the American diplomat who wishes to rise in the hierarchy are those with other Americans, both important American visitors and members of the American missions. Too much association with natives is likely to involve some slighting of this relationship to other Americans and is, consequently, likely to retard promotion.

Knowledge of foreign cultures is of some, although limited, usefulness to the diplomat in securing promotion. If this knowledge leads to the same general conclusions that have been reached by the superiors, who will normally not have a similar knowledge, or if it leads to different conclusions only on matters upon which these superiors do not feel strongly, the existence of this knowledge is obviously of no handicap, and may be helpful. The politician can, through using this special skill, add "convincing details which give verisimilitude" to his reports, and he may gain a local reputation as a sort of specialist. Nevertheless, this is not the usual route to promotion.

High-ranking members of the American diplomatic service tend to be "generalists," persons who neither have, nor claim to have, any particular knowledge of any specific foreign culture. In the normal case, they have been transferred from country to country, and, as a result, they have never had the opportunity to establish and maintain close contacts with the inhabitants of any one country. These people tend to think of the world within which they operate as being, largely, the foreign service itself. Contacts will be re-established at foreign posts, and the foreigners themselves can be ignored for the most part. The wife of a middle-grade official once summed up this attitude rather well. She had just returned from a tour of duty in Brussels, and she remarked that she had liked the assignment "because the people were so nice." Then, in order to remove any possible ambiguity, she added, "The Americans, I mean."

Influencing foreigners is, of course, one object of the American foreign service, but there is no simple way of determining how successful any particular individual has been in this task. As a result, the Department of State tends to overlook this factor in deciding on promotions. The ambitious diplomat will, if he is wise, confine himself to influencing Americans. His reports should be based on an analysis of the Department of State, not upon the country he is ostensibly reporting. Quite naturally, as a polished diplomat, he will not admit all this, probably not even to himself.

Although I am personally familiar with only the Department of State, there are surely similar phenomena in other parts of the governmental structure. Military ability, in the sense of the skill in winning battles, is not of much use in rising to high position in our armed forces. We fight wars rarely, so that this ability would be very hard to test.[4] Furthermore, rising to high rank requires political abilities which are seldom combined with military genius. Most authorities agree that some of the greatest generals in American history fought in the Civil War. Yet the four greatest, Grant, Jackson, Lee, and Sherman (arranged here alphabetically to avoid argument), could hardly have risen to high rank in Melville Godwin's army. In fact, although all of them had graduated from West Point, and all had distinguished themselves in the Mexican War, none of them was on active duty when the Civil War broke out.

4. It is probably symptomatic of a deep decay in our forces that most recent maneuvers have been "controlled"; i.e., they are planned from the start and make no effort to test the ability of the respective commanders to outwit each other.

Even a century ago, the army had developed to the point where officers of this calibre found difficulty in conforming.

These problems are not inevitable in large organizations. There are means of bringing the criteria for promotion and advancement more into line with the overall "functions" of the organization. In the military services, an increased emphasis on the ability to win war games, on the Prussian model, might be a step in the right direction. Success in war games is not, of course, perfectly correlated with success in war, but it is far more closely correlated with the latter than is social polish, exact obedience to superiors, and the ability to draft brilliant memoranda. In any case the individual politician must accept the environment as he finds it. If the general atmosphere of his organization requires actions contrary to the attainment of the objectives of the organization in order to secure promotion, the politician can hardly be expected to choose a course of action detrimental to his own advancement.

CHAPTER 4

SPECTATORS AND ALLIES

It seems appropriate that the analysis of the strictly human part of the politician's environment should begin with that element which tends to enforce the general atmosphere. All the people with whom a man who tries to rise in a given hierarchy comes into contact or must consider can be divided into two groups or classes. First, there are those who are directly involved in his struggles for power and advancement. Second, there are those who are so far removed that they are not so directly involved. The second group may be called *spectators*. Note that the spectators may still be within the hierarchy. The division here may be depicted graphically as follows, with those persons outside the range of the circle being classified as spectators.

The precise line that divides spectators from the active participants in any particular politician's environment may be difficult to draw. In a strict sense, persons simply become less and less important as the organizational distance from the reference individual is increased. For purposes of our model, and for the most part in reality, the division can be made readily, however, since the number of people concerned is likely to be small and the gaps between particular individuals to be significant.

Individual persons in the hierarchy may shift their own positions into or out of the spectator group for a given politician. Transfers and promotions will bring new persons into the circle and move others out of the group of active participants. If the reference politician is himself transferred or promoted, the whole breakdown must be modified. Less important changes may

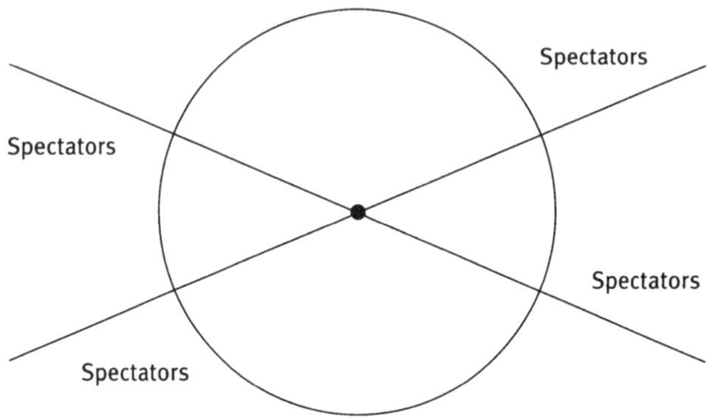

also, on occasion, modify the makeup of the spectator group. Some persons who have previously been spectators may, for any of a number of reasons, take an interest in the career of a given individual and become, in this way, active participants in his struggle. Similarly, some persons previously among the active participants may lose interest and shift to the spectator class.

The term "spectators" may mislead. It might suggest that the people in this group devote a considerable part of their time to observing the activities of the reference individual. This is not the case. The persons who are spectators are interested primarily in their own power struggles, in their own career advancement. Normally, they will give little, if any, attention and energy to the power struggles that are going on around them. In this sense, the relationship between the politician and his spectators is likely to be reciprocal. The reference politician himself is likely to be among the spectators to the power struggles of those individuals in his own spectator group. A person is a spectator, not because this is his principal interest in life, but only because of his relation to the other individual in question. He is, in fact, an "outsider looking in," and the word "outsider" might be a better term did it not imply that members of the group must be outside the hierarchy.

It would be possible to draw yet another circle on the outer edges of the illustrative diagram to indicate that there are persons so remote from the reference politician that they could not even be classified as spectators. This would add an unnecessary complication. As aforementioned, the relationships normally will shade off gradually as the organizational distance from the reference politician increases. At some point, of course, the politician's world has limits, but there seems no need to discuss these limits here.

The number of spectators, like the number of participants, may vary tremendously from hierarchy to hierarchy as well as from position to position. But the number will tend to be reasonably stable for a given politician in a given position. While it is always possible, for example, that a GS 11 in one of the innumerable sections of the Department of Commerce should find himself in the center of attention of a great number of people, such events are rare indeed. Usually he can assume that very few people are sufficiently interested in his private situation to come within the relevant circle. While the number of spectators will, of necessity, be larger, this group, too, may be quite small. His world is simply limited in size. At the other extreme, consider the presidential candidate. To him it must appear that every man, woman, and child (who, after all, may influence a voter) in the country is a direct participant in his power struggle. This is, of course, an extreme case: the normal man, trying to rise in a hierarchy, whether this be governmental, corporate, or religious, will have to consider only a relatively small group.

By definition, the spectators are not directly involved in the attempts of the politician to advance. He must, nevertheless, take them into account in his behavior. Individually, they have little effect on the politician, but they are relatively numerous, and, as a group, they may have power to influence his future career. His general organizational reputation will be largely created by these spectators. Usually the persons with whom he is directly involved are not sufficiently numerous to create much of an impact on the "service opinion" of the politician. Most of us are familiar with the way in which gossip and personal information concerning a person travel through devious channels in a large hierarchy. "So-and-so says that X is a good man" is likely to be more important in reaching decisions on the future of X than any formal efficiency evaluation taken from the files.

General reputation is probably a good deal more important in those organizations where individuals are systematically shifted from one position to another and where individuals do not work for one superior for long periods of time; but reputation is important in any hierarchy. The man who has a name as a "good executive" can shift readily from one large corporation to another. A good reputation will tend to provide an advantage in all spheres of life, since it will serve to ease initial contacts. Reputation is also extremely important in providing data upon which transfers from one section of a hierarchy to another may be based.

The spectators must be taken into account by the politician for a further reason. They serve to enforce the various moral sanctions. Conduct that appears to violate an existing moral code, internal or external, may result in damage to the general reputation of the individual in question. If the violation seems severe, spectators may go to great lengths to become directly involved in the politician's struggle for power. They may become active participants for the purpose of restoring the moral tone of the group by eliminating the offender.

As an illustrative example of the role played by the spectator group, let us consider a typical pre-Castro Latin American revolution. One group of politicians, supported by some part of the army, overthrows another group of politicians, supported by yet another part of the army. The bulk of the population takes no active part in the proceedings. After the revolution, the former government either retires to private life or goes into exile abroad. In any event, its members immediately begin plotting another revolution. Why do the victors not immediately eliminate this threat to their own power by killing or imprisoning the members of the losing group? Such action has been observed to occur rarely, and, when it has occurred, it can usually be explained on other grounds. The reason for this paradoxical behavior can be readily understood if the role of the spectators is considered. In the typical pre-Castro Latin American revolution, practically the entire population falls into this category. They are prepared to go through the motions of hailing the victors, but, fundamentally they are little concerned. If, however, the victors should inadvisedly break tradition they might stir up this previously inert mass.

In sum, the spectators "keep the ring." Although they normally do not take any direct action with respect to the politician, they are the custodians of his reputation. He must consider what they will say and think about any move that he contemplates. Sufficiently great departures from established moral standards may galvanize them into action. They may change from spectators to participants with respect to the politician who overplays his hand and arouses their wrath. Normally, it is within their power to destroy the individual politician since they are so numerous. Action on the part of a politician that displeases the spectators as a group may have any consequence from a minor blemish on his reputation to a lynching.

THE ALLIES

It is now necessary to consider a special group of persons who, while they fall within the general spectator group, take on particular distinguishing characteristics. I shall call this group "allies," although the usage does some violence to the English language. The term "ally" is introduced largely for want of a more suitable one. In my usage, an ally may be friendly, unfriendly, or neutral. I define an ally as a person who is not directly involved in the politician's struggle for position (and, thus, a spectator), but one who may, as an individual, exert some influence on the politician's position. The ally is of the struggle but not in it. The idea that I wish to convey here can be explained by an example. Officials in the Department of State frequently deal with officials in the Pentagon. In various ways, the officials in the Pentagon can help or hinder the officials in the Department of State with whom they have contact, and *vice versa.* Yet the two groups are involved personally in different hierarchies and in wholly different power struggles. This is the relationship that I call that of allies. Graphically, it may be represented as shown below.

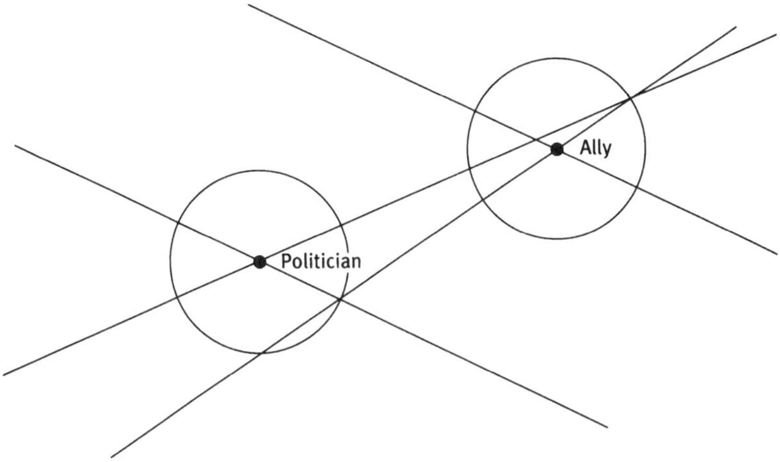

John L. Lewis provides us with a second example. For most of the latter part of his active career, he was an important figure in national politics. Although he could not be elected dogcatcher in his own right, he could influence votes in national elections. Similarly, certain politicians, although they would have no chance of participating directly in the power struggle within the United Mine Workers, could assist or harm Mr. Lewis in various ways. These politicians and Lewis were "allies" by our definition, even though they might be in opposition to each other.

In depicting the ally relationship graphically, I have chosen to place the ally far enough removed from the reference politician so that the circles of active participants do not intersect. This seems to be the usual case, but some intersection is possible. This is especially likely if the two individuals in question are thrown together because of some common concern with the activities of a third party on the periphery of each of their interests. Each one of them may, in such a case, be interested in advancing the cause of this third individual; each may be interested in reducing his influence; or one may wish to advance the third party's cause while the other seeks to retard it. In any event the relationship is one among allies.

As we have depicted the relationship above, the ally is located among the equals of our reference politician. This need not always be the case. There are undoubtedly instances in which fairly close relationships, with considerable superficial resemblance to the ally relationship, exist among persons of very different ranks within the same system. Victor Kravchenko, for example, was a friend of Ordzhonikidze. In *I Chose Freedom*, he makes it very clear that this relationship was of considerable help to him, particularly in his contacts with the secret police.

The relationship between someone high up in the hierarchy and a man of much lower rank will always be somewhat anomalous. As we shall argue later, an efficient executive will always have at least a few such relationships, as a way of finding out what the "lower deck" thinks, but they will always be somewhat exceptional. Such relations tend to set up conflicts and irregularities in the chain of command. Further, the great difference in income, status, and social world of people far apart in rank will normally make such contacts a little uneasy. The relationship is highly advantageous to the man in the lower rank, but the superior will gain much less. Perhaps he will find the unabashed admiration, which he will usually get from the inferior, pleasing, and he may find the problems of the inferior, which are so far removed from, yet related to his own, interesting. Simple friendship cannot, of course, be eliminated as a motive.

My inclination is to term this situation an example of the ally situation, rather than inventing a new word for it. It should be noted that this situation requires quite a considerable difference in rank between the two parties. If they are close enough so that the circles of active participants surrounding each one overlap, then the situation will become one of "multiple sovereignity," which I shall discuss below. A further difference between the situation where allies are superior and inferior and the situation where they are equals should be emphasized. Normally the superior can, if he wants, order his direct inferiors to order their direct inferiors, etc., until any desire of the lower-ranking man is fulfilled. Thus, he has it in his power to do practically anything he wishes for his lower-ranking ally. The lower-ranking person will be aware of this, and realize that the superior is deliberately refraining from aiding him in many cases. Under the circumstances, the relationship can never be the easy, completely confident one which may exist between equals.

CHAPTER 5

THE POLITICIAN'S WORLD— THE SOVEREIGNS

The most important category in the politician's world is that of the *sovereigns.* I shall discuss this category in some detail under five separate subheadings. In the diagram reproduced below, the sovereigns are depicted as occupying the space directly above the reference politician.

I shall define sovereigns as those people who are able to reward or to punish the reference politician, the people whom he must please (or, more precisely, those toward whom he must act in such a manner that they will reward him). It is clear that, in general, the sovereigns invariably make up the most important part of the politician's world.

It must be emphasized, however, that the term "sovereign" refers only to the people immediately above the reference politician who actively take an interest in his affairs. To a corporal trying to make his sergeant's stripes, only his company noncoms and officers are sovereigns. The regimental colonel would, normally, be a shadowy, far-away figure. To the officers, on the other hand, the colonel is a highly important sovereign, while the chief of staff would be merely an important example of the spectator class.

The person who desires to rise in any hierarchy will find that careful study and analysis of his sovereigns is highly rewarding. He will find it advantageous to become expert as regards their likes and dislikes, the activities that they will or will not reward, the activities that they will or will not penalize, and the means of exerting influence over them. Here, as on several

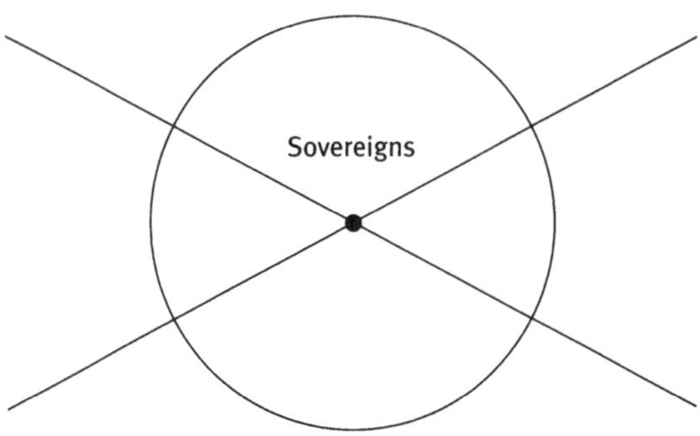

occasions before, it is necessary to discuss the issue of individual morality. The man who desires to advance and who does not discriminate among the various means of achieving this goal will always tend to take the course of action that will most likely be rewarded, regardless of whether or not this is the "right" thing to do. He may, therefore, deceive his superiors deliberately, or he may do things which they really would not approve if they knew all the circumstances because he feels that they will, given their imperfect knowledge, reward such behavior. If his superiors are men of superhuman ability, such opportunities will never arise, but with ordinary humans, at least some such situations will present themselves. Thus, the man who rises most rapidly will tend to be the one who takes advantages of the weaknesses of his superiors.

Of particular interest is the activity of the expert who is called in to give advice in his field of competence. If his career depends on pleasing the superior to whom advice is proffered, the expert will consider both the real situation and the information on this situation possessed by the superior before offering an opinion. It will be more important to him to appear to be right than to be right. Unless the superior is very careful, he may find that experts are devoting their efforts to developing rationalizations for opinions that they think that he holds, rather than producing independent expert advice. This fact explains the very old and respected administrative practice of asking an inferior's advice before indicating an opinion. Unfortunately the intelligent inferior can frequently infer the opinion of the superior.

To this point, I have discussed the sovereign on the assumption that there is only one person above the reference politician, one person empowered to reward and to punish him. In some respects, this situation is the administrative ideal, but it is by no means the administrative norm. It does provide the simplest case, however, and the principles derived from its study may be applied to the more complex, and more common, cases of group and multiple sovereignty. Before examining these situations we must consider the politician who has no sovereign at all. This is a rare occurrence, but since it is usually found at the very apex of power, it is highly important.

THE NO-SOVEREIGN SITUATION

At first glance it appears obvious that the administrative pyramid must have a peak. At the apex there must be some individual or group which is subject to no superior. The word "sovereign" in ordinary speech refers to that individual or group. According to the dictionary "sovereign" means "the person or body having independent or supreme authority."[1] If we accept this definition, however, then the word "sovereign" will have no application to reality. Kings, dictators, and voters have no sovereigns above them, but since the time of Hobbes it has been recognized that their powers are subject to considerable limitations. Kings and dictators may be overthrown when they fail to consider the interests of politically powerful "inferiors," and even the sovereign people may find a more sovereign Caesar. The traditions of despotic government are strong and reinforced by religion in Mohammedan culture, yet Farouk, coming to the throne as a popular young king of a prosperous kingdom, succeeded, through profligacy and inefficiency, in throwing it away.

THE OVERTHROW OF SOVEREIGNS

In order to develop a more realistic notion of "sovereignty," a discussion of the process by which the ultimate sovereign may be overthrown is necessary. It is traditional among students of politics to distinguish between two cases. A king (or dictator) may be overthrown by people who rank high in his government: this is usually called a *coup d' etat.* He may also be overthrown by an uprising of people farther down the pyramid; it is customary to call this a revolution. While it is obviously a matter of degree, this distinction seems a useful one, and we shall retain it. There is no general term in use to describe the overthrow of a democracy, but this has not been uncommon historically, and we must give the situation some consideration.

Starting with the coup, we may consider a king on his throne in a well-governed kingdom. He will be surrounded by his ministers who will obey his orders and who will, in their turn, give orders to their subordinates. There are two reasons why the ministers carry out the king's orders. In the first place, the ethical system in which they have been trained probably puts loyalty to the king high among the virtues (a dictator is less likely to have this advantage), and, secondly, it is in their interest to obey. They hold office only during the king's pleasure, and individual disobedience is likely to result in dismissal. If all of them, or even a substantial majority, should decide to overthrow the king, however, he could do little about it. It is unlikely that this will happen in a well-governed monarchy. While the man who replaces the king in a successful coup will gain greatly, the other ministers will simply be shuffled around with some gaining and some losing by the change. Since at least one probable loser can be depended on to tell the king of the conspiracy, it is most

1. Merriam Webster, 2nd edition.

unlikely that a majority of the ministers can be organized in a plot against the king. Machiavelli thought the risks of betrayal of any conspiracy to overthrow a prince so great that it was marvelous that any ever succeeded.

Yet we know that many kings and princes have been overthrown by coups. In these cases it will usually be found that only a few ministers were involved in the plot, while the bulk of the officials remain passive spectators. The king (or dictator), in such a situation, finds himself without real support when confronted with his enemies and is overthrown. Obviously, a king who wants to keep his job must so comport himself as to minimize the possibility of this happening. He should try both to attach all of his ministers to himself and to prevent the growth of powerful cliques and personal followings among them. His position as ultimate sovereign thus depends on his behavior conforming, to a considerable degree, to a pattern imposed on him by his subordinates. This does not mean that he must please his subordinates in all matters. Measures to attach them to himself will usually require that he do things which they want, but measures to prevent the development of powerful cliques and personal followings may well displease them. Further, a king or dictator will normally have considerable freedom. Many courses of action will be open to him, none of which will seriously endanger his position. It is this freedom, which will normally be several orders of magnitude greater than the degree of freedom of anyone else in the administrative machine, that characterizes the sovereign. His power is not unlimited, and he must consider other people, but nonetheless his power may be very great.

Although coups are common, revolutions are rare. This is probably because most states are well equipped with a formal system to prevent them. The police and army of any state, if only moderately efficient, can prevent or suppress any revolution. If one examines successful revolutions one will invariably find that the police and army either were completely inefficient or stood by as passive spectators during the revolution. Sometimes these bodies may participate in the revolution or be divided among themselves. It may happen, for example, that different parts of the army will be active on opposite sides of the revolution. So far as I know, however, there has never been a case of successful revolution where the army and police were both efficient and active in support of the existing government.

In the American revolution, which comes as close to being an exception as any I know, the British army remained loyal and efficient to the end; but it was always much too small for the task in hand. In the early days of the revolution, the whole British army was small, and the portions of it in the

Americas insignificant. Certainly the colonial militias, on which the defense of this part of the Empire had traditionally depended, were much stronger than Gage's forces. Later, the British mobilized much larger forces, and might conceivably have won if they had not at the same time found themselves at war with most of Europe. Since the Americans were reinforced by a French army and benefitted by the operations of the French and Spanish navies,[2] the basic rule that the police and army can put down any revolution if they are efficient would not appear to apply. The "police power," in any case, had been disloyal to the British from the beginning.

The romantic type of revolution, in which noble heroes conspire to raise a popular rebellion, does not exist outside novels. Any large conspiracy will always be betrayed, since, in any group of, say 10,000, men, there will always be at least one who will sell out. The usual situation does not involve any large conspiracy. What happens is fairly simple: most people become dissatisfied with the existing government to the extent that they will actively or passively support revolutionary forces. This attitude, if the revolution is to succeed, must extend well into the army and the police. If, in this situation, an open organization hostile to the existing government, like the committee of correspondence of the American revolution, is permitted to exist, then conditions are even more favorable to rebel success. In these circumstances one of two developments can occur. Small groups may engage in guerrilla warfare, keeping most of their secrets to themselves (thus avoiding the risk of betrayal implicit in large numbers) and depending on the unwillingness of the bulk of the populace and much of the military and police to engage in actively hunting them down. Or, an incident of some kind may set off a popular explosion—the events in Hungary will provide an example. In any event, success requires that the police and army not engage in actively putting down the uprising.[3] The Chinese, who, through the study of their own long his-

2. The brief skirmish between the British naval force commanded by Graves and De Grasse's French fleet which goes by the rather pretentious name of the Battle of the Virginia Capes can be considered the decisive battle at which American independence was established. Until this action Cornwallis was in no particular danger. He was in a familiar position for a British general, in possession of a port and awaiting the arrival of a fleet. After Graves withdrew, he was doomed.

3. National uprisings against foreign domination appear to be something of an exception to this rule. Apparently the emotions associated with such "revolts" are much more deeply felt than those associated with a desire for democracy, and such uprisings can continue even in the face of extreme repressive measures.

tory, have developed a regular theory of the overthrow of dynasties, consider the internal decay of the government as the principal reason for the uprisings which normally end them. Whether it is the principal reason or not, it is an indispensable condition.

The overthrow of a democracy follows a different path. First, we must distinguish the case of a new democracy from that of a well-established one. The fate of the first French republic, ending in the empire of Napoleon, indicates that newly established democracies may sometimes be easily subverted. It is quite possible that newly founded democracy may simply be unpopular. This seems to have been the case in South America in the nineteenth century. The revolutions against Spain were led by the "aristocracy." The common people, although not feeling strongly enough to risk their lives for him, were loyal to the king. Under the circumstances, democracy was obviously impossible. In any free election the royal viceroys would have won easily. The same situation, although in a less extreme form, has occurred elsewhere. Usually, however, the newly established democratic government will be initially popular. The people, used to despotic governments, may also not realize for several years that they can disobey the democratic leaders. This honeymoon period is likely to be crucial for the future of the democratic government.

If, during the initial period, the people are "educated" in the democratic process successfully, the first hurdle to the establishment of democracy has been passed. If they are not properly indoctrinated, they may end democracy by completely democratic means. More normally, if democracy is new, and not too popular, it will be ended by undemocratic methods. This does not necessarily mean that the people would not, if asked, vote the democracy out. It merely means that the political leaders feel no need to await this development. Most people, except in their capacity as voters, are mere spectators of the political process in such situations. If those members of the community who are willing to fight actively for their political ends are dominantly opposed to the democratic government, then they may end it by direct action regardless of what the passive people think. If history is any guide, however, this is possible only in the early days of a democratic government. In a well-rooted democracy, the people would be jolted into action by such a blatant attack on the democratic process. They would shift from spectators to active participants and eliminate the prospective non-democratic rulers.

This is, however, only true in a well-established democracy. Obviously the transition from a new democracy to an established democracy is a gradual one. If, for reasons of convenience, a line between the two is desired, then

I would suggest that we consider as "new" all apparently democratic governments in which there has been no democratic change of government, or in which the opposition has replaced the ruling party only once. Those democracies in which the shift from one group of democratically elected officials to another has occurred two or more times should be regarded as more or less established. This rule has the additional advantage of distinguishing, rather neatly, genuine from fake democracy. It is quite possible to go on holding elections in which the ruling group wins indefinitely if the ruling group is willing and able to use appropriate methods of keeping their opponents out of power. Fakery which goes to the extent of losing the elections, however, is virtually indistinguishable from the real thing. Looked at from this angle, two changes of government by election are necessary, since a party in power may, erroneously, think that it is so popular that it will automatically win. In such circumstances, the 1950 Turkish elections and the 1956 Korean elections will serve as examples, no precautions may be taken, and the party in power may be much surprised by the results. This type of error is unlikely to be repeated.

The problem of overthrowing a well-established democracy is illustrated by the United States. If the Joint Chiefs of Staff were to issue orders to the powerful armed forces which they command to seize the government, it would cause some confusion, but that is all. Most of the officers and troops would simply not obey when they realized the implication of their orders. The Joint Chiefs would probably not even be court martialed. They would be sent to Walter Reed for observation. There would probably be a good deal of public discussion of the strain of their position in the Cold War, and measures might be taken to relieve this strain in the case of their successors.

Well-established democracies have, nevertheless, been overthrown. Such an acute observer as Aristotle thought them mere way stations on the road to tyranny. Most of the Greek city-states eventually lost their democratic institutions. In many cases, of course, this should be counted as an example of the overthrow of a new democracy, not a well-established one. Looking further, almost all of the "democratic" city-states founded in the late Middle Ages and early Renaissance period eventually gave way to a despotic form of government.

The usual course by which democracies have been overthrown was described by Aristotle. Briefly summarized, some leader arises to convince the common people that the wealthier and more powerful members of the commonwealth are oppressing them. On this platform, the leader will be elected to the highest office, and he will then be able to make various changes in the constitution designed to increase his power. The crucial moment comes when the leader convinces the people of the need for an armed "protective" force, subject to his command, and allegedly needed to protect him from the "oligarchs." In the possession of this armed force, and with the backing of a majority of the people because of his antagonism for the wealthiest among them, the leader is in the position to become the dictator.

This seems adequate as a generalized description of the process through which a democracy might be overthrown. We find essentially the same procedure in many times and places other than ancient Greece. The establishment of the Medici power in Florence is an example. Caesar's subversion of the Roman Republic differs somewhat, but he was the leader of the popular party, and the men who killed him were trying to protect the Roman constitution against that party. The process also has some resemblance to the Marxist program, with its emphasis on developing class conflict between the poor and the rich, and then establishing a "dictatorship of the (most) proletariat."

All of the available historical evidence seems to point toward a fundamental difference between the "sovereign people" and an individual sovereign. Kings and dictators may be overthrown, but well-established democracies must be persuaded to abdicate. If the people are wise enough to refuse to accept any deviation from democracy even to deal with "enemies of the people," then the democratic structure remains safe. The king is never so secure. No single individual is ever completely sovereign. Nevertheless, while the ruler must consider the outside world in choosing policies and in making appointments, he still maintains a wide range of choice. There have been numerous cases where clinically insane men have held supreme power for long periods of time.

THE BEHAVIOR OF ULTIMATE SOVEREIGNS

Having completed a rather lengthy digression on the possible overthrow of sovereigns, a digression which was included in order to emphasize the limitations on the power of the ultimate sovereign, it is now possible to consider the behavior of the politician who finds himself in a position of "ultimate sovereign."

The first, and familiar, point to be made concerns the probable shift in motives, and consequently in behavior, that may accompany elevation to this position from the lower ranks of the hierarchy. Consider a man who has devoted his career to personal salesmanship and maneuver with the objective of rising in some hierarchical system. Eventually, he reaches the top of the pyramid. The motive that has dominated his life to this point, the desire to rise, simply disappears. Some of his energies may, it is true, be shifted into maneuvering to maintain his position, but this task is unlikely to require nearly as much effort and attention as did the struggle to reach the top. In such circumstances, the behavior of the politician may show major change. His attention shifts to objects that he has not previously considered. For example, he may like the good life. He may have been willing to forego such pleasures during his struggle for power, but, once he has attained the top position, this sort of sacrifice is no longer necessary. A marked improvement in "standard of living" is almost universal upon the attainment of supreme power.

Similarly, and socially more beneficial, the politician may have always wanted to behave in accordance with the ethics of his larger social group, to lead a "moral life." This desire would have been subordinated to the desire for power itself, and consequently, it could have been little evidenced during his rise to the top of the hierarchy. Now that he has attained the pinnacle, he can behave more in accordance with his basic desires, although he will rarely carry this to the point of endangering his position. This provides, perhaps, the element of truth in the view that kings, dictators, etc., embody the national will. Even the man who has risen to power in the most ruthless and unethical manner may appear to his subjects as an enlightened ruler. Augustus is probably the most important example of the apparent change in character which may come with the achievement of supreme power.

The politician who has risen high enough so that there is no sovereign above him will find that his principal problem is that of insuring obedience to his commands. This problem can be subdivided into two parts: the negative objective of avoiding being overthrown, and the positive objective of getting things accomplished. The first of these objectives has been discussed in this chapter, and the second will be discussed at length in a later portion of the book. At this point it will be useful to consider an in-between category, that is, people who are not ultimate sovereigns, but who yet are subject to no sovereign.

QUASI-SOVEREIGNS

Even within a well-organized hierarchical structure there may exist persons who are subject to no sovereign. A familiar example is that of the federal judge in the United States. He is appointed for life, and he may be removed only for some serious breach of conduct. In practice, since the only way of removing a judge is a congressional impeachment process, he is almost immune to disciplinary action. The Constitution also protects him from any diminution in salary, and the Founding Fathers thought this last consideration to be of such importance that, at the constitutional convention, the possibility of making the judge's salary payable in commodities instead of in money as a hedge against inflation was seriously discussed. Protected as he is against dismissal, the federal judge is reasonably free from the temptation to rise in the world. Historically, appointments to the Supreme Court from among the judiciary are rare, and an argument of considerable weight can be advanced that the "promotion" of federal judges should be avoided. If such "promotion" is held out as a significant prospect, ambitious men might begin to shape their decisions with this end in view.

Since the latter half of the nineteenth century, other quasi-sovereigns have been introduced into the United States governmental structure. Various boards and commissions have been set up that are intended to be independent of the control of any superior. The Interstate Commerce Commission, the Federal Reserve Board, and the Atomic Energy Commission provide examples. These boards or commissions are usually given jurisdiction over an area of activity in which the federal government wishes to engage, but in which the influence of "politics" is thought to be detrimental. It is frequently provided that members of the board should be more or less equally divided as between the two major political parties. Terms of appointment are reasonably long and are staggered. But, since the members are subject to reappointment, they have considerably less independence from either executive or legislative influence than members of the federal judiciary.

It should be noted first of all that most federal judges and members of the independent commissions are politicians of the ordinary sort at the time of their initial appointments. Appointees to the Supreme Court are almost always prominent in political life, and appointees to the lower federal courts are usually simply less successful politicians. The whole system must, therefore, be based on the belief that the politician is somehow changed by his being appointed a judge.

It seems clear that the Founding Fathers, and their modern successors who have created the various independent commissions, implicitly analyzed the motivations of the politician in a manner similar to that of this book. They recognized that the politician could be predicted to put great emphasis on "getting ahead." Since they were not interested in being tried by judges who were less interested in the facts of the case than in personal advancement, an attempt was made to insure that the judge could not be a politician in the normal sense. The appointments to the bench would, in any case, be made from among those persons who are most successful in maneuvering to get them, so the politician could not be eliminated at this stage of the process. If, however, upon his appointment, the federal judge is effectively removed from political life; if he need not worry further about his position and if he has little hope of bettering it, the former main object of his life—his own advancement—should become irrelevant in his behavior. No particular decision could influence his future career, and he could, therefore, decide all cases "on their merits."

The system has not always worked as it was intended. Judges and independent commissioners sometimes remain active members of political parties, and their party sentiment may influence their decisions. Judges may also occasionally contemplate a return to active political life, and, in a sense, they may "campaign" in their decisions. In the independent commissions, these factors are more significant than in the judiciary. Most members keep the eventual expiration of their terms in mind. Even if they are somewhat more independent of political influence than would be an appointee subject to immediate dismissal, they are not nearly so independent as the judiciary. On the whole, however, the system of the independent judiciary has been successful. It has been widely copied elsewhere, although, oddly enough, not by most of the American state judiciaries.[4]

Independence has seldom been applied uncompromisingly outside the judiciary. The independent boards and commissions are free only within limits from political influence. This is probably advisable in such cases, because independence has its disadvantages as well as its advantages. Theoretically, independence, as such, is always contrary to the basic principle of government. It would be impossible to conceive of a government, all of whose officials possessed the independence of federal judges. In practical terms, this reduces to the fact that the genuinely independent official cannot be made to obey orders. Again, the federal judiciary provides examples.

The federal judges do a poor job of enforcing the laws. This may seem to contradict what has been said before, but it does not. Nor is it a severe criticism of the judiciary. If the duty of the court is the exact enforcement of the laws enacted by the legislature, then the federal courts do a very poor job.

4. I do not intend to give the impression that the independent judiciary is an American invention. It is much older than the United States. But, to my knowledge, the American constitution represents the first formal incorporation of the principle into any nation's basic law.

But, on the other hand, if this duty is conceived as that of doing substantial justice in accordance with the mores of the culture, the courts do a reasonably good job. The two concepts are different. If a statute, enacted by the legislature, when applied to a given case should be in complete accord with the ideas of right and wrong held by the judge, no issue arises, and the judge will follow the statute. The same decision would have probably been reached, however, without the statute. On the other hand, if the "law," as applied to a specific case, should deviate from the ethical norms of the judge, the court will normally give lip service to the law and enforce the ethical norms.

In such cases of conflict, the statute may be evaded in several ways. It may be declared unconstitutional, but this is the most drastic of the possibilities. It may be interpreted so as to give results in keeping with the judge's ideas, but this is not the usual manner either. The more normal procedure is that of finding facts to be different from what they are. Thus, the law may provide that a man who commits a certain crime shall be sentenced to ten years in prison. The court or the jury may feel that this is unjust, and "find" that the prisoner has not committed the specific act, but, possibly, some other, and related, act for which the penalty is lighter. Under such circumstances the law, as written, is not enforced. Appeal courts are loathe to upset lower court rulings of questions of "fact," and, in any event, the appellate judge is likely to have roughly the same ethical ideas as the trial judge.

As a result of this set of institutional interactions, we have in the United States two bodies of "law"—a vast and complex collection of laws and precedents, and a set of ethical behavior patterns of judges and juries. Law schools normally define "law" as "what judges will, in fact, do," recognizing that the judges do not necessarily obey the orders that they receive from the remainder of the governmental system. On the whole, this is probably desirable. No citizen could possibly have a full knowledge of all the laws, written by legislatures, that literally apply to him. Under such circumstances, it seems advantageous that the judges do not, in fact, enforce the laws.

The disadvantage of such a system is that the orders are not obeyed. While this may be desirable in a judicial system, as noted, it could not be applied to most parts of the government. Administratively such a system is grossly inefficient. It would make the carrying out of policies decided upon at higher levels of government difficult or impossible. The Supreme Court's power of invalidating any law that it considers to be contrary to the constitution merely dramatizes the problem. The independent members of the system, by the virtue of their independence, are really outside it. They are themselves sovereigns, instead of being subject to the sovereignty of the whole apparatus. Indeed, they may be much more independent in this respect than the genuine monarch. The judge in an American federal court need not fear that he will be overthrown if he takes an unpopular stand. He is safer in pursuing a course of action to which the populace objects than is the dictator. This independence of the judge provides protection for the citizen from the arbitrary actions on the part of the rest of the government, but, from the point of view of the internal workings of the hierarchy, it is not efficient. And, because of this inefficiency, such independence cannot be tolerated in many positions in the overall hierarchical structure.

CHAPTER 6

THE SINGLE SOVEREIGN SITUATION

The politician subject to a single sovereign has only one way to improve his position in the world; he must act in such a manner as to be rewarded by that sovereign. The individual politician may, of course, be interested in many things other than success. In his novel *The Power and the Prize*, Harold Swigget allows his hero, who has risen to the number two position in a large corporation by the president's favor, to fall in love with a girl of whom the president disapproves. The hero decides to marry the girl, even though the president has advised him that an "unsuitable" marriage would make it impossible for the hero to continue with the firm.[1] In matters of less moment, such hard choices confront the politician frequently. He will find himself in a position where two courses of action are possible, A and B. A, we may say, is that course of action more likely to lead to rewards from his sovereign, while B, for reasons extrinsic to his career, is the course of action which the politician would really prefer. Faced with this choice, he will have to balance off the respective advantages of advancing his career by action A against the desirability, for non-career reasons, of action B. The politician will, by no means, always choose A. The point is that, if he chooses to frustrate his sovereign's desires, he must risk a penalty.

In particular cases, the course of action that is not likely to please his sovereign may be highly rewarding to the politician. The non-career satisfaction gained may, paradoxically, take the form of a feeling of ethical justification for making a personal sacrifice for reasons of "duty." A Chinese story tells of a minister serving a young and extravagant emperor. The minister frequently annoyed his young master by suggesting the desirability of economy. His arguments were always couched in terms of the long-term interests to the emperor himself. Finally, the emperor, in a fit of temper, informed the minister

1. The story ends happily with virtue triumphant. From the standpoint of the theory developed in this book, the plot is interesting as an example of the intrinsic difficulty of maintaining the single sovereign situation. Up to the time of the break between the hero and the villain (the president), the hero is in a strict single sovereign situation. The duel between the two is, however, fought out in a multiple sovereign situation with the denouement occurring at a meeting of the board of directors which is, of course, a group sovereign.

that any further reference to the subject would lead to the loss of his head. The minister promptly replied: "I am perfectly willing to sacrifice my life for your majesty's good." The story is doubtless apocryphal, but anyone familiar with Chinese history must realize that it could have happened. The dilemma facing the minister in the story will, in less extreme form, be present in every political career, and some politicians will make the same choice as the minister.

The situation will usually not be so clear-cut. In the first place, the sovereign will seldom have perfect knowledge of his subordinate's activities. Much can be done without his finding it out. Furthermore, the sovereign will not usually have perfect knowledge of the subordinate's "division" of the total organizational task. A politician may be able, therefore, through deliberately misrepresenting the facts or through carefully choosing the facts presented, to control the sovereign's decisions so as to make them favor the objectives desired by the subordinate. In other words, with care, the politician may cause the sovereign's own decisions to conform closely with his own (the politician's) desires. The danger, to the politician, of concealing the truth from his sovereign should, however, be stressed. It will do a general little good to report continuous victories if he must eventually retreat through the capital city.

As suggested above, the individual politican may take either course of action when confronted with the situation discussed here. Again, it must be emphasized that any hierarchical system will operate as a selection process. People in this system will rise more readily if they always take action aimed at that end. Thus, the people who are successful in moving up the hierarchy are those who are most likely to choose career-motivated action rather than action motivated by other things. As the economist likes to emphasize, everything in the world is obtained at a cost, and the politician who obtains satisfaction from extra-career motivations must expect to pay for this in terms of a slower rate of advancement.

Again, this analysis represents some oversimplification. The politician confronted with the choice must take two variables into account, the deviation between what he really wants and what the sovereign will reward, and the probability that the sovereign will be aware of his action. The problem of weighing the risk of discovery is added to the problem of choosing between the two courses of action. When it is further recognized that the single sovereign situation in its pure form is seldom actually encountered, the choice problem confronting the real-world politician is likely to be considerably more complicated than that one postulated here. In normal cases, even with a single sovereign, there will exist some chance of overthrowing the sovereign, either by the reference politician or by some third party. In order to simplify our analysis, we eliminate this complication by definition. It represents multiple sovereignty rather than single sovereignty as the latter is herein defined.

CRITERIA FOR REWARD

To this point, I have employed the rather clumsy phrase "action likely to be rewarded" or some equivalent to describe the type of action which will be taken by the ambitious and intelligent politician. It is easier to talk of action that is designed "to please," but unless carefully explained, this usage may lead to misunderstanding. The type of behavior that a sovereign may reward is not necessarily that which pleases him in the ordinary sense of this term. Even such a degenerate monarch as Charles V of Spain would hardly have consciously insisted that his prime minister be his queen's lover, yet if Don Manuel de Godoy had other qualifications they have escaped generations of historians.[2] This example is cited to suggest that there are cases in which a sovereign will quite obviously reward behavior that is personally displeasing to him. He may, for instance, dislike upsetting scenes, and he may be willing to give in to, i.e., reward, the man who shows signs of creating such scenes. The last Tsar of all the Russias was, apparently, literally bullied into various courses of action by the more self-assertive of the grand dukes.

The object of the politician seeking to rise in a hierarchy is, to summarize, to take that course of action that will be rewarded by the sovereign, regardless of the subjective attitude of the sovereign. Normally, and over the long run, actions that cause the sovereign pain are not likely to be rewarded. We may conclude that most politicians, most of the time, try to please their superiors because they feel that such a course of action is more likely to be rewarded than any other. The skilled politician may always keep in mind those means of advancing his cause that will not please his sovereign, but he will seldom resort to such measures. For this reason, the statement that behavior pleasing to the superior is likely to lead to advancement does not greatly differ in substantive content from the (tautological) statement that behavior

2. Although Godoy himself was a man of very slight attainments, his self-justifying memoirs are of some interest to a student of politics. His continual emphasis on his own lack of power, when he was the most influential man at court, is a useful corrective to the more self-assertive stand that strong characters normally take in their autobiographies. He never had any doubts that his position depended entirely on the favor of the king and queen, and shaped all of his decisions to the end of keeping that favor.

likely to be rewarded is that behavior likely to be rewarded. Pleasing his superior is *almost* an accurate description of the behavioral goal of the politician who wants to succeed, and I shall use it as an approximation in what follows.

PLEASING THE SOVEREIGN

We may now discuss the extent to which the politician will sacrifice other ends to the objective of pleasing his superior, an objective which, in itself, must be only an intermediate or instrumental one. When we read accounts of life at the courts of absolute rulers, we are often astounded at the extent to which all turns on the desires and the whims of the ruler. The courtier not only follows the least indication of the ruler's will; he also spends a great deal of time trying to discern the ruler's unexpressed desires so that he may respond also to these. There is tremendous interest in everything connected with the personal life of the ruler. How well did he sleep? Is he feeling well today? Who will be his next mistress? Above all, what is his attitude toward me (the reference politician) and toward the task I am carrying out? Each contact with the ruler is carefully planned to give the proper impression.

Some rulers may like to be convinced on policy decisions through argument. Louis XIV of France, for example, wrote a long document that purported to be a guide for his heir. It was, in fact, an autobiography. One day he took the document from its cabinet and prepared to burn it in the fireplace. The skillful courtier who was in attendance immediately interposed himself between Louis and the fireplace and demanded that the king desist. There then followed an "argument" in which Louis several times reiterated his desire to burn the document, while the courtier held that this would deprive Europe of a priceless treasure. The result was as could have been predicted. Louis did not burn the papers, and the courtier found his relations with his sovereign improved until another courtier was able to score a similar coup. (Needless to say, the document in question is not a priceless treasure.)

It is possible that the courtier may have genuinely felt that the preservation of the papers was desirable. But more likely he gave little attention to this aspect of the matter. He acted in the manner that was calculated to please the king and so to advance his own cause. The courtier simply treated the king as most human beings treat the various parts of their environment. In trying to attain their goals, people normally consider the situations in which they find themselves, look at the parts of the environment that may be utilized, and take the indicated measures. In other words, we tend to look upon our environment instrumentally. The politician in our models takes the same attitude with respect to his sovereign.

THE SOVEREIGN'S KNOWLEDGE OF POLITICIAN'S ACTIVITY

If the politician looks at matters in this way, he will become a serious student of his sovereign. The first consideration is the degree of knowledge possessed by the sovereign on the sphere of activity of the politician. This aspect of the relation is most important to the politician because his actions will be judged in terms of this knowledge (or lack of it). On occasion, the superior may have a simple means of judging the success of his subordinates without a detailed understanding of their tasks. The owner of a chain of stores, for example, need know little about retailing. He can consult the balance sheets at the end of each accounting period, and then fire the five managers who show the lowest net profit. This method will, of course, work only within limits, and it will not be the most efficient method of control, but it will work.

In a governmental hierarchy the problem of knowledge is much more difficult than it is in business organization. The type of knowledge problem facing the normal public official is not susceptible to simple mechanical solution, or even an approximation to such a solution. Furthermore, governments are essentially monopolistic. The external check of competition that is present in business organization is absent. Governments can follow inefficient policies for very long periods without being eliminated. The Kingdom of the Two Sicilies, for example, seems to have been governed atrociously for practically the entire period of its existence. The politician is much less subject to pressures for "efficiency" than is the normal businessman.

To the individual politician, "efficiency" is meaningful, not in terms of the organization's goals, but in terms of his own. For him efficiency is measured by the extent to which he is able to satisfy his superior, and this, in turn, depends very largely upon knowledge possessed by the superior about the politician's activity. This knowledge varies greatly from one situation to another. For example, if the superior has only recently been advanced to his position from that which is now held by the politician, his knowledge of the subordinate's activity will be substantially complete. This represents one extreme. In the normal case, the sovereign will possess much less knowledge about the politician's sphere of activity than will the politician himself. In choosing a course of action, he must decide not what would be "best" for the superior in the light of all the information that he (the politician) possesses, but rather what will seem "best" to his superior in the terms of his more limited information. Thus, the politician searches for policies that can be readily and plausibly explained to the less well informed superior rather than for policies which, in terms of the total information available, would be best for the superior.

A factor limiting the difference between policies taken to please the superior with limited knowledge and those that would be taken on the basis of full information is the simple desire of the politician to appear competent. He will avoid actions that will lead to failure. If the policy that may appear best to the superior is known by the subordinate to lead to probable failure, a conflict arises. The politician must weigh the probable initial displeasure of the sovereign produced by his taking action that seems wrong to the latter against the probable displeasure of the sovereign if the policy adopted should fail. Even if the politician secures explicit approval for a course of action in advance, he cannot hope to be rewarded if that policy should fail.

This problem, although important, must not be overemphasized. There is seldom clear and unambiguous evidence that will indicate whether or not a given policy decision is successful. Furthermore, the decision made by the individual politician will almost always be only one of a number of influences on the final outcome. It is nearly always possible that a "correct" decision could be followed by a poor result, and vice versa. Judgment on the politician's actions, then, purely in terms of results is not possible in most situations. This fact is known by superior and inferior alike.

The discussion here may be summarized by putting the matter symbolically. Let us say that a superior knows facts A, B, and C. The subordinate, due to his more intimate contact with the problem, knows facts A, B, C, D, E, F, G, and H. On the basis of facts A, B, and C alone, action X would be indicated. On the basis of the more inclusive set, action Y would be suggested. The situation is complicated further by the recognition that there will surely exist facts I, J, and K that are unknown to both the superior and the subordinate. These other facts can never be known, however, and, in normal cases, the greater information possessed by the subordinate implies that policy Y will be more successful than policy X. Nevertheless, the wise and efficient politician will tend to recommend X rather than Y. He will back up this recommendation by reasoning from A, B, and C, and, if he is artistic, will bring in, say, G, which will reinforce the argument.

The result of such recommendation is that the sovereign will be impressed with the soundness of the politician's reasoning. If, by contrast, the politician should recommend policy Y, this would involve a lengthy and involved effort to educate the superior on the additional facts: D, E, F, G, and H. Even if he is successful in convincing the superior of the appropriateness of Y, this behavior is not likely to endear the subordinate to his superior, who in any event may not have sufficient time to undergo the educational process. As there are usually several subordinates reporting to a single superior, the next promotion is likely to go to the man who has reached "correct" decisions, not to the one who has come up with "peculiar" solutions backed up by a long list of "facts" which appear dubious to the superior.

This analysis suggests that, in a bureaucracy, factual information tends to flow from the top down instead of from the bottom up. This conclusion is contrary to the normal assumption that subordinates in a bureaucracy collect and winnow information and pass on only the most important parts of it to their superiors. This is what "should" happen in the ideally efficient organization, and it is also what would happen if men were machines. Departures from this "ideal" become especially significant in poorly organized hierarchies. In a badly run bureaucracy, the information that is really important to the subordinate does not concern the real world, but rather his superior's image of the real world. As a result, almost no new information that will be relevant for policy will enter the organizational machine at the bottom tier. The typical method through which such an organization adjusts itself to new and changed conditions is through external sources acting on the man at the top, and, subsequent to this, his inferiors finding out from him. In the Department of State, Walter Lippmann, the *New York Times*, and the *Washington Post* are, I am sure, the primary sources of information upon which the foreign policy of the United States is based. The higher officials in the department read these, more carefully than anything produced within the department itself. More importantly, even if they should read departmental reports and papers, they would normally find that these only reflect their own opinions.

As I have suggested earlier, the analytical model does not suggest that typical politicians in an organization are hypocrites in that they consciously follow these practices. In many respects, organizations would run more smoothly if they were. Judgments would in that case be more rational and more predictable. In fact, however, most politicians and most officials would become uneasy if they realized that they recommend policies to their superiors that may be contrary to those suggested by the facts at hand. In many cases the desire to avoid this realization has the result of causing subordinate officials to lose interest in objective factual aspects of their activities. While it is probable that the subordinate will know more about any given situation than his superior, it is also true that the ambitious and intelligent bureaucrat will tend to cut himself off from external reality, unless he is a conscious hypocrite. The official who is not hypocritical about his task soon learns that an active curiosity leads either to quarrels with superiors or to bad conscience; hence, he suppresses his curiosity.

An example may clarify the situation. In 1950, while in Washington, I sat in on a few classes in the Foreign Service Institute which were a part of a course designed to train mid-level officers. One class was entitled "problems arising in the diplomatic service" or something similar, and had as a guest lecturer a high-ranking official of the Policy Planning Board. He was a Russian specialist who had spent part of World War II in Egypt maintaining liaison with and expediting supplies for Tito's forces in Yugoslavia. He chose an incident from this part of his career as the main basis for his lecture. Here I boil his half-hour speech into a few sentences: It seems that Tito had sent two generals of his force to Egypt, and they had brought along a copy of the new constitution which Tito had decreed. The Russian specialist remarked (speaking in 1950) that he had been impressed by these men and the document. He had been particularly impressed by the civil rights provisions of the constitution. He then went on to say that there were rumors that the forces under Tito were using some of the arms which they were receiving in a little civil war against the forces of Mihailovich.

This rumor eventually reached the ears of very important people, and the mission to which the lecturer was attached suddenly received a telegram sent from the Quebec conference asking whether these reports were true. This was the climax of his story; this was the difficult problem. As a matter of fact, he never told us what reply was sent, closing his speech by saying that he still remembered the impact of this telegram. Using our previous discussion as a base, it is clear that, with the receipt of the telegram, the Tito regime changed its character. Before the telegram was received, the Russian expert was impressed by the constitution which parroted the "Great Stalin Constitution" on civil rights, because his superiors were impressed. He was not curious about the reality of the regime, and if he had heard the rumors (the subject was discussed in many American newspapers) about the fighting between Tito's forces and the Chetniks he had promptly dismissed the subject from his mind. Then, like a bolt from the blue, came the telegram of inquiry, and he was confronted with a most difficult problem.

Fundamentally, he was interested not in the situation in Yugoslavia, which had not changed, but in his superior's knowledge of the situation.

The telegram, then, was a major crisis. The fact that it came in the form of an inquiry made it particularly difficult. Did the people congregated in Quebec want these rumors confirmed or denied? Even discussing the question would destroy the elaborate protective mechanism and convert him into a conscious hypocrite. On the other hand, the telegram had to be answered, and the answer could seriously affect his future career. Under the circumstances there would be nothing to do but to carefully analyze the telegram for a hint as to the attitude of his superiors. Probably this led to no definite conclusion, and an ambiguous answer was sent off while soundings were taken through other channels to find out whether or not, in the minds of Washington, Tito was fighting Mihailovich.

Since this was a voluntary choice of topic by a fairly important man, and, since he could have told the story in other terms, terms which did not reveal his complete lack of interest in the real situation, we must assume that his attitude was completely unconscious. He had risen to high rank in the Department of State through following a certain pattern of behavior. He probably had never stopped to analyze that pattern. Furthermore, his audience saw nothing unusual in the story. I discussed the matter afterward with several officers, and none of them thought that the lecturer had done anything unusual. The pattern of behavior which we have deduced from theoretical considerations had been internalized in each of them.

LIMITATIONS ON TIME OF SOVEREIGN

The limitations on the knowledge that a sovereign can possess concerning the activities of his subordinate depend in part on the limits on his time. The politician knows that the sovereign cannot spend all of his time supervising the activities of each of his subordinates. If, for example, a king should have a cabinet of ten equally important ministers, obviously he can give no more than one-tenth of each day, on the average, to supervising a particular one of them. In practice he will spend much less than this. He will have other things to do; and his position of power and wealth makes his access to interesting distractions very great. The Ming emperors, for illustration, during the later period of the dynasty, found life in the palace so interesting and entertaining that they hardly ever gave audience to their ministers. Even in that time of the superior which is devoted to affairs of state, the whole amount cannot be devoted to supervising subordinates. Some time must be spent reaching decisions about general policy questions, and the high officials of the realm may, in fact, spend much more time advising on these than on the concrete operations of the bureaucracy in its several divisions. The situation is the same if we consider a less exalted official. The lower the official in the hierarchy, the greater the pressure that he will be under to be industrious, but a lower official must devote time to his own sovereign, thus taking time away from his activities in supervising his subordinates.

In view of these limitations on the sovereign's time it is impossible (as well as unwise) for the subordinate to educate his superior in all of the facts relevant to a particular problem. Insofar as the sovereign trusts the subordinate to make decisions independently, the latter will take those decisions which are best for him (the subordinate) after considering the whole situation in long-run terms. *The resulting decision will be correct from the standpoint of the superior only if he has so organized his area of control that decisions which are best for his own interests are those that will also improve the position of the inferiors.* This implies that the superior or sovereign must reward "correct" decisions and penalize "incorrect" decisions. The difficult questions as to how this can be done, when both the information available to the superior and the amount of time that he can afford to devote to any given problem are extremely limited, will be discussed further in a later chapter. Here it suffices to say that only approximate measures are possible, and that in some circumstances the best solution may be very poor indeed.

If the sovereign gives direct orders, he will be making decisions on subjects about which he clearly possesses insufficient information. The system will be inefficient because final decisions are made by someone who is less well informed than others in the hierarchy. If the inferiors are ambitious and tactful, they will, of course, conceal this fact, and they will seek to convince the sovereign that his decisions are greatly admired. They must try, in such situations, to act as if they genuinely consider the sovereign to be wise.

The importance of the time limitation will vary from position to position. The head of the Chevrolet Division of General Motors must expect the head of the parent company to spend considerably more time supervising this division's activities than would be the case for the manager of a smaller division. Further, the time limitation is reasonably flexible, and thus may vary significantly from problem to problem. In the case of special developments, the sovereign can always pay particular attention to a single problem within the area of activity of a single subordinate, neglecting temporarily the activities of other subordinates. This potential flexibility in the time assigned by the sovereign must be taken into account by the subordinate.

INTELLIGENCE OF THE SOVEREIGN

As we have seen, if mobility with merit selection characterizes the hierarchy, then those who rise to the highest positions will tend to be the most intelligent members of the hierarchy. The average intelligence at each level should be higher than that at the next lower level. The necessity of effective social mobility for achieving this result must be emphasized. A hereditary king is apt to be less intelligent than his high-ranking ministers, provided only that they have risen to their positions through merit selection. The king's ministers are likely to be more intelligent than the king, even if they have risen to high ranks entirely in terms of their ability to please their master in capacities other than their normal ministerial ones. Thus, if the king should select boon drinking companions and rousing good fellows to head all of his ministries, then the most intelligent and ambitious people will take pains to become good drinkers and wild carousers. Their intelligence may or may not have some effect on their ministries, but it will help keep them in favor with the king.

Let us take an extreme case. Consider a professor of economics and the dullest student in his class. Let us assume that, by accident of gene selection, the dull student becomes a king, and, possibly by inheritance from a previous king, the professor of economics becomes his principal economic minister. As all professors of economics know, many of the duller students never learn what economics is about, even with the best efforts on the part of the teacher. In the assumed situation, the professor, now a minister, can no longer compel attendance on the part of the dullard, nor can he even threaten the latter with a flunking grade. His only refuge is to try to charm the dull king into accepting ideas which would be completely beyond him were he in a classroom.

Such a minister has open to him three courses of action: he can resign; he can stop trying to improve the economic conditions of the kingdom and simply implement the king's stupid ideas on economic matters; or he can try to deceive the king into carrying out the policies that he, the minister, thinks wise while agreeing with the king in council. The apparent preferability of the third alternative vanishes when it is recognized that someone else who wants the position as economics minister will surely tell the king of his current minister's deceit. The intelligent and ambitious man will, therefore, certainly choose the second course of action. A man of intelligence, but with less ambition, might choose the first or the third, either one of which would eventually lead to his removal from the position and to his replacement by someone else who is more interested in what the king thinks about economics than in what economics really is.

Analogous situations to this occur among the relations at various ranks in any hierarchy characterized by merit selection and social mobility. As we move up the pyramid, the average intelligence will steadily increase, but the word "*average*" should be emphasized. The difference between the average intelligence level of one rank and another may be quite small. Among American army officers, very mediocre persons may occasionally rise to the rank of colonel or brigadier general, but major generals are usually or nearly always reasonably intelligent. Lieutenant generals, whatever one may sometimes think about their military abilities, are generally very intelligent. But note that the man who is destined to reach general rank in 1985 is now a junior officer, and the chances are that he is now serving under a superior who is considerably less intelligent than himself.

Thus although average intelligence increases as one moves up the pyramid, at any given time many persons in the structure are serving under superiors who are less intelligent than themselves. The man who has the capacity to rise ultimately to the top will probably have to serve under less intelligent men throughout most of his career. Again we may revert to the example of the economist and his dull student. Assume now that both are in the civil service, and that the dull pupil, having started his career earlier, is the superior of the professor. Like the king's minister, the professor must either adjust himself to the dullard's ideas or get out. Much of the frustration experienced by academics when they attempt to influence decisions within an administrative hierarchy as consultants, advisers, etc., probably stems from their failure to adjust to this situation.

We see, therefore, that the man who has the ability to rise to the very top of an administrative hierarchy will continually confront the problem of dealing with less intelligent superiors. He will, of course, never rise if they should be displeased by his performance. Hence, if he is ambitious, he must try to please these superiors. He will not advocate policies which, to his superior intelligence, may seem wise if he feels that such policies involve complexities too "deep" for his superiors to comprehend. Instead, he will devote some of his intellectual gifts to a careful study of the superiors themselves, as opposed to a study of the objective conditions of his duties. If he should fail to do this, or if he should think mostly of his "duty," and, thereby, be led into disagreement with his less perceptive superiors, he will fail to advance in the hierarchy. High intelligence, unless it be combined with an intense devotion to careerist ends, is a serious disadvantage to a man in, let us say, the civil service. But intelligence is a decided advantage if the man possessing it uses his abilities primarily to further his own career.

THE SINGLE SOVEREIGN SITUATION IN AN ADMINISTRATIVE HIERARCHY

As previously mentioned, the single sovereign situation cannot be treated as a general one, applicable to whole administrative structures. With a specific exception to be discussed below, the single sovereign case in its pure form exists only in the first layer of an administrative pyramid, i.e., at the apex, where the individual at the top is in the no-sovereign situation. The immediate ministers of a king or dictator and other people who find themselves working for someone who, in turn, is not working for someone else; these are the persons in a single sovereign situation. Lower down in the hierarchy, the relationship is almost non-existent. To understand fully why this is true, let us now superimpose our diagram of the politician's world over a more conventional organizational chart.

Note that no circle or boundary has been drawn in the figure separating the participants from the spectators, because the location of this dividing line is the point at issue. If the area of participation is small, and only B3 lies within its upper quadrant, then P, the reference politician, is in a single sovereign situation. If, on the other hand, the area of participation is large enough so that A is also within the limits, P is in a multiple sovereign situation.

The boundary line separating the active participants from the spectators cannot be adjusted simply through administrative order. Although the hierarchy might function more effectively if, somehow, each member of the hierarchy could be placed in the single sovereign situation, no general rule dictating that this be so is likely to exert much influence on administrative practice. Refer again to the diagram, and consider the interests of the several parties.

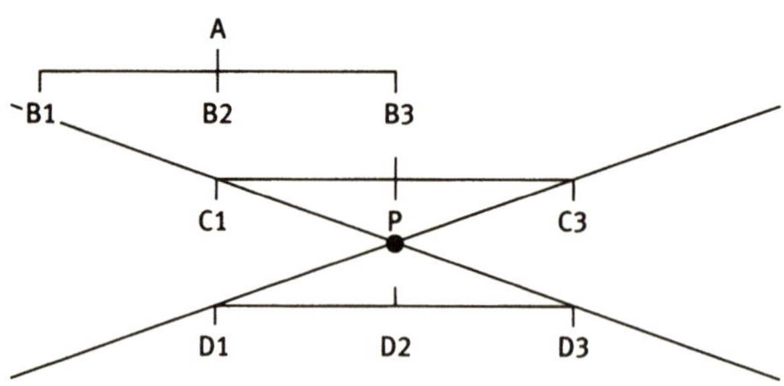

P has everything to gain by placing himself in a situation where he confronts multiple sovereigns rather than a single sovereign. This widens his range of choice; provides him with alternatives; gives him room to maneuver; and is the ideal situation for a politician who wants to rise. P cannot, however, control the upper reaches of his administrative world. His desires in this matter, therefore, are only of secondary importance. Conversely, P would prefer to be in a single sovereign relationship with his own subordinate, say, D2, since this would give him maximum control. In this way, each official in the hierarchy has some motive for maximizing the number of higher officials with whom he has contacts, while, at the same time, trying to keep his own subordinates from having contact with any superior other than himself.

To this point, the pattern shapes up as a straight conflict between superiors and inferiors, with odds on the superiors to win. But there exists one factor which almost insures that any inferior will, in fact, be confronted with a multiple sovereign situation. Refer again to the diagram. B3 desires to maximize his control over P, but he also wants to minimize the time and effort that he must devote to attaining this end. One of the simplest techniques of control is for B3 to form some sort of connection with D2 (and other subordinates of P). P's subordinates can be expected to know much of what he does, and, if the proper channels have been opened, B3 can expect to be told if P does something that is particularly contrary to B3's desires. Further, even the knowledge that B3 consults with D2, and may contemplate putting D2 in the place of P, can be counted on to make P keep on his mark. As a consequence of this logic almost all higher officials maintain some channels of contact with low-echelon people.

The result of the contact between B3 and D2 is clear. D2 is no longer in a single sovereign situation. He now has at least two persons within the upper portion of his circle of participants to his own power struggle, P and B3. Further, A can be expected to reason in a similar way with B3, with the result that P will also be in a multiple sovereign situation. P, who would like to prevent the contact between B3 and D2, cannot do so, because B3 is his superior. In turn, B3 cannot prevent the contact between A and P, because A is B3's superior. As a result, we can see that the pure single sovereign situation can hardly ever exist except at the very top of the pyramid.

The discussion to this point has been basically analytical, but the memoirs of many successful people who have risen in various hierarchies will indicate that our theoretical construct is in accord with reality. The picture is everywhere the same. Any official will have relations not only with those directly above and below him, but also with the next step in both directions. Frequently the circle of participants will be even larger, and relations may extend much farther up or down. The Nazis, in their "theoretical" literature, sometimes advocated the "führerprinzip" for all organizations in the sense that each official would be responsible only to his immediate superior. Here again, however, the memoirs of many former members of various German government hierarchies have made it clear that our generalization holds. Hitler himself did not confine himself to dealing with his immediate inferiors, but regularly went to their inferiors. The less-exalted officials of the regime did the same.

There is an exception to this general rule about the non-applicability of the single sovereign relationship in hierarchies, although the relationship is peculiar to the position and cannot, in the nature of things, be applied generally. This exception lies in the relationship of the aide, the flag lieutenant, the private secretary to the top-ranking official in the hierarchy. Let us call this sort of official an *equerry*. These persons are not really a part of the struggle for power within the formal hierarchy; they are of the "staff rather than of the line." They are helpful to the high-ranking official precisely because of this fact. Such persons are in single sovereign situations, and likely to remain so. Only the one higher official is in the upper reaches of their world. Even if the superior has, in turn, his own superior, the equerry is unlikely to have relationships with him.

FLATTERY

Although from some points of view, the single sovereign relationship is the most efficient administrative arrangement, there are certain specific disadvantages. The first of these I shall call flattery. I should like, in this analysis, to give this term a somewhat broader meaning than it normally carries, but the relationship between my meaning and the normal one is quite close. Consider an ultimate sovereign dealing with his subordinates. Assume that the sovereign is interested only in increasing his own satisfaction. His subordinates contribute to this satisfaction in two ways. They increase his satisfaction in carrying out his desires, in doing the things that he wants done. This is the aspect of the power relation that is usually discussed. But they also increase the sovereign's satisfaction by making their own relations with him pleasant. Thus, in dealing with subordinates, an ultimate sovereign can increase his satisfaction in two ways. Either he may choose subordinates who are efficient in carrying out his wishes, or he may choose those with whom he finds it pleasant to deal. Both desiderata are taken into account in most actual decisions, and the second is what I shall call "flattery."

Everyone, of course, desires to have his personal relations with those with whom he deals as pleasant as is possible. The definition of what is pleasant varies from one man to another, but every man will try to maximize the pleasure he gets from personal contacts insofar as this does not reduce his satisfaction from other sources. The pretty blonde who can also type and take dictation is sure to be hired. But the single sovereign is in a position to place greater emphasis on her beauty than on her typing. He is free to consider his subordinates either as instruments for carrying out his will, and in this way indirectly pleasing him, or as sources of direct satisfaction. He is likely, merely because he is more able to do so, to give more attention to the aesthetic aspects of his relationships with subordinates than will a man in the multiple sovereign situation.

Recognizing the importance of flattery, the subordinate will tend to devote attention to the form of his relations with the sovereign. This will depend upon the character of the sovereign, and vast differences exist between different sovereigns. Straight and open flattery is the best behavior pattern in a surprising number of cases, but something more subtle may be indicated. A skilled courtier can give the impression of greatly admiring his sovereign without ever specifically saying anything on the subject. The sovereign may enjoy being opposed on occasion. He may even prefer to lose occasional arguments or contests. Again the skillful politician will adjust his behavior accordingly. The politician must do more than admire the sovereign, or seem to do so. He must also try to conform to the superior's idea of a pleasant companion. He will cultivate an interest in subjects that fascinate the superior; he will try to develop the "character" type that the superior finds most congenial.

The politician will recognize, however, that flattery, even in the broad sense used here, is not the only desideratum in dealing with superiors and that it can be overdone. In lighter-weight "how to get ahead" books, flattery is sometimes treated as the only route to success. But this is as one-sided as the reverse position that "doing your job" is all that matters. In fact, the sovereign will be interested in both aspects of his subordinate's performance. A charming and inefficient man is as little likely to rise to the top as the efficient boor. The man most likely to advance is the one who combines relatively great talent for getting the sovereign to like him personally with a relatively great talent for carrying out the tasks that are given to him. Such a person will sometimes be confronted with the necessity of choosing which of the two ways to please the sovereign when these two ways come into conflict. He must seek a balance between "flattery" and "performance." Some sovereigns will be interested almost solely in performance; others in flattery. To some extent, the relative interest of the sovereign in these two aspects will be imposed upon him by the external environment within which he operates.

It was noted above that the single sovereign is more likely to be affected by flattery. The reasons for this are not difficult to find. If single sovereignty situations should exist lower in the hierarchy, flattery would be important at these ranks also. But, in any part of the hierarchy except the very top, each sovereign will have at least one other superior over him. The higher sovereigns will be interested only in their relations with inferiors with whom they have relations—this is a deliberate tautology. The personalities of inferiors with whom they do not have relations do not interest them. The performance of distant inferiors will, however, remain of interest to them. Thus, the head of a division, in dealing with his superiors, may make use of both the flattery and the performance techniques. In dealing with his own inferiors, however, as head of a division, he must, if he wishes to advance, emphasize performance, rewarding only those who perform well and controlling his natural impulse to reward those whom he likes. This is because the performance of his inferiors becomes, in effect, his own. His superiors will, in computing his efficiency, simply measure the performance of his division. They will not be able to select out that part of the divisional performance that is the supervisor's own unique contribution, nor would they be interested in doing so if they could.

All of this amounts to saying that the sovereign who is himself subordinate to another sovereign cannot "afford" the added "real income" (nontaxable) that pleasant relationships with his own subordinates can provide him if this "real income" is secured at the cost of performance. The man who rises most rapidly in a multiple sovereign situation will use flattery, but he will not allow it to be used on him. Following our usual analysis, since such people will tend to get to the higher ranks in hierarchies, these ranks will tend to be filled with persons who do, in fact, emphasize performance rather than flattery. This fact tends to insure that flattery, as such, will be less characteristic of administrative hierarchies than appears likely at first glance.

VAGUENESS OF SOVEREIGN'S WISHES

The second special disadvantage of the single sovereign situation is not so readily apparent; it is frequently very difficult for the politician to find out what the single sovereign wants. While it may be hard to predict the reactions of an electorate, even the politician subject to the group sovereign in a democracy is much better off than his compatriot under the single sovereign. Sampling procedures can provide the democratic politician with some indication of an electorate's wishes. The highly efficient single sovereign will rarely leave his wishes in doubt, but this degree of efficiency is not normal. Most sovereigns will have the defects of ordinary men, and defects tend to be magnified when men are placed in positions of power. One of these defects makes it especially difficult for the subordinate to find out the real wishes of his superior.

Persons without experience with absolutist power situations may think that the politician who wants to find out the wishes of his superior may do so by asking. There are two considerations that prevent courtiers from turning often to this expedient. First, the chance that the sovereign will not answer, and, second, the chance that the mere asking of the question will prejudice the career of the inferior. Any sovereign will, as has been suggested earlier, have a limited amount of time to give to the activities of any one subordinate. Thus, there is a definite limit to the amount of time that he can give to answering a given subordinate's questions. Further, one of the reasons for employing the subordinate is to relieve the sovereign of some of the burden of decision making. In addition there may be other reasons that are rationalized on the basis of these quite legitimate ones. The sovereign may be lazy, and he may not enjoy the trouble of reaching decisions. Besides, there are certain decisions that he may want to avoid making. People in general like to avoid responsibility, and absolute sovereigns are no different from their fellows in this respect.

In cases where the sovereign does not really know what he wants or where he does not want to make up his mind, the subordinate is in a particularly difficult position. If he takes action without questioning his superior, he stands the chance of having his decisions disapproved, *ex post facto*. On the other hand, if he asks a question beforehand, he may be penalized. The situation may be complicated even more by an additional behavior pattern which seems characteristic of persons in positions of great power. Many such sovereigns do not think of themselves as acting arbitrarily. They think that their decisions are based on rules or principles. They commonly complain that, "When I do not do things directly, everything is done wrong." What they actually mean is that, "When I do not do things directly, they are done differently."

This suggests that many such people tend to think of themselves as having great power to *do right*, not simply as having great power. Nothing infuriates such persons more than the subordinate who says, "I shall, of course, obey your orders because it is my duty, but I think that you are wrong." If the sovereign, in his own eyes, is doing the right, properly virtuous subordinates will be expected to do the right also, without the necessity of asking questions of the superior. In this case a request for instructions can be looked upon as an indication of incompetence. For all of these reasons, the direct inferiors of kings, dictators, and other people in positions of absolute power tend to be most reluctant to ask for instructions. Farther down the administrative hierarchy, the tendency to refrain from question-asking is less pronounced, but the fundamentals of the problem remain.

CHAPTER 7

THE GROUP SOVEREIGN

The third situation in which our politician may find himself is being subject to a group sovereign, that is, a group of people who, through some voting process, act as a unit. This is the situation we normally describe by the adjective "democratic." In recent years considerable progress has been made in the theoretical analysis of the democratic process. Since it would be tedious to attempt a full summarization of this important work here, I shall confine myself to a very brief indication of the general fields in which this research falls, and to referring the reader to the original sources for further enlightenment.

The first field investigated is the mathematical analysis of voting procedures, especially simple majority voting. This sounds simple to the point of simple-mindedness, but in fact is quite complicated. Further, the results have been startling. Anyone who is able to follow the mathematics of the workers in this field is inescapably led to the conclusion that the traditional theory of democracy is untrue. Since democracy obviously exists, this points to the need for a new theory, and such a new theory is gradually taking shape. William Riker's article "Voting and the Summation of Preferences"[1] presents an excellent summary of the work done in the last decade. Two articles published after his deadline may also be of interest: Dr. Benjamin Ward's "Majority Rule and Allocation"[2] and my own "Utility, Strategy, and Social Decision Rules, A Comment."[3]

A second field which has recently been investigated concerns the theory of constitutions. The workers in this field, so far mostly limited to Dr. James Buchanan and myself, have been interested in the application of the techniques developed in economics to the analysis of constitutions. The basic problem is the relative efficiency of various possible constitutional orders. Again, the methods are radically different from those of traditional political theory, and the results are somewhat surprising. The only book in this very new and underdeveloped field is *The Calculus of Consent*, by Dr. Buchanan

1. *American Political Science Review*, December 1961, p. 900.
2. *Journal of Conflict Resolution*, December 1961, p. 379.
3. *Quarterly Journal of Economics*, August 1961, p. 493.

and me.[4] My recent monograph *Entrepreneurial Politics*[5] is of special relevance to the problems discussed in this chapter.

Neither of these two fields, however, falls directly within the scope of this book. The final field, represented by Anthony Downs's *An Economic Theory of Democracy*[6] deals with the behavior of politicians, and hence falls within our present concerns. This chapter will owe a great debt to Dr. Downs's work, but I will attempt to avoid duplicating the reasoning of his book as far as possible. This will result in my leaving some of the more important matters aside, but since they are so well presented by Dr. Downs, this will be a small loss.

When a politician is directly subordinated to a group of men who always act as a group, he is in a group-sovereign situation. Historically such groups have reached decisions by a wide variety of processes. Everyone has heard that Poland was ruined by the rule of unanimity which prevailed in her Diet (in the eighteenth, not the twentieth century). Something similar to this "consensus" is used successfully not only by the Quakers, but by practically all of the numerous self-governing villages in Asia. Still, the systems with which we are most familiar operate on other principles, and this chapter will consider the types likely to be important to a politician in our society. The type of group sovereign which we will discuss may be exemplified by the electorate, Congress, or the stockholders of a corporation (a very interesting case because the different stockholders have differing numbers of votes).

In order to simplify the discussion we must introduce some distinctions and subclasses. We may first distinguish between a group which is itself the ultimate sovereign, the body of voters, for one example, or the Venetian senate for another, and a group subordinate to some other authority such as Congress or the board of directors of a corporation. The first category we shall call a democratic group, although this may in some cases involve some peculiar uses of the word "democratic." The Venetian government was not democratic in the normal use of the word. The second category, the groups subordinate to another authority, must also be subdivided into two classes, according to their relations with that authority. If the group is composed of a number of individuals who are each subordinated to a different authority, then we have what we shall call a "representative assembly." The American Congress, with

4. University of Michigan Press, 1962.

5. University of Virginia Economic Monograph Series No. 7.

6. Harpers, 1957.

each congressman subordinate to a different electorate[7] will serve as an example of this category. If all the members of the group are subordinated to one outside authority, then we shall call the group a "commission."

From the standpoint of a politician who is subordinate to a group sovereign, the number of members it has is, probably, a more important variable than the particular nature of the group sovereign under the classification given above. The larger the group sovereign, the less attention he must pay to the personal feelings of any individual member; and the more he must play to the gallery. The two types of criteria are not entirely contradictory, however. A numerically large group sovereign will always be democratic. The numerically small, say under ten men, will almost always be a commission. Very small groups of men who attempt to conduct business in a democratic way have almost always failed. Juntas are transitory phenomena, with one or another individual member eventually obtaining predominance and converting the junta into a single sovereign.

Regardless of size or type, the group sovereigns have a number of characteristics in common. In the first place, the procedure of discussion and voting on issues is much slower than the making up of an individual's mind. The total number of decisions which can be taken by a group sovereign will normally be much smaller than the total number which an individual could take. The Congress of the United States passes each year an astounding number of bills, but most of them are trivial matters which are not really decided by the House and Senate. The chairman of the appropriate committee decides, usually without bothering to read it, that the bill is harmless. It is then passed with a long list of other bills which have also not been read by more than a few members of these assemblies. On important matters, where consideration must be given to the merits of the issue, the two houses take much more time to make up their minds than would any normal individual. In fact, the rather normal individuals who compose the American Congress have usually made their personal decisions on the bill long before it comes up for a vote.

Individual members of a group sovereign may also have their views on a given decision influenced by their relations with other members of the group sovereign. The members of the group sovereign will normally have rivalries and differences among themselves, and cliques and less well organized groups will be formed. Further, maneuvering for position within the group sovereign

7. This is a slight oversimplification since both senators from any given state are subordinate to much the same electorate, and there are representatives at large.

may well be the primary occupation of many members of it. In this case, consideration of the merits of a given proposal may be slight. The extent that these phenomena are important varies from group to group, but they will always be a factor. The politician in dealing with the group sovereign, must be well-versed in the cliques and power relations within it, and may find it desirable to attach himself to one of the cliques. He will also normally have considerable freedom to maneuver among the various groups.

In a "parliamentary" government the members of the "cabinet" are also members of the group sovereign to which the cabinet is subordinated. Individual members of the cabinet have greater power, prestige, and income than individual members of the parliament, and most members will be interested in becoming cabinet ministers. Since ministerial rank comes from the parliament's approval, members will try to behave in such a way as to obtain the approval of other members. The result is a legislative body in which individual members, particularly the more important individual members, balance the advantage of pleasing their constituents against the advantage of pleasing other members of parliament. Inter-parliamentary wrangles are apt to be less violent, and sheer obstructionism less common in such a situation than in non-parliamentary representative assemblies. The same phenomena can be observed with democratic group sovereigns which are small enough so that individual members will consider the effect of their actions on their own future chances of office. The Venetian senate or small-scale town meetings will serve as examples.

If single sovereigns are sometimes lazy and/or interested in other things, the same can be said of the members of a group sovereign. In any group sovereign there will be some people who work hard, and some who work almost not at all. Clearly the first group is more important to the politician. The gulf in work loads can be extreme in group sovereign situations, since the members of the group sovereign are apt to be primarily interested in something other than their responsibilities as such members. A rational man in the United States, for example, might decide to pay no attention at all to politics, since time devoted to this end is unlikely to have much effect on his personal future, while the same time devoted to his occupation would bring in real rewards. There are, of course, individuals and groups who stand to benefit from specific government actions and who form pressure groups, but the basic reason for the flourishing nature of our democracy is the fact that politics is our most popular hobby.

Now this might all seem to be an attack on democratic methods. It is quite true that I do not think that the creation of a group sovereign is likely to lead to efficient implementation of some desired policy. A superior organizing his inferiors to execute his will should avoid establishing commissions. The collegial system of administration which was so popular in Europe in the first part of the modern era could be justified as a method "taming" the feudal lords, but it was inherently inefficient, and its replacement by more modern methods of individual responsibility was undoubtedly an improvement. Not only is a commission subject to the disadvantages we have noted, it is also likely to be composed of relatively poor personnel. If we have a given amount of money to use for a given end, and we have a choice of hiring one man or a commission of five with that money, we will obviously be able to pay the individual five times as much as the average commissioner. We will, therefore, normally be able to obtain an individual who is superior to any individual among the five. If we are in a situation where we can direct manpower rather than hiring it, in a totalitarian state or an army, then the same result will occur.

This, however, is a discussion of the most efficient method of carrying out the will of an ultimate sovereign. It has no relevance to discussions of who or what that ultimate sovereign will be. If we feel that the people should be the ultimate sovereign, we can discuss, on the basis of the reasoning exhibited in this book, how the will of the people should be implemented. This book is not seriously concerned with justifying any particular type of absolute sovereign. Speaking for myself, I prefer a government in which I have something, however little, to say, and in which the employees of the government know that their jobs eventually depend on pleasing the voters. It is an interesting fact that almost every advocate of non-democratic forms of government implicitly assumes either that he himself will be in a position of power in that government, or that the people who will be in power will generally agree with him. He looks for a government which will be, not a father surrogate, but a self surrogate. No Nazi believed in dictatorial government headed by a Jew. People who advocate dictatorial governments always assume certain desires on the part of the dictator. The dictatorial government is not really wanted for itself, but in order to carry out certain projects which appeal to the individual who wants it, but which are difficult to accomplish under democracy. Such people should read a few careful accounts of historic despotisms and ask themselves whether the switch to such a system, headed by an average absolute ruler, would really be an improvement.

If it is assumed to be desirable to let the people exercise as much influence on the government as possible, letting them vote on various issues seems the most efficient method of achieving this objective. It is not necessary that they all have the same number of votes. Corporations are democracies (albeit ones in which most of the electors are exceptionally inattentive to their duties), even though various people have different numbers of votes. Similarly, the system which England abandoned only recently, of giving university graduates two votes, is possible. The decision as to how many votes each person will have is a decision which must be reached on the basis of considerations foreign to the reasoning in this book. We are concerned with how the ultimate sovereign gets his will carried out, not with who the ultimate sovereign is.

In most democratic countries, the people elect representatives who then carry on the business of government, rather than directly voting on each issue. This is a labor-saving device reducing both the attention that the average voter must give to politics and the influence that he has. These two considerations must be balanced against each other in deciding whether to adopt it. The oldest and probably most successful of present-day democracies, Switzerland, resorts to referendum procedures to an extent which seems fantastic to an American.

Returning to the main subject of this book, the procedures used to get orders carried out, appointing a commission or board, are usually highly inefficient. The will of the ultimate sovereign, whether the sovereign people or the Great Vozhd, will be most efficiently implemented if it is the responsibility of individuals, not groups. There is one special case where the formation of a commission can be said to be the best way of solving an administrative problem: if we are more interested in the consistency over time than in the actual terms of the decisions in a given area, a board will be a better insurance of such consistency than any individual. Such a board will, in the first place, be subject to gradual replacement, something which is difficult with an individual. Further, such boards have a greater tendency to act in terms of precedent than have individuals. All human beings change their minds, and all collections of human beings are subject to fads and fashion changes, but such a group will be likely to make less-radical shifts than an individual.

Another useful institution which may be confused with a group sovereign is the royal council. Machiavelli puts great emphasis on the desirability of the Prince getting lots of advice. Advice and counsel is widely agreed to be useful in making up one's mind. As a result people frequently consult a number of others whose judgment they trust before they make up their minds. The practice is quite frequently institutionalized by providing a "council" for people, kings, or lesser officials, who must make important decisions. These councils give advice, normally as a collection of individuals rather than as a group, but they are not a group sovereign.[8]

Efforts to establish commissions to act as group sovereigns carrying out the will of a higher-ranking sovereign may result in establishing a council. Each member of the commission will wish to please the sovereign who can reward him and will be likely to take differences of opinion to this higher tribunal. The commission may become simply an organization which conducts preliminary arguments and winnows down the positions which will eventually be presented to the sovereign for decision. If the different members of the commission argue for different courses of action before the higher sovereign, then the commission has become a mere council.

Let us now consider a politician seeking a job from a group sovereign. Let us also, for the present, assume that the group sovereign is democratic, in our terminology, and large enough so that the politician is not interested in the individual members of the electorate. This is the situation which is most readily subject to analysis, and our conclusion from a study of it will be applicable, with suitable modifications, to other types of group sovereigns. The politician may present arguments for his election in two general fields. He can argue in terms of his own personal virtues and in terms of "issues." Most politicians will use both of these techniques, although the relative weight given each will vary. The earlier theory of representative democracy treated the election process as a selection of especially qualified people to make political decisions. More recently elections have been discussed as themselves determining policy. Both processes undoubtedly exist concurrently, and the voter may consider both whether he trusts the judgment of a candidate and the candidate's stand on specific issues. The development of party systems has tended to increase the importance of "issue" voting as compared with "personality" voting. Our discussion will be largely devoted to the "issues" involved in an election rather than to "personality salesmanship," because abstract reasoning leads to more interesting results in this field.

8. The point may be illustrated from Lincoln's comments when he presented his Emancipation Proclamation to his cabinet: ". . . I have got you together to hear what I have written down. I do not wish your advice about the main matter—for that I have determined for myself . . . If there is anything in the expressions I use, or in any other minor matter, which anyone of you thinks had best be changed, I shall be glad to receive the suggestion." *Inside Lincoln's Cabinet*, Salmon P. Chase (edited by David Macdonald), p. 150.

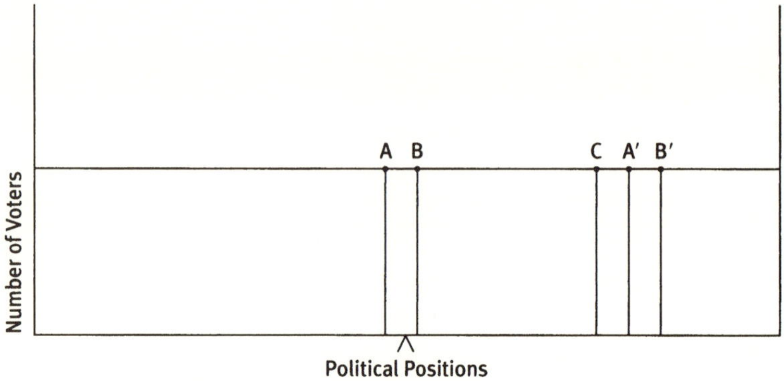

Let us begin by assuming that, with regard to any given issue, each member of the electorate will hold position along a line connecting the two extreme positions. Since their distribution does not in any way affect the demonstration upon which we are embarking, let us assume that they are distributed along the line in the simplest possible way, that is evenly. Let us further assume that all of the individuals have what are known as "single-peaked" preferences along the line. For our purposes this simply means that any individual will always prefer the point out of a collection of points which is closest to his first preference position.[9] Thus the people whose first preference lies at point A of the figure on this page would choose A′ in preference to B′, and B in preference to C, A′, or B′.

Let us consider two politicians, both of whom wish to maximize their support and look upon the issue presented in the figure on this page as an opportunity to do so. The first politician, trying to decide which position will lead to the most political support, chooses B. This is intended to be the exact midpoint of the distribution. If 1 has chosen properly, then 2 must either agree with him, not too good a political position, or select a position on one or the other side of the midpoint, which will result in 1 having more support than 2. Normally, however, the information available to either politician as to the distribution of the populace on this issue will not be completely reliable, and the initial position selected by the first politician is not likely to be exactly at the midpoint. The announcement of politician 1 that he favors policy B is likely to cause some public discussion, so that politician 2, when

9. This rule applies, strictly speaking, only to points on the same side of the individuals' first preference point. This restriction, however, is not relevant to any of the proofs to be presented.

he makes up his mind, will have the benefit of better information on public opinion than 1. If politician 1 has made a slight mistake, which even the most skilled judge of popular opinion may do, he will not have chosen the exact midpoint, and politician 2 can take position A, which is as close to the midpoint of the distribution as is B.

Let us now assume that politician 1 makes a bad mistake in judging the public mood, and adopts position B′. What should politician 2 do? The answer is not to take position B, on the midpoint, because that position, while better than B′, is still not the maximizing point. If politician 2 took position B, then half of the people between B and B′ would support politician 1. If, on the other hand, politician 2 takes position A′, then he gets the support of all the people to the left of A′ and half the people between A′ and B′. Obviously, politician 2 should get as close as he can to politician 1. The only limit would be the necessity of keeping enough space between them so that people can distinguish the two positions. The obvious answer of politician 1 to such a move on the part of politician 2 would be to jump over his head to a position nearer the center, say position C, but in actual politics this type of thing is usually difficult. A third politician entering the race at this point would naturally aim at a point to the left of A′, and beat both 1 and 2, but at present we are considering only two politicians. Thus, if we have two politicians competing for public favor, their positions will probably be close to each other, although they may not be at the midpoint of the distribution of the opinions among the voters.

The essence of political strategy is to seize upon situations where your opponent has made such a mistake and exploit it to the maximum. In the period just before the United States entered World War II, for example, Roosevelt made very shrewd use of this principle. The public opinion polls show that the public was more "interventionist" than government policy. The Republicans, however, had made a mistake, of the sort which they so often made in the thirties, and had taken an essentially isolationist position. Roosevelt maximized the political gains to be made out of this situation by taking a position not far from, but on the interventionist side of, the Republican position, and "leading a vigorous fight" against them. He carefully refrained from pushing his advantage to the point of winning enough legislative victories to completely demolish the Republican position, because this would have deprived him of his advantageous strategic position.

A politician may maneuver his opponents into such an unfavorable position, instead of simply waiting for them to make a mistake. If my interpretation of the events of early 1957 is correct, Eisenhower did just that to the Democrats in connection with his "Middle East Doctrine." Regardless of one's views of the value of this proposal in the sphere of foreign policy, and I have little admiration for it, Eisenhower's tactic was well chosen from the standpoint of the American domestic scene. It was the type of proposal that most Americans like, and in general was approved by almost all sectors of the American public. The method of releasing the doctrine, however, has been described as "clumsy," since it antagonized the Democratic majority in the new Congress. If Eisenhower's objective was the amelioration of conditions in the Middle East, he was surely clumsy; but if he aimed at a victory in the domestic political war, his handling of the issue was tactically brilliant. By annoying the Democrats into opposing this popular measure, he put them in a most difficult political position. It seems to me that the Democratic choler about this measure largely followed from their realization that the President had outmaneuvered them. They had been goaded into taking a false step, and knew it. There was, however, nothing they could do, except to be impolite to Mr. Dulles; and eventually they were forced to pass the resolution. The average man got the impression that the President had proposed a desirable measure, and the Democrats had opposed it for strictly partisan reasons. I may be quite wrong in my interpretation of this particular incident, but it cannot be denied that this sort of thing is part of the stock-in-trade of skilled politicians in a democratic situation.

Returning to our abstract model, there are several likely deviations from my assumption that each person judges various positions in terms of their distance from his own ideal position, and always chooses the one closest to his own position. The first of these is that he applies this system only to positions fairly close to his own; that is, he does not discriminate between different positions if both of them are beyond a certain distance from the position which he considers ideal. Note that this is not the same as simply not caring what position is taken anywhere on the line. There will be many people who don't care what solution is reached in a given problem, but these people are not on our line. The first conclusion which an intelligent politician would draw from this changed assumption is that there is no longer so much pressure to get close to your opponent. Moving toward your opponent's position will, it is true, gain support from people who are located between you, but it may also lose the support of people who would have distinguished your position from that of your opponent prior to the move, but now consider them both beyond the pale.

An interesting variant of this situation is the case where the voters vary in the distance to which they carry the process of favoring the nearer position. If, for example, the people on the right side of the diagram follow our first assumption and always choose the position nearest to them from any pair, regardless of the distance, while the people on the left side follow this rule only with positions which are within an inch of their own, the result is to shift the point at which maximum public support can be obtained to the right. It is sometimes argued that the Republican loss of the House of Representatives in 1954 was the result of Senator McCarthy's followers' refusing to vote because they felt that there was no perceptible difference between the two parties. The result, if this theory is true, was that a composition of Congress which was farther from their position was obtained. A voter who wishes to maximize his power will always choose the position nearest his own, regardless of how distant.

Another variant on our assumption is to consider that voters will choose between positions only if the difference between them exceeds a certain minimum. This is most certainly true, and the politician must be careful to sufficiently distinguish his position from that of his opponent. Again, we can profitably consider the situation in which different people discriminate between positions in different degrees of fineness. Let us support that on a given issue there are five possible positions, A, B, C, D, and E. Among the voters we will consider two groups; one group prefers A to B and B to C, and so on to E. The other group prefers E to either D or C, but makes no distinction between C and D. Similarly, they prefer D or C to A or B, but make no discrimination between A and B. If the general configuration of voters' preferences is such that the politician must choose between D or C (or A or B), he will ignore the second group in making his decision. The voter who wishes to maximize his power should make fine discriminations.

Thus far we have assumed only two politicians and only one issue. Unfortunately we must complicate our analysis. In the first place, a politician who plans to win an election must know the conditions of the election, what type of vote he must get to win. This can vary greatly from country to country. We shall discuss one of the oldest and simplest methods, which we shall call the English system. This system, with greater or small modifications, is used in the English-speaking world and may also be found in non-English-speaking areas such as Korea and India where Anglo-Saxon political influence is strong. In its pure form, one person only is elected from each electoral district, and the person elected is the one who gets the most votes, regardless of whether or not he has a majority.

A politician who considers entering such an election is in somewhat the same position as a manager of a department store. He seeks to attract a very large clientele and hence must have a diversified stock-in-trade. The politician's stock consists in his stand on various issues. We have already discussed how a politician should choose his position on individual issues, but he must also seek a logical balance between his different "lines." Like the department store manager's deciding that a certain type of shoes will bring customers into the store where they may buy other things, each issue will be weighed in terms of its possible effect on all the others. This does not, of course, imply that the politician's stand on all issues must be logically consistent. Possibly a politician seeking election by an exceptionally rational and intelligent electorate might find a high degree of logical consistency necessary, but certainly most electorates put little restraint on a politician in this direction.

We may here briefly digress to discuss certain other differences between the politician and the department store manager which are not directly relevant to our general theme. Our ethical code puts considerable restrictions on the direct charges which a store management may hurl at opposing stores. There are some limitations on the activities of a politician in this regard, but they are much less stringent. Further, there are numerous legal restrictions preventing a department store from making claims which cannot be fulfilled, and the customers are in a position, if they are dissatisfied with the wares, to shift their custom elsewhere without waiting for the next election. As a result, department store managers are on the whole much more honest in dealing with their customers than are politicians.

The politician must also decide whether he will run.[10] This decision will, if it is at all rational, consist in a weighing of the costs of making a campaign against the rewards of victory, discounted by an appropriate risk factor. If no one else has announced his candidacy, the problem is easy enough. If there is one candidate in the field, the politician should consider his chances of beating him. If they are not good enough, he should not enter the race. In the absence of parties, and we have not yet introduced parties into our analysis, single-candidate elections are not uncommon. It should be noted that this situation may be completely democratic. We should always be suspicious

10. He may, of course, first decide to run and then decide on his position, or the two decision-making processes may run on simultaneously.

when we see unopposed candidates, but if the reason for the lack of opposition is simply the known popularity of the single candidate, the situation is democratic, if not particularly healthy.

Since most people tend to think of elections solely in terms of parties, I should possibly stop and explain why I am delaying the introduction of this phenomenon into my analysis. In the first place, there are a number of examples both in history and in the present-day world of democracies functioning without party organizations. In the Southern states of the United States, for example, the Democratic primary is the real election, and candidates for this "election" are normally not organized into parties. They sometimes form transitory alliances, and a strong leader may keep such an alliance powerful for some time, but there are no real parties. An analysis of democracy should be applicable to both this type of situation (and a third situation which we will discuss briefly) and a party system. Secondly, an examination of the history of any democratic system in which there is a party system will normally reveal that there was an earlier period, which may have been very brief, in which there were no parties. The reverse is normally not the case. The American South, to my knowledge, is the only place where a party system has been replaced by a non-party system, and there are obviously special factors at work here. It would appear that the party system normally grows out of a non-party system.

If our politician decides that he has a good chance against the single candidate already in the race, he will enter and take positions on various issues. Now let us consider the problem facing a third politician who contemplates entering a race where there are already two candidates. His basic approach is to weigh his chances of victory against the costs of campaigning. Let us confine ourselves to two cases. In the first, the two politicians now in the field have selected their issues so that they about split the electorate between them. A third politician entering in this situation may be able to take votes from both of them, for example, by taking about the same position on issues as they have, but relying on personality salesmanship for victory. More normally, however, he will have to take a position "in back of" one or the other of them. That is, he will be more extreme on some given issue than is the nearest of the two original politicians. The usual result will be that the third politician and the one of the original two who is closest to him will both be beaten. There is, therefore, no incentive for a third politician to enter such a race.

We have already deduced that, if one politician makes a mistake in selecting his position on a given issue, then a second politician will normally take

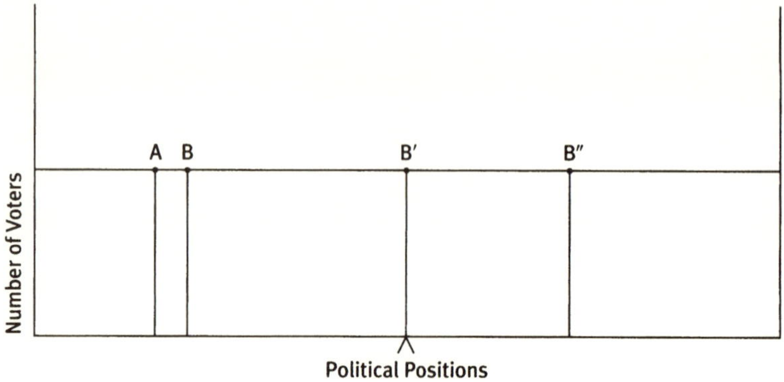

a position very close to that mistaken position. Thus, in the figure above, representing the distribution of the electorate on one issue in a campaign, the first candidate chose position A and the second candidate took up position B; then any third candidate taking a position to the right of B would be in a more favorable situation than either of the first two candidates. In this situation, then, a third candidate would be wise to enter the race.

It should be noted that the second candidate has no real defense against this type of stab in the back, except in special circumstances. In the diagram, if the second politician took position B′, at the center of the distribution, he could still be beaten by a third politician who took a position slightly to his right. Only at B″, far to the right, can he be certain that he will not be beaten by a third entrant on his right. Position B″, however, may be so far to the right that the first politician will beat him, and certainly it will permit the first politician to adjust his error. Jumping over your opponent's head is usually impossible in democratic politics, but taking up a compromise position closer to him is usually quite acceptable. The first politician, then, could move to B′ and win.

But now let us return to the case we discussed above where two candidates have both chosen their positions so skillfully that they divide the electorate about evenly between them. Let us simplify the situation by assuming that there is only one issue in this election, and that all potential candidates have equally attractive personalities. The two present candidates occupy positions A and B on the next figure. No third candidate can occupy a position which will win. Since hope springs eternal in the human breast, a third politician may make a mistake, optimistically miscalculate, and enter the race taking position C. This has as its immediate result the guaranteeing of the victory of A.

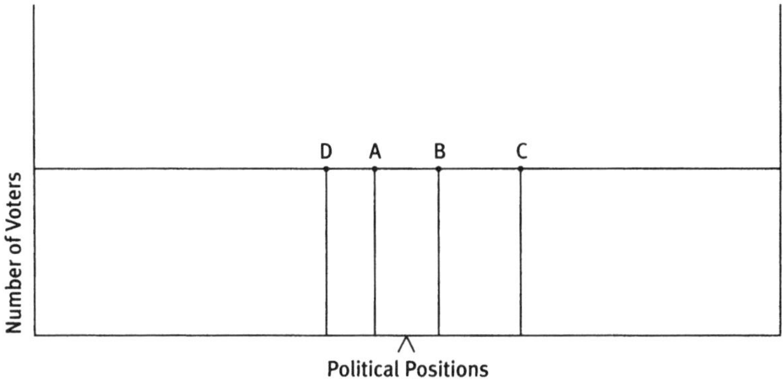

Once the third politician has made this mistake, there is an opportunity for a carefully calculating fourth politician to enter, taking position D and winning. Depending on the exact locations taken by the first four, there may be possibilities of success for a fifth politician, and so on. There is a resemblance between this situation and the standard economic descriptions of oligopoly. No politician can choose his optimum position unless he knows the positions of all the rest, yet he must assume that his choice will affect their positions. As in the oligopoly situation, there is no determinate solution. There is, however, a fundamental difference between this situation and that found in an oligopoly: only one politician can win. There is nothing corresponding to the usual oligopolist assumption that none of the competitors can overcome all the others. On the contrary, that is the only outcome possible, and the only question is which will win. It is the oligopoly problem raised to nightmare proportions.

So far, political parties have not been mentioned, and the model which I have been analyzing has, in fact, no room for them. Individual politicians might, it is true, develop personal followings of one kind or another, but there is no possibility of alliance between two candidates in the electoral systems so far discussed. This can be readily changed. We have discussed only politicians competing for the favor of the same group of voters. If we imagine a number of political offices which are to be filled by people who face different electorates (English MPs each elected from his own district), or if we consider each voter voting for candidates for a number of offices (an American voter selecting his state government), then alliances between these noncompeting candidates are possible. An alliance between a man running for governor and a man running as lieutenant governor can be helpful to both.

This mutual aid takes the form not only of cooperation in various maneuvers, but also in presenting a position on the issues. Thus a candidate for the English parliament who has no allies will probably not convince many of the electors in his district that he will have much power to carry out his campaign promises. On the other hand, if he can present a stand on a number of issues as not only his own, but also that of a powerful group which may well win a majority, the electorate are more likely to feel that a vote for him will improve their chances of gaining their ends.

This fact explains the relative predominance of issues in most elections. If the candidates are organized in parties then it is quite likely that the winning party will be able to pass legislation implementing its promises, and those promises are of much greater importance to the voter. Similarly the qualities of the individual candidate for whom he is asked to vote will be of less importance to him. Alliances between different politicians not directly competing with each other may be limited in scope, affecting only a few candidates, or they may be very wide. They can also vary in the time dimension, lasting for only one election campaign (or even only part of such a campaign) or lasting for some time. We shall ignore brief and transitory alliances, considering them the normal development of a non-party system, and concern ourselves only with alliances which last for some time and concern more than a few candidates in each election. Such alliances fall into two general classes. The first class, which is overwhelmingly the most important numerically, will be called an oligarchy.[11] If all of the politicians who have much chance of winning get together in one alliance, they will be able to maximize their mutual support. Most clubs, labor unions, etc., are run on this system, and it is also to be found elsewhere. The Byrd machine in the Democratic Party in Virginia is a clear case.

Oligarchies have great advantages for the professional politician who gets "inside." Being allied with all the other really competent politicians, he has powerful support in dealing with any local contender for his own office. For the man who is "outside," on the other hand, it is a terrible handicap. But if oligarchies are to last long, they must occasionally change both their policies and their personnel to match the desires of the voters. In most cases where such organizations have lasted for any length of time, they follow a simple

11. Oligarchy is, in a sense, a bad name for this system, and left entirely to myself I would choose another. Since Robert Michels gave the system this name in his *Political Parties*, however, I see no need to further complicate the vocabulary of political science by adding a new term.

system to assure this. It will occasionally happen that an especially talented outsider wins an election against a member of the oligarchy. This indicates that the newcomer is politically more competent than the man he has replaced; the other members of the oligarchy will safeguard their own positions by cold-bloodedly dropping their old comrade and welcoming the newcomer in his place. Thus, over time, the personnel of the oligarchy may completely change, but the system goes on.

An oligarchic situation, like a one-candidate election, may be consistent with democracy, although the members of the oligarchy will normally be subject to less pressure to follow courses chosen with the next election clearly in mind for every tiny detail. But when we see such a system we must be doubly suspicious, since an undemocratic system may well be hidden beneath it.

Although the oligarchical system is common, it seldom provides the basis for the government of a major political system. Essentially, it grows up in situations where the voters are not terribly concerned with the functioning of the political organization. Clubs are probably its natural habitat. In situations of more importance to the voters, they periodically "throw the rascals out." Since the oligarchy depends for its functioning on winning almost every election, it cannot function in such a situation, and there arises either a non-party system, which we have already discussed, or a multi-party system which we must now consider.

To start with the simplest case, let us imagine a political system in which a number of offices are filled by election using the "English" system. Whether these offices are memberships of a representative body, elected by different constituencies, or simply different offices, all filled by the votes of the same electorate, need not concern us now. If the voters periodically vote against the people in power, an alliance of politicians to take advantage of this phenomenon would be profitable. There may, therefore, be two alliances of politicians contesting with each other for election. These groups we call parties. It should again be emphasized that parties are not inevitable. Non-party systems do exist. But while the transition from a non-party system to a party system is fairly easy, the reverse movement is very difficult. In the United States, of course, there are various legal restrictions which make the way of an independent candidate or a "new" party hard.

In a single-member constituency system there is, if the party system has emerged, strong pressure for a two-party system rather than a system of three or more parties. This is because a successful party must attract competent politicians and must give people who vote for it a feeling that they are accomplishing something. Let us consider a situation in which there are three parties. Suppose that, in the average constituency, 35 per cent of the voters always vote for party A, 25 per cent for party B, and 20 per cent for party C. There are two other groups: 10 per cent of the voters vote sometimes for A and sometimes for B, and another 10 per cent vote sometimes for B and sometimes for C. Obviously party C will never win an election. Further, party A will direct its campaign solely to attract the group of voters who switch between it and B, while party B will direct part of its campaign to this group and part to the group that switch between itself and C. B's position on issues, therefore, is likely to be closer to that of the average voter in C than is A's, and, after many discouragements, the voters in party C are likely to slip away into party B. C would shortly disappear.

While we have not discussed the nature of a political party, I have implied that it is simply an alliance of individual politicians. It is this, of course, but usually also something more. Parties may develop into organizations which plan for success as a whole and try to maximize their total number of electoral victories rather than help individual members. In this case, the party management resembles a rational entrepreneur, trying to win the most power possible and willing to sacrifice the well-being of any individual member to this end. Real parties are always somewhere between the extremes of alliances of freely contracting individuals and a rationally functioning corporation. Generally speaking, left-wing parties tend toward the latter pattern while right-wing parties tend toward the former. Occasionally parties are fundamentally, at least in their inception, organizations set up to propagate some political idea. The Republican Party is perhaps the most successful example of such an organization. Originally organized a few months before the 1856 presidential election, it was so successful that it could face the 1860 elections in the mood well expressed by Whittier: "Then furl again the banners, let the bugle call anew; If months have well nigh won the field, what may not four years do?" I suppose I need not remind my readers that from 1860 to 1932 only two Democratic presidents occupied the White House.

The type of party which acts as a rational entrepreneur has a distinct advantage in political maneuvering over the party which is less monolithic. Consider the 1956 elections for the upper house of the Japanese legislature. One hundred fifty members of this house are elected by prefectures. Each prefecture has as many seats in this body of 150 as its population justifies. The method of election is that each voter has one vote. If the particular prefecture is entitled to five seats, then the five candidates with the most votes are chosen.

In Japan the real locus of political power lies in the lower house, and there were two major parties with their center of power there.

Of these two parties, one had a clear majority both in popular votes and members of the diet. The other, the socialists, hoped only to prevent the majority from rising to the two-thirds level which would permit changes in the constitution. The maneuver chosen by the socialists depended on the fact that they were more disciplined than was the governing party. Assume that a prefecture will send five delegates to the upper house. Also assume that the electorate split between the government and socialist parties in a ratio of 7 to 3. The government party, being mainly a coalition of individual politicians, and unable to prevent its members from running if they wanted to, offered five candidates. The disciplined socialists ran only two. It is not a mathematical certainty, but the most likely outcome would be three government and two socialist members. If the government had been able to limit its candidates to four, it could have elected them all.

The question of the type of party organization which might arise under such a system is of considerable interest. Consider a country ruled by the parliamentary system with a one-house legislature, the members of the legislature being elected from, say, forty districts, each of which sent five delegates. Twenty per cent of the votes would insure the candidate a victory, and normally he could get elected on 10–15 per cent. As a consequence, he would point his campaign at a selected segment of the electorate and not try to get half of it. There would probably be considerable differences between the "platforms" of the various candidates.

No candidate could form profitable alliance with any other candidate in his own constituency, but alliances with candidates in other constituencies could be mutually helpful. Thus a party system would be quite possible. There would be at least five parties, but it is hard to say more. Under the English system it is easy to see the pressures which may produce a two-party system, but our present case is more complicated. Whether "equilibrium" would call for five, six, or ten parties is a question which must await a better mathematician than I. Unfortunately, we cannot illuminate this theoretical problem by considering any real examples. Although systems which resemble our imaginary one are common enough, particularly on the continent of Europe, they all differ in one vital respect. The various constituencies are of different sizes, and the number of representatives sent to the national assembly varies accordingly. Further, most of the European nations complicate the situation by other electoral provisions.

So much for what can be done with our simple model. In fact it seems likely that a good deal more research using this tool is possible. In view of the extremely simplified nature of the assumption upon which the model is based, the close fit it gives to politics in the real world is rather surprising. Clearly the development of other, more complex, models is highly desirable. Fortunately this is a field in which there is currently a good deal of research, and in which the amount of work done is increasing. It seems likely that in a few years we will know vastly more about the functioning of democracies than we do now.

CHAPTER 8

MULTIPLE SOVEREIGNS

The situation that I shall discuss in this chapter is the most frequent, especially in the lower ranks of administrative hierarchies. Politicians are far more likely to find themselves in the multiple sovereign situation than in any other. This situation exists when an individual is confronted with several superiors, who do not act as a group, but as individuals. The diagram below illustrates the situation.

The multiple sovereign situation is more complex than any that has been so far discussed, for two reasons. First, there are more sovereigns to be influenced. Second, the objective of the politician seeking to advance is not nearly so well defined as in previous cases. There are several routes open to him. In the diagram as drawn, the politician wishes to move to "y." By so doing he can convert some of his present sovereigns to equals, "peers," but he will also bring more-distant superiors into his category of sovereigns. To advance, the politician must secure the favor of one or more of the higher sovereigns.

The ambitious politician, confronting multiple sovereigns, will try to form a connection with one or more of these superiors. Since the sovereigns will normally compete among themselves, and since each of them can employ the support of lower-ranking personnel in this competition, the politician will have some discretion in choosing among the sovereigns. He may, of course, switch his allegiance as required to further his career interests. In the extreme cases there may exist a sufficient number of sovereigns so that the

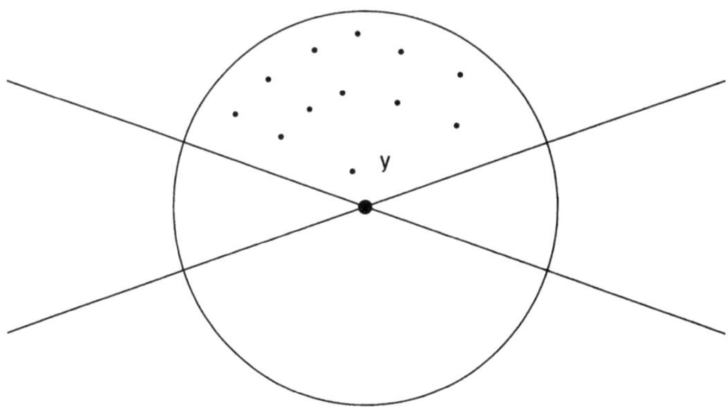

relationship resembles that of free contract. At this extreme, the "political" relationship that we have been discussing merges into the "economic," which is, for our purposes, defined as the availability of a sufficient number of attractive alternatives to make the cost of shifting negligible. In the more normal multiple sovereign situation, the junior politician may still shift to another sovereign, and the sovereign is fully aware of this prospect. Hence, the superior will neither expect such loyalty nor exact such deference from this junior as he would if he were a single sovereign. The basic superior-inferior aspects of the relationship, however, will remain.

Note, that, on the diagram above, the various superiors of the reference politician are not placed in a series of equal ranks. This is realistic. The normal organization chart may be convenient for the outsider who has no working knowledge of the hierarchy, but it does not represent the internal structure. Persons who might appear as equals on an organizational chart differ greatly in power and influence, and the politician seeking to advance will be interested in their actual position, rather than in the spot which they occupy on the organizational chart. He will tend to have a good idea as to the actual position of those superiors who are in his immediate vicinity in the hierarchy, and he will be on the lookout for changes in these positions.

As we have suggested several times, the administrative relationships are apt to be simpler at the apex of the pyramid than farther down the hierarchy. Under feudalism, however, a multiple sovereign system, of sorts, extended up to the top of the structure. The king or emperor was simply one of the most important territorial magnates. Furthermore, there was a continuum of power running from the king on the one hand to the lowest of the petty nobles on the other. There was continuous maneuvering by the various lords to hold or to improve their relative positions. This is similar to what is to be found inside almost any modern hierarchy. The principal difference between the situation of the historical feudal structure and the modern hierarchy lies in the overt manner in which things were done in the former as compared with the latter. This provides a distinct aid to students, and we can find the feudal system helpful in providing examples of the general relationships discussed here.

Let us consider the situation of a young man who succeeds in attaching himself to the train of a major feudal lord. If he is capable, he will, shortly afterward, attract the attention of other followers of his sovereign, including those in higher ranks, and also the attention of other lords. He confronts a multiple sovereign situation, and he will be ready to take advantage of it.

Basically, there are three courses of action open to him: he may try to improve his standing with his present lord; he may assist his lord to rise and to advance along with his sovereign's advance (these first two are not necessarily conflicting); or, he may switch his allegiance to another lord. The first of these elicits the same pattern of behavior that would be expected in the single sovereign situation, although the presence of alternatives open to the politician results in a necessary weakening of the pressures upon him to please the sovereign.

If the politician chooses, instead, the second course, he must take care to insure that his lord's rise will also redound to his own benefit. What counts here is whether or not the superior to whom the politician attaches himself is both willing and able to reward the allegiance given to him. Normally, the feudal lord is engaged in a power struggle of his own, and he will be interested in accumulating support for his position from among those lower down in the hierarchy. In the strict feudal situation, this might actually take the form of military ability, since pitched battles formed part of the power struggle. On the other hand, this allegiance might take other forms. Philippe de Commines and Baldassare Castiglione, to mention two famous men, both rose to high position in what was essentially this feudal type of environment, although neither of them seems to have been particularly skilled in war. Their political and diplomatic gifts were as valuable to their sovereigns as military activities might have been.

In any event, if the follower hopes to gain from the improvement in his lord's position, he must have reason to expect that the lord will pass along to him some of the winnings. This expectation may take the form of an implicit bargain in which the superior promises the reward in exchange for the follower's support. On the other hand, the superior may appoint the subordinate to a position of higher responsibility simply because he has confidence in him. These two reasons for the successful sovereign's rewarding a subordinate are logically distinct, but they are probably mixed in the minds of most sovereigns. The politician, however, need not be overly concerned about why the lord promotes him. It is sufficient for him to insure that he is rewarded when his lord advances. Unless he is assured of this, there is no particular reason for the politician to exert himself on his superior's behalf.

The follower's third alternative is switching to another sovereign, preferably in return for definite commitments by the new sovereign. The possibility that any follower may do this must be a basic consideration in the mind of any ranking lord, and provides one of the major reasons for his trying to keep followers contented by providing them with rewards. The politician must, however, avoid switching allegiance too often. If he has a reputation for sticking with sovereigns even in times of trouble he will be more highly compensated than his rival who has a reputation for switching readily.

Academic readers will be aware of many analogues to this situation in their own environment. One means through which the professor, in an American university in the 1960's, insures that his own salary will be periodically increased is to keep before his administration the threat to shift his "allegiance" to another university. He must establish the feeling in the administration that, while he is loyal, he will "move" unless he is favorably treated. In fact, he may often go so far as to elicit definite pecuniary offers from competing institutions, primarily for the purpose of improving his internal bargaining position.

From this brief discussion of the multiple sovereign situation inherent in the feudal system it appears that there are a number of similarities to the commercial system of free contract. But with the feudal system there was no court to interpret and to enforce contracts once made. Lord Stanley betrayed Richard at Bosworth Field, yet he was highly rewarded for his action. Even if Richard had won, Stanley would have been executed arbitrarily by his king, not as a result of any legal process.

If we shift our gaze from medieval Europe to a modern administrative hierarchy, several differences may be observed. Some of these differences are superficial; e.g., the junior government bureaucrat who has attached himself to some higher-ranking official will not wear the livery of his superior, and his service to this superior will not require technical efficiency in the use of the broadsword. There remains a more fundamental difference. In the historical feudal system, the relationships between the leader and the men who had attached themselves to his train were overt and unconcealed. These relationships were accepted as the basis for the whole administrative structure. In the modern bureaucracy, on the other hand, such relationships are considered to be "undesirable" from an overall global view of administration, and, because of this, they tend to be hidden. The higher-level officials, while building up their personal followings, may try to prevent the lower-level officials from accomplishing the same purposes. Further, the whole organizational structure may be deliberately constructed with the objective of minimizing the opportunity for the establishment of personal relationships of this nature.

Despite such differences, the fact remains that the multiple sovereign situation which is customarily to be found in the lower ranks of modern administrative organizations can be represented accurately as a weakened version of the multiple sovereignty situation that was present in the social structure of feudalism. The same considerations are relevant to the politician, and he must utilize techniques that are essentially the same in the two cases. The difference, to the politician, lies in the degree of his freedom to maneuver. Philippe de Commines would, were he transplanted into the present, undoubtedly find himself fully at home in either General Motors or the Department of the Interior.

Despite the fact that the multiple sovereignty situation is overwhelmingly the most common relationship in which the politician finds himself, a relationship that will tend to dominate his career until he reaches the very top of the administrative pyramid, analysis of this situation in any systematic manner is very difficult. This is because of the great degree of indeterminancy that must remain in any "solution." The particulars of the relationship will vary greatly from case to case, and few generally applicable principles can be laid down. At the one extreme, the situation merges into that of single sovereignty. This extreme is approached when the reference politician finds it difficult to shift his allegiance, or finds that he can do so only at a considerable personal sacrifice. At the other extreme the multiple sovereign case merges into free contract. In such cases, the politician finds that he can shift among superiors without much personal cost, and the competition among superiors for his allegiance will tend to make his relations with any particular one of them almost entirely impersonal. At this extreme, the relationship becomes "economic" and not "political," and the analysis can be left to the economist. The in-between cases are the difficult ones to analyze, and for the reason that they are, in fact, in between. They contain elements of the single sovereign and the free contract, and the particular mixture will determine the result.

This point can be illustrated with an analogy from the theory of markets. The seller of a good or service who is faced with a pure monopsonistic buyer for his product is in a situation closely analogous to our single sovereign situation. He is at the mercy of this single buyer and must, therefore, try to please. This case is difficult to imagine as being widespread in actual markets, but it has, perhaps, more relevance for the theory of bureaucracy. At the other extreme, we may have the seller who is confronted with any number of buyers for his product or service. The individual who sells shares of AT&T on the New York Stock Exchange does not even know the buyer to whom he transfers his paper. And the seller of an old master at Sotheby's may not know the buyer at all well. At least he need not bother to cultivate the buyer in any personal manner. Most market situations are, like the administrative situation, in between these extremes. Most sellers of commodities and services are not confronted with a single buyer, but most of them do not have sufficient alternatives to allow them to remove all personal relationships from the market contract. To the extent that this is the case, "political" elements, in our terminology, enter into "economic" institutional arrangements, just as "economic" arrangements enter into "political" institutional arrangements.

For actual descriptions of politicians faced with multiple sovereigns, literary rather than scientific sources seem more suggestive. Marquand's novels have often treated such situations in a highly perceptive manner. *Melville Godwin, USA*, and *Sincerely, Willis Wade* are particularly useful in this respect. *Executive Suite* by Cameron Hawley is also worth study, and there are several other treatments of the same conflict situation by modern novelists. For more detailed study we must look primarily to historical materials, notably to medieval history, and especially to the stories of second-level figures in this history. A much larger source can be found in Chinese. The biographies and memoirs of leading officials which are so numerous in Chinese literature provide the student with an almost inexhaustible mine of significant material.

CHAPTER 9

PEERS, COURTIERS, AND BARONS

"Peers" are defined as those equals of the politician who are organizationally close enough to participate in his power struggle. The location of the peers on the standard diagram is shown below.

This group will include, normally, the persons who are the main rivals of the politician and also those persons with whom he has the most frequent organizational contact. The personal attitude of the politician toward these persons seems likely to be one of apprehension, but such feelings must be concealed, and this concealment, in itself, may result in an intensification of the normal apprehension. The literary and historical sources of information on the multiple sovereign situations mentioned in the preceding chapter are also useful in the study of the relations of the politician with his peers.

The relations among peers are basically determined by the sovereignty situation. The single sovereign situation places a group of peers in subjection to the will of one man, the single sovereign. The promotion or demotion of each of the peers depends on the decisions of that individual sovereign. The rivalry among the members of the peer group will be intensified by the very simplicity and clarity of the power structure. Normally, the sovereign will not distribute rewards equally among all of his immediate followers; there will arise a hierarchy of "favor" among the peers, and the knowledge of this hierarchy and the attempts to modify it will tend to dominate the plans of most

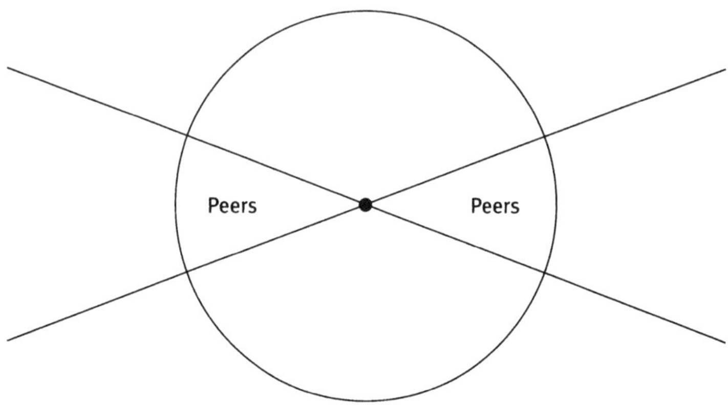

members of the peer group. The individual politician must not only make every effort to please the sovereign; he must remember that his success depends also on the extent to which others are successful in this same objective. The politician is likely, if he is wise and ambitious, to make efforts both to please the sovereign and to undermine the like efforts of his peers. He will try to present his own best image to the superior along with the worst image of his rivals. This double task may prove difficult because, under some moral systems, "running down" others may reflect discredit upon the one who undertakes it. The politician, when carrying tales to the sovereign, must always recognize the possibility that the sovereign does not like talebearers.

The politician may get around this difficulty in a number of ways. One method that seems to apply to a surprising number of cases requires merely that the politician start off with the prototype statement, "I never tell tales," after which he proceeds with the gossip. This procedure often works because the sovereign will realize that his own control over the hierarchy beneath him will be improved if each subordinate reports to him on each occasion that a rival subordinate is detected in an action of which the sovereign might disapprove. Thus, the sovereign may give no more than a formal bow to the general ethical standard of the culture. There are still other ways in which rival peers may be discredited. Kravchenko reports a simple method used in one of the Soviet offices in which he worked. The politician made up a set of notes on a particular rival's behavior "for his own reference," and then he placed these notes in the politician's own safe. Since the secret police knew the combinations of all the safes and made regular checks, this procedure would insure that the politician's views on his rival reached the hands of his superior without directly implicating him. This procedure of having the sovereign "eavesdrop" on a remark or conversation which, purportedly, is not for his ears seems to have wide application.

Yet another method of accomplishing the same objectives involves the skillful handling of conversations with peers themselves. A carefully planned line of conversation with a rival may convince him that the sovereign is already aware of some aspect of his behavior. In this way, the rival peer may be misled into an unnecessary disclosure to the sovereign.

Still another method may be that of leading the sovereign to take an interest in some particular field where the weaknesses of a rival seem likely to be discovered. Or it may be possible for two rivals to be maneuvered into positions of conflict that would discredit both of them to the politician's advantage. In sum, the possible methods are varied and subtle; they need not be catalogued here. The individual politician will, of course, have available to him only such opportunities as the occasion permits. After all, he can fully control only his own actions.

The politician must continually be on his guard against similar activities by his peers. The simplest method of protection is that of never doing anything of which the sovereign might disapprove. This is, however, a counsel of perfection, and is of little practical utility. As noted earlier, what will please or displease the sovereign will depend upon the amount of information possessed by the sovereign. The politician will never know exactly what that information is. Further, one of his rivals may take the trouble of improving the sovereign's information on a matter just after the politician has made an irrevocable decision. Add the additional fact that the politician may be ignorant of exactly what the sovereign really wants, and the problem becomes even more difficult. As a final consideration, it must be recalled that the politician will be serving the sovereign only as a means to achieve ends of his own. If the politician completely, and in every case, subordinates his own desires to those of the sovereign, there is really nothing to be gained from his success in pleasing the sovereign.

The last complexity can be minimized if there exists a clear demarcation between the private and the official spheres of activity. A person might be quite willing to do as another person wills for eight hours each day in return for an appropriate income with complete personal freedom for the remaining sixteen hours. Most sovereigns will, however, exercise some control over the personal lives of subordinates, although this may not always be a conscious process. Palmerston once rejected the promotion of a diplomatic official with the remark, "he beats his wife," and we are familiar with the procedure of modern American corporations in checking out the wife of a prospective middle management employee.

The politician must accept the probability that his peers will arrange for the sovereign to learn about discreditable events in his personal, as well as his official, life. Activities that might readily be concealed from the superior may be impossible to conceal from the peers. They are too numerous, and, more important, they will be on the lookout for possible slips. Under these circumstances, the peer group, so to speak, acts as a proxy for the sovereign, putting pressure on each individual politician in the group to comply with the sovereign's will. The politician must endeavor, therefore, to make his actions appear, not only to the sovereign but also to his peers, as the embodiment of the sovereign's will.

This principle, as with most, is subject to several important qualifications. First, an untrue denunciation by peers may, on occasion, serve to undermine the politician as well as a true one. The sovereign has limited time, and he cannot investigate thoroughly each alleged breach of trust by an inferior. He will normally consider derogatory information on the basis of its initial plausibility in the context of his current information. The aim of the politician must be, therefore, to incorporate a strong image of his reliability in the mind of the sovereign. If this image is sufficiently strong, the politician may proceed to impugn the reputation of his peers with less fear of their reciprocal activity. By contrast, if the politician is thought to be unreliable, he may be destroyed by a transparent falsehood about his behavior, official or personal.

The second limitation on the effectiveness of the peers as an enforcement agency for the sovereign lies in the necessary interaction among the peers' own interests. As an extreme example, if all members of a cabinet should be dipping into the organizational till, it is unlikely that any one of them will advance the suggestion that the books be audited. A sort of implicit agreement exchanging silences on various subjects is not uncommon among peer groups, although it seems doubtful if the wise politician places much confidence in such agreements. The rationale for such agreements is, of course, provided when it is recognized that the politician not only seeks to advance; he must also seek to maintain his own position, to keep from falling. Under many circumstances in the single sovereign situation, politicians in a peer relationship are likely to be reasonably conservative in their behavior.

PEERS SUBJECT TO A GROUP SOVEREIGN

Insofar as the relationships among peers are concerned, the group sovereign situation is not greatly different from the single sovereign situation. The group must, we recall, act as a unit. The group either does or does not select a particular politician for a given task. The various politicians competing for the group's favor will tend to behave in much the same way that they would under a single sovereign. There is the same concentration on determining what the sovereign wants, the same effort to give the impression of meeting this want, and the same attempts to discredit rivals. A presidential campaign is, in many ways, simply an overt expression of much the same process that is found within the private chambers of an absolute ruler.

There are, though, significant differences between the behavior of peers in the single sovereign and the group sovereign cases. An electorate, as a group sovereign, is less likely to be even moderately expert in evaluating the efficiency with which the politician performs his duties. On the other hand, it is probably more difficult for the politician to deceive an electorate than a single sovereign. This generalization may seem strange to those of us familiar with democratic processes, which include the many highly dubious behavior patterns of politicians, but a close study of any autocratic ruler's decision-making procedures will suggest that the opportunities for deceit are greater here than in democracies. The man who wishes to influence an electorate by false statements must, necessarily, make the false charges publicly. Thus, the lie must be exposed to possible refutation. While the truth may not overcome the bizarre lie, it has a fighting chance. In the single sovereign situation, by contrast, no one other than the sovereign and the subordinate who reports to him need learn that a given statement (presumed false in this illustration) has been made. The man who is maligned in these circumstances will have no opportunity for refutation.

Furthermore, while the electorate as a whole will seldom give much attention to any given interchange of charges by rival politicians, there will frequently be individuals within this electorate who will make the necessary investigation. The possibility that these individual investigations will take place serves to inhibit the politician facing the group sovereign in comparison to one who confronts the single sovereign.

A conspiracy of silence among high officials in a peer relationship who cannot easily rise but who can fall is also less likely to occur under a group sovereign. This type of behavior becomes possible only under the single sovereign who, because he is a single individual, must limit his contacts. All of those whom he sees personally must be well up within the hierarchy. A group sovereign, by comparison, really has no contacts at all as an entity. Each member of the group may have personal contacts, and the sum total of these may be very large. Almost anyone who wishes to rise can attract the attention of at least some members of the sovereign group. If the ambitious newcomer has the necessary talents, this attention may be all that he needs. He can readily break any potential conspiracy of silence that a senior group of peers may seek to impose.

PEERS SUBJECT TO MULTIPLE SOVEREIGNS

The multiple sovereign situation presents the politician with a considerably different set of problems when he deals with his peers. Let us once again consider our diagram of the politician's world. The dots indicate the location of other politicians.

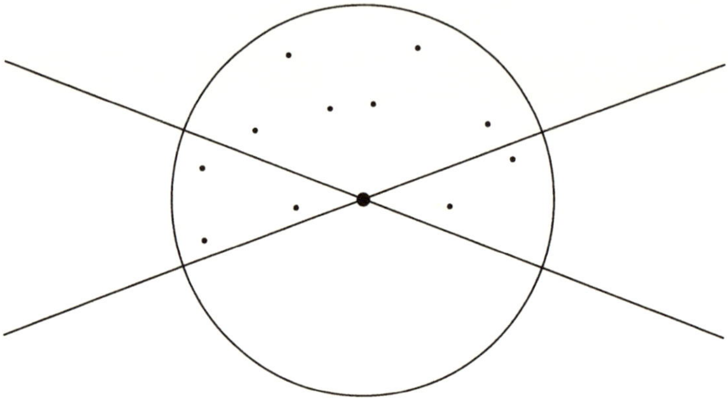

Recall that it is always the purpose of the reference politician to shift his own position upward in the hierarchy, and in so doing to begin to count at least some of the persons who are now sovereign as his peers.

Advance in such a situation will require the favor of one of the higher-ranking sovereigns. The ambitious politician will try to form some connection with one (or possibly several) of these. But in the multiple sovereign situation, these sovereigns are themselves rivals, and they are competing for the favor of still higher sovereigns. In this competition, they can make use of the service and loyalties of lower-ranking personnel. As we have shown earlier the politician retains elements of choice here in the determination of the sovereign to whom he shall attach himself. Furthermore, he can readily shift allegiance among sovereigns.

These facts of the situation, which summarize the earlier analysis, largely determine the relationship among peers. To the reference politician, his peers divide themselves into two groups. First, those that give allegiance to the same member of the higher-ranking sovereign as himself. Second, those that give their allegiance to some other member of the multiple sovereign group. The politician's relationships with these two sets of peers will be different. With the first set, he will be united in the common desire to see that the particular sovereign to whom they are all attached will secure advancement, bringing them up in his train. Within this peer group itself, he will look upon individual members as rivals for the particular sovereign's favor. With regard to the second set, the peers who support some other member of the multiple sovereign, the politician will consider them general enemies and obstacles to the advance of his in-group. On the other hand, he need not consider individual members of this out-group as personal enemies, and the politician may, when the occasion warrants, consider shifting into one of these other sets of in-groups.

There is little more that can be said about the principles of relationships among peers in the multiple sovereignty situation. There will be, of course, infinite variations in real circumstances.

COURTIERS AND BARONS

We shall now introduce a distinction among politicians generally. Among members of any given hierarchy, there will exist some individuals who are almost wholly dependent upon the favor of their sovereigns for their current positions and for their hopes of advancement. There will exist other individuals who possess some outside source of support. The outside "assets" may take various forms. The politician may, as in the United States on occasion, be independently wealthy; because of this he will not be strictly dependent upon his job in the hierarchy. Alternatively, the politician may have powerful personal connections that give him a differential advantage in dealing with his sovereign or sovereigns. Still another source of support might lie in the technical expertise of the politician, whose particular knowledge or skill may be irreplaceable, at least in the eyes of the immediate superior. Finally, the politician may have been able to secure a strong personal following among members of the lower ranks in the hierarchy. Somewhat different from these external sources of independence, the politician may have internal strength of character which allows him to take an attitude of independence regardless of the personal cost.

The point to be made is the obvious one. The man who is not particularly interested either in the rewards that his superior can provide him or in the penalties that his superior can impose is not really dependent on the superior. I shall call bureaucrats of this type *barons*, adopting the name of the medieval lords who seem to have been practically pure models of the type. A sovereign's attitude toward genuine barons in the hierarchy will always be somewhat ambigious. He knows that he cannot readily "push them around" and that, by virture of their status, they will be more important to him than their peers. Barons also present a special problem to their peers. They cannot be easily maneuvered out of their positions, which do not depend, in any strict sense, on the personal favor of the sovereign.

The other type of politician, at the opposite extreme from the barons, is wholly dependent on the good will of his superiors. I shall call these politicians *courtiers*, again because those normally referred to by this name seem to have constituted nearly pure types. Since the courtiers are entirely dependent on the good will of the sovereign, they will be compelled to devote considerably more effort in pleasing him than will the barons. This weakness of the courtiers vis-à-vis the sovereign, however, provides them with some differential advantage. The sovereigns will know that the courtiers are more "trustworthy" than the barons, and will tend to prefer them as subordinates.

Let us consider medieval court. From the viewpoint of the king, the people at court fall neatly into two categories, his officials and the great lords of the realm. His ministers, if the king is intelligent, will not be great territorial magnates. Ministers will, instead, tend to be selected from among the clerics; these would be courtiers in the pure sense and completely subject to the control of the king. The lords, as history records, tend to be a much more powerful group. To them the king would be merely *primes inter pares*, and they would be capable of refusing royal commands if the king should be so ill-advised as to give them a suitable opportunity. In such a structure, it is obviously to the interest of the king to undermine the positions of the barons and to shift power from their hands into those of the courtiers. It is equally clear that it is to the interest of the barons to prevent this movement.

In one sense, the history of all Europe up into modern times may be recounted in terms of this elemental contest. In England, France, and Spain, the king won the struggle, at least initially. At the court of Louis XIV, there were nobles bearing territorial titles, but they were completely subordinated to the king's ministers. In the Holy Roman Empire, on the other hand, the barons won the struggle. During Louis's reign, again, the title of emperor was little more than an honorary one, held by the most powerful of the German lords.

As is the case with all such distinctions, the division between barons and courtiers must be a matter of degree. It is evident that, all things considered, the barons are in a more satisfactory position. They are less subject to the sovereign's will, more secure against personal damage, and generally more powerful than their peers who are courtiers. From this it follows that any courtier should have as one of his goals or objectives becoming a baron. This is simply another means of stating that there will always be pressure for "security" on the part of the politician. The man who cannot be fired or demoted has, in effect, progressed far toward becoming a baron. He remains a courtier only insofar as he continues to be interested in securing further promotions.

The development of a loyal and devoted following among lower-ranking bureaucrats is another means of becoming a baron. For example, Dean Acheson was idolized by the personnel of the Department of State. When the

Republicans won the 1952 elections, John Foster Dulles had great difficulty in bringing the department under his control. In this particular instance, Acheson's position with the department was not owing to conscious effort on his part, but politicians in other areas have been known to utilize this technique deliberately. (Are J. Edgar Hoover and Robert Moses good examples??) A politician can also try to arrange his position so that the superior is dependent on his technical expertise. To the extent that he can do so, he becomes a baron. The file clerk who cannot be fired because he is the only one that knows the filing system may be a bureaucratic legend, but the legend well illustrates the basic point.

With respect to promotion, the distinction between the position of the baron and the courtier is somewhat more complicated. The sovereign, presumably, will not desire to increase the power of a baron in the hierarchy since the latter might defy him on any particular occasion. On the other hand, promotion to higher rank may convert the baron into a courtier. In feudal times, for example, the lord of a minor fief might have been given a high position at court. Since the high position was solely dependent on the pleasure of the sovereign, the lord who might otherwise have remained a baron acted as a courtier in order to hold the court office. A sovereign may prefer to deal only with courtiers, but he may consider promoting barons for the very purpose of reducing them to the status of courtiers. The promotion that will be required for this purpose will normally be, however, somewhat more important than a simple shift one rank up a hierarchy.

Situations may exist in which promotion will not end the baronial status of the person promoted. In all such cases, the sovereign will be reluctant to make the promotion, but he may not have any alternative. Again using feudal Europe as our example, the governmental system required, for its functioning, a high-level nobility. The king might have found it necessary, on occasion, to promote barons to earldoms. A new earl would still be, in our terminology, a baron, even a more important one than before.

The American federal civil and military services also have this characteristic to some degree. It is extremely difficult to reduce persons in rank or to fire them. The only rewards or penalties available to the sovereign are promotions or the withholding of promotion. After a promotion, the inferior can, however, be motivated only by the desire for further promotion. This fact, when coupled with a general rotational system, makes it difficult for the sovereign to secure the cooperation of his subordinates. An officer who has acquired enough seniority for promotion "bucks" for this promotion; that is to say, he begins to devote a great deal of time to pleasing his superiors. After he is promoted, however, he tends to relax and act as a baron.

He does this because he realizes that, by the time for the next step up, he will be serving under different superiors because of rotation. Thus, having been recently promoted by his current superiors, he will have little incentive to carry out their desires.

In this particular case, the solution is for the sovereign to have available numerous gradations in rank, so that the possibility of promotion always exists. The presence in the American civil service of far more grades than can be accounted for on the basis of ordinary chain-of-command theory can, I think, be explained at least partially on these grounds.

CHAPTER 10

THE FOLLOWERS

In this chapter I shall discuss several miscellaneous topics that should logically be included in the discussion of "the politician's world," the subject for this part of the book. The first of these fragments is a brief discussion of the one remaining segment of the basic diagram, that part which lies below the reference politician. The persons in this part of the hierarchy I shall call *the followers*.

A BRIEF LOOK AT THE FOLLOWERS

The followers are less important to the politician in his struggle for advancement than are the peers or the sovereigns. Somewhat paradoxically, however, they are highly important in another sense. In Part 3, we shall largely be concerned with the problem of getting the followers to carry out the will of the superiors, not with the problem of the politician seeking to rise. Much of the discussion of followers can, therefore, be deferred. But followers are also important in the reference politician's struggle to rise, and in ways that are not directly related to his problem of securing their cooperation in carrying out his desires.

To the man who is in a position of a single sovereign few if any political problems arise other than those of getting his will carried out. We may, therefore, leave him out of account. The particular relationships with followers that we want to discuss here arise only in the multiple sovereignty situation. The man who is in a position of multiple sovereignty with respect to a group of followers will recognize that this group can affect his own relationships with peers and sovereigns. The politician will find that men in the lower ranks may want to attach themselves to his train, to give him particular personal loyalty, provided only that his star appears to be on the rise in the hierarchy. Similarly, he will know that, should his star decline, followers will tend to desert his cause. In many cases, the tendency of lower-ranking personnel to join forces or to desert may provide the politician with the first inkling of changes in his own fortunes in the hierarchy. The ambitious politician will also know that the size and the efficiency of the train of followers are important in and of themselves in his relationships with superiors.

These facts suggest that the politician must devote some of his efforts toward insuring the continued allegiance of followers. He must, paradoxically, devote some of his time to pleasing them, and he can do so by using his own power in assisting them to achieve their objectives. This effort on the part of the politician can be undertaken only at a cost, a cost in terms of other time that he might spend more directly devoted to his own advancement. As in all such cases, the politician must reach some marginal balance between the additional effort required to recruit and to maintain loyal followers and the direct effort toward his own more narrowly defined career objectives.

In a similar manner, the politician must balance off the advantages of a large, but loosely organized, group of followers, and a smaller, but highly efficient group. The politician who places few restraints on his followers can always insure for himself a larger group than would be the case if he imposes more rigorous standards.

In his relationships with followers the politician must always remember that each member of the group considers himself as a potential peer. A follower may be willing to join a politician's train, but he would be happier to become his equal or even his superior. The wise politician must try to minimize such opportunities unless, of course, he finds it advantageous to reverse positions with a follower completely. The latter phenomenon is not unknown. When a politician, for any reason, decides that his own talents (or other characteristics) prohibit his attainment of a higher level, he may turn to one of his hand-picked followers and encourage his rise, even to a rank superior to his own.[1]

A VIEW FROM THE OUTSIDE

We have completed our survey of the political-administrative structure looked at from the inside—that is, from the point of view of the politician who finds himself within the structure. Part 3 of the book, beginning with

1. Johnson Hagood, in the early part of World War I, was in charge of a post to which George Marshall, then a subaltern, was assigned. In this capacity, Hagood was called on to draw up an efficiency report on Marshall. Hagood realized that he himself was never going to reach the highest rank of the army; Marshall, on the other hand, looked like a good bet. In making out Marshall's efficiency report, therefore, Hagood said, ". . . in time of war I would like very much to serve under his command" (*Saturday Evening Post*, July 15, 1939, p. 62). This explicit admission by a senior officer that one of his juniors was more capable than he, was probably the strongest recommendation ever given. Had Marshall reached chief of staff before Hagood's career was terminated by his quarrel with certain "New Dealers," he would no doubt have been suitably rewarded. The situation, however, is a rare one, and few men are called upon to choose whether they should attach themselves to their inferior's train.

Chapter 11, will be devoted to looking at the structure from the point of view of the man or group at the top of the pyramid. At this point, and briefly, I propose that we step outside the structure of the hierarchy and assume the position of external observers. This change of point of view immediately raises a major question. The analysis to this point has suggested what a politician *will do*, or tend to do, provided that he is both wise and ambitious. Nothing has been said about what the politician *ought to do*. It should be emphasized that nothing in the discussion to this point should lead to any degree of identity between "will" and "ought."

The analysis is, I think, basically realistic. The successful politician will be the one who chooses the most advantageous courses of action, not those courses which are, by some external moral code, the most righteous. Nevertheless, the objective for which administrative structures are organized is not that of giving a number of individuals the opportunity to rise. There is an "ought" somewhere in the organizational structure, even if only in the dreams of the organizer. Looked at from the outside, this "ought" provides the only justification for the existence of the structure at all. The total absence of this sort of "ought" from our models so far might, therefore, be considered a serious defect. But to repeat, the models seem basically realistic as they have been presented. The "ought" which justifies any organization cannot be found in a study of the type of behavior that leads a man to the top of the administrative pyramid. This man will behave in the manner that is most advantageous for his own career. If this behavior should be the same as that which would further the objectives for which the structure is organized, then from his standpoint this is mere coincidence.

The solution to the positive-normative problem is, thereby, suggested. If a hierarchy is so organized that the politician choosing a course of action in his own frame of references will always choose that course which he "ought" to take, when defined in terms of organizational objectives, then only "desirable" actions will be taken. It is at once obvious that such organizational perfection cannot be achieved. It does constitute a goal, however, that may be approximated in varying degrees. The problem is to so arrange the structure that the politician is led by self-interest into doing those things that he "ought" to do. This is not a problem for the politician himself; rather it is a problem for those who want to organize activity for the achievement of given ends or objectives. This becomes, therefore, the problem of the superior in dealing with inferiors. The "ought" in bureaucracies should not be looked for in the relationships of inferiors to their superiors, but in the converse relationships.

PART 3

LOOKING DOWNWARD

CHAPTER II

SUBORDINATES AND INFERIORS

Except for the few pages at the end, Part 2 was devoted to analyzing the behavior of the politician seeking to rise in an administrative hierarchy. In this part of the book, we shall analyze the behavior of the politician "looking downward." We shall examine the bureaucratic structure through the eyes of a man whose main task is that of trying to get inferiors to do what he wants. These two points of view are not necessarily opposed; they are, rather, complementary approaches in the analysis of bureaucratic structures. In both cases, the politician is seeking to maximize the satisfaction that he gets from his environment. In both cases, he will make use of his relationships within the hierarchy to achieve his goals. In a broad sense, the situation in each case is also analogous to the individual who operates in an economic rather than a political context.

Nevertheless, if we move to more specific levels of analysis, the outlook of the politician in our two cases becomes quite different. To state the matter in overly simplified terms, the politician within the hierarchy seeks power which will permit him to achieve his ultimate goals. By comparison, the man at the top of the hierarchy has the power, but he is confronted with the organizational problem of using that power in the most effective way. In the normal case, the politician will find himself superior to some persons in the hierarchy and inferior to others. The result is that he behaves both as the man whom we have discussed in Part 2 and as the man whom we shall discuss in Part 3. Almost all politicians face some problem of dealing with inferiors. Above the very lowest tier, the politician will have supervisory functions, and his own prospects for promotion will depend partly on the efficiency with which he makes use of his own subordinates.

Consider, then, the problem facing the politician within a hierarchy who is of sufficient rank to carry supervisory functions, but who is not high enough to have become disinterested in further promotions. What he seeks from his followers may be classified in two categories. First, the politician will supervise the carrying out of some assigned function. He may head a bureau charged with collecting crop statistics in Illinois; he may be responsible for supervising the singing of perpetual novenas before the Emerald Buddha; or he may be entrusted with the command of an army. Regardless of the nature of his command, the efficiency with which his subdivision of the hierarchy performs will affect his own position. He will have a distinct interest in improving that efficiency. And insofar as his actions are directed toward improving the efficiency of his particular subdivision, he is, in effect, acting as a proxy for his own superiors and carrying out their will.

Secondly he will also be interested in the efficiency of his followers in another sense. In his competition with his peers for the favor of their mutual sovereign(s), his subordinates can be very useful. The efficiency with which they are organized for this purpose is important to him in his own power struggle, but this sort of efficiency may not contribute to the performance of the assigned function of the bureau. In the ideally efficient organization, the politician would, however, realize that the only way of pleasing his superiors was to organize his subdivision of the grand enterprise to carry out its organizational objectives most effectively. As we have suggested, the degree of approximation to this ideal may be taken as a good measure for the efficiency of an organizational structure. At the opposite extreme from this ideal lies the organization in which the wise and ambitious politician is relatively unconcerned with whether his own subdivision carries out broad organizational tasks. Instead, he is primarily interested in his subordinates as an entourage to assist him in his conflict with his peers for advancement. To the individual politician, these two types of "efficiency" are more or less indistinguishable. He is interested, like the ultimate sovereign, in getting his own wishes carried out. He wants his subordinates to do those things that will most advance him in the organization, and he is not particularly interested in whether or not these activities coincide with his ostensible responsibilities.

THE "IDEAL" SOVEREIGN

We may imagine a man who has nothing to fear from his subordinates, while at the same time possessing less than godlike control over their activities. We are unlikely to encounter any politician with this degree of security, but an analysis of this "ideal type" will be of considerable assistance in understanding the problems of real supervisors. The central problem of this "ideal" sovereign is organizing subordinate politicians so that they, to the greatest degree possible, will behave as their superiors want them to behave. This, in essence, is the principal problem of the sovereign at the apex of the pyramid. It may also be considered, in the more general sense, as the basic problem for social organization. Normally, it must be accepted that it is desirable that organizations work efficiently in the carrying out of the functions for which they are constituted. In one sense, the position of the analyst here is somewhat akin to that of the political economist. We shall try to discover those types of social institutions that will be most efficient in attaining desirable ends with given expenditures of resources. The theory developed will thus be a general normative theory, but, as in all such cases, the theory, to be useful, must be applied to each particular organization separately.

THE GROUP SOVEREIGN IN A DEMOCRACY

The analysis has a special relevance and importance in democratic countries. Here, as we have seen, the ultimate sovereign is the voter. Each and every voter is a member of a large group sovereign, or, more precisely, a number of group sovereigns. Those politicians who obtain their positions through the (collective) favor of the voters will follow the "will of the people" with almost slavish devotion. This basic fact is often obscured. We sometimes speak of politicians as leaders, not as followers. But we must recognize that the slogan: "The mob is in the streets. I must find out where it is going, for I am its leader," is a good one for any democratic politician.

A second factor that obscures the underlying reality of the situation lies in the "official theory" of democracy. It is sometimes assumed that there exists some "volonté générale," and that the duty of the democratic process is to locate this will. Any reasonably careful examination of actual democratic process will, of course, quickly dispel this illusion.

From the point of view taken here, the problem vanishes. A democracy is merely a political system in which ultimate power rests with a special type of group sovereign. The politicians court this group sovereign in much the same manner that they would court any sovereign. They are interested in the "will of the people" only in the sense that they are interested in determining those types of behavior that will be rewarded at the next election. We have, in Part 2, discussed this reaction of the politician to the electorate, and there was no implication that the electorate does not possess power over the politician. But it should be emphasized that the conduct that the electorate will reward in the politician is not likely to be identical with that which would please the professor of political science.

The political leaders thus owe their positions to the favor of the voters. In terms of the relationships herein discussed, the people are the superiors of the politicians. If we wish the politicians to act in specific ways, they must be rewarded for so doing. If, by contrast, we wish to prevent specific types of governmental action, such action must be made unprofitable for the politicians. The democratic electorate will be confronted with much the same problem as the ideal sovereign at the apex of an administrative pyramid. The analysis of this part of the book, therefore, deals with the problem that confronts the voting population.

LIMITATIONS ON HIERARCHICAL TASKS

We shall now discuss briefly the limitations on the tasks that can reasonably be assigned to any given organization of human individuals. This concept of limitation has not to my knowledge been fully explored. No one would, presumably, believe that the tasks assigned to a bureaucracy could be expanded without limits, yet there does not appear to be any serious discussion of that point. Occasional reference will be found to tasks that are "administratively impossible," but this term usually refers to the impossibility of accomplishment due to limitations on manpower available or due to the existence of mutually conflicting sets of instructions. The hypothesis that there might exist tasks which, although free of internal contradictions, might simply be too large for performance by any bureaucracy does not seem to have been examined. Yet once the hypothesis is advanced, no one is likely to contest its validity, although great differences of opinion may arise as to its relevance.

The tendency for scholars to ignore the possible limits on tasks that may be performed through bureaucratic structures suggests that such limits, if they exist, are so high as to prevent the problem from having practical real-world application. Organizations have been set up or projected that imply extremely high limits. Certain socialist scholars of the 1930's and 1940's dream of a world state as a planned society. The Nazis had essentially the same organizational dream, although the objectives were, of course, different. Similar illusions seem to have been fairly common historically. Most regimes of which we have knowledge have incorporated governmentally controlled economies with totalitarian political structures. The limited state of Western society with which we are familiar is a distinct oddity in the totality of human experience.[1] The progress of the West under this abnormal political system can be taken as some indication of its efficiency, but its unusual aspects, historically, should not be overlooked.

Numerous objections have been raised to the various proposals for changing the political order that has been characteristic of the West in the last century or two toward an order conforming more closely to the world norm. But the suggestion that it would be impossible to organize a governmental

1. It was not the Webbs but Mencius who first said, "The government should own the important industries and closely control the rest."

structure that could actually carry out (as opposed to appearing to do so) the task of centralized totalitarian control of the activities of a whole nation does not seem to have been among the more important of these objections. Economists, it is true, have argued that economic planning could be highly inefficient as a means of organizing an economy and that such planning would tend to lower living standards; but this argument has usually been based on strictly economic considerations. There are, however, two important exceptions to this widespread failure to recognize the general limitation of bureaucratic tasks. F. A. Hayek has argued convincingly that the problem of running a planned economy efficiently could not be solved by the planning authority, because it would be impossible for the authority to possess all of the knowledge which would be necessary for the required decisions. Although Hayek uses this objection only with reference to the planned economy, it clearly has wider applications. Administrative problems in other fields could also be of such complexity that the centralization of information necessary to make decisions effectively in a bureaucracy might not be possible.[2]

Michael Polanyi also has offered an interesting mathematical argument against a centrally planned economy, an argument based on problems of control. Although his main interest is economic, his arguments apply to other types of organization.[3] Both Hayek and Polanyi are obviously opposed to the centrally planned economy for reasons other than that mentioned here, but it is interesting to note that no proponent of such an economic order has, to my knowledge, attempted to refute either of them on this particular argument. It is also somewhat curious that no political scientist, again to my knowledge, has recognized the relevance of these studies to the whole subject of political theory. The arguments seem to have made so little impression that even those who are, on other grounds, opposed to totalitarian controls have often implicitly assumed that the centrally planned society is possible.[4]

2. Hayek's article "The Use of Knowledge in Society" first appeared in the September 1945 issue of the *American Economic Review* (519–30), and has been reprinted in his *Individualism and the Economic Order* (77–91).

3. Polanyi's arguments may be found in the last three essays of his *The Logic of Liberty*. I have given no details on either Hayek's or Polanyi's position largely because I see no point in duplicating material which is already in print in a highly elegant form. I will shortly present my own arguments on this point, and as they are somewhat similar to those of Polanyi and Hayek, a separate presentation of their position would result in simple waste of wood pulp.

4. I am, of course, aware of the existence of many historic regimes, which in theory were centrally planned. To anticipate arguments which will be made in more detail later, I believe

A more formal discussion of this whole problem of the effective limits on the size of the task a bureaucracy can perform must be postponed, but a brief introduction may be given here. In later chapters, the nature of these limits will be discussed more thoroughly, and we shall try to determine their general order of magnitude. We shall also find that these limits vary with the nature of the task to be performed and that some types of operations permit the adoption of procedures that materially raise the limits on the size of the tasks that may be accomplished through a single organizational structure. The basic problem is that the degree of internal coordination which is necessary to accomplish a given task effectively may be greater than can be achieved by a hierarchic structure that is large enough to perform the task. If this should be true, the task is organizationally impossible.

To this point, I have used the word "task" largely in the singular. If we think of "tasks" in terms of the multiplicity of things undertaken by large organizations, the concept of limits does not apply with the same force. Different people in any large organization will normally be doing a large number of different things. If these different things are intended as coordinate parts of a single larger function, the limits on the size of the organization which is possible may be severe. If, on the other hand, the organization carries out a collection of unrelated and separate activities, the conception of limit that we mention here need not apply. This becomes obviously true when it is recognized that the carrying out of unrelated and uncoordinated functions is equivalent to converting the single organization into several organizations, united only by the accidental fact that each unit involves some of the same personnel. The center of attention here, however, is organizational structures that exist for the purpose of performing some *coordinated* task, even if this task be the abstractly simple one of carrying out the will of a man or a group. The limits on the size of organizations of this type are much lower than those upon merely formal organizations which exist without effective intrahierarchic coordination.

THE PURPOSES OF BUREAUCRACY

Why do extremely large organizations exist? Most persons would have little difficulty in answering this question. The stockholder in the General

---

that such regimes are, in a sense, optical illusions. Everyone is fitted into a gigantic hierarchy, but most of the actions taken by the vast numbers of people on the lower levels of the hierarchy are not planned by the central authority.

Motors Corporation, for example, understands that the purpose of this particular hierarchic organization is that of making money (of which he hopes to secure a portion), primarily through the manufacture and sale of automotive vehicles. Similarly, most citizens of the United States, if asked the question as to why the national government exists, would reply in terms of various functions such as defense, foreign affairs, etc., all of which are carried out by the governmental bureaucracy. Thus, to the average man the obvious justification for any hierarchical organization lies in its ability to carry out some task. This commonsense understanding of organizational purpose is that which is adopted in this book. Organizations are established, or should be if they are not, as a means of getting certain things done.

There are, however, less obvious justifications for bureaucratic structures. The individual member of a hierarchy is likely to feel, although possibly only subconsciously, that one of its major functions is that of supporting him personally. The attitude is, surprisingly, not confined to members of the bureaucracy itself. In every congressional debate discussing governmental economies, some remarks will be introduced about the "threat" to the livelihood of the bureaucrats employed in the hierarchies threatened with extinction. A proposal to abolish a certain bureau or agency will always raise questions about the dismissal of its employees. Both in Congress and among the voting public this is widely accepted as a valid, although not necessarily conclusive, argument. The same argument applies on the positive side. New organizations are sometimes proposed, not in terms of the functions that they will perform, but in terms of the persons that will be hired, as if their basic function was that of hiring employees.

Still another, and more complex, justification for the existence of an hierarchy is one that I shall call the ceremonial. The hierarchy is conceived of, essentially, as an end in itself. This attitude, seldom conscious, is of considerable importance.

Some people feel that society should be monolithic, or at least that it should have that appearance, and they are apt to feel personally somewhat more secure when they are enabled to occupy a niche in an established hierarchy than they would be in an "open society." As we have already noted, any hierarchy operates largely through personal relationships. By contrast, the free economy, in its ideal form, operates largely through the mechanism of impersonal relationships. Some persons simply feel happier when they can depend on other individuals to decide upon their destiny than when they feel this is determined by impersonal forces. In America, we talk of a government of laws, not of men, but subconsciously many persons really long for the apparent security of the older system.

Our later analysis will deal, almost exclusively, with the first, and commonsense, objective or purpose of organizational structures. If supporting its employees is the primary function of bureaucracy, then obviously the concept of efficiency has little meaning, and almost any structure is as good as another. The desire to "belong" to a monolithic structure represents grasping at a shadow at best. Large organizations are never genuinely monolithic. Nevertheless, the illusion in this respect may be maintained, and a large bureaucracy may be indispensable for its continuation. But this sort of bureaucracy also will not command our attention in the analysis that follows. Essentially, such a bureaucracy would be an experiment in social suggestion. The objective would be that of concealing from the members the real fact that monolithicity is not attained.

The discussion of bureaucracy that follows is based on the simple premise that organizations are established to accomplish an objective. A function is to be performed, and this function is directed toward the world outside the hierarchy. The one exception to this generalization is the all-embracing bureaucracy; the social system in which every member of society belongs to the gigantic organization (such as the ideal state of the pre-1945 socialists or the Inca Empire). This system must, by definition, be concerned with the welfare of its members, or at least some of them. But even here, the system can be analyzed in terms of the well-being of members as individuals and not in terms of the psychic benefits that they may secure through membership in the organization as such.

THE ARTS OF PERSUASION

One additional point requires consideration briefly in this introductory chapter. We shall be largely concerned with getting subordinates in a bureaucracy to carry out the desires of superiors by the devices of rewards and punishments. There are, however, other methods. These methods are extremely various. Hypnotism is theoretically possible, but it probably has been rarely used. Deliberate drug addiction followed by control of drug supplies is also possible and may have been used by the sect of the assassins.

The more normal methods of getting persons to do as one desires, without resort of direct rewards and punishments, can be summarized in the word "persuasion." This covers many and varied techniques, from advertising to fraud to logical discussion. It includes, by extension, what Weber calls "charisma" and also religious influence. Any man who desires to get his subordinates to do things without "paying" them, or who wishes to obtain more from them than he does "pay for," must resort to such techniques as these. In some cases these techniques have the major advantage of being less costly than other methods.

A warning should be inserted for presumptive superiors against an overdependence on methods of persuasion. Due to the ubiquitousness of advertising in modern life, we sometimes overestimate its importance. It may be forgotten that the method is important to business firms only when products advertised are almost identical in quality. "There ain't no difference in soap," and hence the soap company with the best campaign sells the most soap. But shortly after World War II there was a difference in soaps; the detergents were introduced. At that time none of the old companies, experienced and skilled in advertising techniques, tried for long to sell old-fashioned soap in competition with the new detergents.

This phenomenon carries over into political life as well. Normally, individuals know what is, in fact, to their own interest, and are capable of deciding what action will be best. Trying to get persons to do something against their own interests is, of necessity, a difficult job, and it should not be depended on as a principal method of securing efficiency. The simple procedure of utilizing rewards and punishments with the aim of making the person's own interest correspond with the objectives of the superior is far better as a method. This conclusion is, of course, in almost direct contradiction with one of our most powerful current myths.

The view that "psychological methods" and indoctrination can accomplish almost anything seems to be firmly believed by many people. Actually, such methods are always of limited utility, and the myth should be recognized for what it is. Conditioning in childhood makes us what we are to some extent; this much is surely true. But this will be of little assistance to the politician who must deal with adults and tries to get them to do things against their interests. This is particularly the case when he must deal with those politicians who have risen to high positions in a system of social mobility that incorporates some merit selection. Two of the important reasons why these politicians have risen, as we have shown in Part 2, are their greater than normal ability to understand those actions that would, in fact, advance their own interests and their willingness to take such actions. These politicians are particularly poor subjects of psychological manipulation or persuasion of any sort.

CHAPTER 12

KNOW THYSELF

The classical Chinese, when they wrote on political subjects, placed great emphasis on the personal "virtue" of the leader. By "virtue" they meant something quite different from the meaning of the equivalent English word, but there seems no doubt that they were correct in their view. The performance of a man's followers is greatly influenced by his own personal qualities and behavioral characteristics. Because these writers felt that the efficient administration of the Chinese Empire was the ultimate desideratum, they devoted a great deal of their efforts to "preaching" the desirability of "virtue" to various emperors and officials.

THE ABSENCE OF EXTERNAL NORMS

This approach requires the introduction of some external value source. An outside observer may feel that a given politician or bureaucrat should work harder, but the official in question may not, himself, agree with this view. He may be naturally lazy, or he may be interested in other things. We know that many absolute monarchs, including the emperors of classical China, have devoted less time to the business of ruling than to the business of enjoying themselves. To this point we have, in this book, attempted to consider the hierarchy from the standpoint of the real politician, the politician who is assumed to possess the usual human strengths and weaknesses. It would be improper, as well as confusing, to modify this approach and to begin to judge politicians by some externally imposed standard. This is not to deny the relevance of external values for some purposes; the point here is simply that such external standards have no place in this analysis, which is, essentially, positive.[1] For this purpose, we take the politician who wants to maximize the achievement of

1. Traditional political theory has suffered from the failure of many works to make the basic distinction mentioned here. Many writers have not distinguished the theory of political obligation, which is essentially a normative theory for the behavior of either the rulers or the ruled, and the theory of political process, which is essentially a positive theory of the workings of collective decision processes. For a discussion on these points, see James M. Buchanan, "Marginal Notes on Reading Political Philosophy," Appendix I to the book jointly written by Buchanan and this writer, *The Calculus of Consent: Logical Foundations of Constitutional Democracy* (Ann Arbor: University of Michigan Press, 1962).

his own desires, whatever these might be. These desires might or might not include things that would be disapproved of by the average clergyman.

KNOWLEDGE OF OBJECTIVES AND ABILITIES

Nevertheless, it is important that the politician who is in a position of power realize what his own objectives are and also how much effort he is willing to devote to achieving these objectives. The politician should also be aware of his own limitations with respect to such qualities as intelligence, information, and that mysterious characteristic usually referred to as "force of character." If the politician is willing to work hard, he will obviously be better able to control his subordinates than if he gives the supervisory task little attention. (The advantages gained through industry may be offset by other defects in character. George III was a most industrious monarch.) Similarly, if the politician has great force of character, high intelligence, and wide information of the specific fields in which his subordinates are working, he will possess differential advantages in dealing with them.

These points seem clear. The man must cut his coat to suit his cloth. He can control others (or do anything else) only to the extent of his capacity. This is, however, of considerable importance to the structure of the organization. We have already introduced the concept of limits upon the task that an organization may carry out. Obviously, the limits will vary greatly with the personal capacity and the industry of the person at the apex of the hierarchy. It should be noted that the organization that does not attempt to accomplish more than its "capacity" will work more efficiently than one which overextends itself. An incautious sovereign who assigns too large a task to his organization may not realize that a reduction in the size of the task itself provides his only means of increasing his actual accomplishments.

This consideration applies to politicians within a hierarchy as well as to those at the apex. There is, however, a different limit on capacity here. If the organization is one that permits "merit"-type promotion, lazy and incompetent persons are not likely to be found in the higher ranks. The abilities of politicians in these ranks are likely, therefore, to be reasonably high. But the amount of time and energy that can be devoted to supervising inferiors may be low, in a relative sense. In inefficient organizations, especially, the politician seeking to rise may have to devote a large part of his time to dealing with his sovereign at the expense of time that he could devote to supervising his own inferiors. Such a politician may find that his genuine capacities for supervision may not exceed those of the laziest and least able monarch.

We have already made the distinction between the supervision of followers in carrying out "official" organizational duties and supervising them in other activities which will advance the supervisor. From the latter's point of view, these two types of supervision are identical. He devotes energy to supervision in each case instrumentally; that is, to further his own ends and interests. To him, whether or not these advantages come from his followers acting to further the official purposes of the organization is irrelevant. One likely error consists in assuming that the politician can somehow exert closer and more effective supervision in those activities outside the "official" purposes of the organization. This view is, of course, incorrect. If the politician seeks to have an efficient train of followers, in this respect, too, he must limit its size and task to the range of his effective supervision.

REAL AND APPARENT POWER

It is important for the politician to decide whether he wants real power or only the appearance of power, or some combination of these. Real power is, by necessity, strictly limited, and its exercise requires hard and unremitting work. Apparent power, on the other hand, can be substantially unlimited and can be more easily obtained. Provided that the appearance is well preserved, apparent power can satisfy the "power aspirations" of all but the most perceptive of men.

In this discussion of the distinction between real and apparent power of a sovereign, three situations may be noted, more or less arbitrarily classified. In the first, the sovereign is presumed surrounded by inferiors who bow and scrape and inform him that his orders are being obeyed, but who do not actually carry these orders out. There is surely some of this sort of behavior in every organization. Readers of Winston Churchill's history of World War II will recall that he gave orders on an extremely wide range of subjects. Everything, from the cleanliness of the flag at the Admiralty to the amount of exercise for generals, seems to have met his eye. But we can feel confident that many of these orders were quietly forgotten. The generals surely did not tell Churchill that they were deliberately ignoring his orders, but probably few of them altered their daily regimens in order to get the amount of exercise that he demanded. Because they did not inform Churchill of their disobedience, his own morale was no doubt higher than it would have been otherwise. The point to be noted is that Churchill had somewhat less effective control over the British war effort than would have been the case had he chosen to confine himself to a narrower sphere of activities.

In most administrative organizations (including Churchill's wartime government), this deliberate ignoring of the orders of sovereigns is probably a minor factor. More common is the situation in which the specific order of the sovereign will be carried out to the extent that it is possible. The sovereign may be at the apex of a vast hierarchy, and this hierarchy may carry out, or attempt to do so, each single order that he issues. Yet most of the members of the hierarchy may be doing things that are either opposed to his desires or, at best, neutral. The difficulty here arises because a large hierarchy—that is, the persons within it—will be doing far more things than can be ordered by any one man, regardless of his rank, diligence, and ability. Those orders that he directly issues will represent only a very small part of the total "output" of the organization, which must, by necessity, operate largely on the basis of established decision rules. Consequently, the sovereign at the apex cannot, at any specific time, be said to exercise actual control over the hierarchy. Yet, because each specific order that he gives is obeyed, he may think of himself as being in complete command. This situation led Nicholas I, the "Iron Tsar," to say, "I do not rule Russia; ten thousand clerks do." To the perceptive man this sort of situation can be highly frustrating.

This situation also does not represent power maximization. The person who wants to make maximum use of a bureaucracy must find some better means. This suggests that the sovereign should so attempt to organize the hierarchy that its members act, in a sense, as his proxies. He should attempt to make inferiors reach decisions that are in accord with his own wishes without the necessity of issuing specific orders in each particular case. The degree to which this objective for the organization of a hierarchy can be achieved and the methods to be employed will be discussed later in this book. Insofar as this last method can be applied the organization is efficient from the point of view of the sovereign.

In any real organization, the three elements are likely to be intermingled. Some orders by the sovereign will be ignored. Others will be obeyed, but the diversity of tasks undertaken by the organization will overwhelm the importance of the sovereign's orders. Finally, existing decision rules will cause inferiors to act as proxies for the sovereign. In poorly organized structures, the first of these two will predominate; in well-organized structures, the last element will be more important. In any case, the politician at the apex must decide which of these three types of "obedience" he wants to demand.

To most external observers, the third type of "obedience," that which is incorporated into the rules of the organization itself, will probably seem the most desirable. The recognition that power will be effectively maximized by the introduction of organizational rules conducive to this type of behavior obviously takes a type of intellectual courage and penetration that may not be found among politicians at the top of any hierarchy. In the analysis that follows we shall, however, assume that the sovereign desires to achieve obedience of his subordinates in this organizational sense, rather than in the first two senses mentioned above. This type of obedience is, of course, the most difficult to achieve since it must be, so to speak, "built in" to the structure.

CHAPTER 13

PARKINSON'S LAW

When considering the number of subordinates that an intelligent politician will desire to have under his supervision, some attention must be given to the phenomenon of "bureaucratic imperialism." This has been discussed by numerous analysts (*Parkinson's Law* is possibly the most familiar, as well as the most amusing, treatment), but without a full understanding. It is usually treated as something that is inevitable in bureaucratic structures. Although there surely is a tendency toward such imperialism in most administrative organizations, it seems rarely to have been a significant problem when the broad sweep of history is taken into account. It has been awarded more importance than its due, perhaps because of the concentration on recent American and European hierarchies where the phenomenon has been pervasive.

The explanation is simple. As a more or less accidental by-product of a number of policy decisions reached for other reasons, a situation has arisen in most American and European governmental bureaucracies in which a politician is rewarded by his sovereigns for simply increasing the number of inferiors that he supervises. Obviously, this is a pathological situation. The ultimate sovereigns should reward their subordinates in terms of their accomplishments, not in terms of the number of followers whom these subordinates, in their turn, supervise. But, because the situation does exist in many modern hierarchic structures, it warrants a brief discussion here.

Two examples will indicate how the system works in modern American bureaucracy. During one of the reorganizations of the Department of State in the early 1950's, a group of experts from the Civil Service Commission were called in to inspect a particular bureau in the department to determine the appropriate "ratings" for various employees. Apparently, the only concern of the commission "experts" was that of ascertaining the number of subordinates supervised by each employee. Some of the employees in the bureau happened to be highly trained analysts who were supervising no one. Because of this, the commission experts' reaction was to recommend that these analysts be reduced in grade level.

As another example, an engineer invented a shell-loading machine which could have resulted, at that time, in a substantial reduction in the manpower requirements at various arsenals in the United States. He had no difficulty in arousing the interest of the Department of Defense in this project, and he received funds to construct the machine for test purposes. After the machine was built, he failed to get any of the heads of arsenals to introduce the machine. None of these officials denied that the machine would save the government money. The saving in manpower resulting from its installation would have been so great, however, as to jeopardize the civil service grade of these officials, and so they were extremely reluctant to utilize the machine. These men held their positions, their ratings, by virtue of the number of employees directly under their supervision, and any reduction in that number would have had the effect of reducing their pay. These two examples indicate the danger of rewarding individuals for the wrong things, for things other than those that will further the objectives of the organization.

This type of situation can arise only if the higher members of the organization, the ultimate sovereigns, are either ignorant of or uninterested in the functions performed by the subordinates. Only this could account for the practice of using the number of subordinates as a means of evaluating a politician's worth to the organization. If such a system is applied throughout a whole organization, as it is to a large extent in the United States government, the higher officials will actually encourage their inferiors to build up the size of the whole hierarchy since their own position, as well as that of their inferiors, will depend on the number of subordinates. Under such circumstances as these, the politician need be concerned with little else than the size of his "empire." He will attempt to increase this without limit. Efficient management becomes, in this extreme case, a problem about which he need not be concerned. Parkinson's Law may well apply.

This, then, is the real basis of bureaucratic imperialism. Imperialistic activity, as such, may take two forms. First, the politician may try to increase the size of his part of the hierarchy by hiring new personnel. Second, he may try to increase it by raiding the trains of other rival politicians, his peers. Thus, the head of the Command Desk of the File Section of the Ordnance Small Arms Depot may suggest that "efficiency" requires the combination of CDFSOSAD with the Personnel Desk OSAD, under the head of the chief of CDFSOSAD. In this way, he hopes to secure promotion. The head of the personnel desk will probably think that such a change would be "inefficient."

This type of imperialistic activity may be contrasted with that which involves convincing Congress that the politician's bureau or agency should hire more people. As a general rule, bureaucrats will prefer this direct type of expansion to the raiding variety which pits them one against the other. Despite this preference, however, the limitations on the resources that governments possess insure that most persons who have risen very rapidly will be experts in both types. But all bureaucrats, whether successful or not, thoroughly approve of an expansion of the whole bureaucracy. If the army is expanded sufficiently, all present officers can be generals or, at the least, colonels.

The taxpayer, the ultimate sovereign in the case of the United States governmental hierarchy, has opposite preferences concerning these two types of activity. Shifts of employees from one bureau to another, with the concomitant promotions and demotions, do not particularly affect him. General increases in the whole structure are, however, quite different matters since this will be reflected in an increased burden of taxation.

The remedy for bureaucratic imperialism is not difficult to recognize in principle, but is not necessarily simple to implement in practice. It is only necessary that the bureaucrat's superiors concern themselves with his performance and that of his whole division, and reward him accordingly. The bureaucratic supervisor even can be offered additional rewards for accomplishing given tasks with fewer inferiors under him. Measuring performance may be extremely difficult, but it should be possible, at least, for superiors to abandon the nonsensical method of rating inferiors by the number of followers that each is able to accumulate.

At the outset of this reference to bureaucratic imperialism, I stated that the phenomenon was rare except in modern Europe and America. The reasons for this are not far to seek. The more general system has been that of allocating to an official certain revenues along with certain functions. The official is then expected to perform the functions while using the revenues, and his superiors are not interested in the number of men that he may employ. Thus, the high admiral of Spain in early modern history received a harbor fee for each ship that entered a Spanish port and retained a small revenue service to collect the fee. If his ships were kept up to mark, no higher official asked the admiral for an accounting. In other systems the taxes were collected by a centralized organization, but the revenues were then allocated to the various departments on much the same terms. An army commander could expect to receive a given sum of money, but he would not be rewarded for his own efforts in increasing the number of men in his command.

CHAPTER 14

WHISPERING DOWN THE LANE

Early in basic training, the American army used to employ an experiment as a teaching device. Seven to ten soldiers would be arranged in a large circle out of earshot of each other. The remainder of the unit would be concentrated at a point on the circle. The officer in charge of the experiment would then give a simple message to the soldier at that point which would be heard by the "audience" but by none of the other soldiers on the circle. The first soldier would run to deliver the message to the next man on the circle who would pass it along to the third, and so on until the circle was complete. The last soldier would repeat the message, as he thought he had received it, to the officer in the hearing of the "audience." There was normally little resemblance between the message after it had completed its circuit and the original text. The moral that the army drew from this was that messages should be written rather than oral.

For the analysis of this book we must discuss the problem raised by this experiment in more detail. In the first place, careful selection and training of personnel would, no doubt, secure somewhat improved results over that achieved through the use of untrained recruits. But the basic principle is certainly correct. The method *is* highly inefficient as a means of transmitting information. Moreover, the amount of error ("noise" in communications-theory terminology) would increase exponentially with the increase in the number of persons in the transmission chain and with the complexity of the message transmitted.

It should be noted that the cause of this phenomenon is not really the use of oral rather than written transmission. There are probably some errors of simple mistake in understanding, but the main distortions arise within the brains of each man. The man hears a message, mentally interprets its contents, and selects the important points for repetition to the next man. Through a series of such operations, the original message becomes something entirely different. If the message should be transmitted by means of a written note obviously there would be no distortion if each man simply made an exact copy. But if each man should receive a written note, discard it, and then run to the next man and write out the note again in his own words, roughly the same pattern of distortion could be predicted.

THE STANDARD VIEW OF BUREAUCRACY

All of this may appear to have little relevance for our subject of hierarchical organizations. In fact, the experiment does have little or no relevance for the way in which hierarchies actually operate. The experiment is useful in refuting the popular view of the way in which a bureaucracy works. The "normal" or standard version of bureaucracy seems to be something like the following: The lower levels of the structure receive information from various sources. This information is then passed along upward through the pyramid. At the various levels, the information is analyzed, collated, and coordinated with other information that originates in separate parts of the pyramid. Eventually, the information reaches the top level where the basic policy decisions are made concerning the appropriate actions to be taken. These decisions on policy are then passed down through the pyramid with each lower level making the administrative decisions that are required to implement the policies sent from on high. This descriptive scheme has not, to my knowledge, been used by any serious student of bureaucratic hierarchies, but it does seem to be the version held by the "average man," and by most bureaucrats themselves.

The army experiment discussed at the outset of this chapter disproves this theory of bureaucracy. Let us consider a hierarchy in which H is at the lowest level; he reports to G, who in turn reports to F, who reports to E, who reports to D, and so on to A, who is the ultimate sovereign of the particular system. If H sees something that he feels is worth reporting to G, who in turn thinks that the item is important enough to report to F, and so on up the line until it reaches A for a decision, the experiment indicates that the version of the information that reaches A must be materially different from that which H perceived. Suppose that A, on the basis of the "information" that he gets, makes a decision, then issues an order to B, who passes it along to C, and so down the line, until it finally reaches H for implementation. The order will also have undergone major changes during its transmission. Consequently, H will receive from his superior, in final consequence of his original observation, a distorted version of an order based on a distorted version of his original observation. This result can, of course, be altered by converting all of the bureaucrats between H and A into mere postmen who serve simply to transmit reports and orders verbatim. I shall return to this point presently.

The degree of distortion that would arise under such a bureaucratic system would probably be so great that neither the original report nor the issued order would be recognizable in any sizeable organization. This would be true due to the complexity of the information, and of the orders, transmitted and also because of the particular problems in transmission. The members of a hierarchy do not, in fact, think of themselves as mere messenger boys, faithfully transmitting the reports of their subordinates. G would, in our example, not be likely to simply pass along H's report accurately. He would consider it a part of his duty, because of his superior experience and training, to extract the fundamental aspects of the information from H's report, and to add some comments of his own. In addition he could be receiving, at the same time, information from the peers of H that would have to be coordinated with that of H before the preparation of G's report to F. As a result of this structure, reports are transmitted upward under what may well be the worst possible of circumstances.

The same general conclusions hold with respect to an order issued from the top, by A in our example. B is, presumably, only one of several direct subordinates to A. B will have then to decide what parts of the general policy directives issued by A affect his particular division of the hierarchy. He will prepare orders and pass along to his inferiors, C_1, C_2, and C_3, only those parts of A's overall directive that he considers relevant. But to this directive he will add his own detailed administrative instructions. C_1 will do likewise with regard to passing the orders to D_1, D_2, and D_3. When it finally reaches H, at the lowest level, the order will have undergone significant changes. Note also that, in the case of orders issued from the top, the distortion is likely to vary within the organization. Thus, an order received by B_1, B_2, B_3, from A will be passed on in slightly different form by each of them. By the time the general directive reached the lower levels, there might be major differences among the versions received by comparable bureaucrats in different parts of the same organization. Uniformity could not be expected from a bureaucracy that attempted to operate in this fashion.

BUREAUCRATS AS POSTMEN

Let us consider, in contrast, a hierarchy similar to that used for illustrative purposes above except for the fact that all officials between the highest and the lowest levels interpret their duties to be those of mere postmen; the intermediate level officials merely transmit verbatim texts of information upward or orders downward in the chain of command. This system would be similar to replacing all of the intermediate level officials by mechanical transmission devices. If each official has three subordinates of lower rank reporting directly to him, with the chain running from A to the H level, there would be something over 2,000 H's at the lowest rank. A, the single sovereign at the apex of the pyramid, would have to deal more or less directly with this whole mass of bureaucrats. Obviously the single human being, unless he be possessed of superhuman powers, cannot absorb all of the information that 2,000 inferiors would obtain and pass along. This should be sufficient to indicate that the replacement of live bureaucrats at the intermediate levels with transmission machines, human or non-human, will not make the hierarchical system work any better.

Since the errors in transmission will be so large in the first model, and since the capacity of leaders will be so limited in the second, there remains only the possibility of combining elements of both of these organizational forms. We might suppose that each official culls from the reports he receives that information which he deems proper for his superior to have, taking into account duplications and also the capacity of the sovereign to digest information. For the material that is submitted upward suppose that verbatim transmission should be the rule. This system might serve to avoid the distortion that is implicit in permitting intermediaries to interpret both reports and orders, and at the same time it might avoid the hopeless clogging up of the arteries of the hierarchy.

Two objections may be raised to this compromise system, the first of which is perhaps trivial. It is commonly stated that organizations, especially those that specialize in securing information, secure a multitude of individual and particular facts, and then, from these parts, build up a correlated "picture." This procedure would be almost impossible under the compromise system discussed above. If the facts gathered by low-level personnel should be individually unimportant they would be dropped out in the lower stages and hence never correlated.

The second, and more important, objection to the compromise sort of structure considered here turns on the contributions of the various levels of the hierarchy to the final results of the combined operations. If each official has three inferiors, the number used above, and there are eight levels from A to H, there will be 2,000 H's, over 600 G's, over 200 F's, etc. If we assume the compromise system in operation, the H's, who directly collect the field reports, will collect only an amount sufficient to occupy the G's (collecting information will always require more time than reading it and evaluating it). At the lowest level, therefore, enough information will be collected by the whole organization to occupy the time of 600 persons. By a series of operations in which two-thirds of the information held at each level is discarded and the remainder passed along up the chain, this total information is eventually winnowed down to that which can efficiently occupy the time of only one man. The great bulk of the field information originally collected is discarded and no use is made of it. This, quite naturally, raises the question as to the wisdom of collecting this excess information in the first place. If the organization were truncated below the fifth step instead of the eighth, for example, undoubtedly the E's in the system would know less than they would in the larger hierarchy. But would A be in any less favorable position in making the basic decisions for the whole organization?

We are once again driven to conclude that the objective of an organization should be, not the referring of information to and expecting decision from persons at the top of the administrative pyramid, but rather the obtaining of decisions from persons who are not themselves at the apex. The head of a hierarchy, the sovereign, has, as his principal problem in organizational efficiency, arranging the structure so that his inferiors reach decisions which he would have reached if he should have possessed as much information about the particular situation requiring decision as they do. The sovereign should not attempt to centralize decision making directly, but rather to influence his inferiors to make decisions that fit into the grand design of the organization, or, more simply, into his desires.

CHAPTER 15

A MENTAL EXPERIMENT

In the last chapter, the "standard" theory of bureaucratic operation was criticized. This completed, I am obligated to propose a substitute theory. The theory of organization that will be developed is basically normative. It is a theory that attempts to tell *how to make bureaucracies work.*

THE DECISION TO START AN ORGANIZATION

We may begin by considering a person, call him A, who is busily engaged in activities that he judges to be both desirable and important. The particular type of activity need not be specified here. He may, for example, be a wealthy man who is devoting his life to giving away an accumulated fortune in the "best" way, or he may be a dictator. In any case, assume that, recognizing that his own faculties are limited, this person decides to establish an organization to assist him in accomplishing his goal.

As a first step, we assume that A hires B as his assistant. While there may exist situations in which A would exercise extremely close control over all of the activities of B, these are rare. Normally, the man who has decided to create an organization and who begins by hiring a single assistant will want to devote only some part of his own time to controlling and supervising the assistant. The sovereign will have other things to occupy his mind, or he may be simply lazy. The point of transferring some of his functions to an assistant is to enable him to give more time to other matters. This suggests that, in our model, A is likely to devote considerably less than his full time in controlling the activities of B. For simplicity, let us suppose that the time not spent in controlling B is to be devoted to controlling other assistants, $B_2 \ldots B_n$.

ORGANIZATIONAL SIZE

One of the first organizational or structural problems that confronts A will be the determination of the number of direct subordinates to hire. The funds that he has available for hiring these assistants will be highly relevant here, since such funds always are limited. If, for example, A should be willing to devote $20,000 for the personnel expenses of the particular organization that he is forming, he might find that he could hire two men at $10,000 each or ten low-grade employees at $2,000 each. Obviously, there will be major differences in the quality of the personnel that can be hired at different rates. The average quality of assistants must decline as more are hired for financial reasons. It is to be noted that this would remain true even if there were no financial limitations at all. If A should be a dictator with the power to conscript every man in the country, presumably he would get the most highly qualified assistant first, the second most qualified second, etc. The average quality of personnel would, as in the other case, decline as the number of persons in the hierarchy is expanded. This assumes, of course, that A will be able to discriminate among his actual and potential assistants. But, if he can't, he is beaten before he begins. This fact of declining quality must be taken into account in determining organizational size.

In addition, A must recognize that the more direct subordinates that he employs, the less time he will have available to devote to controlling the activities of each single one. The less time that A has to control the activities of a given subordinate, the more likely are the activities of the subordinate to deviate from A's desires. Against this must be balanced that, the more subordinates, the larger the volume of total activity that the organization can handle.

Taking all of these factors into account, A must reach a decision concerning the number of subordinates that he will employ. This number will vary with the type of personnel and the type of activity that is to be carried out. For analytical purposes here, let us assume that A decides on hiring four assistants, each of whom reports directly to him. He can then devote one-fourth of his total organizational time to supervising each one of these assistants. The assistants will, of course, have to devote some time to "receiving supervision." For sake of simplification, let us suppose that each of them devotes, on the average, one-fifth of his time to such contacts with A, his sovereign. Since all of A's time, and one-fifth of each of his assistants' time, is taken up then with internal activities within the organization, this total group of five men will be able to exert only as much influence on the outside world as three and one-fifths men. In other words, by adding four assistants A has only increased his powers of external action by three and one-fifths. But this is still a sizeable multiplication of his powers to act on the external world.

This result, however, is based on the assumption that everything is done by the assistants (B_1, B_2, B_3, B_4) in exact conformity to the wishes of A. This assumption is not warranted. Men will make errors. Even if B_2, for example, wants to do precisely as A commands, he will still make mistakes. Moreover, there is no reason to expect that B_2 will actually be so wholeheartedly devoted to A's interests. B_2 is, after all, an individual in his own right, and he will be more interested in his own objectives than those of A. As we have seen in Part 2, this interest will not, in such a small organization, often lead him to take actions directly contrary to A's wishes, but surely there will be certain occasions in which he will take actions not desired by A. B_2, along with his peers, will find this to be possible simply because A will not have sufficient time to check thoroughly on all of the actions of all of his subordinates. Again, for purposes of analysis, let us assume that for each three actions that B_2 takes that are strictly in accord with A's wishes, there will be one action that will go contrary to that which might have been desired by A.[1] This allows us to divide B_2's activities into three sets: First, he will spend, as we have assumed, one-fifth of his time "receiving supervision" from A. Second, he will spend three-fifths of his time carrying out A's wishes. Third, he will spend one-fifth of his time doing things which are not really desired by A at all. Extending this same numerical calculation to all four assistants, the total organizational group of five men, A and his four assistants, will really devote two and two-fifths man days each day to carrying out activities in the external world that are consistent with the purposes for which A established the organization. Four-fifths of a man day each day will be devoted to activities that A is either unconcerned with or would be opposed to.

If, in fact, A has correctly appraised the situation, and four is the optimal number of assistants for him to hire, either a reduction to three or an increase to five would reduce the overall efficiency of the organization. By reducing the number to three, he could exert closer supervision, but the total "output" of the hierarchy would be reduced. On the other hand, by expanding to five, he could expand the "output" of the organization, but at the expense of less strict control over the members, and a consequent increase in the expected number of "errors."

THE EXECUTIVE OFFICER

Can this situation be improved? For now, let us assume that A is employing the best supervisory techniques (a subject to be discussed at length later). This allows us here to discuss relatively minor organizational changes. Although the model we are discussing here is extremely small, this fact in itself will be helpful in understanding general modifications in structure. In such a small model, modifications are more readily analyzed and, for the most part,

1. This figure seems to me realistic, but the reader who feels that some other figure is better is invited to duplicate the arithmetic which follows using his own estimate.

the analysis can be extended to larger and more complicated structures without difficulty.

The first of the modifications that I want to discuss here is appointing an "executive officer" for the whole organization. In our model, this involves the placing of some "executive officer" between A and the subordinates B_1 to B_4. This being done, A could confine his attention to supervising the work of the executive officer who, in his turn, could directly supervise the subordinates. This actually compounds the problem. The executive officer would not be a perfect proxy for A, and hence the B's, carrying out the exec's orders, would be even farther from perfect execution of A's wishes. We know, however, that systems containing executive officers are quite common to administrative structures. Modern military organizations rely heavily on this office in the chain of command, and the prime minister or vizier has also been very common historically. Some consideration of the justification for this form of organization seems warranted.

One of the primary reasons for the use of the executive officer is probably simple laziness on the part of the superior that this officer is supposed to assist. The caliph of Baghdad, for example, might not want to put in a full day on dull administrative work when he could be enjoying himself in his harem or out hunting. Accordingly, he might appoint a vizier and devote only a small fraction of his own time to supervising the government's activities. The vizier then supervises all the junior officials, while the caliph supervises the vizier. Without doubt, this system serves to economize on the caliph's time, but there are disadvantages. The vizier, like any other official subject to only part-time supervision on the part of his sovereign, will not do exactly as the caliph wants. And because the vizier's inferiors, in their turn, will also evade their sovereign's desires to some extent, there will result a compounding of the deviation from the true desires of the caliph. Thus, the whole system will be less subject to the control of the ruler than would be the case should he devote his full time to supervising it himself. It must be recognized, however, that, if the ultimate sovereign is inherently lazy, the use of the executive officer device may be beneficial. Louis XIV ruled successfully without a prime minister. When his less energetic and less talented successor tried the same method, the result was administrative chaos. Louis XV was neither willing nor able to give his cabinet adequate supervision, and he would have surely been better off with a prime minister than without one.

There is a second reason for the use of an executive officer: to provide a scapegoat for the ultimate sovereign in the case of major administrative errors. This has been particularly important in Persian administrative practice, but, to some extent, it is among the motives in almost all systems. The organization of a naval vessel, in which the captain may be made into sort of a father figure while the executive officer is assigned most of the unpleasant disciplinary duties, provides another example.[2] The situation where the prince is credited with all good results, while the vizier is blamed for all that may go wrong, has been, historically, quite common. For this system to work the presence of a vizier is obviously required, but also his sphere of duties must be wide enough to make such blame plausible.

At the lower levels of administrative hierarchies, something equivalent to an "executive officer" type of organization may be used to help higher-ranking officials retain close control over lower-ranking members. The Chinese Imperial Civil Service, for example, normally appointed officials in pairs. One member of each pair would be senior to the other, although both were of equal nominal rank. The second served as a check on the power of the first, and vice versa. The actual term "executive officer" is not used to apply to such cases, but some of the tables of organization appear surprisingly similar to those of modern military establishments. This motive, that of applying an additional check on lower-ranking officials, is probably present in most modern systems where lower officials supervise "executive officers."

THE STAFF

The second organizational device that is sometimes thought to be able to extend the supervisory ability of the sovereign comes (like so many bad things in the modern world) from Prussia. With the death of Frederick the Great, the Prussian army was confronted with a serious problem. In theory, the king was commander, but none of Frederick's successors had either the talent or the inclination to exercise this command. The problem was that of maintaining the fiction of command while at the same time assuring the army an effective leadership. After a number of false starts, the "staff" type of organization evolved. Generals, for many years, had had personal staffs, usually consisting largely of men we should now call aides-de-camp or couriers. Prussia, one of the most bureaucratized states in Europe, had an elaborate staff organization to begin with. Under Frederick's successors this organization was enlarged. The chief

2. See John Master, *Bugles and a Tiger*, pp. 280–83, for a particularly good account of this phenomenon.

of staff, who was theoretically only an aide and an advisor to the king, became the real and effective commander of the army.

In order to give this fiction an air of verisimilitude, subordinate commanders were also equipped with elaborate staffs, and direct channels of command running through the staffs developed. The system was, of course, asymmetrical. The chief of staff of the whole force, although in theory only the king's aide, was in fact the army commander. The chief of staff of the second corps, on the other hand, was merely a staff officer under the commanding general second corps. But this made the illusion of royal command more realistic.

The device may have been more or less harmless so long as the staff concept was confined to the solution of the Prussian problem. Under the circumstances of the time, the Prussians could afford to waste some resources on a command structure that was of only ceremonial importance. But with the Prussian victories of the 1860's and the 1870's, Prussian military prestige rose sharply. Ibn Khaldun remarks that people usually copy the clothes of their conquerors. Armies seem to copy the organizational patterns of successful military machines. The staff system thus spread rapidly to all of the armies of Europe toward the end of the nineteenth century. "Staff" concepts also began to be taken over into non-military organizations. The division between the "staff" and the "line" became the basis for numerous textbooks in organization theory.

Basically, the "staff" device consists in the sovereign's appointment of persons to assist him in supervising subordinates.[3] In terms of our model, A might appoint a single staff officer to assist him in supervising the B's. But this staff officer must also be supervised, unless A is content to allow him to supervise the B's in terms of his own wishes rather than those of A. If, however, A spends some time in supervising the staff officer, he will have less time free to supervise the B's. Thus it seems to be, at the least, questionable whether the reduction in direct supervision will be compensated through the increased indirect supervision that is gained through the addition of the staff officer.

Furthermore, the new organization results in an asymmetrical arrangement of subordinates. The B's become subject to the supervision of both A and the staff officer, while the staff officer is subject only to A. Thus, the staff officer is placed in a position of relative advantage in the struggle with his

3. It may be objected that this is not what "staff" means in modern practice. I do not dispute this, but I find no common meaning of "staff" at all in modern organizational practice. For this reason, I present my own definition of what "staff" should mean.

peers, the B's, for A's favor. This fact, in itself, may account for the tremendous relative growth of "staff" in comparison to "line" agencies in most modern bureaucratic structures. The head of a section of the staff, with direct access to the sovereign, and with a status requiring that he assist the sovereign directly in controlling line organizations, is in a much better strategic position to secure appropriations than is the head of some comparable line agency.

Will the appointment of a staff or an executive officer affect the number of subordinates under a given sovereign's control? To this point, we have not raised this question. In our model, if A should choose to select one from the B_1 to B_4 group and make him his executive officer or his staff officer, and if he does not replace this man in the "line," then clearly the total external influence that the organization can exert will be diminished. The internal improvement in the organization that this change might make possible would probably not balance off the loss in external accomplishments of the organization. If, however, a fifth man is so appointed, the disadvantages would be those of having an additional subordinate to supervise. Since there would be the same number of men in the "line," there could be no greater total "output" of the hierarchy. There might, however, be some gain in the efficiency with which the ultimate sovereign's orders are performed. Again, the net gain secured from such an administrative change may well be negative. In more complex organizations than our model here, some "staff" might lead to a net gain in overall administrative efficiency. This point will be discussed later.

THE RESERVATION OF DECISIONS

While staying within the confines of the simple model of this chapter, I want to introduce one additional possible organizational change. It might be possible for A, the ultimate sovereign, to reserve decisions on certain issues and give orders that all decisions with respect to these issues be made by him personally, while allowing his subordinates to reach decisions on all other matters. In this way, A could insure that, at least in this reserved category, his own decisions would prevail. But this apparent advantage can be secured only at a cost. Under this system, A will be spending some of his time making particular decisions relevant to the specially reserved category. Accordingly, he will have less time available in supervising subordinates in other activities of the hierarchy. This means that he must expect a higher proportion of deviations from his desires, other things being equal, in those categories of activities that he does not reserve for special treatment.

CHAPTER 16

THE EXPERIMENT CONTINUED

Let us now extend the model and suppose that A, being pleased with his initial results, decides to add four assistants for each of the B's. These we shall call the C's, designated by C_1 through C_{16}. In strict logic, A should hire a somewhat smaller number of assistants for his direct subordinates than he himself supervises. This is because, as we have shown, each of the B's will have less time than A to devote to supervision, because of the necessity of taking some time to devote to dealings with A. But this particular refinement of the model need not trouble us. We shall also disregard, for the time being, the fact that the C's, at the third level of the hierarchy, will probably be lower-quality personnel than the B's.

In this model, as before, assume that A devotes his full organizational time to supervising the four direct subordinates, the B's. And let us continue our earlier quantitative estimates concerning the allocation of the time of the B's. These assistants devote one-fifth of their time to receiving supervision from A, and the remaining four-fifths are devoted to supervising their own assistants. Let us say also that the sixteen people at the third level will devote one-fifth of their time to receiving supervision from the B's, and four-fifths of their time to taking the action toward the outside world that represents the purposes of the organization. The whole organization will, therefore, acting externally only through the activities of the C's, affect the outside world by twelve and four-fifths man units. As with the smaller organization, not all of this contact with the outside world will represent actions desired by A. Assuming, as before, that the B's, in supervising the C's, follow A's wishes only three times out of four, and that the C's, following B's directives, similarly respond positively only three out of four times, we have a compounding effect. By simple arithmetic, we find that of the twelve and four-fifths man units contact with the outside world, only seven and four-fifths will strictly represent the activities that are desired by A. Five and three-fifths units will be devoted to activities that are either neutral or else contrary to A's wishes.

These results seem to be most disappointing. With a whole apparatus of twenty-one men, the total effect that A is able to exert on the outside world is only a little more than seven times as much as he could exert if unaided. But his impact, his capacity to accomplish the organizational function, has been expanded sizeably in absolute terms, even if less than proportionate to the increase in organizational manpower. The central problem lies in the compounding effect: the fact that A's influence flows through the B's to the C's. The element of distortion ("noise" in communications theory) that is introduced necessarily by the C's is compounded by the distortion already introduced by the B's.

We have previously noted a technique which might possibly be of some use here. A can, by keeping open channels of communication with the C level, somewhat improve his ability to supervise the B's. This means that some part of his time spent in supervising say, B_2, will be devoted to B_2's assistant, say, C_5, and in listening to what C_5 might have to say about B_2's methods of carrying out A's original orders. This will surely improve A's control over B_2, but at the same time it will equally surely reduce B_2's control of C_5. Whether the whole organization will be improved in efficiency as a result of such a change will probably vary with the special conditions. Generally speaking, we may conclude that the method will probably result in some improvements in A's overall control. At any rate, few, if any, supervisors have been able to resist the temptation to make at least some use of this procedure.

THE MODEL EXTENDED

If we extend our model organization further, and assume that A adds four assistants for each of the C's, we find that the new organization, composed of eighty-five persons, will be able to exert an external influence equal to fifty-one and one-fifth that of the single individual. Only twenty-one and three-fifths of this activity would be that desired by A, while twenty-nine and three-fifths would represent activity to which he is either neutral or opposed. With this extension of the model, we see that A's total influence on the outside world is being extended as the organization expands, but it is being extended at a rate that is considerably below the rate of expansion in the number of employees in the hierarchy. Also, note that the total time that the organization is spending on matters purely internal to the hierarchy is expanding more rapidly than the increase in personnel. The number of activities undertaken with respect to the outside world that are not within A's desires, too, is increasing more rapidly than the other magnitudes. While I make no claim that the numerical values in this model are more than very rough approximations, the model does, I think, represent a reasonable description of reality. Even if this much is not accepted by the reader, the model can still be helpful in developing a more comprehensive overview of the administrative process.

LIMITS TO ORGANIZATIONAL SIZE

It should be clear that, should we further expand our model, the trends outlined above would continue. A's influence would continue to increase in total, as the organizational size increases, but this influence would increase less and less rapidly. If the objectives for the establishment of the organization were unbounded, and A sought merely to expand his influence through the use of the organization, there would be no definite maximum. In reality, of course, many other considerations would arise to limit sharply the growth of organizational size. Costs increase with increasing size, and it would seem that costs would increase at least proportionately with size. It seems clear that the declining "marginal efficiency" associated with increasing size would guarantee that a point would be attained at which the further gains from expansion would be less than the added cost.

In real-world situations, the expansion of organizations should probably be stopped short of even these theoretical limits. The sovereign will have mixed motives in any case, and he surely will not relish the notion of a large organization devoting a substantial portion of its time to activities outside the range of his interest. Furthermore, large organizations are, in part, social aggregates that take on lives of their own. The man who finds himself at the apex of such a large organization may find that his action is as much controlled by the organization as vice versa. Various unpredictable feedbacks are likely to occur. The "power maximizer" may remain satisfied with a comparatively small organization.

THE TASK OF COORDINATION

The model of organization that we have introduced has been extremely general. We have assumed that its contacts with the outside world take the form of individual actions carried out by the lowest-level members of the hierarchy. We have not specified that these actions must be coordinated in any manner. Nor have we specified that these actions be such that they can be supervised by simple methods of accounting. As we have previously indicated, we propose to defer discussion on the latter point, but we shall raise the problem of coordination here. Normally, when an organization is established, the sovereign will realize that it must perform a large number of individual operations carried out by individual members, but he will not consider these activities as such but rather will think in terms of the overall general task that he hopes that the organization will perform. This serves to increase greatly the complexity of the supervisory job, and it lowers considerably the limits that might be placed on organizational size. If, for example, A's desires should be such that each lower-level action requires the perfect coordination of three persons, using our previous numerical values, it can be computed that there will only be roughly a fifty-fifty chance that such perfect cooperation can be obtained.

This result may seem, at first glance, wildly improbable, but it is not unrealistic. The fact is that organizations are almost never set up in which this degree of coordination is required. It is difficult, sometimes impossible, for one man to coordinate his own actions so that these lead to the accomplishment of a desired goal. Such coordination should not be expected from a group composed of several separate individuals. When we read or hear occasional accounts of the functioning of an administrative apparatus (for example, the Soviet economic system) which is alleged to be perfectly coordinated, we may rest assured that we are hearing a mythological, not a realistic, account of its performance. Coordination will always be much less than perfect. Administrative organizations cannot be assigned tasks that require perfect coordination, or even some approximation of this. Furthermore, due to the compounding effect arising from the interactions of the separate command levels, the larger the organization, the less coordination of activities to be expected.

There may, however, be varying degrees of coordination among the individual activities that represent the "output" of an organization, and we shall discuss here methods of obtaining coordination. The usual method is simple. An official who confronts an issue that requires some coordination of his decisions with those of his peers, simply refers the issue upward to his superior who, if all the interacting officials are within his jurisdiction, makes the decision required. The issue is thus shunted up the line, so to speak, to the point at which the interactions are "internalized" within the jurisdiction of a single official. This system, although ultimately necessary, has a serious disadvantage. If a substantial number of decisions are referred to supervisors, not only will these superiors find their time entirely taken up with them, leaving no time to supervise inferiors in other tasks, but also they will have no time for the problems appropriate to their rank level. If, for example, each of four subordinates should refer to his superiors one-half of his problems, the superior would be confronted with decisions amounting to two man days of work. From this simple example, the point seems clear that devices must be invented to reduce the coordinating load on higher-level personnel.

The first and simplest device is that of reducing the amount of coordination actually required in the organization. The lower-level officials will be permitted to take independent decisions in areas where a perfectionist might counsel coordination, merely because the higher officials in the hierarchy do not have the time to coordinate more than a fraction of the subordinates' activities. This process can be applied only to general tasks that do not require a high degree of coordination; that is to say, those in which the interactions among individual actions may not be great. This device seems to be almost an unavoidable expedient in large organizations.[1]

A second method of securing coordination without reference to superiors is that of allowing politicians at the same level to coordinate their separate activities directly. This procedure is subject to two serious limitations. In the first place, it will work only when the officials concerned are able to reach agreement. If agreement cannot be reached, there are no mechanics for resolving the issue except that of referring it to a superior for decision. This probably explains the emphasis on "reaching agreement" in much discussion of administrative procedure.[2] This particular difficulty might, it appears, be resolved by the introduction of some sort of an arbitration process. This might involve the reference of an issue requiring coordination to another official at the same level, rather than up the chain of command to superiors. The second major problem that would arise in allowing junior officials to coordinate their separate activities is that, in order to do so effectively, these officials would have to know what all of their peers are doing. This would become a serious problem in large organizations. More and more time of the junior officials would have to be put into learning about the activities of

1. Footnote by JMB: This analysis has a close analogue in the economist's theory of externalities. It is recognized that the great majority of actions taken by individuals in the marketplace exert some effect, negative or positive, on other individuals. However, when the costs of organizing alternative organizational forms are fully recognized, the market may still remain the most "efficient" organizational form, despite the externalities, in all those cases where the spillover effects are not significant.

2. Footnote by JMB: Continuing the discussion of the last footnote, this too is closely analogous to the theory of externalities as developed by the economists. Even if the market is allowed to operate when externalities are significant, voluntary agreements will normally be reached that will serve to "internalize" many of these externalities. The agreement reached through the market process is accomplished through the mechanism of exchange. The difficulty in the reaching of agreement among politicians, as discussed here by Tullock, probably lies primarily in the absence of some tangible commodity or service that is readily exchangeable, while "side payments" in money are perhaps ethically unacceptable. Even here, however, the exchange of reciprocal administrative favors should not be overlooked.

others at their own level.[3] The method becomes impossible beyond a reasonably small organizational size.

MINIMIZING COORDINATION AS A REQUIREMENT

The discussion to this point should serve to suggest that it is extremely difficult to coordinate activities of any large number of persons. This, in turn, suggests that we consider whether it might be possible to organize an hierarchy so as to minimize the need for coordination. The degree to which this device might work will depend, of course, on the task to be performed by the organization, but, in any case, minimizing the need for coordination seems to represent an acceptable objective in almost any organization.

The method through which the need for coordination in an organization is met is relatively easy to state in broad terms, but it need not be easy to apply in practice. The system calls for a selection of the duties of each person in such a way that he must coordinate his activities with others as infrequently as possible. Thus, in the simplest case, if there are two tasks, each of which will take about half of the time of one man to perform, and these tasks are such that they need to be closely coordinated, both tasks should be assigned to one man. This is easy in principle, but in real-world administrative structures, it may be extremely difficult. Normally it will not be possible to give to each individual bureaucrat a self-contained job. Even with the best organizational structure, there will remain numerous necessary "coordinations" connecting each person's work with that of others. Nevertheless, we should select the tasks so as to avoid as much overlap as possible. In setting up the larger units in the organization, an attempt can be made to group the employees in segments or divisions that are reasonably self-contained. The prospects of administrative reform in this way involve two desiderata. Tasks would be organized so that, say, John Jones would occupy as self-contained a position as

3. A semi-facetious letter to the *Economist* (November 26, 1955, p. 740) commented on the famous "Parkinson" article. This letter, by a scientist at one of the British government laboratories, contained a formula by which one could compute the amount of time available for a researcher to work on his own project after he had completed the necessary "liaison" with other scientists expressed as a function of the number of scientists at a given laboratory. The function was unique in that it eventually became negative. The writer explained that this merely reflected the exceptional enthusiasm of scientific workers who are willing to carry on "liaison" work even after hours. In spite of the obviously humorous intentions of the scientist, the problem is a real one.

is possible. Recognizing that his position cannot be wholly isolated, the attempt would also be made to insure that the contacts that John Jones has with other members of the hierarchy be limited to a relatively small group of closely connected officials, and the contacts between this group, this subunit, and the remainder of the hierarchy be minimized.[4]

Some understanding of the principles developed above seems to lie behind most "theories of organization." I am, however, reluctant to state definitely that the principles are implicit in such theories, because they are poorly expressed if present. Nominally most proposals for organizational improvements are based on "functional" analysis. In practical fact, proposals for improvement are often advanced in the most naive form of essentialism. Things described by the same word are assumed to be the same, and they are, therefore, placed within the same jurisdiction.

Defenders of more conventional organizational theory are likely to say that I have set up a straw man. They will claim that they do not believe in organization according to mere vocabulary. Presumably they will, once the subject is brought up, agree that this would be silly. After all, any given phenomenon is likely to be described by many words, not all of which have the same *other* phenomena also included. Thus the bears at Yellowstone are included within the term "bears"; they are also included to most Americans in the term "Yellowstone Park." The English language doesn't really offer any guide to organizational problems.

It could, of course, be maintained that "functional organization" means essentially the same thing as "minimizing the need for coordination." I submit, however, that the discussion of the principle in explicit terms of the coordination problem itself represents an advance in clarity. Modern organization specialists often propose the setting up of "functional" units, which are supposed to perform some specific function, say, "intelligence." The danger is that such emphasis will tend to shift largely to definitional disputes concerning whether or not a unit is engaged in "intelligence." The principle developed above may be restated. If two tasks must be carried out in closely coordinated fashion, the ideal solution is to assign them to the same person; the

4. Footnote by JMB: Again, the analysis of Tullock here finds close analogues in the economist's theory of externalities. One means of reducing the importance of externalities in the economy is that of redefining property rights in such a way that these externalities are effectively internalized. This is equivalent to the proposal made here by Tullock with respect to bureaucratic hierarchies.

next best solution is to assign them to two persons working in the same subsection; the third best solution is to assign them to two subsections in the same section, etc.

If one looks at the world's collection of administrative organizations, it is difficult to avoid the conclusion that, like Topsy, they have "just growed." They show no real signs of any organizing principle or plan. At any given time and with any given system, the structure in existence probably seems "right" to those who have become accustomed to it, but in the normal case, the explanation can be found only in history. During the latter part of the nineteenth century, a number of British colonies, particularly those located in Africa, were administered by the Foreign Office rather than the Colonial Office. Not to be outdone, the Colonial Office appointed Her Britannic Majesty's Consuls in The Levant. Similarly, in the British navy, the electrical parts of a ship (but not the electronic) were called the Torpedo Department. I cite these instances only to indicate that the organizational patterns in existence at any given time are likely to be more readily explained by their history than by any analysis of their "functions." This is, of course, as true of American as of British bureaucracy. The point, I think, is that there should be no presumption that present organizational arrangements are representative of any sacred organizing principles and not subject to criticism and change.

CHAPTER 17

LIMITATIONS ON ORGANIZATIONAL TASKS

The prospects for improving organizational efficiency through the method outlined in the last few pages of Chapter 16 are severely limited. Any general organizational objective that requires some coordination among its separate aspects will simply not lend itself to the sort of factoring out that was discussed there. Thus, while the attempt to arrange the duties of the various members of the hierarchy so as to minimize the need for coordination will surely result in some improvements, this, in itself, cannot be considered to be a satisfactory solution in more than a small number of instances. There is, of course, no "solution." We shall discuss later some of the improvements in the techniques of control that might allow the sovereigns to achieve a somewhat greater degree of control, but these, too, are only applicable in special cases, despite their total importance. In general, efforts to set up administrative structures to perform sizeable tasks will always fail. An administrative structure may be set up, and it may accomplish something, but it will not perform the task for which it is designed.

The basic reason for this negative conclusion lies simply in the fact that the talents of individual human beings are all of comparable orders of magnitude. This is not to deny that there are great differences among men in their capacities to carry out various tasks. As we have seen, men who rise to the top of a hierarchy are likely to be, on the average, much more capable than those who remain at the lower levels. There is also, in all probability, a considerable difference in talent among the members of a hierarchy at each particular level. But the difference in ability between a superior politician and an inferior is seldom great enough to permit the administrative structure to perform in the manner that the prevailing mythology would suggest.

Most governmental tables of organization would, if taken literally, require a level of talent for the higher officials hundreds of times as great as for the lower-ranking personnel. This point may be demonstrated by taking almost any governmental structure and considering the problem of supervising a lower-level official. For purposes of analysis, assume for the moment that the superior is not in any way more talented than the man whom he is supposed to supervise. Assume also that there is no easy way to determine, by examining the results of his work, whether or not the subordinate has carried out this work properly. Under these assumptions, it would take the superior as long to obtain information and to make up his mind as it would for the inferior to do so. Then, if the superior is to insure that the inferior does exactly what is required of him, the superior would have to put the same amount of time into supervision that the inferior does to performing the task. Thus, if the superiors at the lower levels are normally given two inferiors to supervise, they would have to be almost two times as capable as those whom they supervise. If they have three subordinates, almost three times as capable, etc., the officials at the next highest level would have to show a similar degree of superiority over their own subordinates, and so on up to the top of the hierarchy. Obviously, this degree of differentiation in talent is impossible. No one expects the higher officials to know more than a small fraction of the things that the organization is actually doing.

In practice, high-level officials frequently demonstrate publicly the most egregious ignorance concerning the area that they allegedly supervise. The first battle of Ypres, in the fall of 1914, for example, occurred as a result of decisions made by both Allied and German high commands, decisions to start an offensive at the same place and at the same time. Joffre's offensive was a decidedly modest one, with the troops consisting largely of the small British Expeditionary Corps. Falkenhayn, who had replaced von Moltke after the failure on the Marne, had much bigger ideas and threw major forces into the area. The result was that the English, instead of advancing, found themselves desperately clinging to their original positions. The courage and military skill exhibited by the English was exemplary, but this is not the point of the story. For several days after the Germans had started their attack, when the British were holding their positions only by the skin of their teeth, Joffre and French, the commander of the British force, went on issuing orders to "continue the advance." It took nearly a week for them to realize that their own forces were defending, not attacking.

In spite of the opportunity to learn about the geography of Ypres during three years of war, by 1917 the British high command had not yet discovered that it was an exceptionally muddy area. The mud turned the third battle of Ypres into a nightmare, which seems to have completely escaped the notice of the staff until after the battle when the chief of staff, at last visiting the area, exclaimed: "Good God! Did we really send men to fight in that?"

Nor are such exhibitions of ignorance confined to the military. One of the reasons for the North Koreans' initiating hostilities in Korea, and the principal reason for their early successes, was the extreme weakness of the Army of the Republic of Korea. One—only one—of the reasons for this weakness was American government policy. The American government officials implementing our policy in Korea feared that President Rhee, if he had the military means, would attack north. They therefore decided to keep his army so weak that this course of action would be impossible. Obviously, this was a foreign-policy decision of great importance, and one which, regardless of whether it was right or wrong, had very serious consequences for the United States. Acheson, who was our secretary of state at the time, was heavily involved in Asiatic problems and had taken an active part in setting up our aid program for Korea. Yet at the MacArthur hearings, he testified that restricting the power of the Korean army had never been the policy of the American government, and that he had never even heard the policy advocated. (The facts, as in the battle of Ypres, had been widely reported in the press.) Acheson may, of course, have been deliberately lying, but it seems equally probable that he actually did not know what policy was being followed by his subordinates. If so, this would provide another illustration of the impossibility for the administrator of a large hierarchy to retain control over the organization.

Accordingly, we see that, in practice as well as in theory, there are very distinct limits to the supervisory capacity of a high-ranking official (or of the electorate in a democracy). These limits, it should be emphasized, are ***limits on what can be done***, not on the size of the bureaucracies that can be built. Furthermore, these limits are much lower if the task to be accomplished requires a high degree of coordination than if it does not.

HUMAN FRAILTY

Any statement implying limitations on human capacities seems likely to be criticized. It remains an article of faith with many people that the human society can accomplish anything. The analysis here, of course, provides no evidence for or against this basic proposition. The capabilities of the human race have, in fact, increased tremendously in the last few centuries, but this does not prove that there are no limits ahead of us. A debate on this particular subject is as absurd as a tribe of Australian Blackfellows who had explored one hundred miles in all directions from their tribal area and had found nothing but "bush" discussing whether the "bush" went on forever. There is no need for this sort of metaphysical discussion about the limits to human capacities. The limitations that I am analyzing here restrict only what can be done ***with a certain specific technique***. Further, these limitations are themselves based on essentially human factors, i.e., human desires.

The belief that each human being is an entity with desire and capacities of his own, and that he will make efforts, possibly feeble ones, to bend his environment to suit his desires is not at all a belief that belittles man. Yet this belief is all that is necessary in order to develop the concept of limitations on the functioning of organizations. The superior will try to bend his inferiors, to change the environment in the direction that he wants. The inferior will do the same thing, and the superior and his desires will form a part—but only a part—of the environment as the inferior sees it. A superior may be capable of controlling completely some individual inferior; but he will be, in almost all cases, outnumbered and incapable of controlling the activities of the total number of inferiors. He can, at best, exert an influence over them; just as they can influence him in return. The superior's influence over his inferiors will steadily decline as the number of inferiors increases, while he will find himself more and more influenced in his own decisions by their actions and desires. The limits are not the limits on the power of the human being, or the human race, but limitations on the power of individuals and groups to influence the actions of other individuals and groups.

NON-ORGANIZATIONAL TECHNIQUES

Furthermore, as suggested above, I am discussing here only one technique of influencing the behavior of others, the organizational hierarchy. One of the most influential men who ever lived was Mohammed. Most of his influence, however, was exerted after his death when he could hardly have headed an hierarchic organization. Although he did build an hierarchy before he died, his post-death influence was less pronounced in the development of that hierarchy than in almost any other aspect of Islam. The successor Mohammed chose was eliminated, his family was substantially exterminated, and the caliphate eventually fell into the hands of the Abbasids, descendants of one of Mohammed's great enemies. In other areas his influence was great, and remains important to the present day.

This book itself represents, to some degree at least, a modest attempt to influence people by non-organizational techniques. The point is that there exist other means than organized hierarchy through which influence over people may be secured. On occasion, the head of an hierarchical organization becomes also a "charismatic" leader, and he may use the hierarchy to carry out his commands. But this would seem to be exceptional. No sovereign at the apex of an administrative pyramid can depend on such means to control his followers. In fact, it is normally because he cannot influence others in this manner that the sovereign decides to construct the organizational hierarchy. The head of General Motors or the Department of the Interior cannot depend on exerting the fascination over his followers that has been successfully employed by Father Divine.[1] He must rely on more humdrum, and often less effective, techniques. This book is about such humdrum techniques, not about the more exciting methods used by certain exceptional people with special talents (and, I suspect, extremely good luck).

THE MARKET MECHANISM AS A TECHNIQUE FOR COORDINATION

The analysis has demonstrated that a high degree of coordination among the separate aspects of a task or set of tasks is impossible to achieve through the mechanism of an organized hierarchy. Society does possess, however, other methods of achieving coordination, and one method in particular needs to be noted here. The market is in one sense an organization, but it is to be distinguished sharply from the hierarchical type of organization discussed in this book. As an institution or an organization, the market in reality is likely to be far from perfect in its operations. Individuals will make mistakes, and the result will involve wastage of resources. But it surely seems true that no comparable mechanism even approaches the market in terms of functional efficiency. There is no place here for a treatise on economics, and the student may be referred to any standard textbook, but it will be useful to provide a comparative illustration of an administrative and a market organization.

The United States Army owns a tremendous number of motor vehicles, ranging from jeeps and motorcycles to the special carriers for "atomic cannon." Leaving aside the strictly special-purpose vehicles, these vehicles are purchased in standardized lots of large size. Instead of buying from a number of manufacturers each year, an order for the entire requirement will be given to one manufacturer who will then produce all of the trucks of a given type to specifications without model changes.[2] These vehicles, after purchase, are distributed among the various army units in a standardized manner. Efforts, not always successful, are made to insure that, say, all of the trucks

1. Even Father Divine felt that his "charisma" needed the fortification of an organizational machine and built a very good one.

2. Actually, small improvements are incorporated in the design from time to time, but "in principle" the design remains unchanged.

of the 502nd truck battalion are of the same model. The purpose of this standardization is, of course, that of simplifying the problems of repair and spare parts. A further system for simplifying these same problems is that of the motor pool. Each unit will keep its vehicles in a motor pool when they are not in use, and this pool will have repair facilities. All routine maintenance and repair work is done in the motor pool, and vehicles are normally used within the area in which the pool itself is located. For more complex overhauls, vehicles may be sent to the more complicated repair facilities maintained, usually, by some ordnance unit which is a part of the command structure above the unit possessing the single motor pool.

This system does serve to minimize the problem of spare parts. The number of types of vehicles for the army as a whole and for each motor pool is minimized. Each motor pool has full knowledge of the number of vehicles that it must keep in repair, and the make and model of these vehicles are known in advance. Furthermore, the design of military vehicles is such that ruggedness and simplicity are stressed; these additional factors minimize the repair problem generally.

In spite of all these favorable factors, however, the problem of spare parts for army vehicles has, at times, seemed to be almost insoluble. The task would seem simple. Parts should be purchased from the manufacturers, shipped along to the appropriate major depots, then shipped to the subordinate depots, which, in turn, pass them along to the ultimate consumer, the motor pools. In practice, the problem has proved extremely difficult. Vehicles were continually held out of use because parts were not available; all this despite the large sums spent on maintaining parts inventories. Add to this the complication that vehicles become obsolete and are discarded. Each time that this happens, vast supplies of spare parts for the abandoned vehicles are found in the various depots. The difficulty clearly lies in the task of getting the spare parts to the vehicles that need them.

The spare parts problem has bothered the military organizations since the end of World War II, and various expedients have been tried. Consultants of many sorts, particularly economists, have been called in to advise, and numerous organizational changes have been made. If anything, the problem has probably gotten worse rather than better. Currently, a large computer is being employed. This computer stores in its memory the inventories of all depots, and it will send orders directly to each depot for the movement of parts. This problem is, of course, "made to order" for a computer, and there is no reason to be skeptical of the results that this method might achieve.

In this particular case, the use of the large computer eliminates some of the problems involved in coordinating the actions of large numbers of people in an hierarchic organization.[3] Through this method, the hierarchy is, in fact, abolished. From the standpoint of the computer, there are no intermediaries between the top and the bottom of the structure. The computer will receive the information from the lowest level, and it will send orders direct to each depot. The distortion that is involved in transmitting reports and orders through channels will thereby be abolished. Also, orders from the computer will be of the most elementary character: "Ship 500 spark plugs to depot 78"; "Order 5,000 tires from the Firestone company," etc. These orders will be based on reports concerning the amount of stock on hand; these reports will be of an equally uncomplicated nature. Nevertheless, the computer will rely on the normal chain-of-command techniques to make certain that the depots inform it properly of their inventories and obey its commands. To this extent, the computer is dependent for its functioning on a conventional bureaucracy and to this extent it is fallible.

Let us contrast this rather dismal picture, which is only slightly brightened by the introduction of modern computer techniques, with the supply of truck parts through an ordinary market mechanism. In the United States, trucks are not particularly standardized, either in design or by fleets. Furthermore, they frequently make long trips, San Francisco to Chicago, for example, and they require repairs in many cases far from their home shops. Spare parts are distributed through a chain of jobbers and wholesalers to parts supply houses and "truck stops." They are obtained by the truck company (or by the truck driver if he is away from base) by direct purchase, usually by individual items. The problems of operating this far more complicated system efficiently would seem insurmountable looked at from the standpoint of the comparable military problem. Even larger computers would seem to be necessary here.

In fact, however, little or no difficulty is encountered. The total number of parts in the "pipeline" between manufacturers and trucks is, by military standards, very small. Yet trucks are seldom idle for any significant period of time because of the unavailability of spare parts. This despite the fact that the total number of parts of different kinds far exceeds the number needed by the more standardized military vehicles, and despite the fact that these parts are distributed through a much greater number of "depots." I shall not here

3. The "span of control" is enlarged to several thousand in this case.

discuss the details of the mechanism through which this is accomplished. This is best left to the economists. The point here is that there do exist non-bureaucratic methods for coordinating the activities of human beings which may be more efficient than bureaucratic methods.

This is not to suggest that there are market solutions for every problem, or that these should be recommended if they do exist. While there certainly are governmental functions, such as the post office, that are in the public sector primarily by historic accident, the bulk of the traditional governmental functions are not suitable for market organizations. For example, it is difficult to imagine how the police services could be organized along market lines. And even with the vehicle parts for the military, there is no suggestion here that it would be wise to shift to a market-organized method of supply. Military organizations are, however, making more and more usage of market techniques, and, in many cases, they are occupied with creating market-like situations even when effective market organization is not possible.

The problem of coordination is difficult at best, and the advantage as well as the disadvantage of all methods must be thoroughly understood before organizational decisions can be properly made.

CHAPTER 18

RELAXING REQUIREMENTS

In this chapter, I propose to discuss certain types of organizations that are widely employed and which evade the limits that have been discussed in the last few chapters. Essentially, there are two ways of avoiding these limits. The hierarchic organization may be confined to those special areas where the problems of supervision become relatively easy and where, therefore, the head of the hierarchy has little difficulty getting his desires carried out. This type of organization will be discussed in later chapters. Secondly, it is possible that the requirements for the bureaucracy be relaxed. The requirement that the hierarchy carry out "orders" from above can be discarded, and the organization can be allowed to function on its own. No attempt will be made to defend this form of organization as such, but any comprehensive study of bureaucracy must recognize that such a procedure is frequently followed.

THE EXTERNAL VERSUS THE INTERNAL VIEW OF BUREAUCRACY

Before discussing this procedure one particular point must be made, even at the expense of digressing slightly from the main argument. Modern bureaucracies are often attacked on the ground that bureaucrats do nothing. A more sophisticated version of this complaint is that, while bureaucrats may be furiously busy, they are, like the Chinese laundrymen on the desert island, simply taking in each other's laundry, and that their effect on the outside world is no different than it would be if they did nothing.[1] Obviously, an organization of such bureaucrats would pose few problems of supervision.

There is, without doubt, some truth in this charge. People outside the bureaucracy dealing with it may be impressed with how little "work" gets accomplished. For example, much of the work within the Department of State consists of employees' preparing reports and analyses which are then read by

1. Nikita Khrushchev, explaining his administrative reforms to a rally at Pilsen, said: "We have reorganized our industry and freed hundreds (sic) of persons from paper work. Some filled in forms, others sent cables, while others received or read them. And who was doing the real work? Very little time remained for the real work . . . Suddenly they had to stop writing and cabling but the factories were glad because they had fewer letters to deal with and could do more work." *New York Times*, July 16, n.d., pages 2, 57.

other employees who then prepare papers which are, in turn, read only by the writers of the first papers, and so on. Nevertheless, the charges, basically, are superficial. Looking at the bureaucracy from the outside and judging it by what it is "supposed" to do, such charges surely seem to be relevant. Looking at the bureaucracy from the inside, from the point of view of the individual bureaucrat, it can be seen that, usually, the members of the organization are doing those things for which they will be rewarded by their superiors.

This may be far from obvious in certain cases. During the latter part of the Kelly regime, I worked as a law clerk in Chicago, during which time I became familiar with several of the various offices in the city and county government. It was evident that not all of the employees on the payrolls of these offices found it necessary to report for work with any regularity. It was also obvious that none of those who did report were in danger of overwork. A judgment that these particular persons were doing nothing would have been, however, incorrect. They were hired by their superiors to "get out the vote," and they were quite active and efficient in this capacity. A man who considered only their activities in their formally assigned positions might have easily come to the erroneous conclusion that these people were idlers. Nothing could have been more wrong. This particular personal example demonstrates that, in judging whether or not a given organization is or is not doing something, the real desires of the superiors, the sovereigns, must always be taken into account, not what the external observer may think that they should want.

The common view that bureaucrats in Washington merely shuffle papers suffers from this same error. Since the papers produced by, say, the Department of State's Office of Intelligence Research may almost never be read by anyone of any importance, it might be deduced that the whole thing is wasted effort. Actually, the superiors of the organization have a definite need for these papers, even though they seldom read them. One of the high-ranking members of the organization, for example, wrote a good essay of fourteen pages. Since the essay, independently, seemed unlikely to attract attention, he got each of his subordinates to prepare a paper on the same subject. After this, he collected these papers into a mimeographed volume amounting to one hundred fifty pages and put his essay labeled "Introduction and Summary" at the head of it. In this way, the wise and ambitious politician was able to impress his abilities on his superiors. Even though no one probably read the volume in its entirety, the "Summary" was read quite widely. The book thus was of considerable use to the superior who commissioned it. Blank pages or excerpts from *Pilgrim's Progress* would not have served this purpose.

Normally, however, the situation is considerably more complex. Dependence on sheer bulk is less noticeable. Here, again, the point is that the outsider might see the long series of reports that remained unread as unnecessary activity, whereas these reports, from the point of view of the insiders, might be quite necessary. The situation in which the outsider deals with the bureaucrat who seems highly interested and polite, but in which nothing seems to get done, may be explained on similar grounds. The bureaucrat may be sincerely interested in helping the outsider with his problem, but if the solution requires that he raise some question with his superior, he will be very careful. The bureaucrat will appear very reluctant to take final action. The difficulty lies not in the laziness of the individual bureaucrat, but in the undesirability, from a career standpoint, of his putting pressure on other members of the hierarchy unless this pressure promises to yield him some benefit.

BUREAUCRATIC FREE ENTERPRISE

Having digressed briefly to defend modern bureaucracy against a common criticism, I now propose to discuss what I shall call "bureaucratic free enterprise," and the "imperial" system in bureaucracies. One or the other of these situations exists in bureaucracies which have greatly exceeded the limits of control and which, consequently, are not really performing the functions for which they were organized by their sovereigns. The particulars in each case may be quite complex, but we may simplify the analysis by thinking of two pure types, which represent the two extremes of the spectrum. There are historical examples which come close to each extreme, but most real organizations will involve some mixture of both elements.

"Bureaucratic free enterprise," as I shall define it, is a system that more or less develops naturally when efforts are made to extend the size of an hierarchical organization beyond its practical limits. As the analysis of this book has repeatedly shown, the larger the organization, the smaller the percentage of its actions that represent directly the desires of the ultimate sovereigns of the organization, its higher officials. Think of a very large administrative structure or pyramid with, say, ten steps or levels between the apex and the men who are on the "firing line," that is, the men who carry out the organization's functions with the external world. The single individual or group at the top will surely have little or no control over those at the bottom if we accept, as a rough approximation, the quantitative estimates introduced in Chapter 15. In a large organization of this type, each link in the "chain of command" will introduce some modifications and changes on the order received from above, and as a result of the series of these changes, which compound each other, central control will be eliminated.

It can only be concluded that, in a very large organization of this type, for the greater part of its specific activities, the bureaucracy will be "free" from whatever authority it is allegedly subordinate to. "It," the bureaucracy, will do things, will take actions, not because such actions are desired by the ultimate authority, the center of power, in the organization, but because such things, such actions, develop as an outgrowth of the bureaucracy's own processes. This is not to imply that the various individual persons in the bureaucracy are free to choose their own individual courses of action. On the contrary, by our assumptions, each person will be controlled in three out of every four of the actions he takes by his direct superior. The remaining 25 per cent represents a very limited degree of freedom for individual action. The actual degree of individual freedom of action will vary with different organizations and with different levels within the same organization, but our assumption that 75 per cent of the individual's actions are controlled by superiors is probably about the median.

It is difficult to offer any rational justification for this system, or any organization characterized by this sort of pattern. In one sense it appears to achieve the worst of all possible worlds, combining an absence of effective central control with an absence of individual freedom of action. As has been mentioned before, these systems normally develop by accident rather than design or conscious choice; they are the results of efforts to undertake tasks that cannot be performed.

The Department of State, for example, seems to approximate closely the pure type discussed here. It is the natural result of a tremendous expansion of the idea of what constitutes foreign policy for the country. Until quite recently, foreign affairs was a very limited field. As it was operationally defined by the world's foreign offices, it included only the relations among some states. No nation attempted, again until quite recently, to maintain diplomatic relations with all of the other states of the world. Among the states with which any given nation did maintain diplomatic relations, in many cases these relations would be purely formal. The great bulk of the ambassadors and ministers served largely by standing and waiting. They were expected to become familiar with the country to which they were accredited; but would take an active role only if that country should, for some reason, become suddenly important. At any given time, only a few ambassadors would be engaged in implementing foreign policy actively. The foreign minister or secretary of state, therefore, would find himself with the fairly easy task of supervising the diplomatic activities of three or four ambassadors. The task was, under the old system, a manageable one.

In addition, until recently, diplomacy was limited in scope. Even in its relations with those powers that were most important, a nation under the old system would concern itself with only a few aspects of other nations' affairs. This is not to suggest that many of the elements of modern propaganda, subversion, espionage, bribery, loans, economic aid, and technical advice were not present. The difference between the older system and the modern one is largely one of scale.

Today the Department of State not only tries to maintain active relations with almost all of the nations in the world plus many international organizations; it also gets involved in the most obscure features of the domestic life of these countries. The American government, through the department, attempts to have "policies" on (or, more accurately, gets drawn into) such matters as the curriculum for the third grade in Iran, or the location of a glass factory in Korea. When an attempt is made to implement a conception of foreign policy that calls for dealing with such a vast range of problems, bureaucratic free enterprise is the inevitable result. Individual bureaucrats make decisions in terms of their own ideas concerning what their superiors want. Decisions will be made in terms of "policy," but there will exist no *coordinated* "policy" at all.

The system of bureaucratic free enterprise has such obvious disadvantages without offsetting advantages that arguments in its favor seem difficult to make. Yet proposals that are made to reduce bureaucratic structures of the type—the Department of State, for example—normally meet with considerable resistance. This resistance is probably based in part on a simple devotion to hierarchies and in part on a feeling of "we must." The latter position is inherently irrational. I have, for instance, discussed the American foreign policy apparatus with various persons who have agreed with my analysis. They accept the fact that there is no real coordination, that there is a tendency for the various units to move in opposing directions, and that there is, in general, a rather complete failure to carry out its objectives. When I then propose to these persons that some drastic curtailment in the scope of the foreign policy task should be made, they will almost invariably reply that this is impossible in the modern world. To support this continuation of the current establishment, they will then proceed to employ arguments that require that the Foreign Service function in an impossibly efficient manner. When they are confronted with the contradiction in their position, they may show irritation and uneasiness, but nothing more.

IMPERIAL BUREAUCRATIC SYSTEMS

The "imperial" system is based on the fact that persons with the same cultural background tend to solve practical problems in much the same way. The ultimate sovereign at the apex of such a system, instead of trying to enforce his own ideas as to what should be done within his "empire," merely appoints subordinates who come from a similar cultural environment. Once appointed, they are allowed to do more or less as they please. The job of supervision may be limited to that of eliminating the occasional deviant personality, and that of making certain that none of the subordinates secures sufficient power to threaten the sovereign's position.

As an example familiar to everyone, the British Empire, during the period of its greatest strength, was operated almost wholly without direct orders from Whitehall. The various colonial governors were known, since school days, in many cases, to all members of the cabinet in London, and they were sufficiently trusted to be left alone. These colonial governors, in turn, followed the same system with their own subordinates. The "district commissioner" received little in the way of orders or instructions from his superiors. He had been originally selected because he was "sound," and being "sound," he was left alone in the operation of his office. This system allows the span of administrative control to be extremely broad. Almost thirty colonial governors reported directly to the Minister for Colonies, and, again, in the grand days of the Empire, this minister had almost no staff in London. His primary task, other than getting votes for the party, was that of appointing governors and, on occasion, removing them.

This lack of concern with centralized control can be seen in the British West Indies, where Britain controlled a large number of islands, many of them very small. "Administrative efficiency" would obviously have suggested that they be grouped into a large unit under a single governor who would then appoint subordinates for each island. This was not the course followed. By historical accident, some of the islands were grouped in small clusters, but most of the Leeward and Windward islands had their own governors responsible directly to London. Obviously, under this system, the Minister for Colonies could not be expected to pay much attention to the developments on Barbados. The system worked because the governor was simply left to his own devices.

Close approximations to the "imperial" system were employed in the Roman Empire, by the Persians, and indeed by almost all of the great empires that we know about in human history. It was an important part of Chinese administrative practice, and there it was combined with an educational structure that insured that all prospective governmental employees would have gone through an intensive and identical training in political philosophy, along with an examination procedure which guaranteed that those who were most successful in absorbing this education would be appointed to political office.

This "imperial" system of bureaucracy can usually be readily identified because of the width of the span of control. Governmental hierarchies that make a serious attempt to control subordinates usually allow a superior to supervise three, four, or five subordinates directly. If the superior merely appoints and dismisses, however, he may "supervise" a much greater number, and spans of control that range from ten to fifty may even be expected.

It could, I think, be argued convincingly that the American diplomatic effort would function more efficiently if it were to be explicitly based on such an "imperial" principle of organization. The poor supervision that does exist in the American system leads to some combination of the "imperial" system with that of "bureaucratic free enterprise" that was discussed earlier. The official often finds himself in a situation where his own superiors care little about what he does. Nevertheless, the present system, as organized through the Department of State, is vastly inefficient if it is viewed as a variant on the imperial system. Instead of a few thin threads of command, there are numerous and complex chains. The system approximates imperial method only when these chains of command become so complex as to break down completely. A direct shift in the direction of an imperial system would allow drastic reductions in the size of the organization with considerable gains to be expected in the total effect on the outside world.

The imperial system of organizing a very large bureaucracy has, however, a number of disadvantages. In the first place, it is not really an organizational system at all. It is a system for voluntary cooperation, but with little actual cooperation implied. The system will work only in those situations where the required degree of coordination can be obtained because of the common cultural heritage of the system's members. In such matters as the government of separate and distinct territories—our British example—individual differences on policy issues, which must always exist, need not create serious problems. The system does not work nearly so well within a single territorial unit. The various parts of a governmental hierarchy must be more highly coordinated than is the case with the government of adjoining, but geographically separate, territorial units. This explains, at least in part, the fact that great empires have almost always been organized in terms of geographic rather than functional divisions.

The imperial system is not, therefore, possible for an organizational structure that requires any significant degree of coordination between the various officials. For example, it could not apply at all to a system of centralized economic planning. In addition, the system can be applied only to those tasks of bureaucracy where there is a common outlook on matters of policy among all, or substantially all, members of the parent organization. There is no conceivable way, for example, that such cultural-ethical agreement could exist on the amounts of steel, manganese, and aluminum that should be produced. Bureaucrats in the planned economy might, it is true, have instilled in them some respect for certain "welfare criteria," some conception of an "ideal" allocation of resources, but this would lead them to establish some specific coordinating system—perhaps bureaucratic free enterprise—or else to try to set up the socialistic equivalent to the free functioning of markets, the Lerner-Lange type of economy which dispenses (with varying degrees of completeness) with any organizational structure at all.

Perhaps the most serious limitation on the imperial system of bureaucracy lies in the fact that the accepted ideas of the ruling groups may not be suitable to the tasks that are confronted. This has been the case in the overwhelming majority of instances where attempts have been made to found great empires. The Roman, British, Persian, and Chinese empires are examples of a small class of successful empires. The achievements of these shining examples of successful application of the imperial system are reflected not so much in the fact that they were initially constructed, but rather in their abilities to continue in existence for long periods of time. More normally, empires soon begin to flounder in domestic revolts, minor military defeats, and, frequently, conflicts among the members of the imperial administrative system.

If each member of the "imperial class" should be equally ambitious and anxious to rise to the peak of the administrative system, then internal conflicts of the sort mentioned seem certain to occur, and they will tend to be continuing and bitter ones. Some kind of class structure that effectively limits mobility seems, therefore, desirable for the functioning of the imperial system of bureaucracy. Moreover, something of this sort will be found in most of the successful applications of the imperial principle. But the basic disadvantage (and advantage) of the imperial system lies in the absence of any conscious control. It depends for its "coordinating principle" essentially on the relevant ruling group having gone to the same schools some thirty years past. In this way, the system seeks to avoid the problems of policy formulation and implementation intrinsic to most bureaucracies, but it avoids these at the cost of being uncontrolled.

The imperial system, as such, will be consciously chosen only on rare occasions and to meet special circumstances. The system may accidentally develop under a wide range of circumstances, but then its success will depend on the coincidence of a set of ideas in the minds of the administrators. Otherwise, the system will surely abort. Over time, anything approaching the imperial system will tend to degenerate into that which we have called bureaucratic free enterprise. This change will normally take the form of the central hierarchy increasing gradually the number of orders passed along directly to the inferiors, accompanied by an increasing reluctance on the part of junior level officials to act without orders.

This process can be seen in the history of the Roman Empire. Historians have used the correspondence between Pliny the Younger, who was a provincial governor, and the emperor Trajan as an illustration of the decline of the Empire. Pliny seeks Trajan's advice and assistance on a wide variety of local administrative problems. It has been customary for scholars, while deploring Pliny's failure to solve problems that a governor during the days of Augustus would have solved, to exculpate Trajan of all blame for the situation. But it seems clear that he, and his predecessors, were as much to blame for the process as those who tried to carry out their will.

Pliny did not ask Trajan's advice on the construction of aqueducts in his district because he felt that Trajan was particularly qualified as an engineer, but because he felt that this was the standard operating procedure. Furthermore, Trajan occasionally complains of the fact that he is overworked, but he never discharges Pliny for his failure to reach decisions independently. Pliny was probably correct in his estimate that his behavior was the sort most likely to keep favor with the emperor, and had he taken the imperial admonitions toward acting independently seriously, he might have found himself a private citizen. This failure of the imperial system seems at least as much to blame for the downfall of the Roman Empire as any "decline in the moral fiber of the Roman people."

Similarly, the elaboration, in this century, of the Colonial Ministry in London and the tendency of the governors of the various remaining colonies to depend more and more upon the central office for instructions, does not indicate that the governors themselves are less capable than formerly. It means only that the central government now tries to exercise more control over them than previously. Presumably, if the British Empire had not declined from other causes, this gradual breakdown of the imperial system of bureaucracy would have eventually brought its end.

Although many governments have developed bureaucratic structures that more or less resemble imperial systems, the system in its pure form is only one end of the spectrum. At the other extreme for very large organizations is bureaucratic free enterprise. Almost every large administrative structure will contain elements of both of these systems. Historically, there seems to be discernible some tendency to shift from the imperial type toward the other extreme. This is because of the tendency to bring bureaucracies more and more under control. In some cases this amounts to a gradual shift from an essentially uncontrolled but tolerably "efficient" system to one that is essentially controlled but considerably less "efficient." In neither case will the man or group at the top have much control over the bulk of the activity of the organization, although it will be possible to provide the central authority with control over any given subordinate in any specific action.

THE GROWTH OF BUREAUCRACY

Few persons will consciously advocate either of these bureaucratic systems. Bureaucratic free enterprise grows up as the result of an effort, frequently undertaken with the best of intentions, to have a single organization perform more tasks than can be done by hierarchical techniques. A governmental unit, for example, decides to expand its sphere of control over the national life and takes on a sector that was previously organized outside governmental processes. If the government was at or beyond the "critical" size before this experiment, this addition of a new task will reduce the efficiency of the existing bureaucracy, and the first step toward bureaucratic free enterprise will have been taken. A series of such events and the system blossoms full-blown. No one plans the result; no one desires it; yet most modern governments are gigantic examples of the predictable result of the growth of bureaucratic structures. The final outcome makes no one happy unless it be those who feel some strong psychological need to be a part of a monolithic structure. The structure is not, indeed cannot be, monolithic, but it perhaps satisfies the psychological needs just the same.

Such progressive building up of a bureaucratic system normally results from a series of individual expansions that are discussed one by one, and each on its own merits independent of the whole structure.[2] Similarly, no one defends large bureaucratic structures on the ground that they are inherently good in themselves. Normally, the arguments for maintaining the structure proceed in terms of the defense of each particular segment. Let us consider the problem that might confront anyone who tries to "sell" Congress on the desirability of abolishing a given agency in the vast federal bureaucracy. Let us begin by acknowledging that the agency does some task and that someone, even if only the agency's employees, derive some benefit from its continued existence. The agency may, for example, be attempting to expedite the processing of immigration visas, and there may be evidence that its operations do cut the amount of time taken to "visa" the average applicant to some extent.

This particular action may, in the whole scheme of government, be more than offset by other bureaus that act in such ways as to slow down the issuance of visas. The abolition of the particular agency will, nonetheless, be opposed on the ground that its abolition will slow the process of issuing visas. The whole problem of delay in visa issuance may arise because there are already too many bureaucrats in the field of visa-issuing, but it can be argued that the abolition of any one particular agency will disadvantage certain people unless it is accompanied by other radical changes in the whole structure. Thus, the first step toward a radical change can be objected to because it is not a radical change.

The abolition of the agency will, by simplifying the supervisory problem, in and of itself, improve the functioning of the governmental hierarchy. This effect, however, is dispersed and difficult to see, while the abolition of the particular agency or bureau represents a conspicuous and obvious action, the effect of which is concentrated and evident to all concerned. This asymmetry gives to the defenders of the agency a strategic advantage. The problem posed may remind economists of the tariff problem. Everyone loses from a system of tariffs, disregarding largely spurious special cases. Yet attempts to repeal individual tariffs meet determined resistance.

2. No one seems to like large bureaucracies except a few doctrinaire leftists. Even they show signs of uneasiness on this issue and appear to feel that defense of such organizations is a duty rather than a pleasure.

The reason is widely understood. The reduction in the tariff on watches will hurt the watchmakers and help everyone else. More precisely, it will hurt the watchmakers in their profession as producers, while it helps them along with all other groups as consumers or purchasers of watches. The gain to the nation as a whole from abolishing the tariff will be much larger than the loss that would be suffered by the watchmakers through the change. But the loss is concentrated and easy to see, whereas the gain is dispersed and does not affect any particular person very much. The watchmakers are, therefore, likely to prevail in the ordinary political processes that characterize democracies. We should not, however, despair about the prospects for either a reduction in tariffs or in the size of modern bureaucracies. One of the glories of the nineteenth century was the progressive elimination of tariffs and other restrictive measures over the flow of goods and services among nations. It is not impossible that we might see a similar development in the second half of the twentieth century. Future historians may see the return of most nations to mercantilist policies in the period from 1875 to 1950 as merely a passing phase.

The situation is similar, although not identical, if we consider any proposed extension of the size of an hierarchy. Suppose that some new function is proposed. This function will be clear, and some direct beneficiaries will be obvious. The reduction in the efficiency of the whole apparatus that the addition of this function will entail is much harder to perceive. The "Illth" produced by the change will not be visible, whereas the benefits will be open for all to see. Only after a whole series of such changes will there come to be a general recognition that the structure is not performing properly. Even then the cause is not likely to be correctly diagnosed.

An additional factor that may contribute to the establishment of new tasks for a hierarchy is the inefficiency of the system of bureaucratic free enterprise itself. We have noted previously that, in this latter system, the ultimate sovereign can usually get any particular act performed by his subordinates through the issuance of a direct command. But in such cases, the decision as to the proper officials to handle the specific act may be a difficult one. The easy way out for the sovereign is for a new official to be appointed to carry out the specific action desired. This seems particularly likely to happen in those bureaucracies in which employees cannot readily be dismissed. Under this system, as in the federal governmental bureaucracy, the ultimate sovereign is not likely to be defied openly, but its policies may be subjected to serious sabotage by existing administrative agencies. The sovereign, knowing this, will tend to set up new bureaus and agencies to insure the carrying out of its desires. The new bureau, so established, will probably remain strictly under control for the first few years of its operation. This provides the element of truth in the statement frequently heard that administrative agencies work well only within the first five years of their establishment. The whole situation is highly paradoxical. The inefficiency of the overexpanded bureaucracy leads to still further expansion and still further inefficiency.

Most modern governmental hierarchies are much beyond their efficient organizational limits. The damaging effects on the efficiency of the whole organization caused by the addition of new elements is a function of the total size of the organization. With a very small bureaucracy, a given expansion may bring gains that more than outweigh this efficiency factor. As the apparatus grows larger, the reduction in efficiency for the whole organization that is to be expected from each additional unit will increase in magnitude. Eventually, the system will degenerate into bureaucratic free enterprise. Once this stage is reached, the effect of an addition to or a reduction from the bureaucracy will again be slight. At this level, only a radical reduction in the size of the whole apparatus, or else the specific creation of still new agencies, will get specific tasks accomplished.

The analysis here seems, to me at any rate, to suggest clearly that the stage of bureaucratic free enterprise that most modern governmental hierarchies seem to have reached is undesirable. Most observers probably agree on this count. Advocates of expansion talk either in terms of individual particularized interests or else in terms of a completely mythological coordinated administrative pyramid that can never have existed. The only counter to such arguments is a careful analysis, and, if possible, some direct contact with the actual workings of bureaucratic process within one of these administrative structures.

CHAPTER 19

THE PROBLEM OF CONTROL

In previous chapters the difficulties and complications involved in getting an organization to do what is wanted of it have been discussed at some length, but little has been said about the techniques that might be employed to minimize the effects of these difficulties. In this chapter, and in those following, I propose to examine this question.

The present discussion should indicate the sorts of problems that can be most easily met by bureaucratic organizations, and it should also give some idea as to the order of magnitude of the bureaucracy that might be applicable to each task. Chapters 21, 22, and 23 will discuss special techniques which will permit quite large organizational structures to be constructed in certain circumstances without the dangers of bureaucratic free enterprise or imperialism.

INFANTRY EXAMPLES

Let us consider the captain of a company of infantry in two different cases. In the first, he commands "left face"; and his company, ordered on a drill field, all execute the command in the prescribed manner. This is the simplest type of obedience to obtain. It is doubtful if the control of one man over a group is ever greater. The order has been issued, it requires no interpretation or application to the given situation, and the nature of the order is such that the captain has only to glance at his company to assure himself that every soldier has carried it out. It is possible to say, in this case, that only the captain thinks and reaches decisions, that only he "wills" the action: his subordinates merely carry out his decision. Even if we consider this an oversimplified interpretation of the situation—after all the troops could mutiny, and it is likely that at least one of them may make a mistake—still we must admit the captain does have exceptionally great control over his subordinates.

Now let us consider the same captain commanding the same company in a combat situation. He has sent out five patrols to obtain information about the position of the enemy. Although they constitute part of a larger pattern, each of these five patrols has its own separate mission. In addition, each will encounter its own special problems. Even if the captain could be provided with some instantaneous and secure method of communicating with each one, he still could not give them orders in the same sense that he gave the company orders on the drill field. He cannot hope to have the knowledge of the specific situation of each patrol that the patrol leader has, and even if he had such information, he could not give to the problems of each patrol the amount of thought that the commander of that patrol can.

What the captain wants from the patrol commanders is not the simple and uncomplicated obedience which we find on the drill ground, but something much more difficult to obtain. The captain wants the leaders of his patrol to reach decisions on the host of problems with which they will be confronted which will conform to his general strategy; but he cannot tell in advance what their decisions will be. In this situation the company commander is making an attempt to multiply his mental powers by giving a task to subordinates which requires that they think and act on their own. The patrol commander, typically, will be given some general instructions as to where he is to take his patrol and what he is to look for, but there will be emergencies where it is his duty to disregard even these general instructions. In the more normal situation, he will obey the general directive, but he will have to make numerous decisions about the detailed implementation of the order.

The patrol situation has the advantage over the parade ground situation in that far more decisions can be made by the whole organization, because each of the subordinates must reach decisions in addition to the single superior. The disadvantage is that some of the decisions made by the subordinates will inevitably be contrary to the desires of the commander. From the time that a patrol leaves the lines, it is out of view of the superior officer. Patrol leaders may willfully disobey orders without being found out, or they simply may make mistakes. In yet another case, they may encounter a situation for which none of their specific orders apply. In these circumstances they may reach the wrong decision from the point of view of the unit commander.

The drill field and the patrol situations are merely points on a continuous spectrum of administrative control situations. We may designate the extreme end of the spectrum illustrated by the drill field as the "simple" situation and the situations at the opposing extreme as "complex." The simpler the task, the larger the organization which can be designed to carry it out. Tasks that are more complex will require smaller organizations if they are to be carried out effectively. A simple organization is generally limited to carrying out the decisions made by one man. More complex organizations will actually carry out a mass of decisions too large for one man to have reached. These more numerous decisions should conform to some general design if the organization is to have any unified purpose at all, and is not to represent an example of bureaucratic free enterprise. The central problem facing most administrators is that of maximizing the number of decisions taken by subordinates that do, in fact, carry out the general "policy" of the whole organization.

All that may be hoped for here is some approximation to perfection. The first step toward bureaucratic wisdom lies in the recognition of this fact. If it is accepted, reasonably satisfactory results can be achieved through the application of statistical methods of control. This solution, which I shall discuss in detail later, may seem peculiar and radical at first glance, but it is an innovation only in its theoretical aspects. This is the method actually employed by most successful administrators.

COMMUNICATION

A sovereign in getting his inferiors to carry out his will has two central problems: communicating his desires and seeing that these are carried out.[1] These two problems are not only separable theoretically; good administration requires that every effort be made to keep them separate in practice. These two problems are, however, intermingled in many modern administrative structures, and, perhaps because of the existing situation, some analysts have concluded that such an intermingling is desirable.

The reasons why these two problems are so closely tied together deserve discussion. There are some occasions in both business and government hierarchies (many in the latter) where no clear policy for the organization has been laid down in advance. The policy, as this word is normally employed, develops out of a series of individual decisions in concrete cases. These decisions are made, in the first instance, by lower-ranking personnel. Of course, the decisions made by the higher ranks as to who among the lower ranks shall be rewarded and punished are the crucial set. To some extent, this practice is unavoidable—and it may even be desirable—but in most cases it arises because of inefficient administration.

Let us take initially a situation in which this type of intermingling between the communication and control problems cannot really be avoided. Assume that the assistants to a given sovereign normally are called upon to make decisions about various things upon which the instructions received from above are not complete and comprehensive, but assume also that it is possible to

1. The sovereign must also devote time to deciding what he wants done, but we are now concerned only with the methods of carrying out his desires; not with how he came to have them.

apply certain general principles of the organization to the decisions in each case. However, given the rush of events, new problems and issues are continually emerging which the general organizational principles cannot always be expected to cover. The subordinate, in this sort of position, will find himself occasionally confronted with issues upon which he must make an initial effective decision. If the sovereign agrees with this decision, the organizational policy may then grow out of this particular lower-level decision process. If the sovereign disagrees, no policy generalizations will emerge.

There is no way that this sort of ultimate policy formation by low-ranking personnel can be avoided; it will arise on occasion in all organizations, no matter how efficiently these are organized. The more normal case in which decisions are reached by lower-ranking personnel is, however, different. Not only the initial decision, but all subsequent decisions, may be made by men operating at the lower reaches of the hierarchy. The sovereign neither ratifies nor disapproves of these decisions, either because the chain of command is so clogged that he does not hear of the issues at all, or because he is lazy, or because he fears that any decision on his part will, in turn, annoy his own superior in the hierarchy. In such an organization as this, the lower ranks, after perhaps vainly trying to get the higher officials to take action, may be forced to make decisions. Out of a series of such events, a sort of organizational policy may develop by precedent, and the higher officials may never have to make any choices of significance at all.

It may be argued that this system is desirable on certain grounds. The common law system of judicial law making depends on a similar process, and there are admitted advantages to the common law process. The fact remains that the common law is not intended to be the result of any central organization. While it may be argued that allowing individuals to make personal decisions under the rule of *stare decisis* is a desirable means of developing a legal system, it cannot be urged that this is a desirable means of applying a centrally directed policy.

There are other organizations in which policy may appear to come from low-level decisions, but in which it actually does not. The "policy" that gives rise to this phenomenon is what might be called "administrative hypocrisy." It not infrequently happens that the "official policy" of an organization differs sharply from its real policy. Peter M. Blau's *The Dynamics of Bureaucracy*,[2] for example, examines the functioning of a state employment agency.

2. University of Chicago Press, 1955.

"Interviewers," the principal type of employee in such agencies, on being hired are subjected to a training course in the duties attached to their positions. This course has, however, virtually nothing to do with their actual duties. The training, as Blau explains, is in the theoretical policy of the agency; the actual policy is something different.

In more complex situations, the practice of administrative hypocrisy may be a major barrier to efficient operation, particularly for new employees. If the performance pattern actually expected from the employee and the "theoretical policy" of the organization are both complex, understanding the theoretical policy can only be a hindrance to the new employee. There seems to be no need here to discuss in detail the practice of administrative hypocrisy as such, except to mention that it seems to be a very common system in large organizations. Its effect, for purposes of this section, is that of giving the appearance of decisions originating in the lower levels of the organization when actually they do not. In a system of administrative hypocrisy, there are two decisions that must be made whenever a new situation is confronted. First, what must be done and, second, what is to be the rationalization of what is done. The first decision may require immediate action, but the second can frequently be deferred. Because of this lag, the lower-level officials may appear to be doing things for quite a considerable time before "policy" is formed.

There may, of course, be situations in which decisions need to be made by men at the lower reaches of the hierarchy. To the extent that this is so, the raison d'etre for the hierarchy itself ceases to exist. In the analysis that follows, therefore, I shall continue to assume, as before, that an hierarchy is an organization designed for getting centralized decisions carried out through lower-level personnel.

As suggested above, the first problem is that of communication, that of letting the lower orders of the hierarchy know what the policy (or policies) of the organization is (are). I have stated that this function, as such, should be divorced from efforts to enforce that policy. The reasons here are simple ones. Bentham, in describing the common law, referred to it as "dog law." By this he meant that the law ruled people in the same manner that a man trains a dog. The dog is punished for doing things that he ought not to do, but not, for obvious reasons, told what these things are in advance. It matters not whether Bentham's view of the common law is accurate; few will deny that if it were it would be an undesirable system. We are able to communicate with human beings, and it surely seems best to tell them in advance what is desired and then to punish or to reward them for their behavior rather than to let them deduce what is wanted by observing which types of behavior are, in fact, rewarded and which punished.

This all seems clear. In practice, the separation is not so simple. The very reaching of general policy decisions may be difficult, and verbalizing them may be even more troublesome. But the importance of providing inferiors with clear instructions should never be overlooked, nor the fact that failure to do so will, undoubtedly, lead to a lower degree of organizational satisfaction of the sovereign's wishes.

Giving instructions is not an easy task. People seem to possess an almost infinite ability to misunderstand. The Chinese Maritime Customs, an international service organized by Sir Robert Hart, was justly renowned for its efficiency. Sir Robert was an excellent administrator, and his subordinates were mostly men of exceptional merit. Yet if one reads the circular instructions that were sent by Sir Robert to his various offices, one cannot help but be struck by the frequency with which he repeats ideas. Either he was wasting his time, or else he felt that this amount of repetition was necessary to implant his ideas into the thinking patterns of his subordinates. The latter explanation is more likely to be correct, and it seems probable that even more repetition would be required in a less "elite" organization.

The same phenomenon can be seen in the desire of most employers for "experienced" help. Many simple types of employment, restaurant waitresses, salespeople, etc., do not appear to involve any high degree of training on the part of the worker. Nevertheless, experienced people are given preferential treatment by employers. This seems to be the result of the realization by most businessmen that the time and effort which management must devote to training personnel even in such simple jobs is considerable. Here again it would appear that effectively communicating desires to subordinates is no easy task.

There are many devices that will assist the sovereign in communicating with his subordinates. Clarity of expression, repetition, apt similes, and all of the other means of "getting the message across" are of considerable importance here. Even with these devices, there will clearly exist some maximum order of complexity in a task beyond which it becomes impossible for the subordinate to form a clear idea of the desires of his superior with respect to that task. To put the same point differently, the control that may be exercised over a subordinate is limited in the first instance by the limits on the ability to communicate with him. If the superior should be lazy, or if he should not enjoy giving instructions, he must then accept the consequence that most of his subordinates' efforts will not be closely related to the activities that he would desire to see them carry out. Either this, or the superior must be willing to confine his orders to tasks that are so simple as to require little or no instruction before they can be readily understood by subordinates. This suggests that those sovereigns are better administrators who are able to communicate effectively with other people.

Two mechanical methods of simplifying communication with subordinates may be mentioned, although these may be applied only in certain specific command situations. This means that more complex tasks may be performed by organizational hierarchies when such situations are present. The first of these mechanical means is simply that of giving the same task to all inferiors. Let us return to our model of a sovereign with four assistants. Assume that he has assigned to each of these four assistants a different field of activity. Let us say that the overall problem is that of governing an area, and that the sovereign has divided the task into the four functional areas of police, tax collection, public works, and education. If we assume that the sovereign gives one-fourth of his supervisory time to each of these areas of activity, and that this one-fourth is divided between giving instructions and seeing that these instructions are carried out in the ratio of two to three, we can compute that the sovereign would be devoting 10 per cent of his total supervisory time to giving orders to each of his assistants and 15 per cent of this time to supervising the performance of each of them. In total, 40 per cent of the sovereign's time will be devoted to giving orders and 60 per cent to enforcement.

Let us contrast this situation with one in which the sovereign, still with four assistants, limits his activities to only one field, say, police. Here he may be able to give substantially the same instructions to each of the four assistants. This implies that he can devote up to 40 per cent of his time to the careful composition and transmission of orders to his subordinates. The degree of complexity of the ideas that may be transmitted is materially increased in this way. The procedure will work, however, only with certain situations. It must be possible that the assistants do substantially the same thing without duplicating or interfering with each other. Furthermore, the total number of things that the organization might do is severely restricted.

This system is usually applied in practice through the geographic or organizational unit separation of the spheres of activity of the assistants. The sovereign in our example could have given each assistant a specific geographic area to police in accordance with a common set of instructions. A large corporation sets up a series of sales districts, each with a district manager, in order to be able to follow the same pattern of organization. Substantially identical administrative units may be set up which do not involve geographic boundaries in order to achieve similar results. During peace time, a corps commander may deal with division commanders on this principle. In active combat, on the other hand, most of his orders must relate to the specific activities of individual divisions. Note here that the result is the reverse of what might be hoped. It is important for divisions to be able to execute complex orders in combat, yet orders that are too complex for use in wartime may be easily carried out in garrison.

The second mechanical method of simplifying the problem of communicating orders or commands also involves imposition of uniformity on the orders given, and also can be applied only in certain circumstances. In the first method the uniformity suggested extended through different parts of the hierarchy; it was uniformity in space. In the second method, the uniformity extends through time. If a task is such that the instructions required may be left unchanged or substantially unchanged for long periods of time, the instructions may be more complex than otherwise, and still be communicated to the lower ranks of the hierarchy. This is because of the simple and obvious fact that these ranks will have more time to learn these orders. This method is, of course, that of laws and regulations. Almost all hierarchical organizations, no matter how rapidly changing the situations in which they must operate, will have at least some internal regulations and standard procedures which remain more or less unchanged over considerable periods.

The scope of this method of communication is not without limits. Even with a completely stable and unchanging set of instructions, there remain limits on the complexity of these instructions, if they are to be understood and obeyed. In the Anglo-Saxon world, each man is assumed to know the law, and "ignorance of the law is no excuse." In fact, the law is so complex that no one makes any real pretense of knowing the whole of it. As a result, stories about "forgotten" laws being found are regular features of our newspapers.

CHAPTER 20

ENFORCEMENT

When the problem of communication is satisfactorily met, when the subordinate understands the orders given to him, the problem of insuring his compliance remains. The primary device depended upon to "motivate" the subordinate is the simple one of rewards and punishment. In order to award the rewards and punishments properly, however, the superior must have correct information concerning the activities of the subordinate. As we have seen, this knowledge may be very difficult to obtain. In the simplest of all cases, close order drill, no problem arises. Simple orders are matched with an equally simple "inspection" task. Unfortunately most problems of supervision are not this easy. Complexity in either the task to be carried out or in the procedures for determining whether the orders are, in fact, being obeyed is the rule. Frequently both kinds of complexity are present.

Let us suppose that the superior devotes a fourth of his total organizational time to each subordinate. The supervisor must decide on some breakdown between time spent in deciding upon and giving orders to the subordinate and time spent in insuring that there is compliance with the orders that are given. As a general rule, the more complex the task, the greater the amount of time that the supervisor must take in making the initial decisions and in issuing clear orders. This implies that less time, proportionately, is available for insuring compliance. Thus, it must be concluded that the more complex the task the less well will the orders to the subordinate be explained and the less well will his carrying out of these orders be supervised. There is a direct relationship between the inefficiency of a given organization and the complexity of the tasks that it is expected to perform.

How can the sovereign make the best use of the time that he does have available for insuring that a subordinate will carry out his orders?

First, it should be emphasized that, in the context of our model, the sovereign is supervising decisions made by the subordinate; he is not taking individual decisions himself on matters relating to the outside world.[1] He must, therefore, allow the subordinate to reach decisions in individual cases.

1. Decisions taken by a subordinate are intended, of course, to be controlled by the more general "policy" decisions previously taken by the sovereign and transmitted down the line.

If, for example, the sovereign should merely examine the facts in each of a few cases confronting the subordinate and announce the decision that he would make, he will have no way at all of checking on the behavior of his subordinate in those cases where the sovereign is occupied elsewhere.

A STATISTICAL METHOD OF CONTROL

The sovereign must rely on some criteria for judging the behavior of the subordinate on the basis of decisions that the latter has already made. Furthermore, it is clearly undesirable that the subordinate be allowed to know in advance which of his particular decisions or actions will be examined by the sovereign. If he did possess this foreknowledge, the subordinate would devote a disproportionate amount of time and effort to pleasing the sovereign for these particular cases, tending to disregard the sovereign's wishes for the remainder of his task. If there should be any pattern at all in his choice of areas to "inspect," the assistants will recognize this pattern, and they will tend to act accordingly. The sheer inability of the sovereign to investigate all of the actions and decisions of subordinates forces him to rely on some sample of these actions, and he must insure that such a sample is selected in a truly random fashion.

To some observers, a method in which the individual subordinate is not informed as to which of his actions will be subjected to close scrutiny may well seem "unfair" or "unjust." There is little to this argument provided that all assistants in a given hierarchy are treated in the same fashion. If it is accepted that the aim or objective of the sovereign is that of getting inferiors to carry out a policy, these inferiors must be kept in doubt as to which of their particular actions will be examined carefully by the sovereign. An inexperienced or misguided sovereign might, under this scheme, penalize subordinates for each deviation, but any sovereign of normal administrative intelligence should recognize that perfect compliance is not to be expected from subordinates.

This implies that any procedure for formal inspections at stated intervals and for stated criteria should be avoided. It might lead to the satisfaction of the sovereign through deceit. The United States Army has a system of regular inspections in which both the time of the inspection and the matters to be inspected are known in advance. As might be expected, units are always well prepared for each inspection, despite the fact that the same units may be seriously deficient normally. This formal inspection system has the advantage of furthering something akin to administrative hypocrisy. The higher officers can pretend that the subordinates' level of compliance is much higher than is actually the case.

The principle stated to this point says only that the sovereign should examine the decisions of an inferior after these have been made and that the inferior should not know in advance which of his decisions are to be examined. This principle tells us nothing about the criteria that the sovereign may use to judge the decisions and actions of subordinates. One rule seems evident. The sovereign should avoid judging the actions of an inferior in an area where his own relevant knowledge is less than that of the inferior. Since, as we have shown, the inferior will, by the nature of the hierarchical structure, tend to know more about any particular instance than the sovereign, when the instance is first brought to the attention of the sovereign, this rule suggests that the sovereign must undertake some inquiry into those matters that he proposes to examine closely. Before he makes a judgment on the actions of a particular subordinate in a particular case, the sovereign must, within limits, become "expert" in that case. This rule, despite its evident validity, seems to be violated by all but the very best administrators. There is, instead, a tendency for the sovereign to assume that he already knows all that needs knowing about a particular issue. This tendency leads the sovereign to take decisions concerning the behavior of many subordinates when he does not possess sufficient information to evaluate such behavior properly.

This point is illustrated by George Kennan's comment that high-ranking foreign policy officials normally make decisions on matters about which their information is inadequate. In one sense this is true of all important decisions. The special problem emphasized here is that the superior, in his evaluation of subordinates, tends to substitute his own ill-informed outlook for that of the subordinate who might be, and probably is, better informed.

How can the sovereign find out enough about a particular case to judge properly whether his subordinate has reached a "correct" decision? He may, as one method, undertake his own investigation. But there is a less onerous method available. The subordinate may simply be requested to provide the facts for particular cases. As we have already noted, this method is not infallible since the subordinate may not provide information that will tend to cast doubt on his decision. Some distortion in the picture presented to the superior in this way would surely arise, although the degree of distortion would depend both on the personal character of the subordinate and upon the methods of supervision employed by the superior. If, as we saw in Part 2, the sovereign is known to trust his subordinates, then the inferior who is dishonest is placed at a distinct advantage with respect to his more honest peer. If, on the other hand, the sovereign acts on the presumption that, at least for some of the time, his subordinates are likely to twist the information to some extent, this disadvantage of the honest man will be reduced. For our analysis, we shall assume that the sovereign will not rely solely on the faith that men are, by nature, good.

How, then, does the sovereign control the possibility that his inferiors may misinform him when he tries to examine the consequences of their decisions? Again the use of statistical methods seems to be suggested. If the sovereign should check up on all that is passed along to him, he would have gained nothing over his own onerous method of fact-finding. If he painstakingly checks on the factual information provided to him in a specific number of cases selected from all cases in some random fashion, then the sovereign can surely economize greatly on his time. The inferior would be confronted with a situation as follows: out of each one hundred decisions taken, the sovereign can be expected to ask me to provide him with a full accounting of the information upon which my action was taken in twenty. These twenty cases will be selected by some process that I cannot predict in advance. From among these twenty cases, the sovereign will select five, say, in which he will carefully check upon the accuracy of the information that I submit to him. Again, I have no way of knowing how these five will be selected from among the twenty. Furthermore, the sovereign will probably impose more severe sanctions on me for providing incorrect factual information than he will upon me for having reached incorrect decisions. Finally, in some cases I may expect him to carry his own investigations further than I have carried mine.

This method would seem to place what is probably the maximum practicable degree of restraint on the behavior of the inferior in an hierarchy. The sovereign must take particular care not to be led, by least resistance, to check on information that happens to be easy to check, or to check on cases in areas where his own knowledge makes him especially well qualified. Perhaps the most difficult task for the sovereign in this respect is the necessity of shunning deliberately any particular or disproportionate examination of cases in the areas of his own interest.

A unique problem is raised in those cases where the subordinate happens to be "expert" in an area where the superior is not especially well informed. Here understanding the inferior's analysis of the "facts" which led to his own decision would require an education for the sovereign in the particular field of specialization. If each subordinate should be a specialist in a different subject field, the sovereign cannot be expected to learn all the fields. In such command situations, the sovereign will simply be unable to make an independent judgment about the decisions of his inferiors unless he can resort to "judgment by results," a method that will be discussed in the next chapter. Only if his subordinates should all operate in roughly related areas of specialization can the sovereign exercise real control under the methods discussed here.

The sovereign should, in some instances, carry an investigation much farther than the point at which the normal investigating procedure of the inferior making the decision has stopped. This will permit the sovereign to judge the efficiency of the search process itself, to judge whether the inferior stopped too soon, or put too much effort into making up his mind.

The analysis of Part 2 suggested that the sovereign will normally make arrangements with the peers of the inferior to check on the latter's activities. Such arrangements are also to be recommended normatively when we think of the efficiency of the hierarchy in carrying out its basic objectives. The telling of tales should be rewarded and encouraged if efficient administration is the end; this is the result of thinking about the administrative process, not ethical standards. If, on the other hand, the sovereign should wish to uphold ethical standards in this respect, he must be prepared to accept a less efficient organization. Ethical principles themselves often come into conflict. If it be assumed that doing one's duty consists in helping the superior carry out the goals of the hierarchy, then telling on someone may be doing this duty. Furthermore, if the sovereign's information about the behavior of inferiors is improved by such arrangements, then the whole system of rewards and punishments is likely to be more in accordance with commonly accepted ideas of "justice" than if the sovereign's information is less complete. In any case, efficient administrators will normally make some use of subordinates to report on other subordinates.

REASONABLE EXPECTATIONS

Let us now consider briefly the nature of the results that a sovereign might expect when he looks carefully into the activities of one of his assistants. That he should not expect perfection, however defined, seems obvious. No two persons will agree on the proper decision to be reached in a whole series of instances. Furthermore, the frequency with which the two people, the sovereign and the inferior, will differ is dependent on the complexity of the decision involved. In our numerical models developed earlier, it was suggested that the sovereign should be reasonably satisfied in the average case with an equivalance of his views and that of a subordinate in three out of four events. This ratio seems reasonable for most of those situations where the degree of complexity is such as to be characterized by the term "decision making."[2]

In extremely complex matters, an even lower correlation between the sovereign's and the subordinate's decisions might be expected. If we allow, for purposes of analysis here, that the sovereign cannot expect much more than a three-fourths compliance ratio, he must, of course, refrain from dismissing inferiors each time that a specific decision is proven to be wrong. The sequential nature of the decision process must be kept in mind. Either the sovereign may offer large rewards and penalties to persons who, over a period of time, are relatively successful or relatively unsuccessful in reaching "correct" decisions, or else he may offer small rewards and penalties each time a decision is checked with the expectation that, over time, these rewards and penalties will average out to a reasonable pattern. The point is that, under no circumstances, should either large rewards or large penalties be tied to any particular individual decision or action.

The method of supervision that I have analyzed in this chapter is, I submit, the best available system. Little is probably to be gained by discussing various alternatives and pointing out the comparative defects. Almost all of the other proposed systems of control are based upon illusory ideas concerning the mental powers of sovereigns. These ideas are seldom verbalized, but they seem to be present implicity in most theories of supervision and in many tables of organization. It is possible for a sovereign to organize his train in such a manner that he is deceived into believing that he achieves better results than that which can be obtained through the control procedures suggested here. In fact, the sovereign may have to show real ingenuity to avoid being seduced into thinking that his organization is more efficient than the real facts warrant.

It is also possible to organize the hierarchy in such a manner that most of the subordinates are assigned tasks that do not really involve the making of independent decisions. In this case, there may be an illusion of control over a much larger organization than that which actually exists. In the American diplomatic machine, for example, a vast amount of time is spent in writing, distributing, and reading various reports which have little effect on any decisions made by the secretary of state. Since many people are busy with

2. In fact, almost any action requires a decision. A bank teller deciding whether a signature is genuine, however, operates on a much lower level of intellectual effort than does a bank vice-president deciding whether to grant a loan.

these reports, and since these reports appear to be related to the decisions that are made, the illusion that everyone is busy creating foreign policy is widespread. Few persons realize that "the higher they get, the less they read." The same number of effective decisions could be made with a smaller organization, and the decisions would be based on equally good information. While in a smaller organization the total amount of information held by the system might be smaller, there seems no reason to think that the people who actually make decisions would be any less well informed than they are in the larger organization.

In a positive sense, the conception of the administrative process presented here seems reasonably accurate. The system seems to be that which accurately describes the manner in which efficient administrators think and act, although it is not the system which rationalizes their actions. In any event, in a normative sense, the procedure discussed here represents a meaningful objective for improvement in organizational efficiency. Surely administrative hierarchies could function more efficiently if they were explicitly constructed along the patterns outlined here.

CONTROL IN MULTI-LEVEL BUREAUCRACY

The analysis has for the most part been confined to a single-stage hierarchy: a sovereign and a set of assistants working directly under his supervision. In the larger organizations, the same principles that have been developed hold, and the position of the individual with respect to his inferiors is the same as in the single-stage system. The difference in the two cases is that, in the multistage hierarchy, the activity to be supervised at the intermediate levels is itself supervisory activity. If we assume a three-level system in which a sovereign has four assistants, each of whom, in turn, has four assistants, the sovereign will issue instructions in the way that we have previously analyzed. The assistants will then give instruction to their own assistants. These instructions of the intermediate bureaucrats will normally involve decisions concerning the divisions of the general task among their subordinates and concerning the greater detail required in the issuance of lower-level orders. These decisions by the intermediate bureaucrats must be supervised by the sovereign of the hierarchy, and he will tend to use the techniques that we have discussed above. The supervision activities of the intermediate-level bureaucrats will also follow the same general principles.

There seems to be little point in discussing more and more complex administrative pyramids. The principles of control remain identical, except that it must be remembered that the real control exercised over the whole hierarchy by the ultimate sovereign declines steadily as the organization grows in total size. The organization depicted in the analysis is, however, an ideal one. The levels of efficiency that may be suggested by a concentration on this model organization may not be attained if administrators fail to behave rationally. Recall that we have noted previously that the sovereign may not be interested in maximizing real control; rather he may seek apparent control. The analysis here has been in terms of real control over the hierarchy.

EXISTING BUREAUCRATIC STRUCTURES

Given an acceptance of the analysis in this book, the question may be asked: How does the presently existing bureaucratic apparatus in many modern instances function at all? The answer seems to be twofold. In the first place, much of modern bureaucracy is simply a mistake. Various ends have seemed generally desirable. The question as to whether a bureaucratic hierarchy or organization could be designed to reach these desirable ends was not even raised. The bureaucracy was simply set up to accomplish things that seemed to be expedient. The continuing failures of bureaucracies are met in part by continuing reorganizations, the reasoning being that the failure has resulted from the organizational details. In part, the failures are met by concealed shifts in the objectives for the organization. As an experiment, if one examines the original arguments for the establishment of almost any government bureau and compares these arguments with those that may be currently offered for the retention of this bureau, one is likely to find that a considerable shift has occurred in the specification of the objectives that the bureau is supposed to attain. The governmental bureau becomes the permanent fixture, with the objective continually changing. Over time the vested interests of the bureaucrats themselves become more and more important in justifying the organization, although this can never be the sole argument in discussion with outsiders.[3]

3. I once participated in a rather large conference in which the only subject discussed was the necessity of performing certain functions if the organization concerned was not to lose a large part of its appropriation. Not only was the desirability of the functions themselves not canvassed; most people present thought them, as defined, undesirable. Needless to say, no one suggested declining the funds.

CHAPTER 21

JUDGMENT BY RESULTS

The numerous large bureaucratic organizations that can be observed to exist in the world today are not all to be explained as mistakes. There are organizational devices, available only under certain circumstances, which will permit the exercise of substantially more efficient supervision than is ordinarily possible. Many of the existing large organizations reflect the exploitation of such opportunities. This chapter will be devoted to a consideration of these methods.

RESULTS AND ACTIONS

To this point, when discussing the activities of a superior in obtaining desired decisions from his inferiors, we have implicitly assumed that the superior must consider the same set of facts as the inferior and determine the correctness or the incorrectness of the inferior's action on the basis of this consideration. The vast majority of tasks in bureaucracies demand this type of supervision. Simple tasks, such as digging a ditch, can be supervised much more easily, however, since the sovereign is interested solely in the result, in this example feet of ditch dug, and this sort of result can be readily observed. Complex tasks, unfortunately, are seldom of the type to which this system can be applied. There are, on the other hand, certain classes of situations in which it may be possible to evaluate the performance of rather complex tasks by reasonably simple methods. The large organizations which function with high degrees of efficiency normally perform this sort of tasks. In such cases, the sovereigns are able to make judgments concerning the behavior of subordinates, not through judging their *actions or decisions*, but through judging the *results of their actions*.

This procedure sounds much simpler than it actually is. It may appear that most actions, like ditch digging, can always be judged in terms of results. It is not difficult to demonstrate that this is not true. Let us assume, by way of illustration, that the American people gave the Roosevelt administration the general instruction to "improve the common good." Let us now suppose that the Roosevelt administration, as in fact it did, establishes the Social Security system. Can we then judge this particular action by its results, by its contribution to the common good? The answer is in the negative, although this might, at first glance, be disputed. If, however, one should ask a man who believes that this measure has benefitted the country, how he has reached his conclusion, his answer will not be "looking about I can see that the general welfare is improved in comparison with conditions that existed before the measure was enacted." He is far more likely simply to repeat the arguments that were employed by the advocates of the measure before its enactment. In other words, in judging the action after the event, he will tend to repeat the line of reasoning that led to its being taken in the first place. Quite similarly for critics; they will not normally point to any objectionable results, but rather they will tend to repeat the arguments originally advanced against the system. The point seems clear; the correctness or the incorrectness of the decision cannot be evaluated solely by examining the results.

A large number of actions can be judged only in this way. The observer can perceive that an act has taken place, and that the world is somehow different thereby, but whether the decision to act was well- or ill-advised can be decided only by considering again the reasoning processes through which the decision was reached. In this type of situation—which seems to typify public policy issues—the behavior of bureaucrats cannot be judged by results. Only through the consideration of the whole set of circumstances surrounding the actions and decisions taken can it be determined whether the behavior of public officials meets our desires.

This seems to apply to basic decisions, but, once these are made, the more specific decisions of the bureaucracy may be subjected appropriately to judgment by results. To return to the Social Security example, once the basic decision to institute the system is made, certain other actions must be made to implement and to operate the system. The vast majority of the decisions required to keep the system operating from day to day are of the sort that can be judged by results with a high degree of accuracy. As a result, in the Social Security Administration, we have a very large bureaucracy which is performing the sort of function that is quite suitable for a very large bureaucracy. While it is not suggested that this agency is highly efficient, elements of bureaucratic free enterprise do not seem to have appeared and, by and large, it appears to be accomplishing the objectives for which it was established.

The mere ability to judge the result of an action is not, in itself, sufficient to simplify the supervisory task in the sense mentioned here. Many results stem from the actions of more than one person in the organization. If the purpose of judging results is that of being able to reward or to penalize particular persons, it must be possible to separate the components of the final result that may be attributable to each individual decision maker. Often this is not at all possible. Think, for example, of the president of an automobile company after a particularly good year. Some members of the organization, in addition to the president himself, should be rewarded. The candidates may be three men: the designer who produced the new model design; the works manager, who succeeded in keeping costs down; the sales manager, who sold the product. It seems clear that there is no direct way of comparing the net contributions to the results made by these three men. Their functions, although wholly different, are indispensable to each other. Poor performance on the part of one might have been completely concealed by the outstanding performances of the others. The particular automobile might have been, for example, so well designed and efficiently produced that it "sold" even with terrible mismanagement in the sales department.

The president will, of course, make some sort of *ad hoc* decision, but there is no way that he can know that his decision is the "right" one. Further, supplementary decisions concerning the contributions of members of the hierarchy down the line will be even harder to make. In all such situations, judgment cannot be made in terms of results, not because these results are not visible, but simply because these results cannot be readily allocated to any single source.

A third difficulty arises in trying to extend the judgment-by-results criterion to actual situations. Even if the results can be readily observed, and even if a particular individual's contributions can be measured, it is not easy to reward or to punish any one inferior unless his performance can be compared with that of some of his peers. If two people are doing quite different things, their comparative efficiency cannot be judged in terms of results, since the results cannot be compared. How, for example, would one compare an author and a mechanic? The performance of two authors or two mechanics could be compared, but not the performance of widely heterogeneous tasks.

In order that judgment of results may be used as a device in supervising subordinates in an hierarchy, the task assigned to these subordinates must fulfill three separate requirements. It must be such that the results can, without great trouble, be measured. Secondly, it must be possible to attribute the result to particular persons who are responsible for it. Finally, the results from the activities of one subordinate must be comparable to those obtained from others.

These three requirements seem to rule out many of the things that a sovereign, individual or group, might seek to obtain with an administrative apparatus. The tasks that are suitable for attainment through the medium of large administrative hierarchies are decidedly exceptional. The great majority of human activities probably can best be done by individuals working on their own or in mutually agreed-on cooperative arrangements or else through an organization in which superiors must consider the activities of subordinates, not results.

THE INTELLIGENT SUBORDINATE

Before turning to an analysis of the various technical methods that might be introduced to apply the system of judging by results, one special advantage of this system may be noted. The system of judging by results rather than by actions is the only system in hierarchical relationships that permits a supervisor to judge at all adequately the activities or the performance of a subordinate who is his superior in intelligence or knowledge. This does not imply that the sovereign need recognize the inferior as his better in such matters. He may understand the subordinate's comparative intelligence, but there is no need that he consider him his own better. If the sovereign must judge the actions or decisions of a subordinate on the basis of the circumstances under which action was taken, he must try to be as well informed and as intelligent concerning the available alternatives as the inferior. If the sovereign is, however, markedly inferior to his own subordinate in this respect, he may decide that errors have been made in many cases where he is simply incapable of following his subordinates' reasoning. If, by contrast, the situation is such that the sovereign can judge merely by results, he simply observes the better results secured by the highly intelligent subordinate and rewards him accordingly. He need not try to penetrate the processes of reasoning that might have led the more intelligent inferior to his actions.

This advantage always attaches itself to judgment by result, and one particularly clear illustration may be cited. One of the characteristics that would seem highly desirable in a diplomat is foresight, and by this I mean only the ability to make better-than-average predictions about the future course of events. This ability seems surely to be one that should be taken into account when considering whether a junior diplomat should or should not be promoted. It is, however, impossible accurately to judge predictions at the times that they are made. If the sovereign should himself make a prediction and his subordinate another, the sovereign may draw the conclusion that the subordinate lacks foresight. The man who is best at determining, not what will happen, but what the sovereign will predict to happen, seems likely to be advanced over his peer who might have significantly better insight over the future course of real events. If, however, predictions should be judged only after some period has passed, judgment would become relatively easy. If this simple change should be made in the administrative structure, the system would be modified so that those persons with the greatest ability to predict would tend to be promoted. Under the present system, by contrast, the diplomat who seeks to rise in the bureaucracy will not pay much attention to the real world, but rather he will concentrate on his sovereign's image of this real world.

MAKING RESULTS COMPARABLE

Efforts, obviously, should be made to organize an hierarchy in such a way that this labor-saving device can be employed whenever possible. But even in areas where the tasks to be performed meet the requirements, comparison of results may not be easy. Let us consider the simple case in which the sovereign seeks to determine which one of several men can jump the highest. He puts up a bar and lets them jump over it, gradually raising the bar until all jumpers but one have been eliminated. Note that all of the jumpers must be assumed to start from the same level. If there are irregularities in the ground, the method would not work. The track coach would solve this by seeing that all jumpers start from the same spot. In the administration of hierarchic organizations, the analogous problem is not so easy. If, for example, two detectives are sent out to investigate two murders, one of whom makes an arrest within the hour, while the other takes four months, there is no presumption that the first is the better detective.

In the terms of our athletic analogue, the sovereign may level the ground. He may try to arrange things so that each person starts with the same basic situation. This is a desirable objective, but in many administrative situations it is not practicable. It is, of course, the scheme used in tests and examinations.

A second method may be that of measuring the exact distance from the ground to the bar in each instance. But this would seem to bring the sovereign back to judging the whole action, not the result alone. There is, however, a difference. This method consists in looking at the starting place and end, with little concern for what has gone on in between these two points. There is one very important administrative technique, cost accounting, that involves this method. It will be discussed in the next chapter.

CHAPTER 22

LABOR SAVING DEVICES— COST ACCOUNTING

Cost accounting is of interest here only as a technique of supervision. The procedure has, of course, other functions than those of assisting higher-level officials in their evaluation of the efficiency with which lower-level members of an organization perform their assigned tasks. Cost accounting may be used in computing tax liability, in providing the basis for investment decisions, in helping to fix prices, or in numerous other ways. The supervisory function of cost accounting is not, however, unimportant, and it appears to have been a decisive factor in shaping the structure of large corporate hierarchies. Concentration on the supervisory function of cost accounting allows us to ignore one of the most difficult conceptual problems in this field, that of capital accounting. The particular problems here arise largely from the difficulties of evaluating property on hand at the beginning and end of accounting periods. Supervisory personnel, however, normally hold positions for a number of accounting periods. In attempting to judge the efficiency of an individual in charge of, say, a Chevrolet assembly plant, the accounts of that plant under his management for several years would normally be available. Errors in evaluation due to capital accounting difficulties would tend to cancel out.

EMPHASIS ON PROFITABILITY

It should be specifically stated that the only result that cost accounting adequately measures is *profitability*. This serves to restrict sharply the usefulness of cost accounting as a general managerial tool. In our earlier analysis, we have referred to organized hierarchies as means through which the sovereigns attempt to get their own desires carried out, but we have not specified what these particular desires might be. Cost accounting is an aid in supervision only insofar as profitability, in a pecuniary sense, is a major desire of the sovereign. Not all sovereigns, of course, will want to place such primary emphasis on profitability, and few sovereigns will want to give the profitability criterion sole place in measuring results. The owner of a business firm will surely seek other things from the behavior of his subordinates than profits, despite the fact that only the latter can be adequately measured by cost accounting techniques.[1] The device must be considered as providing the means of measuring performance of only one objective of an organization, one out of possibly several.

If the objective for the organization is primarily that of making money, not only does the supervisory method allow for great efficiency, but the task of getting the desires of the sovereign transmitted to the subordinates is greatly simplified. The only effective order that has to be given is "make money." This coincidence of a simple objective with a sure-fire method of enforcing obedience tends to make economic organizations, as a rule, the best-operated hierarchies.

But, to repeat, the whole system works only so long as the making of money profits remains the primary objective. This explains why, normally, governmentally operated economic enterprises do not seem demonstrably more efficient than other government hierarchies. The government normally enters a line of activity precisely because the public is not satisfied with the results of the operation of the profit motive in that particular field. In any case, the government enterprise will not normally be operated explicitly for profit, with the result that cost accounting as a means of control is substantially less effective than it otherwise could be. Other and less effective methods of supervision, common to other government activities, must be introduced. Hence the government economic enterprise will suffer in its record of comparative efficiency with private business organization. There are, of course, examples of highly efficient enterprises operated by governmental units. Usually these enterprises are operated in similar fashion to private enterprises, with profit-making a primary objective.

SUPERVISION THROUGH ACCOUNTING

The actual process through which the sovereign uses accounting techniques to evaluate the performance of subordinates is simple in principle. He should merely look at the accounts of the various subdivisions of the organization and proceed to reward or to punish the subordinates on the basis of what he sees. The sovereign will not make any attempt to determine the particular contribution of the subdivision manager to the profitability of his subdivision. He will, instead, reward the whole subdivision as a unit. The

1. It may be argued that the ultimate sovereigns in any business organization are the consumers who must buy the goods produced. In this view, the owners and managers become simply high-ranking subordinates of the ultimate sovereigns. This modification would have little effect on the analysis here, and I have chosen to disregard it.

manager is thus rewarded not for his unique contribution, as such, but for the performance of his part of the hierarchy. In turn, he will reward or punish subsections in the same manner.

This analysis of modern corporate procedure would not likely be accepted by the corporation executive who chanced to read it. His reaction might well reflect an "optical illusion" that affects men of affairs. The balance sheet is so much a part of their basic thought patterns that they do not realize its importance for their own behavior. They think of themselves as, for example, dismissing a junior executive for "not being up to his job." If specifications are asked, the sovereign will list the personal defects of the employee. Thorough examination of the case should reveal, however, that the inferior was dismissed because he was not contributing to the profits of the organization, and that the ultimate measure of performance in this respect is the balance sheet. This illusion represents no conscious hypocrisy on the part of the average corporation executive; it represents only a lack of introspective clarity.

The accounts of an organization do not, of course, measure the performance of the separate divisions of the hierarchy with complete accuracy. This fact is well recognized. Many problems arise, all of which are compounded by the simple fact that accounting itself costs money. The full technical possibilities of accounting control are not normally realized, because the costs beyond a certain degree of complexity begin to outweigh the additional gains that might be expected from greater accuracy. The fundamental limitation upon the utilization of accounting techniques is, therefore, a cost limitation, not a technical one. Quite apart from cost limitations, however, the accounting process cannot precisely allocate all costs among the separate parts of an integrated organization. There will exist joint costs that must, by necessity, be allocated by arbitrary rules.

The difficulties here are accentuated by the attempts of the various divisions or subdivisions to shift costs onto other parts of the same organization. These attempts take the form of continual discussions over changes in accounting procedures within large corporate hierarchies. To some extent, however, the efforts of the separate divisions in an hierarchy are mutually offsetting. The negotiation of changes in the accounting methods of an organization should be recognized by the sovereign as essentially a political process. He should recognize that the most successful negotiator among the subordinates is likely to be able to advance his own appearance of profitability somewhat at the expense of his peers.

All of the above is by way of saying that there are certain intrinsic problems connected with the use of balance sheets for supervisory purposes.

Nevertheless, the simple process of rewarding those division managers whose divisions show up well and penalizing those division managers whose divisions perform badly may be taken as the objective of cost accounting, insofar as this is a technique for supervision. Defects are present in this procedure, but the technique does, in most cases, provide a close approximation to the relative profitability of the various divisions of an organization. It permits the comparison of the relative efficiencies of persons who might be doing widely different things.[2] The same organization can, through the use of this technique, carry on many diverse activities. Cost accounting is the best-known technique for supervision, and modern industrial civilization very largely depends upon it.

Efficient sovereigns will, nevertheless, not rely solely on figures provided by the cost accountants in rating the performance of subordinate officials. This is due in part to deficiencies in the accounting process, but mainly it is due to the realization that relative profitability is affected by things other than efficiency of management. Luck arising from wholly unpredictable changes in the environment may account for relatively great differential profitability for particular divisions. More commonly, the various parts of a given corporation may be of inherently different potential profitability, due to such things as age of equipment, raw material supply, markets of products, etc. The track coach analogy applies here. The corporation executive will not expect a manager of a semiobsolete steel plant to make the same profit as the manager of a newly constructed plant.[3]

The profit figures taken from the account must, therefore, be accompanied by some judgment as to the extent to which this profit or loss reflects efficiency of subordinates. Thus, a sovereign may reward or penalize his subordinates according to their "profitability," but he must also make decisions as to the

2. General Motors, for example, can weigh the relative contribution to the total corporation profit made by the Frigidaire division and by the division that makes locomotives. The A&P, a second example, can decide whether the manager of a store is more efficient than the manager of a canning factory.

3. Stockholders are probably the only group of any significance in the economic system that normally judges solely on the basis of accounting records. In large corporations, the management is free to do almost anything it desires, provided only that it returns a profit comparable to other companies'. On the other hand, losses, regardless of their cause, will tend to result in changes in management. Stockholders also illustrate well the point that, in such cases where measurement of results is possible, uninformed ultimate sovereigns can effectively supervise more-informed and more-intelligent inferiors.

policy for the organization to follow in the future. These latter decisions, being predictions of what will happen, cannot be exclusively based on past records. Nevertheless, the sovereign's own superiors, his sovereigns, will judge the correctness or incorrectness of his policy decisions on the basis of accounting records after events have occurred. Here, as we suggested above, even dull and unimaginative superiors can readily judge the comparative merits of a number of brilliant subordinates.

LIMITATIONS

There are two additional reasons why accounting records should not be depended upon too much in evaluating the efficiency of inferiors. One of these is based on cost considerations; the other is not. To take the second reason first, most people who find themselves in positions of power will not be solely or primarily interested in using that power to increase their wealth. For this reason, a corporate official will normally be inclined to judge his inferiors by criteria other than simple contribution to organizational profitability. Insofar as these other criteria are introduced, cost accounting becomes unreliable. If the superior simply promotes the subordinate who shows up the best in the accounting measure, this will tend to insure that his personal control over subordinates is eliminated. Knowing this rule, subordinates would be under no compulsion to act in a manner personally pleasing to the sovereign. Only if promotion is made to depend on some criteria other than profit can the man in a position of sovereignty in the organization insure some personal attention to his private nonpecuniary desires by his subordinates.

The other restriction on the use of the balance sheet alone lies in the nature of competitive society in general. Net profits can be secured in such a system only by persons and by organizations who perform better than average. There will be constant pressure toward the reduction of profits. The demonstration of superior efficiency will surely attract other organizations and other persons to imitate the practices used by the initially successful group or person. Undue concentration on net profits as the sole criterion for judging the performance of subordinates may, because of this constant pressure toward attrition of profit positions, cause the innovating individual to be poorly rewarded relative to the highly efficient but unimaginative individual.

AREAS OF APPLICABILITY

In spite of these limitations cost accounting is a remarkable organizational technique, and it does permit a degree of efficiency in supervision that is fantastically greater than that which is possible through any alternative method. As we have said, cost accounting applies only to certain areas of activity. The discussion may, therefore, appropriately be concluded with some consideration of the areas for which the technique might be applicable.

First of all, the fact that the technique is *cost* accounting should be emphasized. Determining the profitability of a given economic organization, a corporation or a part of a corporation, requires two figures: cost and value. Cost accounting, as such, gives only one of these. Value is derived, in most cases, from prices at which products and services are marketed. In very large corporate organizations difficult problems arise because items, instead of being sold to outsiders, may be merely transferred to other units of the same organization. Thus, let us say that Hypothetical, Inc., purchases a certain raw material for $1 per unit. This material is then passed through nine different processes, and at the end of this series of operations it is sold to outsiders for $10. Cost accountants can determine the costs that are incurred by each stage or division processing the item. Let us say this cost is $1 at each point. Do these figures provide sufficient information to evaluate the efficiency of a particular division? The answer is clearly no. Nor would the fact that, say, the B division spent $1.05 instead of $1 be of any help. Some additional information is needed concerning the value added by each division.

Judgment on value added may, in some cases, be possible by comparison. If there is an external market for the semiprocessed product at each stage, the price at which the product in this state could be sold in this external market provides a means of determining the value added at each stage. Similarly, if one of the divisions produces a component that could be purchased on the market externally, the cost of that component on the market can be taken as the "value added" by producing that item internally. It is obvious, however, that the vast majority of operations performed by manufacturing enterprises are not of the sort which can be judged in this way. Usually, a company will purchase from outsiders those components which are commercially available and will restrict its own operations precisely to those which it cannot purchase.

This fact seems to have had a major effect on the organization of major companies. Large corporations are organized on a product rather than on a "step-of-production" system. General Motors has a series of divisions producing various products; it does not have divisions performing various operations on similiar products. This scheme of organization permits top management to make judgments on the efficiency of the various divisions which would be impossible if the divisions should be organized on the alternative, step-of-production, basis. The costs of Chevrolet, for example, can be determined by the accountants; its value can be determined by the price for which it is marketed. Thus, it becomes relatively easy for the corporation's higher officials to determine the contribution to profit made by the Chevrolet division. It is not possible, however, to determine accurately the contribution to total profits made by the subdivision of the Chevrolet division that makes engines. This is because there is no simple way of valuing Chevrolet engines alone since these are not directly priced.

Every corporate management must face problems of this nature, and they must reach decisions as to the relative efficiency of certain divisions that do not produce outputs that are directly marketable. It should always be recognized that these decisions are based on less-accurate information than in the cases where prices are readily available. It is, therefore, technically impossible to administer a large organization, the various divisions of which perform successive operations on the same product, with as high a degree of accuracy as one of similar size that is organized into divisions producing discrete products.[4]

This analysis, if correct, resolves one of the minor mysteries of economics. It has always seemed probable that economies of scale resulting from larger and larger productive processes would lead to large companies growing steadily larger, with the small companies' being destroyed. This has not occurred. There seems to have been no pronounced trend toward bigness in any relative sense. Furthermore, the very large concerns, such as General Motors, the House of Mitsui, or Jardine Matheson, are not built up through the use of production economies of scale. They more normally consist, in fact, of a collection of much smaller economic enterprises that are simply owned jointly.

General Motors and General Electric not only produce a vast range of different products; they even have divisions that compete vigorously with each other. If the economies of scale are a significant factor, it seems clear that some countervailing factor must be present that prevents these corporate giants from taking advantage of them. The intrinsic limitations on accounting as a means of supervision provide this factor.

4. In any given case this consideration may be counter-balanced by the possibility of using certain technical processes which are only available if production is on a large scale. The size of any corporation must be the result of these two countervailing considerations.

CHAPTER 23

LABOR SAVING DEVICES—MISCELLANEOUS

In some cases it may be possible for organizations whose objective is not long-run-profit maximization to introduce systems that are similar to accounting systems for purposes of evaluating the performance of subordinates. Such pseudo-accounting techniques can never be as efficient in this respect as accounting techniques in the traditional sense. The latter alone can measure the relative efficiency of men doing wholly different things, and these alone can consider both the initial conditions and the final results in such a way as to permit reasonably accurate judgments on the performance of individual or organizational units. The pseudo-accounting methods that will be discussed here share with the non-accounting methods of supervision the problem of comparing the performance of persons doing different things.

As an example of a quantitative technique, we may consider the system examined by Blau in *The Dynamics of Bureaucracy*. Blau studied an employment exchange. This particular exchange used a statistical method of determining the efficiency of some of its employees. Blau's account of how this method worked is as follows:

> Until the beginning of 1948, or while jobs were relatively plentiful, the only operation recorded for each interviewer was the number of interviews per month. However, when the labor market became tighter, this single criterion had a detrimental effect on operations. In the interest of a good rating the interviewer tried to maximize the number of interviews and therefore spent less time than was needed during a period of job scarcity on locating openings for clients. This rudimentary statistical record interfered with the agency's objective of finding jobs for clients.
>
> In March 1948, two months after a new department head was put in charge, she instituted new performance records with the following eight indexes for each interviewer:
>
> (1) Interviews: The number of interviews held with job applicants
> (2) Referrals: The number of clients sent out to apply for a job
> (3) Placements: The number of such referred clients actually hired
> (4) (2)/(1): The proportion of interviews that resulted in referrals

(5) (3)/(2): The proportion of referrals that resulted in placements
(6) (3)/(1): The proportion of interviews that resulted in placements
(7) Notifications: The number of reports to the unemployment insurance office of clients' alleged misbehavior
(8) Application forms: The number of forms filled in for job applicants.

While the number of number of job openings available was beyond the department's control, the proportion of these openings it filled provided an index of the effectiveness of its operations. Immediately after the introduction of these records the proportion of job openings filled through the agency increased from 55 to 67 per cent.

Statistical reports influenced operations by inducing interviewers to concentrate their efforts upon the factors that were measured and thus would affect their rating. Because of the percentage figures included in his record an interviewer had not only to place many clients but also to exercise care in selecting a qualified client for each job, for otherwise the proportion of his referrals that resulted in placements would have been low. This curbed the tendency to send out clients quickly and indiscriminately in the hope that a large number, though a small proportion, would be hired—which would have constituted inefficient service to both workers and employers. On the other hand, an interviewer's rating would not be improved by being overmeticulous and referring only perfectly qualified clients, for then the proportion of his interviews that resulted in referrals would have been low.

The interviewers reacted to the introduction of performance records with as vehement hostility as manual workers do to production quotas. For these white-collar workers this attitude was intensified by the fact that "working on production like in a factory" had negative status implications. Interviewers often protested that the "statistics" measured "quantity" but not "quality," but this complaint was not justified. The performance records measured not only the amount of work done (the number of interviews) but also whether certain objectives were accomplished (the number of placements) and whether this was done by prescribed methods (the proportional indexes). The records tended to include all the elements that superiors considered important, and their omission of a factor also influenced operating practices. Thus, since counseling interviews were not included in the departmental report, interviewers rarely asked permission to give one, for these time-consuming interviews would only have interfered with making a good showing on the record.[1]

The above citation from Blau may be taken as a classic description of a system of pseudo-accounting that was both well thought out and intelligently administered and applied to a situation that is almost ideal for the use of this method. Since the advantages in such a situation are sufficiently obvious, I shall, here, confine the discussion to pointing out, first, the limitations of the method even in this more or less ideal situation. Secondly, I shall try to show why the system can seldom be applied so effectively as this to administrative problems generally.[2]

The principal limitations of such systems of pseudo-accounting fall into two categories: the impossibility of applying the system to the whole of an organization, and the inaccuracy of the system in measuring compliance with the desired norms. In the first place, the organization studied had twenty-four employees; only fifteen were interviewers. The system thus permitted a comparison of the members of the group of fifteen only. There was no way to bring in the other nine employees of the organization. Even among the fifteen, however, the system did not accurately measure their accomplishments. The numerical quantities were not comprehensive, in that some things desired of the interviewers could not be included in the statistical variables computed. This meant that supervisors must have been forced to rely on other aspects of performance than those indicated by statistical results. Therefore, although the statistical computations undoubtedly simplified the task of the supervisors, they did not do so to the extent that a genuine set of accounts would have done.

Moreover, since the statistical computations were made regularly, and since they were a recognized measure of performance, there was a strong tendency of the interviewers to try to maximize their own point totals in the computations rather than performance of their total duties, including those

1. From William Peterson, *American Social Patterns*, Anchor, Garden City, 1956, pp. 230–32. The chapter is an abridgement from Peter M. Blau, *The Dynamics of Bureaucracy*, University of Chicago Press, 1955.

2. In the discussion which follows I will attempt to confine myself to a consideration of the general limitations on the method. Blau discusses in the latter part of the article from which the above quotation is taken a number of difficulties involved in applying the method in this particular case, and since these difficulties may recur, a reading of the article in *American Social Patterns* or his book *The Dynamics of Bureaucracy* would be a desirable preparation for anyone planning to set up a pseudo-accounting system.

that were not included in the measurements. In this way the use of the system was, itself, a distorting factor which had the effect of directing some of the efforts of the organization into channels which were contrary to the desires of the sovereign. This diversion, in the case studied by Blau, took the form partly of accentuating certain aspects of the total complex of duties to be performed, because these duties were measured by the index while other duties, not so measured, were slighted, and partly of simple fraud. The latter consisted of the taking of action that would prevent other persons from performing their own duties while easing the task of the bureaucrat.[3]

These two problems in the use of this method are complementary, in a sense. If the supervisors are efficient, they can counteract both of these effects of the pseudo-accounting devices. But this counteraction, in itself, impairs the labor-saving advantages of the device. The result is likely to be that the device, while improving the general administrative picture somewhat, will, to some extent, distort the total operations of the hierarchy. All of this is true even in the ideal setting for the use of such devices, such as that case studied by Blau. Most real administrative problems will not be nearly so readily amenable to this sort of procedure.

In order to demonstrate this point, consider the advantages that the employment agency possessed for introducing this device. In the first place, it was possible to find numerical measures which came reasonably close to measuring desired performance. In most cases, such a high degree of approximation could not be expected between desired performance and an appropriately constructed quantitative criterion. Most bureaucratic tasks are simply not so readily measured as that of interviewing, referring, and placing employees. A second special advantage lay in the fact that three-fifths of the total number of employees were doing substantially the same job. In the more normal situation, where the duties of the employees are more varied, any such system would have more limited applicability.

3. *Footnote by JMB*: The limitations on this system discussed here by Tullock are familiar to all academicians in the form of a close analogue. The "publish or perish" rule for promotion and advancement on university and college faculties represents an imperfect attempt to introduce some sort of quantitative criterion for judging performance that is, at base, not quantifiable. Where the rule is applied, in fact, if not in announcement, there is surely a tendency for faculty personnel to neglect teaching and other educational duties in order to write for publication. Even recognizing this, however, the rule may still be better, if carefully applied, than no rule at all.

APPLICATIONS OF THE LAW OF LARGE NUMBERS IN SUPERVISION

In those cases, the great majority, where direct pseudo-accounting methods are of little or no value, some comparison of results must proceed without mechanical aids. The supervisor simply "looks at" the results of his various subordinates' actions and decides whom to reward and whom to punish. This task will never be easy for the sovereign, but certain elements of the law of large numbers may be helpful. Although there is no way of judging the opportunities for successful performance in unique or discrete cases, the supervisor may, in certain situations, decide that, over a sequence of actions, comparative results become meaningful. With this method, the larger of the number of unique instances of performance the better will he be able to judge. This point is, of course, obvious, but it seems worth pointing out that this law of large numbers has the paradoxical result that high-level supervision, in the same organization, is easier than low-level supervision precisely because there are more events to evaluate the higher the level of supervision in the hierarchy.

For an example, consider the problem of police administration. One function of the police is that of investigating crimes and arresting criminals. The head of a small division of the police, the "squad," has the difficult job of deciding which of his subordinates to reward or to penalize. These subordinates will be working on cases of widely differing type, and the superior cannot judge simply by results unless he is willing and able to wait for a very long time before reaching a decision. Such a superior must, normally, consider all of the circumstances surrounding the actions taken by his subordinates rather than rely solely on quantitative results.

A higher officer assigned the task of judging the relative merits of several squad leaders has an easier job. In the first place, the total number of cases solved by a squad must be considerably greater than that handled by a single individual member of a squad. This means that a statistically reliable number of cases can be accumulated in a shorter period of time. Furthermore, although the cases confronted by each squad will not exhibit the same degrees of difficulty, these differences here are likely to vary less than those among cases handled by different officers of the same squad. It becomes evident that, whereas the squad leader can make little use of judgment by results in his supervisory task, his superior can make some considerable use of this system in ranking the squad leaders. The supervisory task, in this respect, grows progressively easier as one moves up the administrative pyramid. At the very highest levels, it may be quite possible in some cases to depend entirely on some quantifiable criterion, some method of pseudo-accounting.

THE "MILITARY SYSTEM"

Before leaving the general discussion of judgment by results, some attention should be paid to a special category that I shall call the "military system." In history, the military machines of the various political units have been incomparably the largest hierarchical organizations. The careless observer might then conclude that these organizations had, somehow, solved those problems discussed in this book better than other administrative hierarchies. Most persons who have, themselves, served in the armed services realize that such a conclusion would not be accurate.

Armed forces exist only to fight other armed forces. It is only necessary, therefore, for an army to be as efficient as its opponent, and, if the argument of this book is accepted, neither one of two large armies is likely to be very efficient in any absolute sense.[4] War, when it occurs, is likely to consist of a struggle between two gigantic but poorly coordinated organizations. If one organization is better coordinated than the other, it is likely to win. But the point here is that the standard of achievement is strictly comparative, and that victory does not imply a high degree of efficiency in absolute terms. This is well illustrated in the traditional view that the route to victory is that of making fewer mistakes than your enemy.

Nevertheless, there are special features about military organizations which we shall call the "military system." Let us consider the problem that confronts a general in trying to decide who from among his subordinates will be promoted to an important command. Judgment by result is not likely to be possible, because wars are bloody but infrequent. Even if "combat records" exist, these are not likely to be sufficiently lengthy to eliminate chance factors. The situation confronting the superior is insoluble on almost any of the considerations discussed earlier. In consequence, the sovereign here will be likely

4. Those military writers, like Marshall Saxe, who believe that very large armies are apt to be beaten by smaller ones, normally rely on the greater administrative efficiency of the smaller force. The historical record on the point is not clear. Most battles have involved forces which were not numerically equal, and there does not seem to be any pronounced tendency for either the larger or the smaller of the two contending forces to win. Nevertheless, most modern authorities seem to feel that large armies, in spite of their less efficient operation, are likely to beat more efficient but smaller forces. For a contrary view see Charles de Gaulle, *L'Armée de Métier*.

to select for promotion the man who most closely approximates the sovereign's idea of the type of man who would do well in combat. It will be recalled that one of the minor themes in Marquand's *Melville Godwin, USA* is that a man who plays a musical instrument or sings is unlikely to be promoted. This pattern of behavior may seem completely confused on its face, but as a general rule it is probably true that musicians are less capable military leaders than non-musicians.

To a large extent, this system is founded on irrational considerations, but it does have some basis in those situations where there is simply no other criterion upon which the sovereign might rely. If it is decided that a particular type of person is the type that is likely to do well in some given future situation, the selection of personnel in terms of approximation to that type is not unintelligent. In practice, this system of selection is, of course, highly uncertain. The decisions regarding types may be wrong, and persons selected by types may shift from one role to another as they are advanced. Nevertheless, in the face of the complexities that confront the sovereign in supervisory situations of extreme uncertainty, the selection-by-type rule may be preferable to no rule at all.

CHAPTER 24

EXTERNAL CHECKS

Persons outside a given hierarchy are likely to know less about its operations than its members, and their interest seems likely to be sporadic. On the other hand, these people are not likely to consider the effects on their own careers which the passing on of a particular piece of information will have. Information obtained from outsiders will be defective in certain respects, but these will be defects that are different from those that characterize internal information available to the sovereigns. Inaccuracy rather than distortion is likely to characterize external information. The sovereign will find it useful to compare internal and external sources of information.

USE OF THE PRESS

This external source of information need not consist solely of gossip. If the hierarchy operates in a country with an active and free press, and if it is important enough as an institution to make "news," articles in the newspapers are likely to be useful. Such accounts will normally be both more reliable and more detailed than mere gossip, but, unless the organization is extremely important, such articles will be rare. In the United States, with its vast "trade" press, almost every large organization is mentioned occasionally in some publications. Insofar as this occurs, it often is accompanied by organizational efforts to control the information available to the press, and hence to manipulate what the public reads about the workings of the hierarchy.

Generally information that appears can be divided into two classes by the politician: that which informs him about the activities of his inferiors and thus improves his control over them, and that which reflects discredit on his own part in the operation and which, in turn, damages him in the dealings with his sovereign, whether this be Congress, consumers, or other groups. The intelligent bureaucrat will try to promote the first type of information and to suppress the second type.

In practice it will be difficult for the bureaucrat to encourage the press in its provision of information to him and to discourage it in its exposé of him. Generally speaking, any criticism of one member of his hierarchy will reflect upon all members, including the sovereign. Because of this, the attitude of the politician on information about his subordinates will be ambivalent.

He will welcome the opportunity to learn about incorrect behavior by subordinates, because in this way control over them can be increased. At the same time, the bureaucrat will find his relations with those to whom he must report endangered. In each case, the bureaucrat must try to balance these two considerations against each other. Most modern executives tend to place too much emphasis on the negative aspect of press information. Organizations would probably be more efficient if executives took the lead in encouraging journalists to poke around through the lower levels of the hierarchy.

THE USE OF PETITION

Even in countries without freedom of the press, formal institutions for obtaining the opinion of persons outside the governmental machine usually exist. Most absolutist governments in the European tradition had a parliament, council, or advisory board of some sort, the bulk of whose members were not members of the government as such. The use of such institutions varied widely, but their existence was based on the recognized need to check on the king's ministers. The right of petition also served this function. The presentation of a formal petition to the king in which his ministers were alleged to have done something injurious to the petitioner was common practice in most European monarchies.

It is interesting also to note that this technique is retained and developed in Communist states. Letters to *Pravda* in Russia, or the *Jen Min Jih Pao* in China, serve this function. Such letters must, of course, concern themselves exclusively with the conduct of lower-level officials. But the letters are read, and something in the way of an investigation is carried out, and some action is frequently taken. It should of course be recognized that the petition system in absolutist governments can serve as a control on only lower officials, not as any protection for the liberties of the people generally. Only if the lower-level officials do things which oppress the people *and* which are contrary to the desires of the rulers does the petition system provide any assistance.

A somewhat similar function is performed in the United States by the custom of writing to congressmen about the conduct of particular governmental agencies. This is not a petition in the sense of that used in absolutist governments. The people who write the letters here are members of a group sovereign actually writing to one of their hierarchical inferiors, and the time and energy put in by most congressmen in dealing with constituents' letters is an indication of this fact. Nevertheless, such letters serve as an external source of information to higher-level officials in the government bureaucracy, information about the performance of lower-level officials that might not otherwise be readily obtainable.

ORGANIC CHECKS

Most governments also make some usage of organic checks—that is to say, external checks that are built formally into the overall bureaucratic structure. The inspector general's role in the army provides an example. Perhaps the most efficient of all such systems was that of the Imperial Chinese Censorate; a brief description of its functioning will serve as a general explanation of all such systems.

The censorate consisted of an hierarchy of bureaucrats separate from, much smaller than, but parallel to the regular governmental organization. These officials (censors) had only one function: to catch regular bureaucrats in some form of misconduct. If the censors decided that a certain official was dishonest, disobedient to imperial commands, or incompetent they could impeach the official to his superiors. This impeachment was normally followed by a formal investigation, after which action was taken against the individual impeached or against the censor for false accusation. In order to make the system applicable for all levels of the line hierarchy, each censor had the right to send a sealed letter to the emperor. Such letters could not be intercepted, although if the high official accused in one of these letters should convince the emperor that the charges were false, he could have the censor punished.

The system included an "incentive plan" for the censors since the quickest route to promotion in the censorate was a successful denunciation of a high official. Promotion in this case might mean movement out of the censorate altogether and into the top of the regular hierarchy. A censor who failed to find anything wrong with the area of the regular bureaucracy that he was assigned to investigate was likely to be overlooked in future appointments to higher posts. On the other hand, the possibility of severe punishment (usually beheading) for false accusations made the censors consider the situations investigated carefully before bringing an impeachment.

The initial selection of the censors was also highly rational. China operated with a system of civil service examinations, and appointment to high office was more or less restricted to those who had passed these examinations successfully. At each national examination, the three top scholars were especially honored in some way. Quite frequently this took the form of appointment to the censorate. Thus, the appointee was normally more intelligent and better indoctrinated with the traditional political philosophy of the bureaucracy than the average official who entered the regular line. The appointee to the censorate was also young and idealistic, and more important, since he had not served in the regular bureaucracy, he had had no opportunity of forming strong attachments to other officials. He was, therefore, ideally qualified to watch other officials.

The overall effects of this system of checks can be imagined. It was a brave official who took action that would cause him serious damage if it came to the emperor's knowledge. At the same time, the emperor was not bothered by the necessity of continually inspecting the administrative apparatus. It should be emphasized, however, that this system was not designed, nor did it function, to provide protection to the citizens or subjects. The system put pressure on the officials to carry out their orders, and it protected the subjects only insofar as the sovereign's orders were beneficial to them. It is to the credit of the censors, however, that they not infrequently sent in petitions in which they criticized the emperor's own conduct. Such petitions, ritually, ended with a supplementary request for the execution of the petitioner for his presumption. This latter request was granted often enough to make the submission of such a petition an indication of considerable moral courage.

Outside China such complex and well-designed external checks are rare. This is a defect in non-Chinese systems. The censorate surely caused the Chinese civil service to function more in accord with the policy of the sovereign than would have been the case without the censorate. Similar institutions could be expected to serve the same purpose effectively in other systems of bureaucracy.

The only major example in Western societies of an institution at all analogous to the Chinese censorate is the auditing process. The hiring of an outside firm or, in large hierarchies, the maintenance of a special auditing department, to check on the larcenous propensities of the lower-level employees, the yearly audit by an independent accounting firm on behalf of the stockholders; all of these in form look rather like the censorate. This external check is, however, confined to one aspect of the business, and it does not check on "policy" matters. The cost accountants, who may be lumped with the auditors organizationally, do check on policy matters, and, as we have shown, provide to management much of the basic information upon which supervision is exercised. The cost accountants occupy, however, a position more or less in line of command, and cannot really be considered an external agency.

	Plane design A	Plane design B	Plane design C
Engines			
Airframe			
Electronics			

THE CRISSCROSS SYSTEM

There is one method of obtaining external checks that has been incorporated in most modern organizations. I shall call this the crisscross system, but it might be more generally recognized if it were referred to as the staff system. The name "crisscross system" seems preferable here for three reasons: In the first place, the term is a more general one than "staff." The system has existed in many places (including China, where it existed alongside the censorate) without being called the staff system, and the use of this latter term might be overly restrictive. Second, crisscross is a more descriptive term since the crossing of the channels of command is the distinctive characteristic of the system that I wish to emphasize here. Third, the term "staff" carries with it, in popular usage, several implications that are misleading.

The crisscross system is characterized, as I have said, by the crossing of command channels. The organization of the Department of State may be cited as illustrative of this system. In the department, in addition to the geographical subdivisions, there are various "functional" divisions, such as the economic division, the visa division, etc. In this manner, the activity of an individual bureaucrat in the foreign service, say, is subject, ideally, to his geographical superiors at various stages of the hierarchy but also to the superior in charge of the functional division covering the field of the activity.

Superficially, this scheme has a great deal of attractiveness, and this appeal probably accounts for its presence in many large bureaucracies. As another example, one of the major aircraft companies, a few years ago, put its engineers in a very large room. The floor of this room had been painted with lines forming a matrix. The engineers were then placed in this matrix as their tasks dictated. A simplified model of this system is shown in the matrix above. Again the idea behind this organization scheme seems superficially to be an attractive one.

There are several drawbacks. The first problem concerns the choice facing the individual bureaucrat who receives contradictory orders from the two

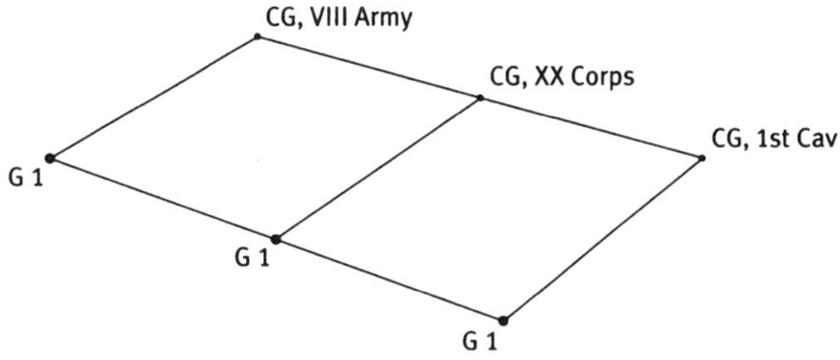

chains of command to which he is subject. It can be imagined that orders would never conflict, but surely it would be much more realistic to say that orders would never coincide. If the system is to function at all well, there must be some "rule" that determines which of the chains of command will be the primary one and which one secondary.[1]

This problem is one for the individual politician within the hierarchy. Looking at the system from the point of view of the sovereign at the apex of the whole administrative pyramid, there are additional problems. In the first place, the establishment of what amounts to a dual chain of command involves manpower difficulties. Twice as many supervisors are required. In reality, this is probably one of the reasons for the prevalence of the system. There is clearly the possibility of having more high-ranking officers. With a sufficiently elaborate system of staff organization, everyone can be a general. This dilution of quality of the higher-ranking personnel can be taken as a desideratum from the point of view of junior officials. The fact that the standard organization chart places the staff, not as directly subordinate to the sovereign, but almost as a part of the sovereign, may also increase its attraction. If such charts were drawn as illustrated above, staffs would perhaps seem less desirable.[2]

Another illusion that appears to be common and which contributes to the growth of the staff or crisscross concept of organization is the feeling that,

1. A complex rule under which the orders received through one chain will be obeyed in certain circumstances, and the orders received through the other, in other circumstances is theoretically possible, but is probably not practical. A system under which one chain of command confines its orders to one sphere, and the other deals with matters outside that sphere, is quite possible if there is some clear and unambiguous method of demarcating the two spheres.

2. The diagram contains only one staff section and only one "substantive" chain of command, largely because more than one of each would produce a hideously complex diagram. If even diagraming the system in two cases, however, would be too complex, consider trying to operate such a chain of command.

somehow, the "functional" chain of command requires no internal coordination. In fact, of course, various functional specialists require coordination as do other bureaucrats. The specialist on the interpretation of Clause 5 in the Standard Treaty of Friendship, Commerce and Navigation may be able to enforce world-wide conformity in the American government's interpretation of this clause, but this does not mean that our commercial policy is integrated. His activities must be meshed with those of the bureaucrats interpreting the other clauses, and with those involved with other aspects of our commercial policy. Regardless of the method of organization, coordination problems arise, and under the crisscross system additional problems are encountered since the two command structures themselves must somehow be integrated.

The failure to realize this simple fact derives from certain factors that are more or less implicit in the evolution of the crisscross system out of ordinary administrative hierarchies. Let us assume that there exists a simple administrative pyramid. Suppose now that a series of roughly similar problems arise at different parts of the hierarchy. The sovereign feels that these separate problems should be treated on an integrated basis; accordingly, he creates a new position and appoints a person with the explicit task of coordinating these separate but related activities. This new man will find his own channels of command crossing those of the basic organization. No particular problems may arise at this stage. But if the sovereign is satisfied with this solution, he is likely to create other cross-channel officials to deal with similar problems. He will tend to overlook the fact that coordination will be needed among these new positions. The problem of coordination among the various staff organizations will become progressively more important as the number of these organizations mounts. The sovereign, failing to recognize this, may feel inclined to create still more organizations to solve coordination problems.

Another illusion is that staff organizations do not require supervision, because they are a part of the commanding officer, organizationally speaking. Since World War II there has been a steady growth of staff functions of the military organizations, combined with an intermittent but real decline in the fighting part of these organizations. There are a number of reasons for this phenomenon, but certainly a misunderstanding of the staff is one of the more important. If, for example, Congress cuts the army appropriation, instead of making up his own mind how the cut will be borne, the commander orders a staff study. Not unexpectedly, the staff reaches the conclusion that the line organizations should be cut.

As is perhaps evident from the above discussion, in my opinion the criss-cross system of organization is overexpanded in the modern American bureaucracy. Nevertheless, there is a place for the system in an effectively organized hierarchy. Two chains of command do work as external checks on each other. Moreover, this provides two channels of communication from the top to any given person within the hierarchy with the result that any intermediate may be bypassed either in giving orders or in obtaining information. These features are advantageous, but they may be more than offset by the disadvantages previously discussed. The amount of confusion created is likely to exceed the added efficiency that is produced unless great care is taken with the organization of staff functions.

PART 4

CONCLUSION

CHAPTER 25

WHAT TO DO? WHAT TO DO?

It is surely suitable to close this book with a cry for reform. We are saddled with a large and basically inefficient bureaucracy. Improved efficiency in this sector could, looking at the matter economically, raise our national income and improve our rate of growth. Politically, it could both increase the degree of control the citizen, qua voter, has over many fields of our national life and enlarge his personal freedom. This apparent paradox is the result of the peculiar form taken by the inefficiency of bureaucratic free enterprise. This system, which characterizes our present government, leads to a reduction in both individual freedom and central control. A shift to more efficient methods could increase *both* our liberties and our ability to control our future. Reforms are clearly needed. Some possible improvements have been discussed in Part 3, but these have mainly been administrative in nature. The purpose of this chapter is to outline briefly two changes in basic policy which could greatly improve efficiency.

The first of these changes is simply a wider use of local government. This rather simple alteration of our present techniques substantially reduces the "supervisory load" of the average voter. If the voter must elect officials on the basis of their dealings with a thousand problems he will exert less influence on the average problem than he would if there were only a hundred. The great advantage of a federal system of government is that it permits the reduction of the number of problems with which the individual voter must be concerned without reducing the total number of problems dealt with by government. As an illustration let us imagine a government which performs ten services for each of a hundred voters who make up the total population subject to its jurisdiction. The government structure subject to this group sovereign must be large enough to perform a thousand services, and the voter must make judgments of politicians in regard to their efficiency in performing these services. If we resort to a federal system this total can be substantially reduced. Let us suppose that we leave to the central government two services per voter and create ten "local" governments which each perform the other eight services for ten voters. Then each voter must judge candidates for the central government on their ability to perform a total of two hundred services and candidates for local government on their ability to perform eighty.

Even though the second system will require two elections and two sets of candidates, it obviously puts less strain on the voter's ability to supervise his government. If carried to extremes by creating, say, ten levels of government, then the additional elections would probably be more bother than they are worth, but used in moderation this device can very materially improve the voter's control over his subordinates by reducing his total "span of control." Technically there are limits on the possibility of dividing "services" in this way. If diplomacy were devolved to the states, we would cease to have an American policy and acquire fifty state foreign policies. Still, the general objective should be to push governmental functions to the lowest possible organizational level. City and county governments should be given as wide a jurisdiction as possible. State governments should take over as many of the functions which cannot be performed locally as possible, and only the irreducible minimum should be left to the central government. In this way, for any given total scope of government action, we will reduce to the minimum the supervisory task of the voter and maximize the probability that the government will, in fact, do as he wishes.

Switzerland is widely regarded as the best administered of the world's nations. There are a number of reasons for this, but their extensive dependence upon local government units is not the least of them. Starting with a nation which is about the size of one of our states they have radically decentralized governmental functions. Their communes and cantons correspond roughly to our local governments and states, but in general the Swiss canton carries out more governmental tasks than our states, and their communes have a wider scope of activity than our cities and counties. Their federal government, on the other hand, engages in comparatively less action than does our national government. This makes the task of the Swiss voter considerably easier than that of his American counterpart, and he naturally performs it better. Another lesson we might learn from the Swiss concerns the organization of local governmental units. American local governments tend to be complex, not to say chaotic. The voter characteristically must elect a large number of officeholders. Sometimes the list of local candidates at a given election will exceed one hundred. There is no need to make an exact copy of Swiss local governmental institutions, but we could seek an equal degree of simplicity.

These reforms would improve the functioning of our bureaucracy, but it still would not work well. If we, as voters, are to control adequately the activities of our servants in the government a sizeable reduction in the total amount of activities attempted by the governmental apparatus is necessary.

Today most things done by the majority of government employees are not really subject to the control of the people, because it would be beyond the physical capacity of the people even to know about them. Some of these things which the people as a whole do not supervise are carefully watched by various pressure groups, but the bulk of governmental activities are substantially unsupervised. Only the most obvious catch the public eye. We, as the sovereign people, have established a gigantic system of bureaucratic free enterprise, and, as is the rule with such a system, we have little control over the bulk of its activities.

Consider our elected representatives; it is well known that the volume of bills passed by Congress is so great that the average member has no time to read, let alone seriously consider, more than a small fraction of them. The quality of the debates so depressingly reported in the *Congressional Record* emphasizes the impossibility of giving adequate consideration to such a large number of decisions. Not long ago an Indian tribe obtained title to a park in Kansas City by slipping a bill through Congress without the Kansas delegation hearing about it. This is merely a particularly striking example of the results of trying to deal with many more bills than the average congressman can hope to digest. The congressmen would, in fact, exercise more control over the nation if they attempted less.

The bureaucracy itself is a further illustration of the point. The lack of control by our elected representatives over the departments is duplicated at a lower level by the lack of control by the cabinet members over their inferiors. The vast and unwieldly departments are almost beyond the control of their nominal chiefs. Sometimes an extraordinarily intelligent and aggressive secretary will leave his mark on one of these vast organizations, but normally most of the activities of each department are the result of bureaucratic free enterprise rather than central decision. The efficiency experts tell us that the largest possible shovel is not the best tool to move the maximum amount of coal. A man equipped with a reasonably sized shovel can get more work done than a man who attempts to take the maximum amount of coal with each shovelful. Similarly, the largest possible bureaucracy is not the best way to get the most done. If we attempt tasks which are beyond our capacity we will accomplish less than if we tailor our plans to our abilities. Our present bureaucracy is well above the optimum size, and we would have more real control if we were willing to accept more realistic objectives.

The same problem exists, albeit on a smaller scale, at the local level. The City of New York, for example, is really a very large governmental unit and would be hard to run under the best of circumstances. In recent years it had added a collection of new activities with the result that the governing bodies have much less time available to control such basic local government activities as police and sanitation. The City of New York operates a vast collection of apartment buildings, and it is dangerous to walk in Central Park after dark. These two facts are not unconnected. By attempting to do too much the city government is losing its power to carry out even its minimum responsibilities. In local governments as well as in the state and national we must cut our suit to fit our cloth. Only by frankly recognizing the limits on our ability to control giant organizations can we obtain the benefits which can be bestowed by a well-functioning government.

If there are strong rational arguments for dismantling the present overgrown bureaucratic apparatus, the political difficulties are obviously very great. Still, the "historic forces" seem to be working toward this end. From about 1875 to shortly after World War II a trend was visible in the Western world toward attempting to centralize control of all aspects of society in the government. Socialists were, in a sense, the leaders of the movement, but it penetrated into almost all spheres of political thought. During this period problems were normally "solved" by being handed to a government bureau. This movement developed an almost religious mystique, and a fully "planned"—or almost fully "planned"—society was widely thought of as both desirable and inevitable. The drive and sense of direction have now gone out of this movement. I do not believe in extrapolating historical trends, and this one has hardly had time to get established, but we can say that few people now favor expansion of central control in principle.

The general situation, then, is not unfavorable. The drastic reform of our administrative system which is necessary if we are to reach our full potential no longer seems politically impossible. The needed changes are radical, and it is always hard to rearrange institutions dramatically, but the "ideological climate" is more favorable than it has been for many years. The world is an uncertain place, and general predictions are hazardous in the extreme, but there are good prospects for radical reform.

Economic Hierarchies, Organization and the Structure of Production

PREFACE

Many economists have examined the corporation, but in general they have dealt with the size of the corporation and its relationship to the rest of the society. The structure and the interior of the corporation receive much less emphasis in economic writings. It would be fair to state that most economists think if we have a system that keeps the corporations competitive and makes it possible to displace inefficient management, we will be okay.

I don't want to quarrel with this as a statement of general policy. These two criteria are important. Nevertheless, the internal function of the corporation is of interest and perhaps it can be improved, although the reader will find relatively few suggestions to that effect in this book.

In a way, I have turned away from the more general considerations that one thinks of in connection with the work of Coase, Alchian, Demsetz, Jensen, and Meckling, and to the more detailed examination which we get in works such as those of Chandler and Drucker. Chandler is a somewhat odd person to bring in here, because apparently he considers himself a historian, and certainly his work has been of great historic value. On the other hand, he has great insight about the internal functioning of the organizations he studies. He doesn't produce many generalized descriptions of corporations, but he does describe individual corporations and the way things change over time. Nevertheless, his level of insight regarding the functioning corporation is significant enough to be noted by all students. The same is true of Drucker, although he does not claim to be a historian. His work, however, shows deep insight into the functioning of corporations.

The collection of economists named before Chandler or Drucker are much more conscious economic theorists. Nevertheless, they have mainly dealt with the external relations of the corporation, counting the relations between the corporations and whoever is residual claimant as part of the external relations. This is not a criticism of their work, but it is not what this book is about. My objective here is to turn attention to the interior of the corporation. The reader may think that my questions outnumber my solutions; and I won't quarrel with that. The questions are, however, important. Asking questions, frequently the first step, is as important as resolving them.

I have deviated from the current fashion of books by not providing much in the way of mathematics or notation. Although in this I follow my own personal tradition, the elimination of formal mechanism is perhaps more sizable here than usual. Organizing my thoughts into formal notation would do little or nothing to aid readers. In most cases, data are presently insufficient for actual calculating or, even when they are, the strict relationship between various variables is unknown. Therefore, many different equations could be written for the same English language proposition.

Adding these equations in might mislead by implying that the particular relationship shown by the chosen equation is the one that exists. In any event, there aren't many of them, nor are there many figures or tables. I hope this will not cause any great difficulty for the readers even though it does give the book an appearance different than most of the more modern books in these fields.

In conclusion, I should apologize briefly for one aspect of my style. I regularly tell anecdotes. One reason is that I believe it makes for easier reading. The other reason is retention: a given idea will often be retained in the reader's memory longer if attached to a mnemonic. Because this style is currently not in vogue in economics, however, my use of anecdotes has been criticized. In response, I would like to point out that the singular of ***data*** is ***datum*** or anecdote. If the reader warms up to these anecdotes, and therefore finds the book easier to read and remember, I will have achieved my objective.

In closing I should like to thank Margaret Chacon and Shirley McEwen for their assistance, as well as my research assistant Josh Gotkin, and two anonymous referees selected by the publisher who had very helpful comments.

CHAPTER I

INTRODUCTION

The first book I ever wrote—although the second book to get published—was *The Politics of Bureaucracy*, a study of large hierarchies. Although it is now partially obsolete, many of its parts have still not been fully integrated into the existing literature. This book is not a sequel, but is an effort to reconsider the whole problem from the beginning. It will deal with a number of problems that were not considered there: for example, why we have large hierarchies. There is also the problem of why so many hierarchies are small.

Indeed, if we look at most human activities, we will find a mixture of different-sized hierarchies. For instance, my house was built by a large company that builds houses all over the United States. When it needed minor repairs I hired a painter, an individual entrepreneur who normally works with one helper. Incidentally, this painter works for the large corporation as well.

Governments also have this extreme mix. Liechtenstein and the government of the Soviet Union are different-sized hierarchies, of course, and do not perform exactly the same function, but they are both governments.

If we turn to the other parts of the economy or the society, we find the same kind of complicated arrangement. Family organizations vary between the extended family of some oriental societies to the tiny and rapidly shifting "family" that we see in Colombia. Church organizations range from the gigantic centralized hierarchy of the Roman Catholic Church to the usually quite small (sometimes even tiny) organizations in the evangelical Christian movement. Presumably all of them are at least reasonably efficient since they all stay in existence. Any theory of hierarchies must deal with the various sizes. It must also explain why we have hierarchies at all.

It is traditional in studies of this sort to begin with the survey of the existing literature. In this case, the existing literature is not very large if one considers theory rather than description. Descriptive accounts of various hierarchies, together usually with some general statements about how well they function or how they could be improved, are common throughout the history of social literature.

Polybius, for example, devoted some fifty pages to discussing the constitution of the Roman Republic and the military organization which was in those days the largest part of the Roman government.[1] A similar impulse to describe various government organizations and remark about their positive or negative qualities has persisted to the present day; indeed, the literature on the subject is extensive. The formal theory, however, is extremely thin in this literature as it was in Polybius's time.

Since Ronald Coase's seminal article,[2] the idea that firms in the economy exist to minimize transaction costs has been important. As far as I know, no one has formally applied that particular model to either governmental hierarchies or such things as the Roman Catholic Church, but surely the ideas behind it have wide application.

The internal structure of all hierarchies have at least some structural similarity. William Niskanen, who for many years was employed by the Department of Defense as a research economist,[3] became director of economics for the Ford Motor Company. He told me that sociologically the two organizations were almost identical.

But if the transaction model has not been much applied outside of the economic area, it has already developed difficulties there. The Yarbroughs,[4] in a very thorough survey of various points of view, list five theories that have developed out of transaction costs, although only one of them is listed as "transaction cost."

A significant characteristic of all five is that they are more accurately described as points of view, or perhaps observations, than as theory. In fact, their first category, "transaction costs," contains a number of different strains. First is the view normally credited to Williamson and his students, that highly specified forms of capital may lead to problems of exploitation that can best be avoided by vertical integration.

Although true to a considerable extent, individual enterprises also exist where this viewpoint does not seem to be important. For this reason Coase has separated himself from Williamson on this matter. Furthermore, in any

1. Ian Scott-Kilbert, trans., *The Rise of the Roman Empire* (London: Penguin, 1979), 302–51.

2. Ronald H. Coase, "The Nature of the Firm," *Economica* 4 (1937): 386–405.

3. Strictly speaking, he was employed by the Institute for Defense Analyses, but since that is paid for by the Department of Defense and his work was mainly military, this is not a matter of much significance.

4. Beth V. Yarbrough and Robert M. Yarbrough, "The Transactional Structure of the Firm—A Comparative Survey," *Journal of Economic Behavior and Organization* 10 (1988): 128.

event, it is hardly a general theory of organization, merely a statement that one particular condition would lead to a particular type of organization.

The Alchian-Demsetz view that organizations exist in their present corporate form largely to monitor shirking undoubtedly has much to commend it, but, again, it is only a partial theory. It argues that ultimate control should be in the hands of the residual claimant, but tells you little or nothing else about the organization. Both of these theories, as indeed the rest, will be discussed later in the book.

Having dealt with these transactional costs theories, the Yarbroughs turn to the "X-efficiency" literature. This is an intriguing literature in which Leibenstein has been arguing that corporations frequently are not as efficient as they could be because people do not work as hard as they could. It is interesting that at the beginning he normally recommended piecework and now recommends improvement of internal loyalty, bonding, good morals, and so on. To engage in a little long-distance psychoanalysis, I suspect the reason for the change is that in the moderate left (which is his particular milieu), *piecerate* is a bad word, and *bonding*, *loyalty*, and so on, are good words. In any event, this again is not a theory of organization but is a simple statement of one aspect.

The fourth type is the "principal-agent" approach in which it is usually pointed out that the principal and the agent do have at least some difference of interest; hence, control is not likely to be perfect. This is true (and certainly it was emphasized a great deal in my book *The Politics of Bureaucracy*), but again it is not a general theory.

The next view, the "sociological," deals with group organization and the interaction of these dynamics with market forces of the firm-market interface. It is not very theoretical, but anyone reading this literature can certainly learn a good deal about how corporations work in practice.

The final theory is a very abstract area, the "mechanism-design" studies which usually deal with organization in the presence of asymmetric information.

All of these things are interesting and, intriguingly, they are not inconsistent with each other, although students generally regard them as mutually exclusive. All of them could be simultaneously true; all of them are largely correct. None of them, however, can be referred to as a general theory.

Admittedly, this book also will not be a general theory, but it will be much more general than any of the before-mentioned studies. It might be referred to as a general picture in which a large number of pieces of theory are integrated, although the integration is not rigid enough to be referred to as one large theory.

Another difference between this study and the others we have described is that I do indeed plan to deal with all hierarchies and not confine myself to large business corporations. I want to emphasize the things that all hierarchies have in common, and I also want to deal with the many differences between the various kinds of hierarchies.

Before closing this first chapter, I want to devote a few words to eliminating a problem—not one that is difficult, but a problem that often agitates newspapers and their readers. Recently, there have been a number of drastic capital reorganizations. For a while, they were mainly takeover bids, but lately the leveraged buyout has developed. Discussion of this issue in the newspapers tends to be rather alarmist, assuming the rather odd view that buyouts involve literally eliminating parts of the economy.

Let us suppose that the management of some large conglomerate arranges a leveraged buyout in which it borrows immense amounts of money in order to buy all the stock in the corporation, and then sells parts of the conglomerate in order to repay some of the loan. The view is frequently canvassed that the parts sold off will somehow cease to exist and that this immense waste of capital should instead be invested in productive equipment.

The error in the first view is obvious; the error in the second is less obvious because not everyone realizes that when you borrow a lot of money from the bank to buy something, you do indeed reduce the lendable resources of the bank you borrowed it from, but you surely increase the lendable resources of the bankers of the people from whom you buy. There should be no change in the total amount invested unless there is some systematic difference between the amount of money that is normally saved among the purchasers and the sellers.

In general, economic reorganization should be considered as something that may or may not contribute to efficiency, but does not basically change the situation of the customers, the workers (including management), and the people who put up the capital. Of course, these three groups of people overlap. The total number of people working, the total value of the capital, and the total number of customers and the amounts they put up are not greatly changed by even drastic reorganizations such as leveraged buyouts, takeover bids, mergers, bankruptcy, and so on.

Arguments exist about the efficiency of one organization or another, and there are individual winners and losers, but real resources remain unchanged.

Whether the consumers are satisfied or not will depend on the efficiency of the two regimes.

To a degree, the same thing holds true when democratic governments are reorganized. The present move in England to emasculate local governments and shift their power to central government will not totally change the power of the individual English voter or civil servant, although it may well change the efficiency with which the views of the voters are implemented. Similarly, the radical decentralization of governments of both Germany and Japan imposed by the allies in 1945 did not actually reduce the government in size. It switched from a dictatorship in Germany to a democracy and, of course, that radically changed the voters' power, but a switch to a highly centralized democracy would have been just as much of a change. Thus, in general, drastic reorganizations affect efficiency but do not change the physical structure of society.

You can think of the economic hierarchies as a set of organizations in which capital holders, workers, and customers are organized to produce things that the consumers want with—we hope—minimum cost to the workers. Since workers and consumers are basically the same people, there is a question of the tradeoff between their two characteristics. A change from one organization to another can be evaluated in terms of efficiency, or aesthetic or moral characteristics, but it should be realized that these aspects all have the same goal.

Such is also the case with democratic governments and, I might even say, with dictatorships. In the dictatorship, of course, the average person does not have very much weight, but changes in the structure of the dictatorship—once again, mainly in matters of efficiency—do not change the relative importance of the dictator or common citizen. Whether the same could be carried over into religious organizations, such as the Roman Catholic Church and the evangelical churches, I do not know. All churches argue that there is a higher power favoring their particular organization. Conceivably, one of them could be right.

But this is enough of an introduction. Let us now study these various forms of organization. Because of space limitations, this book will deal briefly with various special topics attached to extensive bodies of literatures (for example, what I might call "Williamsonism"), but I do not think the brevity will misrepresent these topics. Students know how to find the detailed literature. Meanwhile, let us go on with the analysis.

CHAPTER 2

WHY HIERARCHICAL ORGANIZATIONS? WHY NOT?

The human race throughout most of its *civilized* history had one large hierarchical organization—the government; under that were several small, and mainly family, economic units in each "state." There was a powerful religious order as well, but usually it was closely integrated with the state. The situation in Europe during the Middle Ages in which the most powerful hierarchical organization was indeed the church, with the governments being a set of relatively smaller hierarchies, was unusual.

Much more common is the close connection of the state and church found in places like Hindu or Islamic principalities. Situations like ancient Sumer, in which the temple was in essence the government of the city-state, are also fairly common.

In general, however, over the history of man, what we think of as purely economic activities were carried on either by one big centralized organization which we can refer to as the state, the church, or the state-church, or by a large number of families working more or less on their own, although frequently with a good deal of supervision from the state. These families might be organized—normally at the behest of the state—into professional guilds, but they would carry out production in a semihousehold way. Occasionally, there would be larger economic enterprises, but they were rare[1] and small compared with the state.

It is still true that the largest organizational hierarchies are governments, but nongovernment hierarchies of great size also exist. McDonald's, for example, is now the world's largest private employer with more than a million people working for it (mostly part-time). General Motors and Exxon are also monster hierarchies that are not part of the government. Historically there were cases of private companies which actually were governments, too. The most conspicuous case is the Company of Merchant Adventurers to the East, with its Dutch equivalent nearly as important. No modern corporation

1. Ships large enough not to be crewed by one family were needed for long voyages from quite early times. Whether experience in operating such ships was important in the organization of other enterprises, I do not know.

is as significant in the world economy as those two organizations were in their time.

Although the traditional order was one large hierarchical organization backed by a number of small groups, today the geni curve of organizational size would be much more shallow. On the average,[2] governments are still the largest organizations,[3] but there are very large private organizations. Why the mix?

If we look at governments alone, the problem is similar. In the first place, there are many large, medium, and small states at any given point in time. If we take some specific period, we will normally find some trend for the average size to get bigger or alternatively for the average size to get smaller, but there is no obvious long-term trend at all.

Of course, it is true that the world's population is now much larger than it was in the days of Sumer and is more integrated by efficient transportation. As a result, almost by definition the average size of the state today is larger when measured by population. China, however, has a smaller percentage of the world's population than it did in the reign of Chien Lung. With respect to geographic area, the largest state that ever existed was the Mongol Empire in the thirteenth century, and the combined Portuguese-Spanish Empire ruled by Philip II was the second largest. Both fell apart.

The twentieth century has been a period in which large states have fallen apart and have been replaced by small states. Russia is the unique example of a state that increased in effective size, and its gains were modest. In addition, its empire is currently disintegrating.

Thus, if we look at nation-states in the large, we find the same phenomenon as in the market: that is, a wide mix of different sizes. In this case, however, it has been characteristic of almost the entire history of mankind, whereas, as I said before, until recently the economy was organized into two size categories: the state in its economic manifestation, and the households.

But even this does not give adequate emphasis to the radical size differences that we see in political areas. Some believe, simply by definition, that only one government can exist in a given geographic area. Sometimes American political scientists say this, which is astonishing.

2. There is a significant overlap, with Liechtenstein much smaller than General Motors. As far as I know, however, in each state the government is the largest hierarchy.

3. This may not have been true in the late nineteenth century in the United States. The combination of the railroads, as the first really gigantic private enterprises, and the federal system may have led to the largest organizations being private rather than governmental.

Geographic decentralization, which we call federalism, is quite common. It is not even restricted to such democracies as the United States and Switzerland. Most governments that Karl Wittfogel discussed in *Oriental Despotism* granted the individual farm-villages self-government in a wide range of activities.[4] Indeed, as a general rule, even a large city would officially be a federation of such self-governing villages (what we would call neighborhoods) taking care of many things which in Tucson (the city where I live) are the responsibility of the city government. The result is that in respect to certain minor matters, a citizen of Peking actually has more control over his government than this citizen of Tucson whose vote is diluted by votes of 200,000 others in a single unified government.

Here again is variety. The Communist Russian government, unlike the Communist Chinese government, did not permit this kind of local autonomy, although it made some sort of pretense toward doing so.[5] In democracies, France has always been notable as an area of great centralization, although it has less right now than it once did. England, if anything, is increasing the degree of central control over the local government. Again, the question of why we observe these different forms of government is an open one.

Note that when we are talking about governmental structure of this sort, the citizen does not have as much control over the size of the governments to which he is subject as he does over the size of the economic hierarchies with which he deals. The individual is completely free to decide to invest his money in a fruit stand operated by one man (perhaps himself) or in stock of General Motors. He does not have the same freedom to decide the size of his government.

If we consider the individual in the market as an employee rather than as an investor, then his freedom to decide on the size of the organization he deals with is not quite as unhampered as it is for the investor, but it is still pretty free. In Tucson, I could take a job in a local restaurant or with American

4. Karl Wittfogel, *Oriental Despotism: A Comparative Study of Total Power* (Yale University Press, 1957).

5. I do not wish to exaggerate the Chinese case. There is no doubt that the village under the old empire had a good deal more control over its affairs than it does under the Communist government. Nevertheless, it is still true that local people have quite a bit of control over local matters. Wittfogel explained the system under the ancient regime as a result of declining marginal utility of administration. He argued that large hierarchies simply did not work very well in their bottom levels; hence, it was sensible to abandon the bottom levels.

Airlines. In order to get an equivalent choice of governments, I would have to move.

It used to be said that the government must have a monopoly of the means of coercion. Certainly there is no such government in the United States. If I commit a crime, I might be arrested by a local policeman, state policeman, or federal policeman, depending on various details of the charge against me. All three of these levels of government institute coercion against their citizens, and the whole thing works out reasonably well.

We have here a rather astonishing difference in organization of coercion. In the United States, if you live in a city, you will have a police department where the head is an appointee of an elected government. The state and national police forces are similarly organized. If you live in the county, on the other hand, the police department is headed by a directly elected official called a sheriff, who in many cases is the most important official in the county. On the other hand, in many states both of these police forces will bring you before the same judges.

In other states the police force as a whole is fairly centralized. France is one example. France does not require anything in the way of despotic government, although the despotic government in Russia does, indeed, have a centralized police. When talking about decentralized police, I might mention Mexico, a neighbor to Tucson. They have two police forces: one deals solely with traffic and the other with all nonvehicular crimes.

It is not obvious that the state should or will control all the things we normally think of as state activities. In traditional Islamic communities, the law is not subject to legislative control by the state; it was laid down in the Koran as interpreted by an immense number of Islamic scholars. Furthermore, the judges who actually enforce the law are theologically trained and, although the local despot (and Islamic states are normally despotisms) appoints the actual judges, the selection is made from among a narrow list of people who have the necessary theological background.

The great world conqueror Tamerlane, for example, was not in any real sense master of his own household when it came to law or, for that matter, to the organization of the Islamic church in his area. Although the despots could cut people's heads off, and in fact did so, it did not mean that they could change the law as it applied to the ordinary citizens.

Nor is it even necessary that everyone in the state be controlled by the same law. The old Turkish Empire (and for that matter, a number of other countries, although the Turkish Empire had the most formal arrangement) was federalized on a nongeographical basis, that is, by religion. For the Maronite Christians, then, many of the laws that controlled their lives were those of the Maronite church. The church, in fact, maintained a small police force and had a tax system to support its governmental activities. These laws would be quite different from those imposed upon, say, the Jews by their religious organization.

Once again we find an immense variety of different organizations of various sizes and different structures. The question of why this diversity exists is important.

Throughout history most people seemed simply to have thought that this was the feature of things and did not ask any questions about it. As far as I can see, the first serious inquiry was confined to the question of why we have different kinds of economic organization, and that was asked in 1937 by Ronald Coase. He not only asked the question in his famous article "The Nature of the Firm," he gave a partial answer. His originality in even asking the question should be emphasized. The article went totally unnoticed at the time, and then for many years was footnoted but apparently not read.[6]

The significant problem that Coase dealt with was probably not raised before Adam Smith wrote *The Wealth of Nations* in 1776. Before Smith, the market was thought of as simply a disorderly process, and when you thought of economic or social order, you thought of government structure or perhaps of the church. Smith pointed out that the market itself is an orderly process, and most economists would argue that it is more orderly than most other organizations.

But the question that Coase posed to himself was why we have large organizations that produce automobiles, say, instead of a large number of small enterprises, each of which performs some particular operation in connection with the automobile and then bargains with other people. For example, General Motors buys the frames for its cars from A. O. Smith of Milwaukee. Its car bodies, on the other hand, are produced by a wholly owned subsidiary, Fisher Body. Why the difference? Indeed, why do we not have several tiny

6. Ronald H. Coase, "The Nature of the Firm," *Economica*, n.s., 4 (1937): 386–405, esp. 392.3 and note 5. That Coase's answer is only partial is a fact apparently known to only a very few people, but Ronald Coase is one of them. See, for example, the R. H. Coase lectures in *Journal of Law, Economics and Organization* (Spring 1988), particularly lectures 2 and 3, pp. 19–47. In lecture 3 he says that he is working on a complete answer to this question (pp. 33–47).

specialized enterprises, each performing one task on either the frame or the body under supervision of a general contractor.

Many economic enterprises have been and are decentralized; indeed, most buildings are put up this way. Monster contracting organizations may actually have comparatively few direct employees, most of them engaged in supervising the subcontractors. The garment trade in New York is another example, with large numbers of specialized enterprises that perform just one operation on a bundle of textiles and then pass it on to another organization to perform another operation.

Before Whitney revolutionized the arms industry, it was organized in this way, with Birmingham, the center of the world arms trade in those days, having no large enterprises and a large number of small-scale entrepreneurs who performed particular procedures. Indeed, the whole putting-out system was an example of that kind of thing.

If we look at the world today, we find that there is not only a wide diversity in size of economic enterprises (we will confine ourselves to that field for the time being), but that it changes from time to time. Not long ago, there was a fad in which large conglomerates were set up to deal with different types of business under the same corporation. Special theories, in fact, were developed regarding the efficiency of this situation (to be dealt with later).

At the moment, these conglomerates are rapidly being dismantled by people who have discovered that the individual units in the conglomerate, if sold off, are worth more than the conglomerate as a whole. Clearly, this is a case in which we do not have a sound argument for any particular size of organization. Furthermore, the answer to the question of whether conglomerates are efficient in their approach to the capital market (which was earlier thought to be true) or whether the disintegration of them is efficient (which is the current fad) is by no means obvious.

We can go further here. Most American businesses started as small, closely held enterprises and only became public later in their expansion. Again, general theories were developed as to why public holdings and the stock exchange were a highly efficient method as opposed to the closed corporation with a few active managers owning all the stock. At the moment, the leveraged buyout, in which management converts a publicly held corporation into a closed company which management owns (subject to immense mortgages), is all the rage.

Note that these two changes are correlated to some extent. Some of the managements who built up big conglomerates are now organizing leveraged buyouts for the specific purpose of selling off large parts of that conglomerate and then running the smaller unit. Altogether, it would appear that we need a good deal of improvement in our understanding of the theory of hierarchies. As we proceed in this book, we will find many more puzzles as well as some fairly simple and straightforward answers.

Even if we turn to internal organization, we find a somewhat similar diversity. I mentioned before that McDonald's was now the world's largest employer. Strictly speaking, this is not true, because McDonald's, although it does indeed own a large number of its hamburger stands, operates an even larger number by way of franchise. Other companies are almost entirely franchise operations; still others are almost entirely managed directly. There are also organizations like Ace Hardware that operate by "reverse franchising" where the individual stores own the central organization.

There are arguments for the efficiency of all these types of arrangements, and if we look at the world in general we normally find that there is a change in one direction or the other going on: some companies will be buying up their franchises, and other companies will be selling owned retail units to potential franchise operators. La Paloma, an immense and expensive resort hotel in Tucson, originally was built as a Westin franchise. Now it has been bought by Westin and is to be directly operated in the future.

This apparent lack of stable rules as to what size hierarchy is most likely to survive in business is duplicated by a similar lack of stability in government. Changes in government tend to be much slower and reverse themselves less frequently. In the United States, certainly since about 1930, for example, the central government has been slowly (some people would say *very* slowly) growing. On the other hand, France, since de Gaulle became dictator in 1958, has been moving in the other direction.

In both the United States and England efforts to move toward more decentralization have been under way, but these efforts have had little effect. If we turn to centralized states, Yugoslavia, which was a centralized despotism under Tito,[7] has been disintegrating. Russia may be following the same road.

The major example of governmental shrinkage in recent years was the abandonment of their empires by France, England, Belgium, and Holland. A myth claims that these new states won their own independence by fighting. With few exceptions, this is untrue. The British army still maintains that the

7. He organized his despotism geographically, but the different governments of the "federated states" did as they were told.

only colony they lost was the United States. This is not entirely correct; in some areas there was enough fighting so the British rather got tired of continuing. Malaya and Ireland, and possibly Kenya, are examples. In general, however, the independence movement was essentially British. The Congress Party of India, after all, was started by the British.

Even the nation-states in Europe are showing some slight tendencies to break up. England and France are making gestures to Scotch, Welsh, and Breton nationalism. At the moment these are only gestures. Spain, of course, has a decentralized constitution, and nationalism in both the Catalonia and the Basque regions is a real phenomenon.

Most of the new countries carved out of the colonial empires have little or no reason for their present boundaries. They are simply administrative units set up for the convenience of the colonial power and have little to do with linguistic or economic coherence. So far they have largely remained intact, but the general inefficiencies of their governments are such that this may not continue. Angola was, and may be again by the time you read this, in the grips of what can be regarded as either a civil war or an invasion by a neighboring power, with the main fighting being between two linguistic groups.

In other words, we do not know what an optimal size is in any of these areas. In order to avoid disappointment, I should explain that the reader will not find a complete answer in this book. What we will discover is that a number of factors point toward larger entities, and another number point toward smaller. Also, a number of factors indicate that changes, regardless of what they are, *may* cause improvements in efficiency. Factors that point toward either large or small jointly produce wide ranges in which there is little difference in efficiency, and the efficiency that is obtained shifts back and forth.

But the title of this chapter asks the question of why we see these hierarchies, and so far I have merely discussed the existence of many different kinds and sizes. We now turn to some preliminary thoughts on why they exist.

Students of ancient history have almost certainly seen the famous picture produced by Egyptian artists somewhere around 3000 BC, showing a gigantic stone block for one of the pharaoh's pyramids being towed by what looks like several hundred peasants pulling ropes; a man with a whip stands on top of the block supervising them.[8] We can all agree that this is a hierarchy, and

8. There are also some fellahin putting rollers under the stone, pouring water on the road, and so on. To simplify my example, I leave them out.

we can also see why it existed—granted, of course, that a pharaoh had the power and desire to create the pyramid.

In this case, matters are simple. The hierarchy consists of one overseer and a large number of peasants, who, as far as we know, were conscripted for this activity. This hierarchy was, however, only part of a much larger one.

But consider the situation if a somewhat different organization had been followed. Suppose that the overseer, instead of simply ordering a labor gang, stood on his stone and offered whatever he thought was a suitable amount of money to every laborer who was willing to grab the rope and pull hard. We can even assume that instead of using a whip to encourage laggards, he simply fired them. Would this be a hierarchy? I think the answer is no, unless the particular combination of workers and overseer lasted for some time.

My definition of *hierarchy*, then, is a large number of men/women who stay together for some time, are organized into various ranks of leaders, and are led. The reader is free to use other definitions in different contexts, but if he wants to understand this book, he should remember my definition.

Suppose that the overseer had bargained with a set of small labor gangs, each of which would pull on one rope. Suppose each of these gangs had a manager and totaled ten men. Twenty such gangs are necessary to move the stone. Here is a set of small hierarchies that is each permanent but that makes contracts with various overseers to move stones.

Clearly, the small groups are hierarchies, but is there a hierarchy the whole made up of twenty of them pulling a given stone? I would say not. Provided that this grouping is purely temporary, it is a market organization. Thus, we can have small hierarchies organized for large projects by the market. The opposite is also true. When large corporations hire casual labor for specific tasks, we would have an example.

The building industry is an extreme example of market organization. Consider the situation that I, as a householder in Tucson, face in the event that I need some kind of professional assistance around my house. Since I moved in, I have hired a landscape gardener, a plumber, and a painter. The painter works on his own, owns his own capital equipment, and has many different customers.[9] The plumber is part of a quite small company, and the same is true of the landscape gardener. All three of them operate in highly competitive environments, and in a real sense, so do I. I have to compete for

9. He also has a helper for most, though not all, jobs.

their services by offering them prices and conditions of work that are as good as they can get elsewhere.

Note that there were only small transaction costs in dealing with these people. I asked a couple of neighbors who would be a good painter and then took their recommendation. I did not even chaffer significantly with the painter about his price or the details of his job. He had a good reputation and presumably wanted to keep it; hence, I accepted what was at that time the market price. I imagine if he had been hired by a big building conglomerate in Tucson such as Fairfield (and he does do work for them), they would have done somewhat better than I. On the other hand, Fairfield has to pay the salary of an expert to make these arrangements.

I simply selected the plumber from the Yellow Pages. The woman who answered the telephone gave me their basic price level almost immediately when I told her what I wanted. I assumed that this was the market price. Shopping around did not seem worthwhile, just as it does not seem worthwhile for me to shop around when I go to a supermarket.

The landscape architect was a somewhat more complex case because I was going to have my yard completely redone and that would cost money. I got three bids from three different landscape architecture firms. The transaction costs here were, I think, quite good because all three firms produced drawings of what they proposed to do.

All of this appears very different from the pyramid stone. The obvious difference is that literally the only technologically available means for the pharaoh to move his stone was to have it pulled by a large number of human beings or animals. He had to have them all doing the same thing at the same time. But the difference is not as great as you might think. Many highly integrated jobs require people either to do the same thing at the same time or, more commonly, to do a number of different integrated things in an appropriate time pattern, and these jobs are based on contracts with small entities.

Fairfield, a company constructing many houses in the vicinity where I live, needs to get all the work on any given house done in the right time sequence. There can be no long delays between the completion of one job and the start of another nor can there be long overlaps where the workers on one job wait for the previous job to be finished. Nevertheless, they use contracts with several small specialized contractors rather than maintaining a large hierarchical organization themselves.

Fairfield is not the only case in point. Near where I live, a new bridge is going in to replace an older one. There, too, is much skilled labor and complicated capital equipment. In any event, the capital equipment is owned by a number of enterprises which, because of the expenses involved, can hardly be called small, but certainly smaller than the contractor who is building the bridge.

Presumably, everyone who is reading this book has read Coase's "The Nature of the Firm," although many of you may not have read his more recent thoughts on the subject in the *Journal of Law, Economics and Organization.*[10] His position on the theory of the firm is frequently somewhat oversimplified into the view that the firm eliminates the costs of chaffering and bargaining between parties, that is, the transaction costs; hence, the firm is an effort to substitute hierarchical control for direct bargaining. Coase is, of course, a strong proponent of the market, as were the people under whom he studied and who originally published the article. Nevertheless, they feel that a larger organization—in many cases, skipping the market process and substituting a hierarchy—will do better.

Note that I said "in many cases." Coase is fully aware of the existence of many other cases in which this does not work well, and I think he would agree with my contracting case as an example. With competition, particularly competition on both sides of the market (as there is in the contracting case with many contractors and many people who, say, own steam shovels and are looking for specific steam shovel-type contracts), the process of bargaining and contracting and chaffering is apt to be short and quick. The market itself will provide information as to an appropriate price and an appropriate quality. The fact that both parties can easily switch to another agreement with someone else means that across the market relatively little attention is devoted to attempting to make specific bargains in each case which are superior to those normally found. Note that I say "relatively little." There still is some, and indeed the fact that some people are attempting to do a little bit better than the existing prices is what keep those prices in accord with shifting conditions. Many people, however, free ride on other people's surveying of prices, chaffering, bargaining, and so on.

Still, transaction costs are significant here. If the pharaoh had his stones moved by the market method I suggested earlier (in which a supervisor

10. Ronald H. Coase, "The Nature of the Firm: Origin," *Journal of Law, Economics and Organization*, 4 (Spring 1988), 3–17; "The Nature of the Firm: Meaning," *Journal of Law, Economics and Organization*, 4 (Spring 1988), 19–32; "The Nature of the Firm: Influence," *Journal of Law, Economics and Organization*, 4 (Spring 1988), 33–47.

simply hired people one at a time for movement of one stone), there would be considerable delays while the work gangs were being put together, and these delays would be significant enough so that the work gangs themselves would develop into semipermanent institutions with only a little movement of labor from one gang to another.

The same thing develops to a considerable extent in building contracting. A number of independent contractors work mainly for Fairfield and are assigned the same supervisor. To anticipate what we will be saying later in Chapter 10 on rent seeking, however, Fairfield is a well-managed company and would see to it that these arrangements are not truthfully permanent. Too-close relationships between the supervisor and the people he supervises are apt to lead to "family" arrangements under which costs may be somewhat higher and productivity somewhat lower than if the situation is always kept in a state of at least some strain.

We can make up a list of situations in which a large relatively permanent organization is best fitted for the job. One set of cases contains situations where for some technical reason—whether it is the size of the pharaoh's stone[11] or the production line first introduced on a large scale by Ford—individual bargaining with each single person at each stage is likely to evoke large costs; hence, the optimal structure is a large unit.

Even here, however, it is unclear whether these large units are necessary. Perhaps one could simply offer prices that would include as part of the contract a fine for breaking off the contract when the stone has been moved only half the distance. Contracts of this sort are rare. Mainly they are confined to actors, singers, and so on. The advantage of a large organization here is nevertheless clear.

It may be that very large organizations like General Motors or Exxon are in fact examples of this high-bargaining-cost situation, although they certainly do not look like it. Perhaps there are advantages in having a central control, but they are by no means obvious.

On the other hand, it is possible to have many purchasers and sellers of discrete entities, whether those entities are restaurant meals or drywall contracting for housing. The market operation would be certainly feasible and highly efficient. The strength of competition on both sides of the market makes it fairly cheap to arrange contracts; hence, transaction costs are small. Obviously, there is a continuum between these two cases.

11. Some of them were above twenty tons.

Oliver Williamson has introduced (and others have followed his lead) the idea that under certain circumstances large organizations are relatively immune to certain types of cheating and lying. I call it "cheating" and "lying." Williamson calls it "opportunistic behavior" and "impacted information."[12] The large hierarchical organization, by bridging a particular gap, eliminates the necessity of complex contractual arrangements which would be desirable without the unified control.

This large organization, however, raises other similar problems. Nevertheless, there is considerable truth in Williamson's analysis, and there is a body of empirical evidence that his theory is a factor in establishing large hierarchical organizations in the economy.

I believe, however, that none of these theories are the basic reasons for the large hierarchies evident throughout history, which we call governments. Most governments have been despotisms of one sort or another.[13] Their leaders normally believe that one major function of the government is to get their wishes carried out. As a matter of fact, a large hierarchy is by no means perfect in this regard, as we shall see later, but it does work better than the market.

At the time the organization is set up, the despot usually does not know what his wishes will be next year. An organization that will simply obey orders, then, has its attractions. If the despot waits until next year and then offers monetary rewards for people to do what he wants, he puts himself in the situation where his bargaining power is weak, particularly if his wishes must be kept secret. Thus, a plot to assassinate a neighboring despot, for example, probably would be readily carried out by the previously existing intelligence organization, but advertising for assassins[14] would make it impossible.

Even in cases where secrecy is not necessary, the problems would be real. A despot, after all, has many things on his mind and can only devote a certain amount to each individual project. This gives him disadvantages in dealing

12. Actually, "impacted information" is not exactly the same as lying, because a person on one side of the market may never ask the person on the other side details of his operation. The reason he would not is because he knows he would not get a truthful answer and so "lying" is not a bad term. "Opportunistic behavior" is also not exactly cheating, although it is close enough so that creation of a new word seems unnecessary. I suspect that the use of the two new terms is simply an effort to avoid strong language.

13. See my *Autocracy* (Boston: Kluwer, 1988).

14. The Serene Republic overcame this difficulty. Apparently in its entire history, the Council of Ten never turned down an offer to assassinate one of its enemies by free enterprisers. On the other hand, it did not get very many of them actually assassinated.

with his own bureaucracy, but it gives him even greater disadvantages in an effort to get the market to do something it was not doing before. Thus, the decision which was made by whoever ruled Jericho in 7000 BC to build a strong wall around the city could have, if he had relied on market procedures, put him in a distinctly difficult situation in which probably he would have faced high prices. But simply calling out the citizenry and putting them to work—which presumably is the way it was done[15]—is much simpler.

Thus, it seems that the large state hierarchies in their early days were better adapted to carrying out the wishes of the despot than a market would have been. Note that I am not criticizing the hierarchies in this case. I have no doubt that even such an oppressive government as the Assyrian was, in fact, beneficial for the average person who lived within its bounds. (Note that I say "average." Many probably would have been tortured to death while Assyria was expanding its bounds.) Roads, domestic peace, the prevention of invasions, and a regular system of taxation as opposed to arbitrary exactions are all valuable, and the Assyrians provided them just as the Romans did later.

A similar situation exists with our modern governments. A democracy is not trying to carry out the will of the despot but the rather poorly articulated will of a large number of people. Not being able to predict next year's agenda, however, except to know it will be on a large scale, means that use of the market is difficult.

In one sense, of course, all hierarchies are market organizations. They use market procedures to obtain the individuals who work for them. This, of course, only applies to those in the society who are free to make their own decisions or who, as slaves, are owned by people other than the government, but these people are always a very large part of the government, and in particular they include all the high officials of the government. The pharaoh made his pyramids with conscript labor, but his architects were not drafted.

Large private organizations may be a comparable example. Writers on corporate organization frequently refer to the Napoleon complex of the managers. Even the current tendency to have leveraged buyouts of corporations would mean that individual managers—although they will be managing a smaller corporation—have much more control over it; hence, one could call

15. Of course, this was long before the invention of writing. We know about the wall only because parts of it still exist. It is also possible that the city was governed by democratic means, but if so, they still surely relied on conscription rather than the market to get the wall built.

that another expression of the Napoleon complex. There are, however, very strong market forces that will keep this motive in check.

Another prospect here (to be discussed in detail later) is simply that the large corporation may be more efficient in providing information for potential investors. Actually, we normally know relatively little about the corporations in which we invest, and the Securities and Exchange Commission (SEC), by making ordinary advertising illegal, probably reduces the amount of such information further.[16] Because only a relatively modest number of large corporations exist, however, the investor can more easily invest in a company that is roughly equivalent in prospect to any other large company. The market for control, first discovered by Henry Manne, is important here.

Still, smaller organizations can be effective using relatively temporary contracts, as many cases show. This chapter is titled "Why Hierarchical Organizations? Why Not?" and I cannot say I have given a definitive answer. I take considerable consolation, however, in the fact that Ronald Coase himself has also not definitively answered the question.[17]

16. The SEC, of course, would claim it increases information, but as far as I know no one ever reads the brochures. Indeed, all brochures are required by law to carry in large print a false statement on the first page. This statement, which is required for SEC approval, says that the SEC has not approved the brochure. There are usually other false statements because the writers of the brochure feel that if they make accurate statements of their hopes and plans, the SEC will regard that as too strongly favorable; hence, they put in a falsely modest view. Those rare people who actually do read brochures know this and allow for it, but it is not obvious exactly how much allowance one should make.

17. See the last few pages of his third lecture, "The Nature of the Firm: Influence," 46–47, mentioned before in this text. Both he and I hope to have such a solution eventually, and it is quite possible that one of the readers of this book will do so first.

CHAPTER 3

PARALLEL PROBLEMS

Long ago when I wrote *The Politics of Bureaucracy*, I devoted considerable attention to the loss of control as orders go down or information comes up through a bureaucratic hierarchy.[1] The man supervising three people really cannot know as much as each one does about a particular problem or work unless it is very simple. He is also unable to determine how much attention each person is giving to the job. If he is supervising three people and each of them is supervising three people, the problem is compounded.

Since supervisors do not have perfect control at each stage, to some extent the people in the next stage below will be doing things which their immediate supervisors do not want, which has already deviated from the man at-the-top's position.[2] The deviation increases exponentially as the number of levels is increased.

If we assume, unrealistically, that the individual is able to get his inferiors at each level to do 90 percent of the things he wants and that they only follow their own preferences for 10 percent, then if there are ten stages in this bureaucracy, at the bottom level only 35 percent of the output will be in accordance with the wishes of the top supervisor. On the other hand, if we have a ten-stage hierarchy with each person at each level supervising three at the next level below, we have almost 60,000 people at the bottom, and if 35 percent of their activity is that desired by the man at the top, he receives slightly more than 20,000 times as much activity of the type he desires as he would if he depended on his own labor. The attractiveness of such a hierarchy from the standpoint of the person at the top is obvious. Furthermore, as we will show later, there are a number of techniques whereby he may partially be able to outwit the exponential series.

Nevertheless, hiring 60,000 operators together with nearly 30,000 people in various supervisory roles in order to get a desired output equivalent to

1. Gordon Tullock, *The Politics of Bureaucracy* (Washington, D.C.: Public Affairs Press, 1965; reprint, Lanham, Md.: University Press of America, 1987).

2. By coincidence the deviations from the desires of the lower-level supervisors might lead to accidentally following the desires of the top supervisor in some cases.

TABLE 3-1. *Performance with Different Levels of Control Efficiency*

CONTROL EFFICIENCY	95	90	85	80	75	70	65
No. of people in level 10 carrying out wishes of top-level superior*	35,335	20,589	11,625	6,340	3,325	1,668	795
Percent of people in level 10 carrying out wishes of top-level supervisor	59.9	34.9	19.7	10.7	5.6	2.8	1.3

NOTE: The total number of people in this organization is 88,573 of which 59,049 are at the bottom level actually engaging in activities with respect to the outer world. The remainder are supervisors of one sort or the other. The table makes no attempt to estimate how many times accident would lead to deviation from one of the lower-level supervisor's desires by his inferior to have the inferior force doing what the higher-level supervisor wants.

*Coincidentally, the mistranscriptions of the orders of the supervisor in level 9 might cancel out exactly opposite similar mistranscriptions in the higher level. Thus, the number of people in the lower level doing what the ultimate superior wanted might be greater than shown. But it is equally likely that some of the 40,000 would be doing what the top man wanted if there were no hierarchy at all.

only 20,000 people[3] may not seem to be terribly good performance, and it could be argued that we should do our best to minimize bureaucracy forthwith. Moreover, 90 percent compliance may be too high. Table 3-1 shows the results for a number of different levels of control efficiency. The point of my next few pages, however, is to demonstrate that other forms of organization have similar difficulties of control.

We will begin with a small bureaucracy engaged in an activity that permits division of labor but which is nevertheless reasonably standardized, that is, one in which control problems should be minimal. Let us assume a small task and deal with its small problems with several different organizational structures. Say that we know of a landowner on the outskirts of Tucson who is building houses on his property. In the standard procedure, the houses at any given point in time are at different stages: while some workers are putting in the foundations on one house, other workers are putting up the structure of another house, and still others. There is some resemblance to a production

3. In more exact terms, there are a total of 88,573 people in our hierarchy. Of these, 59,049 are in the bottom layer where they have contact with the outside world.

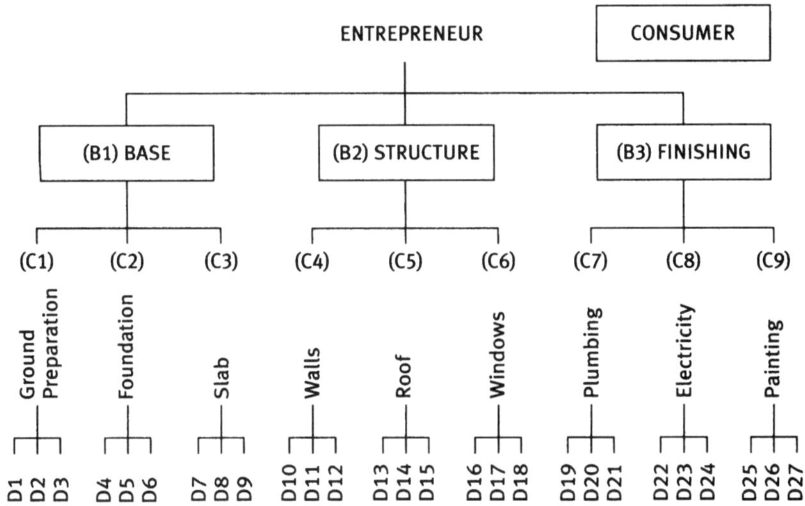

FIGURE 3-1
Structure of the building industry.

line except that the product—the house—stays still and the producing apparatus moves.

For simplicity, I shall assume that the owner hires three superintendents, each of whom hires three foremen, each of whom supervises three laborers as shown in Figure 3-1. Napoleon thought that three was the optimal span for military matters, but there is no reason except for the sake of simplicity to believe it is optimal for our problem.

This structure per se leads to considerable labor that does not have a direct output. The three superintendents and the nine foremen are engaged in supervising rather than directly producing, and the owner is supervising them. Therefore, there are fourteen people whose physical work has been dispensed with because it is thought they are more productive as supervisors than as workers. The apparatus contains forty-one men, but only twenty-seven of them are actually lifting tools.[4]

Superficially, this organization might be regarded as inefficient. Only about 70 percent of the labor force actually is doing anything on the houses, though the supervisors are earning their keep by organizing the work and

4. I have somewhat oversimplified the problem. The bottom-level contractor with three employees may quite frequently spend only part of his time supervising them and part directly working.

making certain that those 70 percent work carefully and continuously. With the supervisors lifting tools instead of supervising, the total amount of useful work might be considerably less.

How should we organize this tiny structure: market, hierarchy, or some compromise between the two? Let us look at Figure 3-1. A customer off to the right is, in a real sense, the ultimate employer of these people. He will, if the enterprise is successful, buy the house; and if no customer can be found to buy the house, the whole enterprise will collapse. Moreover, the more satisfied the customer is, the higher the price is that can be charged him; hence, the more prosperous the whole affair will be.

In most circumstances today, the customer buys the completed house from the entrepreneur. Let us begin with that system and inquire into different ways in which the entrepreneur could organize his production technique. First, he could simply hire the complete hierarchy we show in Figure 3-1. For the building trade, this is quite unusual although you may have to be a little perceptive to note it. People in the trade will frequently refer to hiring someone, when, as a matter of fact, it is an independent contractor that they are dealing with even if that independent contractor is just one person.

My painter, with his single assistant, probably would tell people that I have hired him, not that I have entered into a contract with him, although there is a bid arrangement, and I do not even see him while he is working. The only reason I know that he usually has an assistant is that I talked to him briefly when he was working on the house next to mine and he introduced his assistant.[5]

As the second system, the entrepreneur could hire superintendents for roles B_1, B_2, and B_3, and then actual foremen for C_1–C_9, with them contracting the work out to individual laborers. This is not a common arrangement, but it is theoretically possible. In a way, employment in the building trade does tend to resemble this system because, although we do have someone who, say, owns a bulldozer and does ground preparation with the aid of a couple of assistants, he does not guarantee them permanent employment. If he does not get a contract, his assistants are normally laid off.

Another procedure would be simply to hire the B_1, B_2, and B_3 people and have them arrange contracts with C_1–C_9, who could have permanent relations with their employees within their little organization. This is essentially

5. My painter is an American citizen of Mexican ancestry, but very Americanized. His assistant is, I suspect, an illegal immigrant whose English is very poor.

the way Fairfield operates. No one person is in charge of one particular house. Specialists in various activities contract the work out for several houses at a time.

Interestingly enough, these specialists are not necessarily all that competent. Most of the houses in the particular subdivision where I live have had their roofs re-tiled, courtesy of Fairfield, because the contractor who did the original tiling had not paid careful attention to the local building code. Apparently, the supervisor had missed it.

Last, but by no means least, the entrepreneur could contract out everything, that is, the B_1, B_2, and B_3 levels, or alternatively, could actually skip those levels and take on C_1, C_2, and so on. Many of the so-called intermediate-sized building projects are done this way. If, for example, you want a swimming pool you will go to someone who (after you have accepted his bid) agrees to build your swimming pool, but who will contract out a large part of it to various other entrepreneurs. Sometimes he himself does one part. Let us suppose that the entrepreneur digs the hole using his own equipment but contracts out everything else. Many other mixes of direct operation and contracting are not only possible but common.

Also, within this same structure, the entrepreneur might contract things out at the B level, and the Bs would have permanent hierarchies working for them. As far as I know, this practice is not common in the building trade, but a lot of clothing—particularly hats—are made this way.

So far, we have dealt with only one possible variable because we have assumed that the customer buys the finished product from the entrepreneur who organizes his production even if he does not produce it. There is no intrinsic reason why this is necessary. It would be quite possible, for example, for the base contractor B_1 to prepare the land, sell it complete with foundation and slab to B_2, who would build the structure and sell it to the finishing contractor, who would then sell it to the customer.[6] This particular organization is not common. In Tucson, for instance, many building lots for commercial use are prepared for construction by the owner before he sells them. Indeed, one company is advertising space near my house with the slab and foundation provided.

6. The only pure case I know of where each stage of "production" is completed by an owner who then sells the product to the man who performs the next act, is the production and shipping of stone axes by some backward tribes in northern Australia. See Lauriston Sharp, "Steel Axes for Stone-Age Australians," *Human Organization* 2, no. 2 (1952): 17–22.

Furthermore, the same thing could proceed with the Cs. In other words, a series of sales could transfer the property from one specialist to another, with the painter actually selling it to the final customer. Again, this procedure is not seen very often.

Outside the building trade, however, a large part of the ultimate object sold to the customer has actually been purchased rather than manufactured by the organization who makes the sale.

Leonard Read wrote a famous piece, "I, Pencil,"[7] in which he demonstrated that the lead pencil, composed as it is of a number of products—specialized wood, special paint, lead (which itself is a compound of several things), the rubber eraser, and the metal holder that attaches the eraser to the wooden shaft—is such that no one knows how all of these items are made. The pencil manufacturer buys most of these various things without paying much attention to how they are made, and the people who produce each material do not know too much about the others.

This situation is not abnormal. "Value added" by any given manufacturing process is characteristically a long way from 100 percent of the sale price.[8] I pointed out in connection with Table 3-1, control tends to gradually evaporate or attrit in descent through a large hierarchy. The same phenomenon will be found in purchase and sale.

First, as I pointed out, a large part of the hierarchy will not actually be doing anything other than supervising and coordinating. Similarly, if we have a purchase and sale arrangement under which, say, C_1 prepares the ground, sells to C_2, and so on, a large number of people will themselves be involved in the transactions: salesmen, purchasing agents, and so on. It is not obvious which group of "nonproductive"[9] personnel is larger. In the real world we do not see the kind of straight-line production shown here, with the project moving from C_1 straight through to C_9, but it is still true that large volumes of intermediate goods are purchased by the "manufacturer."

Not only is the chain of supervisory personnel a source of attrition, but market stages are also. The first stage will rarely be exactly what the customer wanted. I recently bought one of these Fairfield mass-produced houses in

7. Leonard Read, *I, Pencil* (Irvington-on-Hudson, N.Y.: Foundation for Economic Education, 1958).

8. I am involved in a small company in Iowa in which the value added tends to be about 20 percent of the wholesale price.

9. The Marxists actually do believe such people are nonproductive.

Tucson. I am satisfied with it, but if I had been able to control the production, I would have designed it differently. Although we usually do not notice it, almost none of the articles that we consume in our daily life is really optimal from our standpoint.

There are several reasons for this. First, as Oliver Williamson has emphasized, if there are monopoly-monopsony relations between the purchaser and seller of some intermediate good, then the transaction cost is apt to be high. Furthermore, the probabilities that the good will not be exactly what the purchaser wants is also high since the seller has strong motives to save money and then conceal the fact that he has done so.

There are various ways of getting around this. I am on the board of directors of a small company in Iowa that has recently put a large piece of capital (large from the standpoint of the small company) into purchasing a special machine which will be used solely to produce a special product for a large company, one of our customers. We will be this product's sole source, and chances are slim that we will be able to sell the product of our machine to anyone else. An elaborate contract has been drawn up to protect both parties against what Williamson refers to as "opportunistic behavior." Still, the problem is real.

Suppose that we have competition, however, as in the case of the building trades. You can buy lumber from one of many suppliers; the same is true of cement blocks, backloaders, and so on. Furthermore, local contractors engage in all stages of construction, and they are also in competition with each other. Cases of what we might call "Williamson problems" are of relatively little importance in home building, a fact of which Williamson is aware.

Another problem is that the final purchaser has little control over what goes into his/her house, swimming pool, or whatever. At each stage, the competitive market is producing things thought to be saleable not to one but to a large number of people. This has advantages, obviously, in that mass production permits lower costs. In addition, aiming at a large number of people enhances the company's reputation for producing high-quality goods.[10] Retail stores are also important in the reputation of the individual producers.

10. In this case, the reputation is normally not the reputation with the final purchaser, but the reputation with various intermediate purchasers. Fairfield recently discontinued the use of the type of sliding door that is on my house because it required a 2¼″ screw which is hard to get even for a company as big as Fairfield. This is a minor defect in which the sliding door manufacturer has no direct contact with the ultimate customers.

Thus, the customer, in dealing with Fairfield or the retail store, depends on the reputation of the large ultimate seller and not on the reputation of the producers of the various intermediate goods.

But from the viewpoint of the ultimate purchaser, the products are (1) standardized at all stages, and (2) do not exactly fit his desires. The ultimate outcome is that we are all much wealthier than if everything were perfectly designed for our purpose and had an equivalent price. I am not complaining, but this lack of exact fit does have strong resemblance to the attrition of control that we showed in Table 3-1.

Thus, the hierarchical control and the market transmission appear to have similar defects. First, both require many nonproduction employees. In the hierarchy, they are supervisors, inspectors, and so on, and in the market, they are the sales and purchasing officials. Second, there is a loss of control. The people at the top of the hierarchy cannot depend on the people at the bottom to do exactly as they wish; in the market transmission the people purchasing the later stages of production cannot always know that the earlier stages have been done according to their wishes.

Which set of problems is most important in any given area? If we look at the real economic world, we find radical mixes of different forms of organization. For example, for a long time IBM made all of its computers from scratch. Only recently have they begun buying chips. Other computer companies have been as successful (they started smaller and still are smaller, but their rate of growth has been impressive) by buying almost everything—even contracting out final assembly. In summary, the efficiency of these various methods is not vastly different.

Figure 3-2 will seem familiar to any economist since something similar was drawn by Cantillon about 250 years ago. It shows the situation in a general form. We have a group of people who are both the producers and the consumers, and some kind of productive apparatus which I have listed as "black box." Black box is the collection of industrial and commercial organizations included with the government and churches, since I intend to cover all hierarchies, not only the markets, that convert people's property and labor of the people into items of consumption.

In the standard economic diagram, there is another set of arrows going the opposite direction which indicates the flow of money. I left them out because in many hierarchies there is no flow of money. To take one conspicuous example, after the October Revolution in Russia, Lenin turned his attention to organizing a communist state. He adopted what he thought to be the

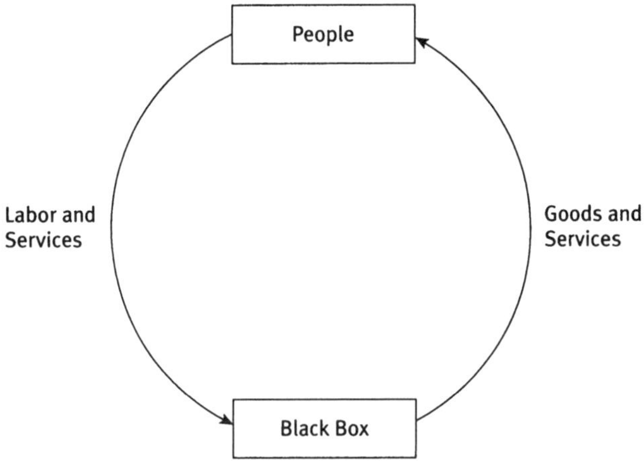

FIGURE 3-2
Cycle of production.

efficient way: to simply abolish the market and have everyone do things as a result of direct orders from the center.

The system was a catastrophe. After a short period, Lenin announced that the failure was caused by the war. He renamed it war communism, and switched back to a modified form of capitalism called the New Economic Policy (NEP). It is still true, however, that a great deal of the productive activity in communist states is the result of direct orders rather than the transmission of money. Gorbachev is trying to change this at the time of this writing.

Nor is it only in the communist states. I served in the U.S. Army in World War II, and although they paid me a small sum, this pay had substantially nothing to do with my military service. I was ordered in.

As a successful example of this same system, the highly efficient cotton plantations of the Old South had slaves composing their labor force who were not compensated in the form of money for their work. As part of the economy of the plantation, they produced most of what they themselves consumed, as well as the principal export good, cotton. In the off periods of the cotton labor demand, they built their houses, produced their food, and to some extent, their clothing.

Indeed, a certain amount of production by noncompensated producers is part of almost every economy. Governments regularly order people to do things in addition to paying taxes. Dukakis urged that instead of having a government health insurance program, private employers should provide it. Most government activity, in fact, has this characteristic. The ultimate consumers of government activity, assuming that we do not regard the employees as the sole consumers, get the services free and are then taxed.

There is no effort whatsoever to bring the taxes paid by any individual person into equality with the services and goods that he/she receives from the government. Indeed, most modern writers in this area would regard such equality as positively wicked. Redistribution is considered as one of the most important purposes of government, and certainly is one of its major acts.

The black box in Cantillon's diagram is something we usually do not investigate. Actually, it is a box containing many smaller black boxes. Organizations take some resources, perform some particular act on them, then transfer them either to the final customer, or more commonly, to another organization within the black box that performs further steps, and so on. Eventually, the customer gets the product.

Note that this diagram is extremely general. Suppose that one of the people is Louis XIV after his famous confrontation with the Parliament of Paris. A lot of the consumption that he received was simply reports of activities of his armies somewhere in Germany. Nevertheless, he counts in our agreement both as a provider of resources (because after his famous meeting with the Parliament, he, for all intents and purposes, owned everything in France) and as a consumer. Furthermore, his direct consumption in the form of the Palace of Versailles was pretty small potatoes in terms of the total budget he allocated.

With solely economic activities, however, hierarchies are frequently engaged in different activities relatively unrelated to each other. One example of this is any large retail chain, whether it is direct or franchised. These chains do other work in addition to supervising their stores. They may provide canned goods and have warehouses, but basically they are a large collection of stores with a hierarchy above them. Individual stores do not perform services for other stores in most cases.

Many corporations are diversified in the sense that although they engage in manufacturing, they manufacture radically different things in radically different places. I am personally involved in a mild way with a small conglomerate of this sort which is in four businesses, three of which are in the same two-digit (but separate three-digit) brackets, and the other—which, interestingly enough, is the largest in terms of gross volume—is in another two-digit area. There is nothing particularly unusual about this arrangement.

Large conglomerates are frequently in the news because of their tendency either to be created by takeovers or to be disintegrated by selling off their units, whether from leveraged buyout or directly. In many cases, there is substantially no connection between the various enterprises except the management. That is true of my little company if one is willing to concede our single computer as part of the management.

There are two explanations for this kind of unification other than simple historic accident.[11] First, management may be a highly skilled group whose talents would be wasted if they were confined to one division of the larger organization. It is even possible that there are economies of scale in higher management. Thus, if your company producing, say, automobiles is not large enough to absorb the economies of scale, you will buy an electronics company and go into the satellite business as Ford did.

Second, this unification is an improvement in the capital market. The management of this conglomerate acts as an intermediate between the people who loan money and the people who buy stock, allocating the funds among its divisions in what it thinks is an efficient way. There is a certain plausibility to this argument, but the details of working it out are quite difficult.

Banks and other lenders are presumably fairly well informed about people to whom they lend the money; stockholders usually are not. Buying stock in one of the five hundred conglomerates is not necessarily any more simple or more rational than buying stock in an investment trust which in turn has bought stock in, say, ten small corporations. Still, it is efficient and could have genuine information advantages. In this case, as in many of the other cases in this chapter, the outstanding conclusion one comes to is that we do not understand why different hierarchical structures exist.

Another problem is who or what should control a hierarchy. Large economic organizations, for example, may be managed by the workers, the stockholders, or possibly by a self-perpetuating board. There have been a number of famous efforts to solve this problem.[12] The whole literature has been destructively surveyed by Henry Hansmann,[13] who demonstrated that the basic argument for stockholder control is full of holes. I should also note

11. I believe in my particular little company, and in many other cases, that it is just that—historic accident.

12. See Armen Alchian and Harold Demsetz, "Production, Information Costs, and Economic Organization," *American Economic Review* 62 (1972), 777; and Michael Jensen and William Meckling, "Theory of the Firm: Managerial Behavior, Agency Costs, and Ownership Structure," *Journal of Financial Economics* 3 (1976), 305.

13. "The Ownership of the Firm," *Journal of Law, Economics and Organization* 4, no. 2 (1988), 267–303.

that his proposed replacement for it (only vaguely outlined in his article) also seems full of holes.

The large, publicly held American corporation whose actual structure was very heavily affected by some rules enacted by the New York Stock Exchange many years ago is not particularly typical of world corporations. Nevertheless, if we confine ourselves to American business, we first notice the existence of a set of large, successful organizations—the mutual insurance companies—which have what amounts to a self-perpetuating board of directors.

Nominally, they are owned by their shareholders, but, in practice, the management is an in-group which selects its own successors. Because many of these corporations have lasted longer and been more successful than the standard corporation, this is a problem for the Alchian and Demsetz, and Jensen and Meckling view.

Let us now turn to governmental hierarchies. Different societies allocate different amounts of their total resources to government control as opposed to private control. They also allocate different parts of their control of resources to religious hierarchies, nonprofit organizations, and families. These will be little discussed later in this book, not because I think they are unimportant, but because I do not know much about them.

As mentioned before, the government has traditionally been the largest hierarchy in any state, the head of which is a single person. In other words, dictatorships or hereditary monarchies continue to be the normal form of government in the world. Let us begin with them and then turn to feudal and electoral systems which are historically less common.

Dictatorships or monarchies, as the case may be, are not all of the same scope. A government like the one in pre-Gorbachev Russia, which attempted total control of its subjects, is unusual. The normal dictator or monarch is interested only in the part of his subjects' lives that contributes toward his security or income.

Rulers have military forces for the purpose of preventing competitors, local or foreign, from removing them from the throne. They also have a police system that assists in collecting taxes and prevents various things like theft, which would reduce the total taxpaying ability of the subjects.

Normally, also from the very earliest days, governments built roads because they were necessary for the various organs of the government. Message systems, which evolved into the modern American post office, were established by the government, although the old Chinese Empire apparently depended extensively on private transmission of government messages from its center.

In addition, there is usually a deep connection between the government and a religion. It is not obvious whether the liaison is primarily motivated by the fact that the ruler believes in the religion or whether the connection is simply a way of firming up government control. In modern times, many dictators have not been particularly religious and in some cases have tried to disestablish religion without re-establishing another one of their own. The Marxists, of course, are simply religious crusaders who do not like competition.

Although the foregoing represent the foundations of most large governments in history, other things have been done: splendid quarters, large harems, and so on. Most rulers are altruistic enough that they also make some efforts to help the poor, improve the economy, and other such acts. Whether they are successful in these matters depends less on their good will than on their knowledge of what would work.

This kind of government has two types of organization: a series of large functional divisions spread throughout the country or a series of geographic subdivisions, each of which carries out functions of government.

Readers of Herodotus will remember in the description of the Persian army that, in essence, each province of the Persian Empire sent a unit; these units were radically different from those of the other provinces. This government depended primarily on geographic distribution of power. The emperor appointed governors but did not insist on uniformity. The Jews, to take but one example, gained a great deal from this policy.[14]

A less common method is one in which the government is divided not geographically but functionally. The ruler maintains an army with garrisons everywhere. A police ministry will have offices scattered throughout; the engineering division will build roads all over, and so on. Normally, most governments have been geographic with some aspects of specialized functional division. The central government of the United States is not dictatorial, but like many other governments in federal areas, it is divided functionally rather than geographically. Of course, that is compensated by the fact that the states make up a geographic division but are not part of the federal government.

The reason for the predominance of geographical subdivisions is that it is probably easier for the central government of the dictator or king to control. It is easier to compare governors and decide who is doing the best job than it is to compare the heads of a set of different functional entities, all of whom

14. The Jews were, of course, reasonably grateful for the favor of the emperor. The Old Testament actually once contained imperial decrees in the original Persian.

have radically different tasks. Still, the kind of attrition of control we have discussed before occurs here.

It is interesting that in the Oriental despotisms which, after all, have controlled most of the human race during most of history, the hierarchy did not go all the way down to the bottom. Villages and, for that matter, small sections of the city, were self-governing in a more or less electoral way. Wittfogel[15] argued that this was because of the declining marginal return on administration, that is, as the administration got bigger, it was sensible just to forget about the bottom levels. These Oriental despotisms were very large and the reasoning behind Table 3-1 was particularly germane to them, though it is difficult to prove.

I have mentioned before the peculiar circumstance of Mohammedan states where the law was not under the control of the government. It should be pointed out that Mohammedan countries, which are in areas where precedents for Oriental despotism has already been established, normally do not permit local self-government by the villages.

Another intriguing example comes from one of the largest empires the world has ever known, the old Spanish Empire. The local municipalities were self-governing, but the people who engaged in the self-government, although residents of that locality, were appointed by the king, or more commonly, by his viceroy. This arrangement permitted genuine decentralization without loss of central control.

Again, we observe a spectrum of different organizational structures and no particular tendency for this spectrum to change over time. With the development of more efficient communication methods so characteristic of the last two hundred years, movement to the functional rather than the geographic method of control has been the dominant change. Certainly, the functional side of this mix of functional and geographic division of power is more prominent now than it used to be. This may also account for the fact that most modern governments make more effort to control larger aspects of the lives of their citizens than they used to. In theory, the old Chinese Empire was a completely monolithic organization with everyone under direct control of the emperor,[16] but in practice the villages were mostly self-governing.

15. *Oriental Despotism* (New Haven: Yale University Press, 1954).

16. As a single example of this, if the magistrate, the emperor's representative in a given county, visited the home of someone, protocol provided that the magistrate was the host because the house, after all, really belonged to the emperor.

Historically, another rare form of government is feudalism. Many people whose background is European think that feudalism is a standard stage in the development of society. This is simply expanding Western Europe to the world. In fact, there are only two absolutely clearcut cases of feudalism: Western Europe and Japan during the Ashikaga. Greece during the period we refer to as Mycenaean, and the Rajputs in India from roughly 1500 to the end of the British raj, could possibly be other examples.

Most of the societies that are frequently called feudal are, in fact, centralized monarchies. In some cases, centralized monarchy collapses; when it does, the individual segments do not have the loyalty to the center that would be called true feudalism, nor are they within their area dependent on feudal inferiors.

The system of feudalism provided that most of the area of the country was governed by people who had a hereditary right to do so; this hereditary structure was similar to a hierarchy. In Europe, the titles emperor, duke, viscount, and count were all ranks in the old Roman army. Thus, the king of England had under him a certain number of dukes who each had under them a large number of viscounts; counts had under them rulers of individual manors, and so on.[17]

The degree to which they would follow orders from above was always somewhat dubious; indeed, there were legal codes as to how long the king could call out the army. It was a disorderly system and a rare one, probably explained by the fact that its lack of a formal structure made it an incompetent form of government. We therefore discuss it only briefly here.

A Knight of Great Renown[18] is a biography of the medieval European knight who was mentioned most often in written sources. The extraordinary diversity of his life is the most impressive characteristic of the book. He was the hereditary lord of Lausanne, then part of Savoy, where he was born and where he died. Most of his life, however, was spent traveling around Europe in the interest of the English king, and in the course of these duties, he also became lord of the Channel Islands.

The other form of hierarchy is one dominated at the top by some kind of electoral system. I say "some kind of electoral system" because one in which theoretically all adults can vote is only a recent development. Nevertheless, since ancient Sumer, we have had situations in which the higher officials were

17. Earl was an Anglo-Saxon title; marquess is a corruption of the German margrave.

18. Esther Rowland Clifford (Chicago: University of Chicago Press, 1961).

selected by voting, with a considerable number of people permitted to vote. This system, like feudalism, has been relatively rare—although not as rare as feudalism—which probably indicates it is not highly stable despite its popular appeal. Still, it has sometimes lasted for long periods.[19] The Roman Republic, for example, endured almost five hundred years from the time the Tarquins were thrown out until Caesar seized control. Athens seems to have lasted even longer, although during at least half of its history, it was simply an administrative subdivision of the Roman Empire. Probably the longest lasting organization of this sort is Venice, which lasted almost one thousand years from the time it was first founded (on the mainland, not in its present location) until its conquest by Napoleon.

We are not as interested in the form of the government itself as in its hierarchical structure. In the case of democracies, the issue of whether to have a central government or a highly decentralized one becomes a rather different issue than in the case of dictatorships. A federal system like the United States or Switzerland, in which a given voter is both a voter in and the subject of at least three levels of government, is perfectly feasible. In this case, the sub black box, which is government within Figure 3-2, itself has a series of black boxes inside it, each of which is called a government or set of governments.

If we contrast a centralized democracy like France before de Gaulle with a decentralized one like Switzerland in the nineteenth century, we see that the principal difference lies in the structure of the higher hierarchy. The centralized one has a big hierarchy, and the decentralized one has a moderate-size hierarchy for the central government and then a set of smaller hierarchies for the local governments. In the United States, during many stages of our development, some individual states probably had more employees than the federal government, excluding government military forces. Even including them, it still may have been true since militias did exist in the states.

Therefore, we must consider not only how large the scope of government will be in a democracy, but whether it will be one government or many. Again, these are questions on which I have elaborated in other publications, but I have only briefly sketched here.

This chapter has certainly raised more questions than it has answered. In my next chapter, I will begin my attempt to solve them.

19. So, of course, has feudalism.

CHAPTER 4

IN THE BELLY OF THE BEAST

Having raised a number of questions in the three preceding chapters, I am now going to try solving them. I do not think I will solve them completely, but, then, neither has anyone else. My strategy might impress the reader as unusual. Instead of looking at the whole hierarchy from the outside, I will attempt to look at it from the inside. We will consider the situation of a person within a large hierarchy.

This strategy must be based on the conviction that from the inside, most large hierarchies are the same. That is, a junior official in the marketing organization of General Motors and a vice-consul in Bogota[1] really face similar situations. They must please their superiors if they want to be promoted. This involves a mixture of doing things that the superiors want done, and simply of politicking.

I mentioned earlier that William Niskanen went from a period of association with the Department of Defense into academe for a short time, and then into a corporate setting as director of economics for Ford Motor Company. He told me, "A bureaucrat from the government moving into Ford Motor Company is all set to hit the ground running." In other words, these structures are much the same.

I can add my own personal experience in this respect since I was in the Department of State for a while, was in private business as a subordinate in a law firm for a short time, and since then, as a member of the board of directors in a small company, have been at the top. To quote Niskanen again, "Sociologically, they are the same."

Niskanen's rapid change is hardly contrary to the general experience of mankind. People switch back and forth from government to private enterprise quite readily in the United States, in England, and in Japan. An extreme case is when generals or admirals become heads of corporations. Usually they do quite well.

1. The vice-consul in Bogota, since it is an embassy, would also certainly be either a second or third secretary, but I have discovered that most people misunderstand those titles. In the view of many people that I talk to, a third secretary is someone who cannot even type, and a second secretary is someone who can type but does not know shorthand.

According to historical judgement, the army of the Roman Republic was the best the world ever saw. It was commanded by successful politicians. Their consuls were roughly equivalent to our presidents, and the largest forces Rome sent out were called consular armies because they were directly commanded by consuls.

One significant difference between activity in private business and in government, however, is that the objectives in private business are better defined and measured. I pointed this out in my original *The Politics of Bureaucracy*. Building on that book, Anthony Downs produced a sensible terminology.[2] He suggested that we use the word ***bureaucracy*** for an organization whose output is not evaluated in the market. The word ***bureaucrat*** would be applied to any individual whose output is not evaluated in the market.

This pair of definitions means that it is possible to be a bureaucrat in a nonbureaucratic organization (for example, someone in the general counsel's office of General Motors), and to be a nonbureaucrat in a bureaucratic organization (for instance, the maintenance workers in a large government office building).[3]

The basic problem is that private enterprises in general have a fairly simple straightforward objective: to make money. Furthermore, the accounting system provides a fairly decent way of measuring the impact of various divisions of the larger enterprise on the larger enterprise's profits. Something like the general counsel's office, to a large extent, escapes this measurement process because, although the costs can be easily evaluated, the benefits are hard to put a price on.

The government agencies, on the other hand, normally do not have as simple and clearcut an objective. Moreover, whatever it is, is hard to measure. Consider the U.S. embassy in Mexico City. The formal instructions it has received are (1) not clear, (2) partially contradictory, and (3) not always being implemented.[4]

2. This comes from a speech I heard him give. He may have published it, but I do not know where.

3. Sometimes the bureaucracy penetrates here, too.

4. When I left the Foreign Service, the general regulations were a set of looseleaf volumes which, if my recollection is right, took up about twenty-five inches on a shelf. One set was kept in the administrative section of the embassy, but neither I nor anyone else of any rank in the embassy had ever read them. Their principal function was to make certain that the accounting data sent back to Washington were in proper form.

This is not a criticism of the embassy. Formal instructions are only a small part of whatever the Department of State wants from its embassy in Mexico City. The problem is not that the embassy ignores instructions, but that its task is so big and vague that it is almost impossible to give intelligible instructions or to understand the instructions that do come their way. Furthermore, it is almost impossible to tell how well the embassy is carrying them out. The government accountants could determine the embassy costs if they tried. Actually, the accounting system used by the federal government is such that the real cost of anything is concealed. In the first place, the capital account is handled in a rather bizarre way in which basic costs are always mis-stated. Second, there is no real effort to allocate the current expenditures by function. Indeed, it is usually quite difficult to determine the exact function of embassy officials who have contact with the native country's officials.

Thus, there is a difference between working in a large corporation and in a large government office. This difference leads toward greater efficiency in the business office, which stems not from the form of organization, but from the simplicity of the objectives. Periodic efforts to improve government efficiency by assigning businessmen the task of applying "business methods" implies a simple misunderstanding of this problem. The embassy in Mexico City is not intended simply to turn a profit on its visa fees, and so on.[5] One reason we have things done by the government is that, in many cases, we do not want certain activities to be run in a profit-maximizing way.

It is an interesting fact that governments can successfully run enterprises in a profit-making way when they want. They give themselves a monopoly to make it easier. The Imperial German railway system, which before 1914 was one of the main sources of revenue for the German Empire, the Imperial Chinese postal service, which also was a major source of revenue, and the innumerable municipality-owned forests that provided revenue for many European cities or local governments of various sorts—these are all cases. A personal example I can provide is the ferry system across Lake Constance—an obscenely profitable business. Indeed, one of the arguments against building a bridge is that bridge tolls could never bring in as much as the ferry does.

Thus, in cases where the government can make cost-benefit analysis, profits may be substantial. It is likely that an employee of the Imperial Chinese postal service in, say, 1890 had a very similar set of incentives and

5. In the present circumstances, anyone who is permitted to sell visas would find themselves in an extremely profitable business.

motives to that of an employee of Jardine Matheson in China during that same period. The Chinese custom service at that time was run on a comparable basis. Historically, tax-farming, which involves contracting taxes out to private businessmen, has apparently been very successful. Rome collected its taxes that way.

But aside from the advantages of having a simple objective and a method of measuring its success, corporation officials must be continually concerned with the accounting evaluation of their behavior. In other words, they must please their superiors. With a junior official in General Motors, say, the ability to please his superiors depends on his directly doing what they want much more than it does with, say, a vice-consul in Mexico City. The reason is because what the GM superiors want their junior official to do is simpler in concept and easier to measure. But if these considerations mean that private profit-making organizations will be more efficient in carrying out the objectives of the people who own them than governments will be in carrying out the rather vague objectives of the people who direct them, it does not explain the various kinds of organization that we have mentioned above. Dramatically different sizes of units and types of arrangements between diverse organizations occur in both government and private enterprise.

In both situations, politicking is important for getting ahead, although more so in a government agency such as the Department of State. I myself was not a very successful member of the Department of State[6] but the people who moved ahead fastest were specialists in dealing with their superiors. Many of them were relatively uninterested in what we might call the substantive side of the department.

I remember one man who went in about the same time I did and rose very much faster. He had just been appointed counselor-minister of an embassy (a small one) at the time that I was contemplating resignation. He kept emphasizing the necessity of improving his bridge game because he had heard that the ambassador liked bridge. My efforts to get him to comment on the political situation (a fascinating one) in his assigned country were completely frustrated. He simply was not interested.

Although this man was typical of those who rise rapidly in the Department of State environment, he would have done badly in General Motors. Not that his concern about mastering his bridge game would have been

6. Not because I had any objection to politicking but because I just was not very good at it.

misplaced if he had moved to a new division where the section head was a bridge fanatic; the fact that this bridge fanatic did not face an accounting test of his department's efficiency is what made the difference. In General Motors, also, if your superior is interested in bridge, it is a good idea to play it well—not enough to regularly beat him, of course. But if you do not contribute to the profit, you will go anyway. There is no profit in the Department of State.

This kind of special interest exists in many market arrangements. If you are a regular customer of an expensive restaurant, before long you will find the headwaiter addressing you by name, sitting you at a table he knows you like, suggesting the wines and dishes that will please you; the waiter may even appear with your favorite cocktail before you have ordered it. This is just like my colleague's bridge game.

What, then, is the difference between a market arrangement of this sort and the government arrangement? It is the ease of breaking contact in the market. For instance, it is not easy for me to cease being a "customer" of Pima County; it is more difficult to cease being a "customer" of the State of Arizona; and it is quite difficult to cease being a "customer" of the United States. Decisions to stop shopping at Smith's supermarket or to replace my current Oldsmobile with a car from another manufacturer are both much easier. The waiter in the expensive restaurant is aware of the fact that I can change his income quite abruptly by changing my tips,[7] but deputy sheriffs in Pima County know that I cannot easily shift to a competing supplier.[8]

Thus, in essence, the difference between a citizen's relations with a customer and his relations with his hierarchic superior is that the customer can shift to another supplier. A hierarchical superior presumably can dissolve the hierarchical relationship or impose a penalty on the individual, but, in general, such a decision is more significant and requires careful thought.

My decision not to shop at Smith's would make little difference to the management, but if a number of people made the same decision, Smith's would go bankrupt. In a democracy, the same can be said with respect to the voters, but there is a subtle difference. My failure to vote for a given party literally has no effect on its future. Rarely would my vote be decisive. With regard to Smith's, however, my decision to shop somewhere else does affect

7. Where there is division of labor, as there usually is in expensive restaurants, some of the people who serve you are not going to get any direct payment out of your tips.

8. As a matter of fact, in my contacts with them they have invariably been polite.

them, even though very little. For them, each customer is significant, whereas in the politics of a democracy, a majority is needed.

This is merely my definition of the two types of organization, although it also fits what most people think the difference is. When I was talking about moving the pyramid stone, I emphasized the difference between a relatively permanent arrangement and a temporary one. That is also the difference in the relationships between Fairfield and its various petty contractors on the one hand and General Motors and its employees on the other. Government is impressive in this area because there a relationship is apt to be permanent, particularly in that relationship we call "citizenship."

Let us now turn to our individual who lies within the belly of the beast, that is the middle-ranking bureaucrat. A middle-level managerial employee in General Motors is presumably in a different relationship to GM than a specialized consultant called in by GM even though their incomes may be comparable. The difference is the permanence of the arrangement and the various things which that implies.

Let me look at this situation from the standpoint of Count Tolstoy.

> When Boris entered the room, Prince Andrey was listening to an old general, wearing his decorations, who was reporting something to Prince Andrey with an expression of soldierly servility on his purple face. "All right. Please wait!" he said to the general, speaking in Russian with the French accent which he used when he spoke with contempt. The moment he noticed Boris he stopped the general, who trotted imploringly after him and begged to be heard, while Prince Andrey turned to Boris with a cheerful smile and a nod of the head.
>
> Boris now clearly understood—what he had already guessed—that side by side with the system of discipline and subordination which were laid down in the Army Regulations, there existed a different and more real system—the system which compelled a tightly laced general with a purple face to wait respectfully for his turn while a mere captain like Prince Andrey chatted with a mere second lieutenant like Boris. Boris decided at once that he could be guided not by the official system but by this other unwritten system.
>
> —*War and Peace*, Part III, Chapter 9

I think anyone who has had any connection with bureaucracies will realize that Tolstoy is an excellent observer. If we wanted to represent the total structure graphically, we would need a multidimensional manifold with the points in the manifold at various levels and distances from each other; we would also need non-Euclidian geometry. To have relationships consistent, we would need many kinds of lines to indicate different types of contact. Furthermore, obviously Tolstoy is right. There are many people who are more important than their official position shows.

When I worked in an embassy in Korea, I came into contact with a number of people in the military organization. I knew one captain, for example, who occasionally had dinner with the commanding general of the Eighth Army, a fact that infuriated the lieutenant-general for whom the captain was allegedly working. There was nothing the lieutenant-general could do about it, however.[9]

An individual within the bureaucracy faces a cloud of other people, some of whom clearly are more important and can affect his career; others are clearly inferiors; a very large number cannot be classified either way. If this individual wants to get ahead, he must either please his superiors or form attachments to some of them so it does not matter if he displeases others. Most large hierarchies have a sort of quasi-feudal structure in which high officials have a number of followers who do their bidding, and not that of the organization.

One particular case is the "ugly genius." This is a brilliant man who has no real prospect of getting ahead on his own, because of his personality. A shrewd, smooth manipulator would regard such a person as a treasure since his only real role in life is following someone else. The genius will provide bright ideas without having the savoir faire to double-cross his superior. I knew several pairs of geniuses and manipulators in the Department of State. If the smooth manipulator was moved to another section, within a month or so the ugly genius was transferred to the same place.

There is another type of relationship between the top and bottom of an organization: the information relationship. High-ranking officials, instead of relying solely on formal channels of information, may attach low-ranking officials with the intent of getting additional information. During the early part of his career, Kravchenko of *I Chose Freedom* was an example of such a

9. Actually, he did take the pro forma step of exiling the captain from his normal post of duty. This meant he had more time to see his fiancee who was in Seoul working for the embassy, and, of course, had no effect at all on the frequency with which he had dinner with the commanding general. It was a foolish thing for the lieutenant-general to do and a little surprising because, although I met many stupid major-generals, and lieutenant-generals were not necessarily excellent strategists, they usually were very bright.

low-ranking official. One high-ranking communist saw to it that they had an evening together once every six or seven months. Kravchenko reports the relationship in terms of awe and great privilege, which I presume it was. But I am sure that the higher official, although he enjoyed associating with a man who so obviously admired him, basically was looking for additional information on the lower levels.

Turning, then, to the Tolstoy view of how large bureaucracies work, we must begin by thinking about our middle-level bureaucrat himself rather than the organization surrounding him. Although with time this man may develop a considerable emotional connection to his organization, he is more interested in himself and his family than he is in Ford Motor Company or the Central Intelligence Agency. This may be concealed by the fact that he spends many more waking hours at Ford Motor Company or the CIA than he does with his family, but that is because he must work there in order to provide suitable family support. The company is mainly a means; his own and his family's consumption is the end.

No one thinks that the ditchdigger who works hard all day to put food on the table for his family is deeply devoted to digging ditches. True, with time he will probably develop at least some rationalizations about the importance of having good ditches dug for society and the right and wrong ways of digging. This is reduction of cognitive dissonance. But he digs for his family, not for itself. The same is true for most officials in the CIA, Ford, and so on.

The higher ranks of the American government are badly paid considering their responsibilities. A certain number of these officials must be viewed as making a sacrifice to meet a public goal. This goal is not necessarily what the government wants or what the people want. It may be more particular to the individual. The fact that these higher officials tend not to stay in the jobs long is evidence that such motives are not overwhelming.

Consider an actual situation—say, the manager of DuPont's sporting powder division. The director of sales certainly will be an important person in his world as will, to a lesser degree, the assistant director, although he has no direct connection. Whether sporting powder is the largest section or the smallest in the explosive division is important to this manager. If, for example, the explosives section is larger than his, then it is likely that the head of the explosive section will probably have some power over him. Indeed, if the head of the explosive section happens to have a particularly energetic and forceful personality, he may have such power even though that division is smaller.

Officially, the contractor's bureau has no direct connection with him, but if this manager is powerful and forceful, he actually has some supervisory control over it in spite of the official organization. In other words, we are now talking about the irregular but genuine structure that we observe. In addition, our division manager undoubtedly has occasional direct contacts to both the general director of sales and the department head. Furthermore, if he is a sensible man, he has cultivated good relations with both of their secretaries.

This discussion merely sketches the complexity of actual relationships, showing that formal organization is only of general use. The individual must deal with both his superiors and inferiors. He must keep firmly in mind that there may be a Kravchenko—or several—in his immediate entourage who, although usually his inferiors, have connections with people of vastly greater rank.[10]

In addition, his closer-ranking superiors and his nominal equals will frequently have contact with his higher-ranking inferiors. Our reference official, of course, will have the same connections with some inferiors of his colleagues. Because large corporations regularly hold large-scale management meetings, even remoteness of physical location does not prevent contact between a supervisor and the inferiors of another colleague, one who may even be that supervisor's rival for a promotion.

Let us confine ourselves here to the structure of the individual's relationships with people who are not working for him—in other words, people who will influence his career other than by increasing or reducing the productivity of his division.

The first thing to be dealt with is what I call *The Gray Flannel Suit* problem. Most organizations have a rather conformist culture, not necessarily in their formal official activities but in their attitude and appearance. The grey flannel suit itself is no longer worn much by officials in corporations, but there is a certain "higher executive look" with, in general, some specialization in each corporate department.

As an example, on one occasion when I was in a restaurant in Washington, D.C., J. Edgar Hoover and one of his high-ranking assistants entered. They were both dressed inconspicuously, but interestingly their clothing was

10. In the days when the Du Pont family was actually running DuPont de Nemours, younger members of the family frequently took junior management jobs in various plants as a way of getting their careers started. It must have been rather intimidating to their formal superiors.

almost identical. Undoubtedly J. Edgar Hoover did not want his operatives to be readily picked out because of their clothing, but his view of inconspicuousness was clearly rather standardized.[11]

As a second example, my first assignment in the Foreign Service was in Tientsin, China. About the fifth day I was there, I was told to go down to the railroad station to pick up an incoming courier. When I asked who he was, they said they did not know and had no idea what he looked like, but that I would have no trouble picking him out. To my surprise, they were right. The fact that 90 percent of the people on the train were Chinese was helpful, but there were also about forty Europeans or Americans. In the future, I was able to continue picking out our visitors just by clothing and manner.

As a third example, when I was in the embassy in Seoul, we occupied a small emergency building. I had a desk near the entrance. A man wearing the uniform of a colonel, but obviously not an army colonel, came in when I happened to be busy. When he stopped and looked around uncertainly, I went up and told him how to get to the ambassador, then apologized for not having given prompt attention to the local commander of CIA. He was irritated to discover that I had detected his organization. He was even more irritated when I said it was because of his uniform. I still remember him saying, "We wear the same uniform as the army."

A person who wants to get ahead in any organization should try to do things for the purpose of promotion and at the same time avoid doing things that might cause trouble. This means that in minor matters such as his clothing, he/she is apt to be conformist.[12]

One might ask why superiors act in such a way as to encourage this behavior. In some cases—for example, J. Edgar Hoover and the head of the Korean branch of the CIA—I am sure that it is quite unconscious. In other cases, it may be moderately intentional. The superior may want to give a certain impression to either his superiors or the general public.

If the supervisor does have some vague subconscious prejudices about how people should dress, he/she can evaluate the true quality of a particular

11. Actually, at that time lower-ranking members of the FBI were not quite so conformist, but it was still true that they were not hard to pick out.

12. In some cases "conformity" involves a deliberate pretense of "nonconformity." It may be that the person who wears an alpine hat, shall we say, scores a little bit over the one who wears a cowboy hat. A man who dresses conservatively in such an environment would be the true nonconformist.

inferior in matters that are important if all of the inferiors are similar along a dimension as irrelevant as clothing style. Although the reason that people tend to look somewhat alike in a given organization is their efforts to get ahead, their superior has no motive to prevent that and may, in a mild way, have a motive to promote it.[13]

Indirect connections, too, can be as important as direct ones. The individual will have social contact with people who are not very close to him/her in the organization but who can nevertheless affect his/her general reputation. My sister and her husband were low-ranking executives working for General Electric in Schenectady at one time. All of their friends were in somewhat similar positions—they held what one might call standard views that they shared. This situation was not necessarily favorable to the company. I was told by a number of them, for example, that I should avoid General Electric's small appliances because there had been too much cost engineering in them. On the other hand, what they recommended was Hotpoint, which is also owned by G.E.

A friend of my relatives was, like many of these people, engaged in auditing which was General Electric's preliminary training stage. He expressed the opinion that the auditors were attempting to be too accurate. In other words, he wanted to depend on statistics to get rid of minor errors. I do not know whether he was right or wrong about this, but the entire collection of young executives was horrified. I suspect that it ruined his career even if he was right.

Superiors are to some extent likely to pay attention to various indirect as well as direct channels of information, particularly in areas where the cost accounting system does not work. When it does work, it is easier to be accurate simply by examining it.

But, again, life is not easy for executives. The cost accounting system will permit you to compare without much difficulty, say, the twenty-five stores that are owned by a given chain. It may be, however, that the best and most aggressive manager is making a much lower rate of return than the manager who is the worst. The skill, talent, and hard work of an individual executive

13. In certain types of organizations, say, creative organizations like the media, there may be a myth that the really good people are nonconformists. Under these circumstances, it might be competitive to exhibit nonconformist behavior. A rigid conformist might turn up in most extraordinary clothing and engage in most extraordinary behavior simply because he is a conformist.

may be offset by the external environment. Accountants measure how much profit is made; they do not tell you how much is due to the external environment, the competitive pressure, and so on.

During the Great Depression, Rockford, Illinois—a machine-tool town where I was born—was badly hurt. A relative of mine had, just before the depression, purchased the Buick agency. From 1932 to 1935, no reasonably expensive cars such as Packards, Cadillacs, Lincolns, or Buicks were sold in Rockford. Buick, looking over the sales and other accounting data of their agencies, deprived him of the Rockford agency. There is no reason to believe that the failure to sell was his fault or that there was anything he could do, considering how extremely depressed Rockford was.

In most cases today, however, the accounting system is a great boon to managers of large companies attempting to deal with their subordinates. But any manager who uses the accounting system and nothing else will be beaten by a manager who is able to use the accounting system as a guide, but then improve on it by considering the degree of competitive pressure and other factors. Even though managers of profit-seeking enterprises are in a much better situation than the managers of the Department of State in controlling their subordinates, the problems are still real.

There is also the question of how much the manager will know about one of his/her subordinates and how accurate that knowledge will be. Turn back to Table 3-1. If we think of ourselves as being a manager at the very bottom of the ten levels, it is obvious that the man at the top cannot have detailed knowledge of what each of the 58,000 people at that level is doing. Furthermore, if for some reason he did become interested in some individual and tried to use that long chain of command to get his information, the distortion would be much the same going up as going down. Therefore, with the 90-percent-accuracy level in the table, about one-third of the information that he got would be accurate and about two-thirds inaccurate. Attempting to judge the efficiency of that low-level official by this method surely would be unwise, even if the higher official could spare the time to do so.

Of course, the 90 percent level is simply one we have used. I would estimate that in the case of the Department of State the 75 percent level would be more reasonable and, at that level, the "information" would be almost entirely random noise.

The lesson derived from this is not that the higher-level people can exercise no control but that the methods must in some way short-circuit the exponential deterioration in gaining information as well as in giving orders.

When I was first introduced to the Department of State as a junior officer, it was explained to me that the officials out in the field collected information that was transmitted upward, digested, and given to policy makers at the top. On this basis they made decisions which were then transferred down to us. It all seemed reasonable, but the moment you began thinking about the actual deterioration both of information and orders transferred through so many people, you realized its flaw.

Officials at the top and bottom are not merely postmen. As information goes up, it is digested and condensed, thus introducing the possibility for distortion. As orders go down, detailed implementation decisions must be made which also creates distortion. Such a simple-minded model will not work, then, and we will devote the rest of this book to methods that will work.

Let us temporarily, however, consider our individual middle-level official and his connections with the people above him. At least some of the information they receive about his actions is subject to his control. He can therefore present a better picture of his efficiency to his superiors than is actually warranted. The manager of the supermarket mentioned before is probably able to tell his superiors various things about the toughness of his competition, the difficulty of hiring labor in his area, regulations of street traffic that affect the number of people who pass by his store, and so on, without the higher officials having direct ways of finding out whether he is telling the truth.

It should be emphasized, however, that simply lying is decidedly risky. Talleyrand-Perigord, an adroit, unscrupulous man, in his activities as a diplomat, never told lies. He was very good at misleading people, but he thought that the danger of being caught in a lie, in the sense of lowering his future credibility, was greater than the advantage.[14] A superior, if you lie to him regularly, will almost certainly discover at least one of these lies and may even fire you for it.

The problem here is that the superior cannot possibly know everything about what you are doing, but he can protect his knowledge about your behavior from you. Your immediate superior has time to supervise you, and by following a quasi-random pattern of investigation, he can make it decidedly risky for you to lie to him. Misleading him without the actual words so that

14. This is true only with respect to his dealings with foreign nations. He certainly misled Napoleon since, during the latter part of his career as Napoleon's foreign minister, he was also an Austro-Hungarian spy. He did not lie to the Austro-Hungarians, because he knew the excellence of their information, but he also trusted their security system.

he believes something that is not true is also somewhat dangerous, but emphasizing the good points and hoping that no one will notice the bad points is always a fact within your control. (See Chapter 9 for further discussion.)

But the immediate transmission of information from you to your superior is not the only consideration. You certainly have rivals vying for favor who will try to find out what you are doing and pass on the bad news. This is in addition to gossip by the cloud of other people mentioned in connection with the auditors at General Electric. (See Chapter 10 for more on this point.)

Therefore, the individual should regard his/her superior as only partially informed about his/her behavior, but as knowledgeable about aspects of it that are unpredictable. By controlling what information is passed on, the individual can influence his/her superior positively, although the degree of influence also depends on how well the superior assimilates these additional channels of information.

Note that from the standpoint of the superior, the additional channels of information are less significant for their specific content than for the fact that they provide a truth check on direct reports. The individual is unlikely to lie directly to his superior if he/she knows of this potential checking system.

It also makes sense to use your (partial) control of information to damage your rivals. The subtle but acute author of *A Practical Guide for the Ambitious Politician* [15] wrote about: "... the calumnies that are used to render us hated and suspected by the Prince. In calumny, two things are to be observed: the first is, is it sufficient to deprive him of the Prince's favor? The second is, is it probable?" This does put the matter clearly. Of course, telling a lie about one of your colleagues in order to cause injury may hurt you if the lie is detected. It is less likely to cause you trouble, though, than telling a lie about your own work. Obviously, you might be badly informed about your colleague. Furthermore, you could perhaps put it in the form of a rumor that you have heard: "I don't believe those tales going around that Jim has been ..."

Kravchenko, in his book *I Chose Freedom*, reported that a number of high-ranking communist officials in the days of Stalin used to deal with their

15. This book is available in a considerable number of different versions and languages, including two different translations into English. Probably the most convenient one is the one that I edited for the University of South Carolina Press (Columbia, 1961). It usually appears in indexes under my name because the author of the original is unknown. Apparently, he was an active courtier in the French monarch's court and felt that his enemies could damage him by pointing out that he was the author.

colleagues by putting in their own safes "notes for my own use," indicating grounds for suspicion of a colleague. The NKVD regularly checked the officials' safes. On the other hand, since the safe owners had not made any accusations themselves, they were fairly safe if it turned out to be untrue.

Most accounts of the interior of larger hierarchical organizations deal with political maneuvering. I do not want to disparage such discussions, but it should be emphasized that actually carrying out the desires of your superiors efficiently is just as important, though nowhere near as amusing. It is difficult to generalize here, however. An official in a hierarchy will have duties, the prompt and efficient performance of which will undoubtedly move him/her upward. In different hierarchies and different times in his/her own career, these duties will vary. It is hard to write a whole book on the classic advice of "Do your job well."

In bureaucratic politicking, however, this is not so. As I have said before, sociologically all hierarchies are much alike inside. Similarly, the bureaucratic maneuvers that propelled the anonymous author of *A Practical Guide for the Ambitious Politician* ahead are also useful to someone trying to rise to the head of IBM.

The maneuvers are not as important, because by way of the accounting system the higher officials in IBM have a better control than the king of France did. The fact that the king of France did not have an outstanding intellect and spent most of his time lounging with his mistresses, hunting, and so on, rather than running the country, is another reason why politicking was more important there. Still, politicking is important in both cases.

It is easy to write an interesting and lucrative best-seller like *How to Succeed in Business Without Really Trying.*[16] If Mead had written instead a detailed account of how he successfully designed advertising campaigns, it certainly would have been of interest at most to other advertisers. It probably would not have been of very much interest to them, because he would have been selling different products. Sales would be limited. The book would not be amusing, although it might, in practice, be of more importance than his actual book.

In our book, we will emphasize the desirability of carrying out orders if you are a lower official. When we turn to the relation between higher officials and lower officials from the higher officials' standpoint, we will discuss more

16. Shepherd Mead, *How to Succeed in Business Without Really Trying* (New York: Simon and Schuster, 1952).

thoroughly ways of getting orders carried out. Generally, the politicking, maneuvering, and so on are widespread topics, whereas the orders you receive and your actions in implementing them out are highly particular.

We are talking about a field that has had quite a bit of economics work done under the principal and agent rubric.[17] I will not elaborate on the principal-agent literature except to say that the principal cannot completely control the acts of his/her agent, and the degree of control depends on the kind of information he/she has about what his/her agent is doing. I will also not delve into the elaborate mathematics and the significant statistics that have been used in the principal-agent investigations—not because I personally disagree with them (I don't) but because I am attempting to go beyond them.

The picture can be told from the chapter title: we look at the organization from the inside, not from the outside; we consider it from the standpoint of the individual in it, sometimes an individual who is head of the organization but more commonly someone who is not. We will also confine ourselves largely to the commonalities of different types of organization.

17. For reasons that may amuse the reader, this problem caused certain difficulties for me when I was, for a short period of time, in active law practice as a junior member of a firm. In those days, law libraries were not nearly as large as they are now; ours consisted mainly of *corpus juris* and, in fact, the first half was from one edition and the second half was from another. If you looked under *agent* under the "a's" it said: "See principal and agent." If you then went along to volume 38, which was in the second edition, and looked under *principal and agent*, it said: "See agent."

CHAPTER 5

LIFE IN THE INTERIOR

Consider, then, the environment of a middle-level official. He finds himself in an organization that has many people, together with various capital items, and that has certain tasks. From his standpoint, the tasks can be divided into those that will aid him in getting ahead, or at least in keeping his present position, and those that will not. There is no ethical difference between the two categories. Indeed, when I was in the Department of State, many people were clearly carrying on agendas of their own rather than attempting to maximize the degree to which the wishes of the higher officials were carried out. These people were mostly well intentioned. They believed that what they were doing was in the best interest of the United States.[1]

But an individual aiming at objectives other than the ones of his/her superiors is, regardless of its possible moral worth, following personal preferences rather than maximizing the well-being of the organization. I call this "hobby" activity because it provides a sense of individual satisfaction. Perhaps the individual gets satisfaction by trying to do good rather than, say, embezzling funds and spending them on a lover. Although in the eyes of God these two types of deviations from orders may be radically different, both are still ignoring the commands given from on high.

The desire to do something really in accord with orders issued from superiors may lead to a serious dilemma for the low-ranking official. Suppose at the top it has been decided that the United States will press for democratic governments everywhere and always. The American ambassador in the country in which our junior official is employed, however, is convinced[2] that removing the present dictator and installing a democracy would simply be a brief way station en route to a communist dictatorship, which will be far worse for the citizens than the corrupt and rather inept dictatorship under which they now suffer.[3]

1. Or, in some cases, the best interest of the Koreans, the Chinese, or whatever country we were in. American diplomacy is very frequently aimed at benefitting countries other than the United States.

2. Whether correctly or incorrectly makes no difference for this example.

3. The removal of Chiang Kai-shek by civil war in 1948, the removal of Batista to be replaced by Castro, and the removal of Samoza and the replacement by the communist

Consider a junior official in the political section of the embassy who must decide whether he should make efforts aimed at overthrowing the dictator or supporting him. Assuming the ambassador thinks that the present incumbent's overthrow will almost immediately lead to a nasty communist dictatorship, what is the junior official's appropriate course of action? Under these circumstances, he can either decide on his own which of the two policies is best and thus pursue that hobby, or he can attempt to guess as to which policy in the long run benefits him the most.[4]

For now, however, we will assume that the official's objective is to follow the course of action that maximizes his likelihood of promotion—or, at least, retention. This assumption is not arbitrary. People who maximize their career goals rise fastest; hence, they are the topmost people in a bureaucracy. Once they get to the top, however, they no longer have anywhere to go; at that point, they may change to a heavy consumption expenditure.

Our reference bureaucrat has contact with people who are his superiors, his equals, and his inferiors. Obviously, this is a rough division. There will be individuals nominally equal to him who, under certain circumstances, may be able to act as his superiors. Other people nominally his equals have special channels of information to his superiors; our bureaucrat therefore gives them careful consideration. Moreover, there will be people nominally his superiors whom he can regard as having no influence on his career or, as in the case of the general being talked to by the prince in the Tolstoy quotation, whom he can regard as his inferiors. The best way to picture this idea is as a cloud of points which we would get if we plotted the data in many statistical operations. A model plot of this kind is shown in Figure 5-1.

The individual himself is shown by the X, and the other points represent other people with their absolute vertical position indicating their rank and their distance from him, and therefore the likelihood they have of influencing his career.

---

government there were all greatly aided by an arms embargo imposed by the United States on the noncommunist side.

4. General Eisenhower was sent to England by General Marshall for the specific purpose of talking the English out of the North African invasion. He ended up as its commander, and, of course, this was the foundation of his later brilliant career. The intriguing feature of all of this, and evidence as to what a brilliant politician Eisenhower was, is the fact that he did not make Marshall angry.

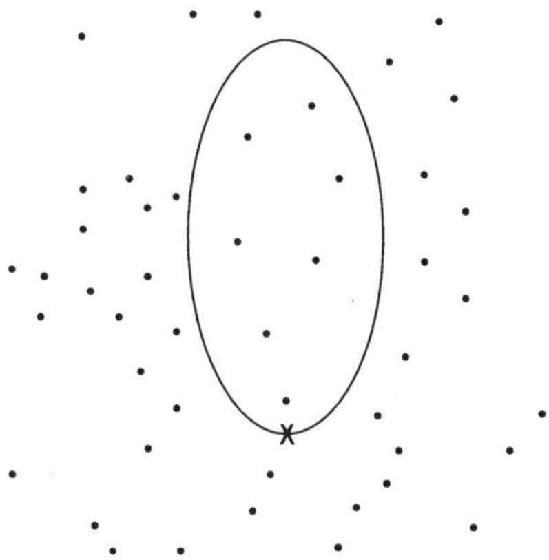

FIGURE 5-1
Structure of command—The view from inside.

I have also drawn on this figure a rough oval representing equal amounts of power over an individual. Thus, all points within the oval are more important to him than similar points outside. We could draw a number of ovals of progressively smaller size[5] representing higher and higher levels of power. The very highest officials are not within this oval. Despite the fact that their power over him could be considerable, they are more likely not to notice his existence.

To make life more difficult, the points are continuously moving. At any given time a particular superior might be able to influence the bureaucrat's career in connection with one aspect of his work and not in connection with others. Correctly, all of this should be in a multidimensional manifold in order to show all the complexities.

Figuring out this set of relationships is a difficult problem, one that the individual must solve. There is no particular difficulty in creating a (or many) mathematical apparatus that duplicates this picture, but it is not worth the trouble. The cloud of points is different for each individual, and it continuously changes. There would always be a "center of gravity," but to locate it would not necessarily be helpful.

5. It is not clear that oval is the correct shape. It would depend on the individual structure. The oval I have drawn goes through the position of the individual, but it would be possible to draw one that passes below him to indicate that even his nominal inferiors have at least some effect on him.

In addition, the figures would vary for different people. Two people may be sharing the same office, but their work is different enough that the shape of the cloud of points for each is radically different from that of the other.

It should be said that the higher our reference politician is in rank, the more likely it is that the people in his cloud are similar to those of an equally ranked colleague because of the roughly triangular shape of the total command pyramid.[6] If two politicians work directly under the dictator, they both have the dictator as an important part of this cloud.

I doubt that absolute rank is vital here. You may know people who are either much higher or much lower than you in terms of absolute rank but who are so remote from your immediate structure that you need not give them your attention. They are, in essence, equals even though they do not appear to be. In some cases, such a relationship may be useful to both parties. Exchange of information may be jointly beneficial even if the information is always somewhat indirect and only of general interest to the recipient. When I was in the Department of State, I had several friends in radically different branches who were, nevertheless, occasionally useful to me, and vice versa. In rare cases, we even dreamed up joint projects.

The people below you may affect your ability to get ahead. They may be information channels for people of higher rank, and this information (or disinformation) may help or injure you. More important, however, is their ability to help or injure you by their assistance in carrying out whatever project you have in mind—whether to maximize your career goals or fulfill some personal desires.

Let us apply this idea to our middle-level foreign service officer who faces various decisions regarding his activities in an embassy. He wants his junior officials to assist him whether he is trying to carry out the orders of his superiors or is trying to implement what he thinks is the ethically superior course of action (even if he is embezzling funds). He may also want to organize an apparatus of propaganda that communicates to his superior systematically biased positive data about his own activities.

This survey of the situation is intended as an introduction to this chapter which, in general, concerns people of higher rank than our reference politician. He is in the interior of the apparatus and if he is to improve or retain his position, the first people he must influence are those above him.

6. In Figure 5-1 the reference politician is far enough down in the pyramid so that its outer boundaries are of little interest to him.

The simplest situation is one in which our reference politician is the direct inferior of the ultimate top man of the bureaucracy. In this case, if we turn back to Figure 5-1, there would be exactly one point in the space above him. Let us further assume that there is no prospect of our reference politician's replacing his superior. His superior is, say, the sole owner or dominant stockholder of a corporation and not a dictator since dictators are commonly replaced in their own regime by high officials.

The individual here, although close to the ultimate sovereign, is not necessarily the highest-ranking official. Anyone who has read about royal courts, or the environment surrounding dictators,[7] or the internal functioning of the large corporations that have a dominant president, will know that the relative power of various individuals is different from their nominal rank. This is true even among small groups who deal directly with the ultimate sovereign.

From day to day the situation shifts, and we can safely assume that our reference politician wants to be the most favored, or at least more favored. If he is the favorite, he wants to maintain that position. He also undoubtedly wants the material rewards that are in the hands of the sovereign.

Obviously, one important thing which the individual must do to a great extent is carry out the desires of the person above him. In doing so, he has some control over the information about his behavior that the superior receives about him. Furthermore, he has more expertise in his particular field than his ultimate sovereign does simply because he can devote more time to it. Thus, the individual is in a position to advise the sovereign on various courses of action.

Other people who work for the ultimate sovereign in a direct way are the individual's rivals and collaborators. Rivalry is obvious, but cooperation is necessary to carry out the objectives of the sovereign. Our reference politician's attitude is a mixture of both. If there is too much rivalry, the individual's ability to control information might be jeopardized by the possibility that these intermediate subordinates will find out something negative and tell his sovereign. It is, however, foolish to believe that you can fool your superior and all your equals all of the time. In general, then, the official should do his best to carry out the wishes of his superior.

7. Accounts of Tito's personal relations with his immediate inferiors when he was living on the island of Vis behind the protection of the British navy during World War II are particularly clear on this kind of maneuvering.

Our reference politician should also keep in mind the fact that his superior will have some channels of communication to his inferiors. Hence, information or misinformation can flow around him directly to the superior. This issue also makes it difficult for him to avoid implementing his superior's wishes. As we shall see later, however, channels of communication of this sort are not very reliable. A friend of mine, who for a short period of time was head of a large corporation, once told me that the corporation chairman must accept a certain amount of ambiguity in everything he is told.

If there are objective measures of the degree to which the individual reference politician is carrying out his instruction from on high, he should try to maximize them. In most cases they will be an approximate measure of what is wanted and not of what is actually wanted. The long and unsuccessful tussle of the Soviet government with "success indicators" illustrates the difficulty of providing objective measures of exactly what is wanted.

In the Soviet Union, the inferiors maximize the success indicator rather than concentrating on what is actually wanted. For a while automobiles were counted by their weight in determining how much a given factory had produced. When they turned to attempting to penetrate the international market for automobiles,[8] it was discovered that the Russian model of the Fiat weighed 25 percent more than it had when the plans were transferred to Russia.

This is also true with respect to accounts although the account purports to measure exactly what the people at the top are aiming at, which is the profitability. There are two problems here. First, current profitability is not necessarily a good predictor of future profitability; hence, maximizing the present discounted value of the future income stream (which is what any economist will tell you a corporation should be doing) is not perfectly measured by the accounting system.

The reason for this imperfection is the extreme difficulty of capital accounting. Accountants find it difficult to measure the net return on, say, a research effort in producing a superconducting computer as IBM once attempted to do.[9] Even if capital could be measured, it is not obvious that it would be optimal, because individuals who are high officials should make estimates of the future and gamble on them. The company should pay off successful gambles and not unsuccessful ones, but the payment should not depend on any single one.

8. They attempt to do so about every fifteen years.

9. This was before the discovery of the so-called high-temperature superconductors. It is possible that IBM will now revive the project.

The second problem is that in large organizations, the division chiefs are doing different things. About the time that Henry Ford II relinquished active control of Ford Motor Company, the high-ranking official in charge of Ford's domestic production was producing very little profit. It would be difficult to blame him; indeed, given a few additional years of work, he began to produce large profits. The difference in profits, however, was undoubtedly due to changes in market conditions.

The problem is intensified if the different divisions are not doing the same thing. Ford was an automobile producer, and the European and American automobile factories had much in common. Ford was for a while, however, producing various components for NASA. Comparing the profitability of that business with the profitability of the automobile business and then evaluating the quality of the executives in those terms would not have been a good technique. If the NASA business was unprofitable, Ford might have wanted to get out of it. But the officials in charge might have done an even better job in difficult conditions than those officials in charge of the highly profitable Argentine manufacturing facility of Ford cars did under easier conditions.

If we move from economic enterprises to more purely political organizations such as the Executive Department of the United States or the former government of Nicaragua, the problem becomes more difficult. There are no effective success indicators here, although in a democracy like the United States, whether you win elections or lose is a criterion somewhat similar to making profits. Since the election process deals with the whole bundle of projects that the government carries out at one time, however, it is difficult to allocate that vote to any particular division.

Therefore, a comparison of the secretary of state and the attorney general in terms of who is doing the best job is nearly impossible. Even defining "a good job" is difficult. The president no doubt gives them specific orders in various areas, and trusts their good judgement in other areas, but he is not really in a situation where he can do high-quality supervision. Under such circumstances, the political ability of the cabinet secretary is of greater importance than the political ability of the division chief in some profit-making enterprise. This is not because business methods are better, but simply because the object aimed at by the profit-making enterprise is somewhat easier to measure.

All this merely indicates that in a corporation the higher officials' control over junior officials is not perfect even if they are simply trying to make a profit. Their advantage is unquestioned over, say, a government official who is trying to determine whether his inferiors are efficient. Assumed, too, is the advantage that a corporate president has in dealing with staff members whose output is impossible to evaluate by accounting methods.[10] The individual in a corporation (even one very close to the top) who finds himself subject to accounting measurement will need to devote more attention to profit-making in that corporation than he would to achieving goals in a government agency. He has much less room to maneuver and to mislead his superior. Nevertheless, even in government, it is safer to put effort into trying to accomplish whatever objectives your superior gives you. Political maneuvering does pay, but so does genuine productivity.

Only a few people are in the distinct position of being immediately inferior to one superior. Another rare circumstance is where an individual is inferior to a group of people which acts through a voting process. In this case, these people have to be the ultimate authority themselves which means they cannot be subordinate to someone else, like Congress to the voters.

Sometimes individuals are directly subordinate to voting boards that are themselves ultimate. For example, I am on the board of directors of a company in which the directors themselves own a substantial majority of the stock. An individual in this case cannot appeal decisions to the higher authority of the stockholders. Of course, he might be able to split the board, but that is characteristic of all groups.

In a way the board has more time than an individual and, therefore, *may* have more collective knowledge, but an individual ruler would probably still be better informed. Even if the board has reasonable information, there is still considerable overlap of knowledge. Therefore, the group as a whole is not well designed to maximize its information-gathering facilities. For each individual in the group, the payoff of becoming well informed on some subject is lower than the payoff for the individual ruler. In acquiring information, each member is generating a public good for the other people. The quality of his vote is improved but not necessarily the quality of the decisions of the board.

If our reference politician were directly under such a group, he would probably receive special attention because of being an inferior. This is the most important characteristic of these groups. Attaching yourself to one or more members of the board as a kind of personal follower could be a high-paying activity. Remember that although all of them have the same number of votes, in practice some votes will be more important than others.

10. Legal counsel and research are two areas where it is easy to measure the costs but very difficult (sometimes even impossible) to measure the benefit.

Though it may be hard to tell which member's vote is the most important, you should try.[11]

Figure 5-1 shows a more general case in which the individual has above him many different people with varying relations among themselves as well as to him. This situation is ideal for the highly political individual because it provides maximum opportunity for maneuver; it is less than ideal for an individual who is highly productive but has few political abilities. It is unfortunate, then, that this is the normal situation. Most organizations are not small enough so that the bulk of the people are immediately under a single sovereign or group.

Before discussing this point, I want to digress briefly to say that many market activities are similar to this setup. The man running a restaurant depends on a large number of customers, some of whom are with him frequently, some of whom are not, some of whom will tell their friends that he runs a good or bad restaurant, others of whom never discuss restaurants with their friends, and so on. One could duplicate Figure 5-1 by putting his customers in the dots above him and get a similar picture. The basic difference is that in most cases there are many more dots than there would be in an organization, and, partly as a result of that, the individual dots are less important to the restauranteur than they are in the hierarchical organization.

So ends our digression. To return to our situation, it is interesting that many people have written about the hierarchical organization in a rather comical vein. Shepherd Mead's *How to Succeed in Business Without Really Trying*,[12] *The Peter Principle*,[13] and Parkinson's work are examples. I presented my *The Politics of Bureaucracy* to the last ambassador I worked for, now retired, who had been very successful in the Department of State. He wrote back saying he was sure that the book was intended as comedy. In fact, it was

11. When Martin was chairman of the Federal Reserve Board, he was never on the losing side on any vote. A number of people thought this indicated he was extremely influential, but the chairman votes last. It is just as easy to explain this phenomenon on the grounds that he was easily influenced.

12. Shepherd Mead, *How to Succeed in Business Without Really Trying* (New York: Simon and Schuster, 1952). Incidentally, the title is a bad misnomer. The person who follows his advice will have to try very hard. It is just that what he is trying to do is not to improve the profitability of the company.

13. Laurence J. Peter and Raymond Hull, *The Peter Principle* (New York: William Morrow, 1969).

a serious book, but perhaps his reaction was influenced by the other books mentioned above.

A more detailed—and more serious—analysis can be found in my bureaucracy book and the earlier *A Practical Guide for the Ambitious Politician*[14] which I edited. Bits and pieces of relevant discussion are also scattered throughout Machiavelli, Castiglione's *Courtier*, and so on.

The basic problem here is an elderly and respectable legal topic called "principal and agent." In recent years it has attracted a lot of interest from economists. It is nearly impossible for the higher official to guarantee that his juniors will, in fact, do what he wants. Here, however, we are talking about the matter from the standpoint of the person who is below and who has his own goals. In general, the way we bring lower-level people into accord with the higher-level preferences is to take advantage of the former's own goals. They want money, prestige, and so on, which are theirs if they carry out the wishes of their superiors. Unfortunately, because of the slippage of control that we have been discussing here, the degree to which they will carry it out is always less than 100 percent.

In this situation, then, the individual should try to make careful estimates of the relative power and interest in his activities of various superiors and, if possible, arrange himself as a conduit of information to someone of high rank so that his immediate superiors are a little afraid of him. He should remember, however, that to some extent they will have knowledge of what he is actually doing. To quote an aphorism I made in *The Politics of Bureaucracy*, it does a general little good to continuously report victories if eventually he is forced to retreat through the capital city.

Thus, hard work on your immediate task is important, even if what you are doing is trivial. Chinese emperors were ceremonial figures, and at various times throughout the year they went to the Temple of Heaven for services in which a designated official read pieces of the Canon. One way to get into high office in China was to impress your superiors by how you read your particular bit of the Canon. To assume the reading was a trivial matter would have been unwise.

Within most large bureaucracies there is a special circumstance that applies to both equals and inferiors: the individual could be either on or

14. Gordon Tullock, ed., *A Practical Guide for the Ambitious Politician* (Columbia: University of South Carolina Press, 1961).

subordinate to a committee. It is important to discuss the nature of these committees before we turn to the individual and how he should behave with respect to his equals. Being subordinate to a committee is quite an unusual circumstance; usually the individual would be subordinated to one particular member of one committee rather than to the committee as a whole.

I am not talking here about a legislature or the entire voting body. These committees have been discussed in detail in other writings and rarely intrude into the bureaucracy. They act as organizations that are sovereign over the bureaucracy.

Nevertheless, if you look at any bureaucracy, private or public, you will find many committees, some permanent and some ad hoc. In general, these committees have had bad press, so we must ask ourselves why they exist if they are as inefficient as they appear.

There are a number of reasons for organizing a committee. On the governmental side, particularly in democratic governments, committees are frequently organized for the specific purpose of delaying decision on an embarrassing matter. President Reagan deferred the reform of the Social Security system until after an election by appointing a committee and telling the members to report to him later on what they thought was a good reform. This example implies that the committee essentially stalls, an easy tactic.

In the governmental process, however, committees are sometimes expected to do other things, and, indeed, President Reagan's committee on reforming the Social Security system did report a number of changes that Reagan and Congress carried out.[15] Normally, however, what is wanted here is not technical advice on what a good thing to do is, but advice on what will go down well with the voters. A committee is composed of people chosen first for their prominence, not for their expertise, and second for their "representiveness"; that is, they are expected to have somewhat the same reactions as the average citizen would. Committees are frequently provided with a technical staff who can deal with the details although not the main thrust of their implementation.[16]

15. As an amusing aspect, the Democratic members of this nonpartisan committee refused to discuss any proposal that might injure the older pensioners until after the election.

16. In recent years, economists acting as staff members of such committees or simply as civil servants have had considerable effect on American government policy. Apparently their arguments, although not very persuasive when offered by way of TV to the general public, have considerable effect when offered in private to people who are well above average in intelligence.

This kind of committee has little direct effect on the career of any given bureaucrat, however, and tends to be temporary. Committees in most large organizations are both permanent and ad hoc. Again, though, they tend to have had bad press.

There are several reasons why such committees may be organized. In the government, they exist to try to minimize the bureaucratic conflicts that are such a dominant feature of Washington life (and that of other capitals). If the five different government bureaus that might be involved in a particular field meet through fairly high-ranking representatives, the fighting will be taken care of at that point, and any decision made by the group will then be carried out. Note that insofar as this is apt to be successful, it is necessary to find a consensus decision rather than simply to decide by majority voting.

In committees like this, an individual member dealing with people who are his equals on the committee should remember that he represents his own bureau, and his job is to maximize its well-being, not to carry out whatever the formal purpose of the committee is. He must also try to have moderately good relations with other committee members. Last, he has the problem of selling to his own bureau an outcome selected by the committee. This last task would be much easier if the outcome is to the advantage of his bureau.

If there were not higher-level people interested in accomplishing a goal, this kind of committee would never reach conclusions. Whether these people are cabinet secretaries, congressmen, or the president isn't relevant; the committee is under pressure to reach some solution, and the individual bureaus represented on it realize their future can be damaged more by lack of agreement than by agreement to a solution that is moderately disadvantageous to them.

Thus, the individual on such a committee has a difficult negotiating position, but if his objective is to impress people favorably and maximize his career development, he can do so. He can also pursue some hobby to his advantage. Membership on such committees is, in general, coveted by junior bureaucrats. Senior bureaucrats normally attempt to switch the duties to junior bureaucrats because they prefer giving orders rather than negotiating.

Committees, by the way, are not always called committees. A colleague of mine who had once been a high-ranking official in a large corporation remarked that one of his corporation's better features was that they had very few committees. He then complained about how, as an executive there, he spent all his time in meetings. Cross-examination revealed that the language used in that organization labeled committees as permanent organizations. Many temporary organizations that held meetings were not called committees.

Apparently, his organization set up ad hoc little groups whenever they confronted a problem. Their committees, on the other hand, were permanent administrative organizations and were quite rare.

Sometimes committees are appointed literally to seek out a solution; they are far more common in the private sector than in government. Since this is so, we shall concentrate here on the large corporation and their web of special committees. The first point to be made was summarized by Shepherd Mead, who once pointed out that the actual decision will be made by someone who is too important to be a member of the committee.[17]

Mead has always tended to exaggerate, but as with so many things he has said, there is an element of truth to this remark. Normally, the results of the committee deliberation constitute advice to higher officials rather than an actual decision. No indication of inefficiency is implied, of course, since turning to lower-level officials for advice is something that any sensible person will do.

Sometimes the committee will make the ultimate decision by itself, but almost uniformly this is done by formally presenting a unanimous report to a superior for his approval. If the matter is technically difficult and the superior has confidence in the committee, he may approve it without giving the matter any serious consideration, and, under certain circumstances, one could actually say that the committee makes the decision. In other cases, he will regard the committee report as simply one input to his own decision process. This process is expensive. A number of people are convening to discuss the matter, to study, and so on. More people are involved than if the task were allocated to a single person. Furthermore, the actual information transfer and study procedure is less efficient than it is for individuals working by themselves. In other words, if, instead of a five-man committee dealing with a given problem, you gave to each of those five men a separate problem, the total net output would be higher. There would be no oral communication, which is less efficient than study; there would be no bickering for prestige among them, which takes a good deal of energy; and there would be no attempts on individual members to free ride on the others' information.

Delegating a task to individuals, however, brings up the problem of supervision. People could hardly be motivated to work hard unless their superior gave quite detailed supervision to their work. On the other hand, the committee in a way supervises itself. Different members will keep track of what the other members say or write, and they are apt to call the attention of

17. Mead, *How to Succeed.*

the higher officials to any default on the part of other committee members. Furthermore (and this will be discussed more fully later), the committee winnows down the total number of ideas, a task that the supervisor would have to do himself if he had five separate workers dealing with the problem.

Moreover, the committee would be much less likely to engage in an effort to replace the superior than individuals would be. This is not because the committee members are less ambitious, but because the committee is a dangerous area to engage in that kind of maneuver. This consideration is more important in the political areas of the government than in the corporation. Indeed, electing large bodies such as Congress and the House of Commons to vote on things, rather than electing a single person who appears to be inefficient, does have the advantage that the society is much safer.

The Aristotelian explanation of the overthrow of democracy starts with the selection of a single high-ranking official to represent the people against the oligarchy; the individual eventually subverts democracy. Although I do not want to endorse this ancient theory, many individual examples do exist, and a single elected leader, even if the election occurs fairly frequently, is much riskier for democracy than a legislature is.

This idea applies to other areas as well. Kings in Europe, when they began destroying the power of the feudal lords, turned to collegial systems under which individual ministries were headed by a board and not by appointed officials. This move disciplined the feudal lords who sat on these boards but who were not in the same position of power they would have been had they been put in charge of a ministry.

The British government, which in many ways is the most structurally conservative of modern governments, has retained all of this in the form of the boards which are at the apex of each of their three military arms. The admiralty, the oldest of them all, has a board called "the lords of the admiralty." The army and the air force have boards who are not all members of the peerage.[18]

Again, this is not very important in most corporations and/or for most governmental boards. Equal-level members of the Department of State who meet to bicker over aid to Bolivia are not likely to subvert the state.

These boards, then, are not confined to the large corporations. Although one can argue that committees in the government—and particularly in academe—represent muddle, incoherence, and confusion, that can hardly be true in large corporations. Most corporations are subject to considerable

18. Not all the lords of the admiralty are actually members of the peerage, although in the long run they tend to be.

competitive pressure to be efficient. Furthermore, most corporations have periodic sharp downturns when they normally trim off a lot of fat.

Another pressure for efficiency in this area is the corporate raider who may decide that the corporation is so organized that, by firing the present management and hiring a new one, the value of the stock will increase enough to pay for the raid. Also, many corporations have individuals who have large enough stock holdings that they personally are very interested in efficiency. Alfred P. Sloan, Jr., who was surely the greatest managerial genius of our epoch, owned enough stock in General Motors that the daily fluctuations of its value on the New York Stock Exchange were of greater value to him than his annual salary. Under the circumstances, he must have had an extraordinary interest in internal efficiency, particularly managerial efficiency. He was a great believer in committee government, and in his memoirs he continually talked about his efforts to set up an appropriate structure of committees.

What, then, do these committees do? In looking through the literature, I have found little in the way of an intelligible explanation and therefore have been forced to turn back to my own ideas. In outlining a theoretical explanation, I should warn the reader that it is not a very good one, although it is as close to the truth as I can get. I urge him/her to conceive of a better one.

I also urge the reader to think about a better explanation very carefully. Almost everyone in the field pops up with an explanation of these committees, and the range of theories is wide. Most of these theories can be demolished as I consider the empirical knowledge we have about the way these committees function. Therefore, I hope that the reader does not simply accept the first thought that comes to mind as a better replacement for my solution.

In my opinion, the management of any large corporation requires a steady inflow of new ideas on various matters. These ideas are not necessarily earth-shaking. For instance, a new marketing strategy for one particular type of portable radio will not be of overwhelming importance to Sony. Nevertheless, it is important that decisions of this sort be considered, that new ideas be steadily developed, and that only the better ones be adopted. To produce quantities of new ideas is not difficult, even though most of them turn out to be inferior.

The ultimate decision on these new ideas will be made by higher-level officials.[19] But in order to economize on their time, these officials would

19. I was intrigued in reading Iaccoca's memoirs to discover that the styling committee, the ultimate decision maker on such things as the color of Ford, is actually composed of the five highest-ranking officials of the company, including the treasurer.

prefer first to have the ideas generated and then sifted out by others. Not that the high-ranking officials themselves don't have ideas which frequently are better than those of their inferiors; it is just that they want a continuous flow and are willing to spend money to get it.

Why, then, is the committee a good vehicle? We have mentioned that individual committee members will not produce as many ideas as they would if the same individuals were dealt with separately. Assume that five junior officials produced some particular quantity of new ideas if they looked at the matter individually, and that when you subtracted the duplication there would be still a total set of, say, twenty-five ideas. The committee would produce fewer ideas, say, fifteen—as many as three individuals operating by themselves.

They then examine this collection of ideas and rate them according to merit, passing on one to their superiors as their principal recommendation with possibly several alternatives. They are fully prepared to switch to another if the superior does not approve of it. The winnowing process will not be perfect; however, it is likely that the top idea passed on to the superior is, say, one of the three best out of our fifteen.

The committee, then, combines a process of generating ideas with a process of winnowing. It does neither with perfect efficiency but performs the combined task better than any other system. It particularly eliminates genuinely poor ideas early in the process so as not to waste time on them.

Careful attention should be given to the opportunity the structure provides for the strategically maneuvering and rather unscrupulous junior officials. The committee is not a good area for him/her to operate because his/her actions will be promptly noticed by rivals. He/she may, of course, be an expert in committee manipulation and may operate very well in committee; hence his/her promotion is promotion for merit. A committee, by guaranteeing much publicity for almost anything that is done, makes the more devious types of political maneuvering by officials less likely to pay off.

This, then, is my explanation of why we see all these committees in profit-making corporations, even those subject to considerable pressure. Normally, committee structure is cut back when the organization is in trouble, but that may simply indicate that they are taking relatively short-range approaches to economy rather than long-range. A company on the verge of bankruptcy is hard-pressed to make money immediately and may be willing to give up some potential for future money-making.

These remarks about the committee, however, are only a specialization of some more general remarks about the nature of corporate headquarters.

Anyone who has had contact with them will be impressed with not only the number of committees there, but the number of people, many of whom do not have highly specified jobs. Indeed, the professional management advice teams that go around the world spend much of their time bemoaning this fact and suggesting that the jobs be sharply defined and that people stop getting outside of their formal jurisdiction. In spite of all this advice, the phenomenon continues.

It seems to me this whole thing—committees and this large collection of offices with various not-too-well-specified duties—is a procedure for generating ideas and then winnowing them as they work their way toward the top. There are many bright people who are heavily motivated to produce profit-making ideas. They work in an environment where most of the other bright people do not really like their colleagues' ideas because they fear the colleagues will be promoted above them, but who are nevertheless interested in increasing the profitability of the corporation. Thus, the other executives will be somewhat prejudiced against any bureaucrat's ideas but not totally unwilling to consider them. The consequence is the joint production of new ideas and winnowing.

The system does not function in a way that, in the eyes of God, would be regarded as perfectly efficient; in practice, however, it would be difficult to improve. The bureaucratic swamp acts as a filter selecting the better (not necessarily the best) ideas for the higher-ups. The fact that these structures regularly and consistently escape the formal specification of job jurisdictions, thereby leaving opportunities for management advisors to tell them they should reform, is evidence that the system is more efficient with this kind of jungle.

One final item to discuss concerns an individual and his/her relation to superiors and equals. By no means are all officials convinced that they are going to advance rapidly. Therefore, many try to buy insurance to protect themselves in their present job. Even those who plan on moving ahead rapidly would like to have some protection on the flanks. The result is the formation of little alliances among different officials of the "you don't tell on me and I won't tell on you" form. I will discuss this thoroughly in Chapter 10, but obviously such organizations do not contribute to efficiency from the standpoint of the corporation as a whole but do benefit the people involved. Well-functioning corporations should try to minimize the formation of alliances.

The picture so far is realistic and coincides with the interiors of most large bureaucratic hierarchies, though it emphasizes disproportionately the need to engage in bureaucratic maneuvering. In any moderately well functioning organization, an individual who wants to rise or to maintain his/her position is under considerable pressure to expend time and energy into carrying out the desires of his/her superiors. Societal or personal views are not relevant here; the objectives of the higher organization are. The best advice is: work hard at whatever you are supposed to do and also work hard at politicking. The former is likely to take up more of your time.

CHAPTER 6

STRUCTURAL REFORM

The last two chapters considered the situation of the individual official inside a hierarchy in connection with his dealings with superiors and equals. Now we discuss his dealings with inferiors. In other words, we assume that he is in a position to have other people work for him within this larger hierarchy.

Juniors will behave toward this official in the same way that he behaves toward his superiors. Furthermore, his behavior toward juniors will be as respectful as his own superior's behavior has been toward him. Just as his superiors will have developed informal contact with some of his inferiors to provide themselves with a better check over his behavior, he will form informal contacts with people several stages down the line from himself to buy similar insurance and control over his immediate inferiors.

We already know that the amount of control he will have over his inferiors is imperfect, just as the control his superiors have over him is imperfect. Let us, however, temporarily consider what he would like his inferiors to do if he had perfect control, possibly through a special divine dispensation.

First, he wants his inferiors to carry out any orders he gives them. But clearly this is only a preliminary approximation. His inferiors will know much more about their jobs and will therefore have to make many detailed decisions without his input or knowledge. Nevertheless, he wants individual lower-ranking officials to make the same decisions he would make in a similar position but with his own interests strongly at heart.[1]

Furthermore, he wants the officials to have these decisions coordinated with those made by the other lower officials. In essence, he wants a collection of robots, each behaving in accord with the higher superior's best interests and each fully informed of the others' jobs. Obviously, this is not feasible.

The individual must settle for less, then, as all large organizations do. Specifically, he must realize that his orders will be distorted as they work their way down the pattern of control. They will also be supplemented by the decisions of lower-level people who know more details about the entire area he is dealing with.

1. Ed Zajac, who used to be a high official of AT&T, always told new employees that they were to try to do what the chairman of the board would have done had he known as much physics as they.

He will, of course, have the problem of obtaining information from below, and here again he must accept a certain amount of ambiguity. The generation of new ideas discussed previously is important, and he must assure that his inferiors do so even if he proposes to seize the credit himself.

This chapter will propose various structural modifications that the individual can make in the organization. Although these changes may help somewhat, they do not solve the problem totally. In other subsequent sections of the book we will discuss ways to moderate demands on his inferiors and thereby elicit better performance from them than if he attempted to implement the robot model described above.

In this discussion, we will think of ourselves as one individual trying to control his inferiors, although in a larger hierarchy things are rarely that simple. Nevertheless, knowledge of the difficulties in this simple structure will be useful in considering the organization of a larger structure. The reader may want to think of our "individual"—here, the whole body of voters of the United States—as a dictator, superior over its governmental hierarchy. In practice, most people who face these problems are fairly low in the hierarchy and have to worry about interference by superiors or equals. This latter aspect will be set aside until later.

We propose first to change the span of control. Table 3-1 showed how the control of a superior tends to attrit by descending organization levels and by the wonders of compound interest; thus, ten steps down, his control was limited. Suppose, however, that instead of having a span of control of three, we have one of ten. Under these circumstances, he can have ten immediate inferiors, each of whom has ten immediate inferiors; he will then have 100,000 people working for him at the bottom level with only five steps down. Thus, with any given level of distortion, the wide span of control would provide a more accurate implementation of his desires at the lower level.

The problem here is that little phrase "with any given level of distortion." Surely, as the span of control grows wider, his ability to supervise each of his inferiors shrinks, and the ability of each of his inferiors to supervise their inferiors shrinks. Therefore, the degree to which he has control shrinks. Table 6-1 illustrates this phenomenon. I have assumed that each of the rates of attrition in Table 3-1 is associated with a span of control, with the 5 percent rate of attrition associated with the span of control of two, the 10 percent with three, and so forth. This table then shows for each of these pairs, the number of steps necessary to get down to a number of junior bottom officials at least roughly similar to the bottom level in Table 3-1. The table also shows

TABLE 6-1. ***Command with Different Spans of Control***

SPAN OF CONTROL	2	3	4	5	6	7	8	9	10
COMPLIANCE	.95	.90	.85	.80	.75	.70	.65	.60	.55
No. of levels	16	10	8	7	6	6	5	5	5
No. in bottom level ≈ 58,000	65,536	59,049	65,536	78,125	46,656	117,649*	32,768	59,049	1,000,000
Total no. carrying out head's intent	60,891	32,699	25,297	21,844	10,675	17,389	4,706	5,634	6,150
Total percent carrying out head's intent	46.5	37.9	29	22.4	19.1	12.7	12.6	8.5	5.5
Total employees	131,070	88,752	87,380	97,655	55,986	137,256	37,448	66,429	111,110
No. in bottom level doing head's intent	28,884	20,589	17,858	16,384	8,304	13,841	3,802	4,592	5,033
No. of bottom level complying $a^L \times$ no. in level	44	34.9	27.2	21.0	17.8	11.8	11.6	7.8	5.0

NOTE: a = percent of compliance; L = no. in level.

*The figure of 117,649 doesn't seem very close to 58,000, but the use of five stages would provide an equal error in the other direction; 58,000 happens to be about halfway between fifth and sixth powers of seven.

the number of people at the bottom level under these circumstances, and the number of them who are actually carrying out the desires of the man at the top.

The reader will note that my interaction of the two variables, the degree of deterioration of command and the span of control, is completely arbitrary. We only know that the attrition would be a positive function of the size of the span of control. This table is intended to clarify thought rather than provide any actual result. What we observe from it is that for any particular type of activity there must be an optimal span of control. The easier it is to see what our subordinates are doing or the easier to give them instruction, the wider the optimal span of control. Thus, we observe that large corporations normally have a wide span of control over individual sales organizations. A division manager may have fifteen to twenty substantially identical stores under his control. On the other hand, within the staff, where it is hard to tell what the lower-ranking people should be doing and whether they are indeed doing anything, we normally observe narrow spans of control.

Each different task, then, presumably has its optimal span of control, and it is a duty of higher executives to see that their inferiors are organized that way. In this connection, the wider the span of control, the lower the number of executives needed. We cannot tell, however, what that optimum is for any given agency. Still, attempting to get an optimal span of control is important for any person trying to control subordinates.

Let us turn to other structural problems. The first one often used, but in a misleading way, is what I call the "criss-cross" form of organization, though it is commonly referred to as "staff and line." In Figure 6-1, I return to Fairfield and look at it from the standpoint of corporate headquarters. Actually, in order to present this figure correctly, I would have to use very large sheets of paper, so the reader should regard this as only a sketch of the higher levels.

First under Fairfield is a set of divisions that builds and sells houses. For the sake of simplicity, I have put in only three such divisions. Their heads are in charge of house building in a particular city.

In addition, there is a set of staff offices in charge of various aspects of building. Once again, I have given only three: foundation, which includes ground preparation and slab; structure, which includes walls, roof, and so on; and finish, which includes plumbing, electricity, painting, and the like. Each staff officer has a connection with the person in each division who is in charge of that particular activity. Thus, the foundation man in Tucson reports

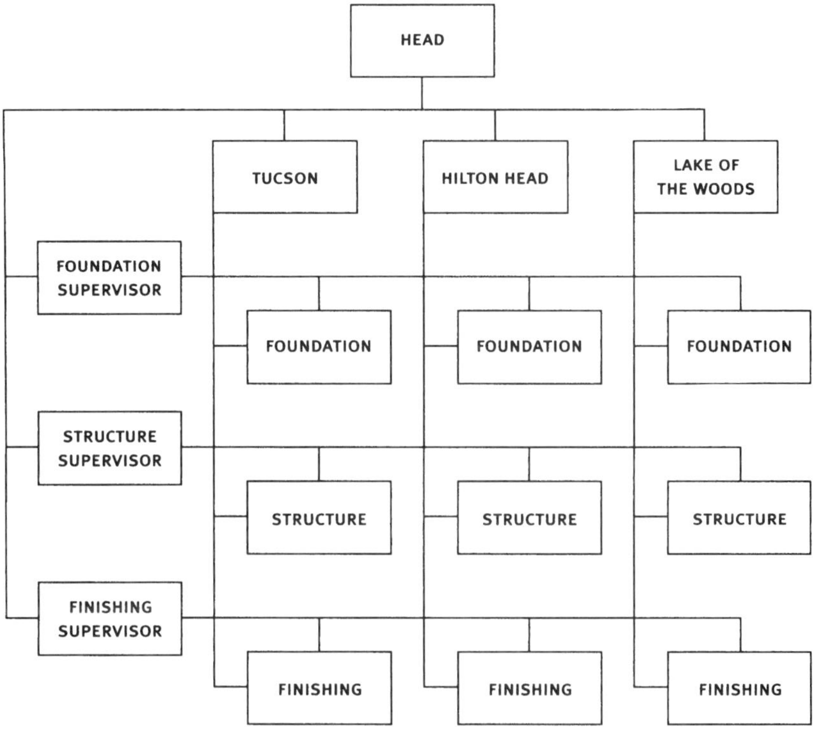

FIGURE 6-1
Fairfield, Inc.

to his superior who is the Tucson manager, but he is also, in a way, under the control of the foundation man at corporate headquarters.

The reason I call this a criss-cross organization is rather obvious: there are two chains of command crossing each other. Furthermore, in all the cases with which I am familiar, there is some doubt as to exactly how these two chains influence any given subordinate. The foundation man in Tucson, for example, will no doubt occasionally find himself in a situation where the orders given to him by his manager are in conflict with the general guidelines from the foundation headquarters regarding how foundations should be built. He undoubtedly will make a choice, and there will be general policies that allegedly solve the problem, with emphasis on the word *allegedly*.[2]

2. Any reader who is interested in how bad bureaucratic prose can get should look into the discussions in military regulations as to the relationship of, say, a division G2 to the division commander and to the Pentagon's G2. The Pentagon G2 is much higher in rank than the division commander.

This structure is much more common in government than in corporations. In fact, I do not know if Fairfield has this structure. In most corporations, with the exception of certain areas where technical advice is needed by lower-ranking officials, this structure has little importance.[3] Normally, the line is dominant; the staff in the headquarters does not have direct authority over the inferiors of the division managers.

One advantage of this system is that it makes certain that the will of the people at the top can be transmitted downward by two chains of command, and information about activities below will come up by two different routes so that in this particular way the superiors have more control over their inferiors. The disadvantage is that in a sneaky way it increases the span of control.

Most discussions on the subject talk about staff officers making it easier for the higher-ranking officers to control the line divisions. This assumes that the staff units do not require any control themselves, which is absurd. In the particular organization shown in Figure 6-1, the span of control for the man at the top is six: three divisions and three staff offices. The head will have less control over each of the six heads there than he would have over each of the three if he only had the line.

This structure, then, is useful only if there is doubt about the far-down inferiors carrying out orders. There are, however, a few cases in which the two channels actually simplify the total command structure. One obvious case is a corporation that deals with a single union and has a single personnel office with control spread throughout the various divisions. When dealing with a single union, a uniform policy is sensible.

Other cases have purely technical aspects. I assume that General Motors has a headquarters division concerned with engine design, which offers technical advice for engines built by many operating divisions. Such a setup is likely to be regarded by the division managers not as a hazard but as a help.[4] Even here, however, confusion could be introduced if an engine designer's views of what a proper car engine is differs from the views of the man in charge of that particular line.

But, again, pure staff activities of the criss-crossing type are not common in the private sector. Even the large staff of large corporations are mainly

3. In AT&T before the dissolution, this structure was very strong. AT&T, however, was a regulated monopoly not subject to the discipline of vigorous competition.

4. Unless, of course, just by accident it happens that the division manager is an engine designer himself.

concentrated in the headquarters or in a few regional offices, and they mainly deal with each other rather than having direct connections to functional areas in the lower-ranking organizations. The staff and line criss-cross is more common in military organizations and, to a lesser extent, in other governmental organizations.

Even in the military, it was a late-nineteenth-century development to provide a large number of high-ranking positions. The U.S. Army, Navy, and Air Force are all examples of many reins and not much horse. But there are more positions for generals and admirals in the reins than there are in the horse.

This structure is not often found in organizations under pressure for efficiency, but a modification of it is widespread. Let me begin with the best government bureaucracy that has ever existed, the old Imperial Chinese civil service. Its members were selected by extremely difficult examinations. The people who excelled in these examinations (people at the very top) were made censors rather than being sent into administrative positions.

The Imperial censorate consisted of a number of officials who originally were very junior although they could be promoted within the censorship ranks. They were sent on roving commissions to all of the major government units. The censor arrived at a provincial government without any formal duties except to watch the other officials. He would be younger with no previous connections with the higher officials. Censors had but one duty: to catch the officials out. If they were able to demonstrate that the lower officials were disobeying the Imperial will, their future was assured. On the other hand, bringing false charges was dangerous because they would be punished by the same punishment that the official whom they charged would have received if the charge had been true.[5]

Note that this system did not expand the span of control very much. The emperor had direct dealings in the capital with the censorate higher officials and had to devote a certain amount of attention to them. But basically he could continue dealing with the regular officials and almost ignore the censorate except when he received messages telling him that various line officials were misbehaving.[6]

5. The more spectacular methods of execution used in China were not applied to officials, but losing their heads was certainly a straightforward possibility.

6. This even applied to the very senior members of the censorate itself. Any censor had the right to send a sealed package that could be opened only by the emperor himself. Thus no one, not even the Board of Censors itself, could actually block criticism.

This is a pure case of criss-cross line of control. It was not a line of command, because the emperor did not give any commands by way of the censorate. In addition to the formal reports that went up through the regular channels, there were always intelligent, bright, and ambitious young men who were watching carefully and who had the right to raise any criticism they thought desirable. There is no doubt that this was a considerable improvement in the efficiency of the system.

Most modern corporations have something similar in the form of auditors. This is shown in Figure 6-2 which, with some relabeling, could just as well be a diagram of the old Imperial Chinese civil service.

Note that the auditors are not even the employees of the company in a permanent sense. Many large corporations do indeed have their own auditing staff for dealing with junior officials, but well-organized large corporations also contract with outside accounting firms for the highest-level audit.

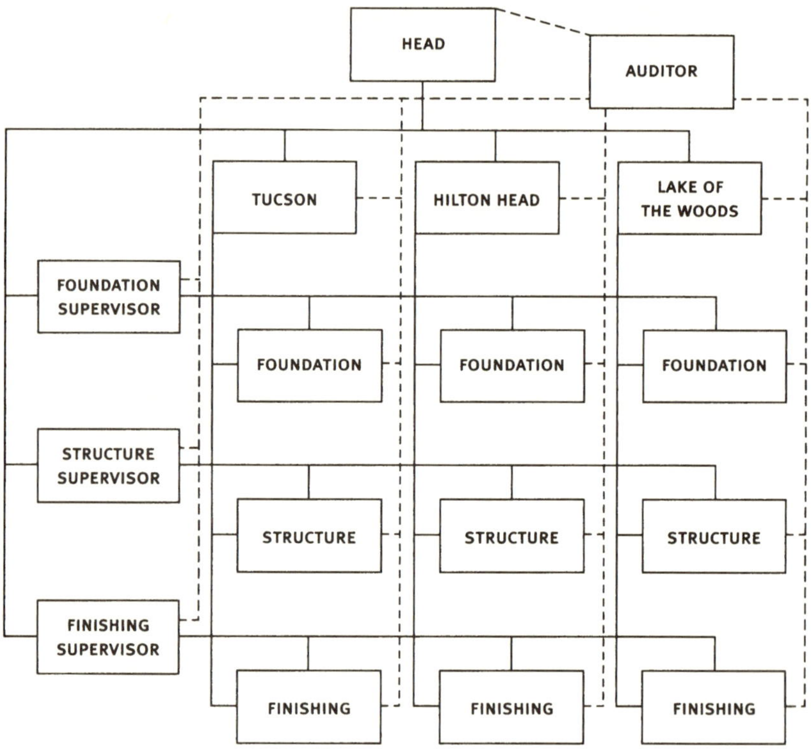

FIGURE 6-2
Fairfield—The role of the auditor.

Furthermore, it is considered good practice to change these outside auditors from time to time. The corporation for which I serve as director does this every five years. But to repeat what has been an underlying theme of this book, the system exists only because of the fact that the corporation is attempting to make money. If it had more complicated objectives, this simple management tool would not exist.[7]

Moreover, to repeat another theme, although this management tool exists, it is not safe to depend on it completely. Nevertheless, auditing definitely improves the control of people at the top just as the Imperial censors improved the control of the emperor.

Other similar mechanisms can be widely used. If some aspect of the work is routine, someone can be put in charge to see that the routine is carried out without the need to devote much time to supervision. The Foreign Service in which I once worked had a set of inspectors who were simply ordinary Foreign Service officers assigned to that job. As far as I know, they were not carefully selected and, in fact, tended to go back to the regular line after a tour of duty in the inspectorate.

Their existence had nothing to do with the higher-level problems of diplomacy. They did make sure, however, that the lower-level functions were uniform. Are the individual Foreign Service officers good at entertaining? Is the expenditure control in the embassy such that embezzlement is difficult? Do they keep their codes safe? Because they dealt with these types of questions, their existence undoubtedly made life easier for the higher officials.

Maybe this point can be expanded. During World War II, there was one lieutenant-colonel attached to Eisenhower's headquarters whose only duty was to travel around Europe calling on intelligence agencies to check if they were keeping their credentials (which permitted them to use a full battalion of infantry) carefully protected. This obviously required some supervision, otherwise he could have simply gone to Paris. But the amount of supervision was slight. It may be, then, that a number of simple tasks can be allocated to people who are good at routine and for which supervision is quite easy and limited.

A special category of this type is the chief of staff, a job that has developed out of military activities but is also found elsewhere more commonly in governmental areas than in a profit-making enterprise. In this case, many

7. The Comptroller General is an attempt to create a similar control for the federal government. It works well for accounting, but when it gets out of simple accounts, we get only certain civil servants' opinions about what other civil servants are doing.

routine activities are put in the hands of one chief of staff, leaving the man at the top more time to deal with the policy issues. Even so, the senior still must supervise the chief of staff to some extent.

Two other cases look similar but are not the same. For one, despots who have various interests other than directly ruling—the harem, for example—frequently have a prime minister as the only official that they supervise. No doubt this means the government is one step further down the hierarchy, and the ruler's control over it is less than it would be if he did not use this short-cut. On the other hand, he does have more time for his harem.

Another similar case involves a high official who acts as a lightning rod for the commander. The commander of a naval vessel is a center for loyalty among the crew, and the blame for various nasty things that happen to them, like enforcing inconvenient regulations, falls on the executive officer. This does not mean the executive officer need not be carefully supervised, but it does mean that the morale of the crew is better than if the captain himself enforced various inconvenient regulations.

The reader might have noticed that these structural possible reforms may be worthwhile, but they still do not solve the basic problems. It is still true that the degree of control shrinks as one goes down the pyramid. There are a few other techniques which, by changing the structure, may lead to the same kind of minor improvement: giving up attempts to get complete control, and aiming for a more limited goal. These methods are also useful when one's goals are more modest.

In the next example, we separate into two categories the orders which are given to junior people: (1) continuing orders (things we want them to do all the time or when some particular contingency arises) and (2) orders for specific problems that arise. In other words, the former can be regarded as general regulations although the latter are decidedly specific orders.

It is easier to get people to understand a set of orders if the same order is left unchanged for some time. Furthermore, it is somewhat easier to find out whether they are obeying, because you can take a random sample over time. For example, you might inquire on 1 percent of the days if an office has filed a report that is supposed to be filed daily.[8]

This method no doubt does improve the degree to which the higher officials can control their subordinates, but again, we must not exaggerate its

8. Grant was removed from command by Halleck the day after Shiloh because he had failed to file a morning report the day before. Lincoln reinstated him.

effect. They still must communicate their ideas to their subordinates and see that their subordinates are carrying out the permanent orders as well as the temporary ones. The effect is efficient, insofar as it is, because there are standing orders. To this extent, the higher officials can get better control by this method. Furthermore, the fact that they can economize on the amount of time spent supervising means they also have more control over the rest of the structure. But again, the span of control problem is not totally solved here. The leader must devote some time to giving the standing orders and supervising their implementation, and that detracts from the number of people they can have under their control for directly carrying out changing policy orders.

My own experience indicates that higher officials have difficulty adjusting these two different activities. Frequently, the fact that something is put into the regulations does not necessarily mean it will be kept a long time. It may only emphasize an order that will have effect only temporarily. Furthermore, as a rough rule of thumb, no one takes the obsolete orders out of the books. Thus, you have immense collections of paper in which only some pages are actually "live."

In a way, then, this system carries with it its own inefficiency. If the higher officials devoted adequate time to continuously changing the standing orders so that they are always in accordance with the desires of the superiors and the current situation, it would be very time-consuming. On the other hand, if they do not (which is generally the course followed), it means that these standing orders provide much freedom for the lower officials who will decide which ones they will carry out.[9]

Although standing regulations are useful, they do not totally solve the problem of control. A couple of other organizational structures can help somewhat. These involve designing the structure in a way that pressure is put on intermediate management to carry out the wishes of the higher management, and then the intermediate management is assumed to be capable of

9. When I first joined the Foreign Service in 1948, we had two volumes of "regulations," and my superiors and other people who had been there for some time were rather unhappy because it had previously been one volume. By the time I left in 1958, there were twelve or fifteen such volumes. They were kept in the administrative section, not anywhere where the higher officials in the embassy would find them convenient. As far as I know, they actually had effect only on the accounting branch of the embassy. Diplomacy does not lend itself very well to this kind of regulation, but nevertheless, I think that a short up-to-date set of regulations would have made it somewhat easier for people in Washington to exert what control they could over individual embassies.

putting the same kind of pressure on their inferiors. Obviously, such procedure will solve the span of control problem only if the intermediate managers are easier to control than the straightforward control we have described above, and there are ways of checking to see that it happens like that.

We have talked about accounting as a way of controlling lower levels of a corporation, because the corporation's goal is simply to make money. Sometimes similar simple incentive structures exist for governmental units or even for parts of the corporation whose output is hard to measure monetarily. For example, for every legal dispute, the corporate counsel could be asked to give an estimate of the outcome and a recommendation for out-of-court settlement. If there are many cases, statistical determination of his/her judgement is possible. If he/she is a good attorney, the court procedures should tend to average out cases that the corporation wins and loses at about the level at which the recommendation for out-of-court settlement is justified.

But note, this system requires that there be some control on the corporation counsel since by providing poor legal performance in the court case, he/she can always lower the number of victories, and hence justify a generous recommendation for settlement. Usually this problem is solved by having outside attorneys handle the cases. Since there is a functioning market for attorneys, it is not difficult to get an idea of their quality by some method other than asking your corporation counsel.

But obviously this is an approximate, not an exact, method. As another example, consider the body count in Vietnam. The reports got negative reactions partly because the army did it badly and partly because most of the people who opposed the war in Vietnam did not like to think of killing.[10]

But the emotional objection aside, the army did fail to take any significant precautions to make the counts accurate and, indeed, apparently hoped that they would be exaggerated. Nevertheless, a combination of the body count and the resources expended by our side, battle by battle, would have made it possible to get an idea of the quality of junior officers commanding those battles. Obviously, again, you need to have a considerable number of such battles to judge any given officer. But that was no great problem in Vietnam, because minor actions were almost continuous.

In both of these cases the numerical measure is not as good as the measure obtained by accounts in the ordinary corporation. We must remember also

10. This was only killing by Americans, of course. Many of them were cheering on the Vietminh.

that the accounting measure is far from perfect, but we must attempt it nonetheless.

We should warn against efforts to generalize along these lines, however. The failure by the Russians to develop suitable success indicators for their economy is merely one example. In general, any government bureau can, if it wants (and it rarely does), save money easily by simply ceasing its operations.

The police department that saves money by discontinuing all patrols would not be functioning efficiently.[11] If the number of people working is not reasonably close to what is wanted, inefficiency will probably result. You will be counting something, and your subordinates will maximize whatever you are counting. If that is not close to what you actually want, this is, in essence, giving them a set of instructions which tells them to do something different from what you want.

During the Korean War, our psychological warfare branch, among its other idiocies, decided that it would deliver one billion propaganda leaflets to North Korea by air in one year. As the end of the year drew nearer, the physical size of the propaganda leaflet shrank. Toward the end, their leaflets were the size of postage stamps. Clearly, this kind of propaganda was not what the person who specified the original number had in mind.

Anyone familiar with the history of bureaucracy can find many more examples. Senior bureaucrats have too much sense to use this method when it will lead to hopeless distortion, but it is still employed sometimes when it should not be, and contrarily, sometimes not used when it should be. It is a highly specialized technique that should be used only in highly specialized circumstances but that may, in fact, improve higher-level control.

The second method of trying to pressure lower-level officials to pressure people below them, without too much span of control structure, consists of dividing the job into a number of divisions that basically do the same thing. This makes comparison easy. Thus, almost all governments throughout history have been organized geographically rather than functionally. A Roman governor in one province had tasks somewhat similar to those of a Roman governor in any other province. The comparison of the output was relatively simple, although there could still be difficulties. In China, the Hsien magistrate was usually the only central government employee in a given county that

11. Long ago, the customs service responded to a reduction in its budget by laying off every single customs inspector and not one single office employee. This was too much even for the federal government, and the civil servant responsible was transferred—not fired.

he ran, being chief engineer, chief tax collector, chief of police, and judge. The central government paid attention mainly to two things, his tax collections and the occurrence of any riots or public expressions of discontent.[12] If he fell behind on tax collections or if there was any public rioting (perhaps about taxes), he was removed. The system was simple and reasonably functional.

This approach made it difficult for the government to get anything else that it wanted done. They used a very wide span of control, roughly ten to one, but the fact that they had these Hsien magistrates as the lowest-ranking, formal, central governmental officials and that these magistrates were subject to considerable pressure along at least two measurable dimensions meant that the central government would largely ignore other local matters. In other words, there were only about two thousand Hsien in China,[13] and direct government control terminated with them rather than the three hundred million individual Chinese. The system worked because these two thousand officials were occupying similar positions, making comparison easy.

Another reason it worked was the simplicity of the orders given. Each Hsien was given almost exactly the same orders as the others.[14] In a way, the span-of-control program had been finessed but not completely. Furthermore, as I have emphasized, it depended heavily on the state's being willing to control the local communities only along a few dimensions.

In this chapter we have been discussing ways in which the span of control, shrinkage of control going down the hierarchy, can be dealt with, on the assumption that you are going to attempt to get perfect control. I presume that the reader is aware of the fact that we have not solved the problem, although almost all our techniques can make control easier. It is important, then, that the higher-ups realize that they do not and cannot have complete control at the lower level. A perfectly integrated, perfectly functioning bureaucracy is a myth; one should simply try to make things work as well as possible. In the next few chapters we will deal with the problem of controlling an obviously imperfect bureaucracy.

12. The censors normally left the magistrates alone. If they did leave the provincial capitals to visit the Hsien, they might have been interested in more than just taxes and riots.

13. This depends on the dynasty and the time.

14. The Hsien frequently were located in portions of quite elaborate irrigation networks. In this case, there were other higher officials dealing with the irrigation network, but the Hsien magistrate would at least be expected to cooperate. Fortunately, this kind of activity in traditional China did not require much change from year to year. The use of the combined tax/no riot criteria nevertheless was a reasonably good measure of Hsien magistrate efficiency.

CHAPTER 7

TERMITES

Long ago, I wrote a manuscript entitled "Coordination Without Command: The Economics of Insect Societies." If it had been published, it would have been the first book in sociobiology. The problem that has made sociobiology a controversial subject is the tendency of O. E. Wilson and his friends to draw lessons for humans from animal societies. I did not think that we should copy the ants and termites, and I made a little restrained fun of an ant specialist who had talked in these terms. Perhaps I could have set sociobiology off on a better start, even though Wilson knows immensely more about insect societies than I do.

My reason for mentioning it is that I developed an economic theory as to how ant and termite nests succeed in coordinating their activities in spite of the fact that they have no central control, and the individual ants and termites have quite literally microscopic brains. This theory was, in essence, a radical generalization of standard market theory.[1] This radical generalization might be of some help in dealing with both private and governmental bureaucracies.

I assumed that ants and termites had very simple preference structures. For example, a given termite has a utility function that differs from ours only in the limited number of simple direct arguments in it. To take only two, the termite "desires" both food and a reasonably well repaired nest (the part of the nest with which he has immediate contact). Both of these desires are subject to declining marginal returns. When the termite attempts to maximize his satisfaction, he[2] either seeks food or repairs the nest, depending on which is most urgently demanded.

In actual practice, I would assume that the termites have ten or twelve arguments in their preference functions. Nevertheless, the termite attempts to maximize this function, which means that whichever of these arguments happens to have the highest marginal utility at the moment is the one it turns to.

1. I have another radical generalization to cover science in *The Organization of Inquiry* (Durham, N.C.: Duke University Press, 1965; Lanham, Md.: University Press of America, 1987).

2. Or she. Unlike members of the wasp family like bees and ants, the termite workers can be of either sex. They also have a royal pair instead of simply a queen. The mole rats, a social mammal, follow the wasps in having only a queen and female workers.

Thus, if the termite happens to be in a part of the nest that is in bad repair and has just eaten, it will repair the nest. If, on the other hand, it is in a part of the nest that is in good repair and is hungry, it will seek food.

Needless to say, the actual pattern of behavior is much more complicated; hence, the preference function must also be similarly complicated. But the system permits explanation of how a decentralized decision-making procedure, provided that the preferences are properly arranged, leads to highly coordinated behavior.[3]

It can be seen immediately that the standard discussion of market procedures is another example of the same kind of thing. We assume that human beings have a number of arguments in their preference function, all of which are subject to declining marginal returns; hence, they are apt to turn to the most pressing one. The basic difference between humans and termites is that humans are able to take indirect measures to meet their preferences. If we find that our front sidewalk is in a bad state of repair, we will very rarely drop everything else and begin fixing it. Usually we will undertake some other activity that permits us to earn money which we use to hire someone to repair it. Still, as I said, these two procedures have a family resemblance.

But not only the market. Public Choice assumes that people in politics also behave in this way. Politicians are motivated by a desire to maximize their preference function and take actions that rather indirectly are intended to that end, and the voters do the same. The basic differences among human beings are different preference functions and different abilities to produce outcomes which directly or indirectly meet those preference functions.

Among the ants and termites, however, if my theory is correct, then the preferences are pretty much identical unless the particular insect happens to have a caste system, in which case they are identical within each caste.[4]

I also think that bureaucrats are like this. They engage in various activities in order to maximize their preferences and they observe the outside environment and take the activity which directly—or in human beings, indirectly—is aimed at making that environment more in accordance with their wishes.

3. In both the ant and termite kingdoms there is a small amount of central control—from the queen in the case of the ants, and the royal pair or the royal group for termites—through the release of various chemicals. These chemicals control, however, a very small part of the total behavioral repertoire of these insects.

4. All of them have at least male and female and many have sexually nonfunctional working classes.

At this radical level of generality, a termite who observes something wrong with a tunnel in which it is moving and stops to repair it is behaving much the same as the bureaucrat who, fearing the budget of his division will be cut next year, produces a minor crisis which is intended to circumvent its occurrence.

The point of this digression is to argue that we can control bureaucrats and, indeed, other people by means other than simply giving them orders. We change their environment. I do not want to allege that an order does not change the environment. Indeed, I was a bureaucrat myself and in a service where travel orders sometimes changed my environment most radically.

That is not the only way in which the environment can be changed. For most human beings the most important part of the environment is other human beings, and they are not necessarily your superiors. Even if they are, they may have chosen to change your environment in some indirect manner rather than simply giving you an order.

Rules enforced by the regular police may be important in bureaucracies. At the time of this writing[5] the managers of the AEC are discovering that just because they are federal employees does not protect them from the FBI.[6] Thus, people organizing large-scale structures have alternatives to direct orders. Unfortunately, these alternatives, although in many ways highly efficient, are also hard to manipulate with precision.

It is also possible to change people's preferences so that they do what the people at the head of the organization want. Military organizations always devote much attention to what they call "morale" which, in essence, is an attitude of mind intended to lead soldiers into behavior that is radically different from what we would normally expect. In modern ground warfare with the units widely dispersed, this is particularly important.

The market is an intermediate situation in which the person's direct personal motives are adjusted to the desires of the overarching hierarchy by providing a set of rewards or punishments. In America, for example, most higher executives have their compensation tied one way or another to the performance of their particular branch of the business. There are many problems with these reward systems which will be discussed below; nevertheless, they are an example of adjusting the environment so that the individual does what you want without direct orders.

5. June 7, 1989.

6. The AEC management of the Rocky Flats plant are accused of various failures connected with the disposal of radioactive waste. I have no idea whether these accusations are true.

Perhaps it is easiest to discuss this environmental correction by beginning with the preference function and efforts to adjust it. Adjusting it is extremely difficult. All of the communist states devoted large-scale efforts to producing the new Soviet, Chinese, and Cuban man. In all cases, the moment the pressure relaxed, it turned out that they had failed. The large-scale welcoming of the invading German troops in Russia is one example.[7] The upsurge of severe criticism of the communist system that has occurred under Gorbachev is another example.

This chapter is being written immediately after the announcement of the results of the first Polish election. The Polish Communist Party, apparently under the impression that it had succeeded in indoctrinating the Poles, made a deal which, although certainly by no means a free election, nevertheless gave Solidarity some power. The result was a catastrophe for the Polish Communist Party which was not able to get its candidates elected even in constituencies where there was no opponent.[8]

Also at the time that this chapter is being written, the students in Beijing are being repressed quite bloodily after they demonstrated that although the bulk of them are children of communist officials and although they are undeniably the elite of the present government, they do not like it. It would be hard to produce better evidence that the indoctrination process, even over many years and accomplished by very skilled people, can fail.

But if these systems have failed, there are other systems that work, at least most of the time and when not subject to too great a pressure. Designers of such systems are well advised to see to it that first, not too much strain is put on these indoctrinated preferences and, second, that there be something in the environment that tends to reduce the strain by rewards and punishments. Stalin understood this; in his case, and in the case of Castro and the Chinese, elaborate methods were put in place to punish those who deviated. In general, communists put much more emphasis on the stick than on the carrot.

7. They made themselves unpopular over time, but it is still true that large numbers chose to flee with them rather than to remain behind and face the Red Army.

8. It has been a rather odd characteristic of "elections" in communist countries that it is necessary to get 50 percent of the votes out for each election in order to have the unopposed candidate (traditional for communists) elected. Occasionally less than 50 percent would turn out even under Stalin, and there would normally be complaints at this point about the poor organization of the election. In Poland, it was not that there was a small turnout, it was that the people crossed the communist name off the ballot. In this case, the peculiar communist method of election turned against them. They were hoist by their own petard.

Indeed, the current difficulties in both China and Russia, and Poland as well, have arisen because the mechanisms for providing penalties had lost their bite. The higher officials themselves had forgotten how the system was intended to work and did not order out the troops and secret police early enough. The fall of the Shah of Iran was caused by the same error.

Pitiless repression will keep almost any group down, and making a lot of concessions may work out reasonably well. Alteration between concessions and repression, however, which was the policy of the Shah, is very dangerous, particularly if, as with the Shah, the repression is rather mildly and inconsistently applied.[9]

But this is a discussion of the reward-and-punishment system rather than the changing preferences or more general environmental construction. Preferences do differ from one culture to another, and most governments make strong efforts to indoctrinate their subjects with whatever preference they think is desirable. The Chinese Empire was perhaps the longest-lasting example, dating back to the Chin Dynasty two thousand years ago. The indoctrination imposed through the educational system (by way of examinations—they did not directly control the schools) in an elaborate philosophy and knowledge of government was, on the whole, very effective.[10] It is notable, however, that although corruption was theoretically objected to, almost all officials were corrupt.

Consider, for example, *A Complete Book Concerning Happiness and Benevolence: A Manual for Local Magistrates in Seventeenth-Century China.*[11] This thick book, which went through a number of editions, was a sort of standard guide for officials who ran counties in China. It does not offer any direct advice on corruption but does discuss ways to keep down the tax payments to your provincial government. It also complains about various obviously corrupt acts by officials other than the head of the county government. Presumably, the readers of the book were able to carry out their corrupt activities on

9. The Shah had called in the International Red Cross to prevent his secret police from torturing suspects about two years before he was overthrown. The work of the Red Cross was not instantly effective, but there was almost no one tortured in the eighteen months before his overthrow. This was nice, but dangerous.

10. Formal examinations are only about a thousand years old, but the selection process in earlier years depended on much the same criteria.

11. By Huang Liu-Hung, translated and edited by Djang Chu (Tucson: University of Arizona Press, 1984).

their own without the guidance of the book. Indeed, if the author had offered any advice on this topic, he would have met a sticky end.

Once again, there is no doubt this had effects. The duties of the officials, particularly the censors, included offering criticism to the emperor of the emperor's own conduct. This was a dangerous task, especially because a memorandum criticizing the emperor ritually ended with a request that the memorialist be executed for his impertinence. The emperor sometimes honored that request.

As another example, the Wanli Emperor, one of the less competent emperors in the later Ming, wanted more than almost anything else to make the son of his favorite concubine his heir rather than his eldest son. It stirred up so much objection from his officials that he did not dare do it even though he violated many other canons for the behavior of the emperor.

In modern structures, similar indoctrination is normal. Efforts are made to indoctrinate people into the policies of the post office or of Smith's supermarket, and our society as a whole has fairly strong procedures for indoctrinating people into its moral code.

Modern educationalists claim that one should not impose moral codes on people, but the only thing that has changed is the moral code they are imposing. The switch from "Homosexuals are unspeakable villains" to "You may not criticize them, and they have a right to live life as they choose" is a change in the nature of the moral system, not an abandonment of morals.

People frequently carry out these changed or imposed preferences when it would not be to their advantage. On occasion we read of someone who found a substantial amount of money and returned it to its original owner instead of just pocketing it. Not all students cheat even when doing so is fairly easy.[12]

Thus, higher-ups in organizations normally have a modicum of control over the preference function of their subordinates. The society in which both the higher-ups and the subordinates operate has more but, again, not complete control. This can make organizing a bureaucracy easier.

We turn now to a way of changing the environment so that the individual is motivated to do the right thing without specific instructions. Another example of this point is an individual's obeying instructions when he/she does not really have to.

12. For evidence as to the quantity of cheating that one gets when it becomes easy, see Richard McKenzie and Gordon Tullock's *The New World of Economics* (Irwin) chapter on cheating, lying, and fraud.

The whole elaborate mechanism of economics is a description of how people are led "as by an invisible hand" to work for the advantage of other people, not because they are good but because the environment is so designed that their own goals will best be met by it. As Adam Smith said, our bread is provided by the baker, not because he has our interests in mind but because he has his own. This environmental coordination is, of course, not perfect. Monopolists are also responding to their environment.

Although the freely functioning market is an example of environmentally coordinated activity, people do not automatically develop efficient markets. Historically, many societies have put their reliance on other institutions. The market cannot simply be left alone to go as it wishes. Careful design, with periodic alternations, is necessary if we want to optimize. Unfortunately, most historic governments have not optimized, and their intervention in market process has often been undesirable. This should not imply that the market by itself operates perfectly.

What happens in the market is that my acts change the environment for other people and thus lead them to do things which, if I have performed properly and if the institutions are right, benefit me as well as them. The market is not the only place where this kind of coordination occurs. If Smith's opens a new supermarket in Tucson, it immediately changes the shopping environment for many people. Smith's happens to be well managed and intends to make money out of this expansion, but its success depends on the environment in which it operates and on other people's attitudes.

The concept of environmental coordination is not usually mentioned in regard to the market. In discussing it here, I am producing a somewhat different but nevertheless perfect mapping of the standard explanation, as the economists will realize.

Human beings have a fairly elaborate preference function, together with considerable calculating ability, which makes it possible for them to use indirect means to meet their most urgent preferences. Like the termite, however, their action is coordinated insofar as it is directly market-oriented by the fact that they observe the environment around them and take action calculated to meet their more urgent needs.[13]

Of course, because human beings have more complicated brains than termites, they may have a large collection of needs in mind and take actions

13. The termite does not calculate and engages in direct action.

intended to maximize this complex bundle, with each one treated in terms of its relative urgency. Taking a job, for example, provides an opportunity to meet many different arguments of the preference function, and the individual knows that. It is dubious that the termite is able to engage in this kind of complex reasoning.

Nevertheless, if we consider a pure market in which a group of farmers, say, trade with each other—a situation found even today in some primitive areas and which in the past was the dominant form of trade—we quickly realize that the farmers' behavior is an effort to maximize their own well-being by acts that are rather similar to those of the termites, although the latter do not ever engage in direct trade.[14]

From this kind of direct trade to the complex types of indirect trade of the modern world, the individual's market-dominated activity is still environmentally coordinated. The decision of Smith's market to stock a certain type of tropical fruit depends on its estimate of an important part of its environment, that is, the tastes of its customers. Shoppers regard the environment in which purchases are made as an important guide for their behavior.

The two "sides" each regard the other as part of the environment, and the coordination takes the form of changing the environment in order to get advantages in the long term. The difference between this and the termite nest is the greater complication of the preference function and the ability of human beings to engage in complex calculations beyond that of the termite.

Environmental coordination occurs in other than direct market operations of the purchase and sale type. The internal structure of any large organization can also be regarded as an example of environmental coordination, especially when superiors give orders and use the carrot and stick on inferiors. If I promise an inferior of mine that for accomplishing a certain task he

14. Among both the termites and the ants, there is a transfer of food from some of them to others. This can be regarded as a trade but only by quite difficult mental gymnastics. If one observes an ant who has returned from a hunting expedition outside the nest and whose crop is full of food, meeting an ant whose principal duties are within the nest, one will observe them tapping antennae, and then the hunting ant will regurgitate some food for the other ant. It can be called a trade in the sense that the ant bringing the food "pays" for the tapping with food, but I think it is more accurate to refer to this as the ant coming in having an argument in its utility function in which delivering food to other ants is something that is positive and valuable. It lays off against the advantages of that particular preference the advantages of consuming the food itself, and takes whichever is most urgent.

will get a bonus, and for not doing it he will get fired, I have changed the environment in which that man operates. He then obviously has the choice of either doing as I say or departing.[15]

Whether this is a convenient way of talking about the matter is an open question, but there are parts of the environment not subject to direct order or supervision by a superior; these are important within an organization. In the first place, simple physical differences make certain types of action easy and other types difficult. All corporations try to establish physical boundaries to make it difficult for employees to steal anything.

Even the location of an office may have a considerable impact on what an individual does. Location affects the people you see and the information flow you receive through informal channels. The equipment an individual is provided may decidedly change his productivity, and the intellectual climate can also have its effects.

Also critical is the accounting system used. The Russians have had immense difficulty over the years in utilizing accounting systems that are not profit oriented. As mentioned previously, the effort to use physical "success indicators" has led to all sorts of severe difficulties. A *Crocodile* cartoon showed a nail factory facing a weight success indicator producing in the course of the year one gigantic spike. The following year it was given a number-of-nails criterion, producing an immense number of almost microscopic nails.

The fact that environmental coordination is one way of describing what goes on in the market and in corporations does have some real consequences, because it reflects on the type of organization we see. With the extreme breadth of different organization types, we do not observe any single most-efficient method of organizing the economy in different areas.

There do exist rare pure market transactions between individuals who work entirely on their own.[16] Here we have pure market environmental coordination. More commonly these days people are involved in some larger structure whether that structure is the government of the United States or the

15. Rommel, when a mere temporary company commander, once gave a platoon leader the choice of obeying orders or being shot on the spot. This changed his environment radically (*Attacks*, by Field Marshal Erwin Rommel [Provo, Utah: Athena Press, 1979], p. 67). Although the publishers give Rommel his eventual rank, at the time he wrote the book he was a lieutenant colonel.

16. As one example, an attorney I used to know had a client who was an inventor of gadgets. Although the attorney had a secretary, he operated on his own, and the inventor depended primarily on inspiration rather than hiring a lot of assistants.

Ace Hardware store franchise arrangement.[17] The spectrum of such organizations is absolutely immense. Corporations may be highly authoritarian in their organization. One example is the Japanese just-in-time automobile factories.[18]

Henry Ford probably had the largest organization with highly authoritarian structure. With his gigantic assembly line, everyone had to behave in exact accordance with the rules, or the assembly line would stop.[19]

I am involved in a minimal way with a small corporation in Iowa that makes clothing. Most of its employees are engaged in either cutting cloth or sewing different pieces of it together. These activities must be closely coordinated with what we can sell since we have many different styles, sizes, and colors. Although the coordination is carried out first by a computer, this computer can be overridden by the higher officials and sometimes is. Nevertheless, the individual working in this plant has specific instructions as to what to cut or what exact two pieces of cloth to sew together with what kind of stitch.[20]

In this case, the coordination takes the form of instructions regarding what work material to place at the elbow of the person sewing and what its disposition will be. In most cases, the sewing machine operator does not receive any oral or written instructions, just a pile of a dozen or so clothing parts to put together.[21]

Environmental coordination occurs in many organizations where an unforeseen emergency is developing. Under these circumstances, personnel may respond to their previous training, but events will occur too fast for them to receive formal instructions.

17. We remember in this case that the franchising runs backward. The "owners" of the stores own the franchising organization.

18. The particular scheme is currently breaking down with a lot of subcontracting.

19. A number of other large-scale production operations behave almost exactly the same way.

20. The stitch is predetermined by the fact that the individual workers use specialized sewing machines. Normally one worker will always sew the same kind of stitch because that is the kind of machine he/she has. The computer directs the work to the appropriate worker as well as telling the worker what to do.

21. The scheme which sounds a priori inefficient and looks inefficient in the factory comes from the extraordinary flexibility that is necessary in a textile operation. The factory holds inventory for the retailers who order small bundles of different sizes, colors, and models for immediate delivery rather than maintaining an inventory of their own. Under the circumstances, long machine runs of a particular size, color, and style of, say, shorts are less economic than this system of a larger number of short runs. At the moment, there are no machines that have anywhere near the flexibility of the human being for this kind of an operation.

This could be an enemy attack on a military unit or a machine breakdown in a factory, or an office facing a major increase in the potential workload. In all cases the environmental coordination is apt to be succeeded shortly by direct orders from above. Still, there will be a period in which the individuals make their own decisions which depend on the environment, including what other people are doing.

In the old days, when fires were extinguished by volunteer fire departments, men would turn up at a fire and begin pumping water without any central control. It was thought to be a sort of contest in which the different independent fire companies attempted to establish reputations by outdoing each other.[22] Nevertheless the fire, the water sources, and the location of the other fire companies involved were the main considerations of a fire company arriving on the scene; central control was not relevant.

I am not arguing that this is an ideal system, but then neither are the ants and termites. However, the latter have no alternative; their system is the only one they have. Human beings can use other arrangements—for example, the carrot and stick for the market. Individuals are environmentally coordinated only insofar as environment determines where they will get rewards and where they will be driven into bankruptcy. On the other hand, we can use authoritative central instruction as, for example, in an army.

Universities are an almost perfect example of environmental coordination. Once a professor has been hired and receives tenure, the university can do little to control him. Indeed, it is a violation of ethics for the university to investigate what he is teaching. People who are actually mildly insane are permitted to continue teaching.[23]

22. It should be pointed out that the pumping of water in this case was a matter of human muscle, and so in a way it was an athletic contest.

23. The subject matter as specified in the catalog is controlled, but I have known at least two cases in which professors came to the conclusion that that subject matter was not really important and simply taught courses in other subjects. In one, a conservative and slightly off-his-rocker individual decided that the standard course in statistics, although no doubt of some rudimentary interest, should be replaced by another course he had written and which no one other than himself had ever succeeded in understanding.

The other case came during the unpleasantness of the late 1960s in which a professor teaching a course in neurophysiology completely dropped that topic and simply discussed politics with his students. Since he gave all the students an A, the course was immensely popular.

Neither of these individuals was fired nor subjected to any disciplinary activity. The first one, in fact, eventually was given an honorary position.

The strength of this ethic in the universities is best demonstrated by another somewhat odd circumstance. When I was at the University of South Carolina, the school of business had contracted an accountant who practiced in downtown Columbia to teach a course in tax accounting. One morning he did not show up for class; he had been arrested for violation of the income tax law on his personal tax form.

The following day I was talking with several other faculty members, including his immediate superior in the school of business, about the fact that the department head had done nothing about relieving this person from his teaching responsibility. The department head was indignant at the suggestion that he do anything about the matter. Whether he would have continued paying the man's salary while in prison we do not know; as it turned out, he was only fined and continued teaching until his contract ran out. Whether arrest is grounds for dismissal is a contingency not usually considered in drawing up a contract. Nevertheless, the department head's indignation indicates the kind of ethical drive.

What, then, does lead professors to teach whatever they teach? They receive a number of cues from the environment and they follow them. They certainly are not subject to any strong control by the carrot-and-stick method or by orders from their superiors. Environmental coordination is strong enough, however, that many professors do not realize just how free they are.

The other aspect of academic life—research—is a clearcut case of environmental coordination, although here it is reinforced by some carrots. I submit an article to a journal over which I have no control whatsoever and which has no direct control over me; either they do or do not publish it. If they do, it is read by various people who regard it either as good or not. Clearly, this is an environmental factor. The university, however, regards the number of articles I have published and the prestige of the journals in which they appear as evidence in determining my salary level. Normally, the bright young faculty member is well advised to pay less attention to his/her teaching duties and more attention to writing articles to get ahead in the academic world.

Environmental coordination can lead to bad performance as well as good performance. Indeed, all social insects are subject to various problems in which the environmental coordination causes them to die off, and the whole nest is destroyed. Certain circumstances can lead bees, ants, or termites to respond to an environmental stimulus in a destructive way. Of course, if this happened very often that particular set of genes would be eliminated by evolution.

The same is true of human beings. I think environmental coordination "just grew" in the case of the academic environment, but in many other cases it is carefully designed and imposed. We should not assume that environmental coordination is a solution, nor should we assume that the carrot and stick or the system of direct orders is ideal. People, as many courtiers in the past have discovered, can win great rewards for action that is contrary to the interest of the king. Strict obedience to orders may on occasion lead to disaster for the person giving the orders.

CHAPTER 8

A GENERAL PICTURE

Consider any society. We find that within it many of the possible human interactions do not exist; for example, I have no contact whatsoever with any man living in San Francisco. Among the social interactions that do exist, many are quite casual and do not take up much time; others are more important. Of the important ones, some are direct bargains in which something is traded for money, products, service, and so on.

Many others, however, are long-lasting relationships in which the same people have contact with each other over time. Of these, many are simple contractual relationships of the type you obtain when you buy a car on credit or when you enter into, as I have, a contract with a gardening company. Among this group, however, we will see cases in which a number of people are grouped together into permanent organization and in which the relations between them are not the result of bargaining. Although an employee can always quit and his employer can always fire him, while they are engaged in their cooperative endeavor, their relationship does not normally center around specific bargains about each individual step. Some nonhierarchical relationships have this same characteristic. I have mentioned my contract gardener, and on occasion I ask him to do something special or complain about something that he has done.[1]

Let us simplify this structure radically to begin our discussion of why we observe these different types of organization. Assume that we have a society where there are no monopolies and no externalities,[2] and in which, for reasons which we will not now discuss, property rights are maintained.

Since division of labor pays, we would anticipate that different people would be producing different things and would engage in exchanges. Our experience indicates that there are economies of scale in many types of activities; hence, that for many activities, large hierarchical organizations would exist,

1. Actually, it is not obvious in this case whether I should say he or she/he. My original contract was made with the wife of the man who right now is doing most of the supervision. The apparent explanation of the switch in the people I am dealing with has to do with a new baby.

2. Of course, many economists regard monopolies as an example of an externality-generating activity.

and there would be a whole set of small hierarchical organizations at different levels of economies of scale. There is no reason that this type of operation could not develop quite spontaneously from people simply wanting to maximize their well-being, with some people choosing to organize lots of others into large organizations, other people choosing to work in the large organizations for salaries, and still others remaining as independent operators.

In any existing corporation, people can be divided into four categories. First and absolutely vital are the customers who, for some obscure reason, tend to be left out in the usual discussion; second, the workers, and the workers are normally broken into managerial and nonmanagerial types, with the people at the top frequently called entrepreneurs. In the final category, we have the people who put up the capital.

There is no intrinsic reason why the fourth category has to be separate. If one looks at the average American corporation, the employees, if they put their entire personal wealth (equity in their house, insurance policy, car, and so on) into the pot, could buy control of the corporation. If they do not, the apparent reason is that they are risk-averse. "Don't put all your eggs in one basket" is a sensible bit of folk wisdom.

As an aside, I should point out that there are employee-owned firms. The case most discussed in economic literature is the law firm, which is unusual because it does not have much nonhuman capital. The present-day large law firm, a recent invention, apparently is a byproduct of the extraordinarily complicated law which has developed in recent years. It provides specialists for each particular branch of the law so customers do not need to track down suitable specialists themselves. In systems where the law is simpler and an individual lawyer can know the whole law himself, these big organizations are not needed.

The other cases of employee-owned firms fall roughly into three categories. One is the small group of cases in which a wealthy man has died and bequeathed his enterprise to its employees, a system that usually does not last very long. Parallel to it are a few cases in which the company itself has had bad luck and has lost a large part of its equity value. If the cause of its loss is a powerful union that has kept wages above the equilibrium level, then transferring the company to the union may be a convenient way of lowering the wages.

The final case is the rare situation where a company has actually developed under employee ownership. The plywood cooperatives that used to be so important on the West Coast are examples, but they, like the others, are tending to disappear. Their basic problem, from the owner-operator standpoint, is that they are risky investments. Understandably, these people would prefer to be employed by one firm and put their money into something else.[3]

A certain number of people do start corporations, investing all their money into them. As an extreme example, Ray Kroc in his fifties sold a small company that he owned and put that capital together with an immense amount of work on his own part into what must have seemed an extremely long-shot gamble. Of course, McDonald's paid off. Most of the businessmen who do this, and it is not too rare, lose their shirts. We are fortunate that a considerable number of people in our society are willing to take this kind of risk.

In most cases, however, the capital is provided by a separate group of people who are not actually employed by the firm although some higher managers may possess considerable capital.

In family corporations, some of which still exist, some substantial stockholders may be members of the lower management. These are young men starting in the business and learning it from the bottom up.

Looking at the world, then, we observe a number of large organizations engaged in, say, manufacturing and selling automobiles. In addition, there are a number of individuals working entirely on their own and in all of the intermediate stages. There are also governmental organizations, but by (temporarily) ruling out externalities, we have in large part made them unnecessary.[4]

The relationship of these large groups to exterior groups is also important. In a real sense, customers act as an important police force for the efficiency of any firm. Only if the firm can produce and sell its products at a price that permits covering all costs, preferably with something left over, can it continue to exist. Another police force is the employees. They must be paid a wage and be provided with working conditions so that they will want to stay.

Last, the capital providers—which in our society are normally separate from those two groups but could be melded with either one[5]—must all be satisfied by this entity. This is different from the individual operator working on his own who can accept low personal returns if he wants. This large entity cannot afford to provide output that is of poor quality or too high in price, to provide wages and working conditions to its employees that are less than

3. For the average worker, that means a house.

4. Property enforcement and enforcement of contracts are traditional government activities, but in both cases it can be argued that their real reason for existing is externality reduction.

5. Consumer-owned cooperatives are not a very significant part of our economy, but they do exist.

competitive, or to produce a return on capital below that of its competitors. It is subject, then, to fairly stern disciplinary activity. Again, this does not require any government activity although government is also important in the real world.

The management must make the decisions and carry out general policy directives in this organization. The problem of making certain that everyone is working hard and trying to do their best is, as Alchian and Demsetz have correctly argued, best left to the residual claimant. The problem with this is that anyone can be the residual claimant. In most American corporations, the profits of the corporation go to the stockholders who are the residual claimants, but there are other possible organizations.

An obvious case is a worker-owned firm where the workers are the residual claimants, and we do occasionally find situations in which the customers are the residual claimants. One such case is the consumer cooperative; we earlier mentioned the rather peculiar organization of Ace Hardware in which the individual stores were customers of the central franchising and wholesaling organization and were also the residual claimants. In each of these cases, the residual claimants are legally the people who have control.

Traditionally, there was a situation in which bankers, who simply loaned money to the corporation, were the people in control. The House of Morgan in 1900 was one example. During that period, a lot of the money was invested on the reputation of the bank rather than on the reputation of the company. It seems likely, however, that the bankers themselves made their decisions in terms of the size of the equity held by the common stockholders. If it was large, the company was worth more loans; if it was small, it was not, and the management had better be changed.

Why in most cases do the stockholders have the ultimate right to fire the management? It isn't so in management-controlled firms, but among established firms, management control is comparatively rare. The answer, I think, is simple. The stockholders, a group of people who know little about the corporation, pay little attention to it, and can easily get out of the corporation by selling their stock, are almost the only ones whose activities cannot possibly be at fault for the corporation's poor functioning.

One reason the corporation is not doing well might be that it is paying its workers too much, and the workers would hardly fire the management for that. Similarly, the corporation might be charging too low a price to its customers who would also not fire the management. The management itself, almost by definition, is likely to be satisfied with its own behavior and will not fire itself. The stockholders normally do nothing whatsoever about the corporation except to change the management occasionally. Their sole interest lies in the company's profitability, and they do not have the same conflicts of interest as all the other possible final claimants.

Another aspect to consider is that the stockholders are apt to be relatively lacking in risk aversion. Insofar as they are risk-averse, they can diversify their investment; therefore, they are usually willing to make sizable gambles on any individual stock. Furthermore, their effect on the organization of the corporation can be registered by simply unloading the stock that they think is doing badly or by voting against the corporation. In the past, corporations sometimes faced proxy fights to get rid of the management; now they face takeovers. The takeover is a better method provided that the financial market is organized well enough to assemble the money for it. Apparently, this last condition has only recently been met.

In any event, the management itself is apt to respond to threats of either a proxy fight or a takeover by making changes within its structure. The efforts of management in recent years—unfortunately, very successful—to protect themselves against either form of discipline, and in particular against the takeover bid, are no doubt reducing the efficiency of our system. It is a case in which supervision is clearly failing.

But to say that supervision is failing because the managers are beginning to protect themselves against being thrown out for inefficiency[6] raises a question about the general supervision. The corporation stockholders normally have to approve these various measures, or, alternatively, the measures are enacted by a legislature in which the corporation stockholders certainly have more potential influence than the management does.[7] It seems simply to be poor supervision. Most stockholders, because they can readily switch from one company to another, are relatively uninterested in the management of a particular company.

If the supervision is failing and a proxy fight (the older technique) develops, stockholders can probably decide casually which way to vote, and that necessarily puts the management under pressure. In the more modern

6. This is not, of course, their explanation for why they are protecting themselves.

7. This would not be true with respect to any given corporation. Stockholders are spread all over the world while the management is concentrated in the headquarters state. But the total number of stockholders in any state will normally outnumber the total management, and these laws affect all corporations chartered by the state. In many cases, the headquarters is not in the chartering state at all.

method, the takeover fight is a good way of making money.[8] In this method, the stockholders, by selling their stock, depress its price; some "pirate" buys the company, fires the present management and replaces it with a better one, then sells the company again with a potential capital gain.

All of this indicates that stockholder supervision is decidedly less than optimal if we think not of the well-being of the stockholders but of society as a whole. However, if we rearranged the corporation so that the residual claimants are the workers, the customers, or the management itself, the situation would be worse.[9] Furthermore, if we consider the utility of the stockholders as part of the value for society, their decision not to spend much time on the job of supervising may more than pay for the inefficiency of that supervision.

So far we have been talking about the environment that surrounds the corporation and how it polices the efficiency of the corporation. We have not talked about the hierarchy itself which starts at the top with the management and works its way down through the workers. That hierarchy faces a difficult task because it is subject to severe competition.

In government the competition is much less thorough. Also, competition in government is not always aimed at a socially desirable goal. The competition of different companies for customers means they are under continuous pressure to cut prices and improve quality. The competition for laborers means that they are pressured to improve conditions at work and raise wages. Finally, the competition that they face to keep the stockholders satisfied and to arrange to borrow money from the banks, making certain that the net value of the stockholders' equity is sizable, tends to make capital in society invest in its most highly valued use.

In other types of activity—government and nonprofit organizations—these pressures are much weaker. Thus, the government and the nonprofits operate in a less vigorously controlled environment, and one can anticipate that they will not work as well.

Even though in this book we concentrate on government and private profit-making bureaucracies, there are other bureaucracies in our society such

8. One of the byproducts here is the development of the specialized industry in which a "pirate" threatens a takeover and gets paid a significant amount of greenmail in order to not carry the threat out. The fact that the stockholders do not prevent the greenmail payment is another example of poor supervision by the stockholders.

9. For a great many European corporations, particularly in France, the latter condition is true, and this may indicate why their economy is not really flourishing.

as the nonprofit portion in which I work.[10] In general, the nonprofits are small organizations. Even if we consider Harvard University, its size is trivial compared with a moderate-sized corporation. It does not have a large bureaucracy, but it sometimes behaves in a bureaucratic way. Custom and individual preferences of employees seem to be its primary controlling variables.

Nonprofit organizations can, however, operate under highly controlled circumstances. The current legal problems of the Jim Bakker family come from the fact that they set up a large nonprofit organization and diverted its revenue to management perquisites. Granted the objectives they had, it was efficient. What we object to are the objectives.

In general, the present organization of nonprofits exists almost entirely to prevent money from being diverted in a similar way to that of the Bakkers. Certainly a self-perpetuating board is not likely to be an efficient organization, particularly if its members are selected primarily in terms of their ability to raise money rather than for their knowledge of the subject matter.

Most of my readers and I have been for a long time in organizations governed in this way. Most state university boards are not self-perpetuating but are selected by the government of the state in terms of whether they have reasonably good political connections but are not actually candidates for anything. This gives us people similar to those, say, on the board at Harvard, except our people do not have as much money. Since they have considerable influence on the state legislatures, however, the net effect is that they provide more money to the university than the board does to Harvard.

To repeat, these nonprofits do not operate particularly efficiently. Their tax exemption, together with the fact that they are able to get free or cheap labor because of their charitable names, could make them able to compete successfully with regular business. Bennett and DiLorenzo have, in fact, written a book on the subject.[11] Nevertheless, it is hard to argue that this is a good system; also, it has no true residual claimant.

10. I am, of course, an employee of the state government, but the academic portion of our society, even though now largely dominated by the government, still continues to act in much the same way as it did thirty or forty years ago when it was dominated by private organizations. In a way, it is a private nonprofit organization that depends on a state legislature rather than on John D. Rockefeller for its economic support and gives about as much control to the legislature as Chicago did to John D. Rockefeller.

11. James T. Bennett and Thomas J. DiLorenzo, *Unfair Competition: The Profits of Nonprofits* (New York: Hamilton Press, 1989).

Consider the standard art museum. It benefits a considerable number of members of the upper class who like to visit it, regard it as a social center, and so on. It also probably benefits a certain number of the lower-class individuals who have artistic desires and can get them filled cheaply.[12] A number of middle-class housewives whose children have gone off to school find useful activities around the museums such as running the museum shop. If they are wealthy they may be on the board. But these people are not the residual claimants despite their probable influence on the management.

Ultimately, the influential people are those in a position to provide further funding. A board member who is thinking vaguely of giving the museum a Rembrandt is a man whose every word is listened to with bated breath. But neither are these people residual claimants; in a way, they are residual sources of money.

The staff in a nonprofit organization has much more influence than in a private corporation simply because the objectives are not as clearcut and measurable as they are in a private corporation. It is not true that the people who visit the museum or the artsy-craftsy types who make up its board are as ignorant of the museum's affairs as the average stockholder is of his company. It is true, however, that the simple bookkeeping number that determines the success or failure of the company is brought to the attention of various people who might be interested—raiders, for example—where nothing like this happens at museums.[13]

When we have a scandal in a museum or church, then it is similar to the situation with the Bakkers in which money has actually been diverted to the management. Scandals in private companies normally take the form of irregular activities that the management undertook to increase the profit of the company, not to add to their own personal rake-off.

Having said this, however, I should say that the lower part of the hierarchy in nonprofit organizations is usually not very closely supervised. Fortunately,

12. Actually, the members of the lower class normally are not much interested in such things. It is the upper class that goes into them. But, no doubt, some lower-class people or poverty-stricken people do patronize these subsidized museums.

13. See William Dyer Grampp, *Pricing for the Priceless: Art, Artists, and Economics* (New York: Basic Books, 1989; Bruno S. Frey and Werner W. Pommerehne, *Muses and Markets: Explorations in the Economics of the Arts* (Oxford: Basil Blackwell, 1989); and Edward C. Banfield, *The Democratic Muse: Visual Arts and the Public Interest* (New York: Twentieth Century Fund, 1984).

it also is usually small since most of these organizations are not big. Although inefficient, there appears to be no better way.

In regard to a larger part of our society, the government, as mentioned previously, suffers from not having any clearcut measure of efficiency like accounting; but in a democracy it does have another measure—the number of votes it gets. This differs from the number of votes that the current management will get at the next election in a corporate organization, because usually there is no opposition in the corporation. When there is, it frequently takes the form of some kind of intermittent pirating technique in which the existing management will be displaced.[14]

Furthermore, although the voter in a political election is typically badly informed, he/she is better informed than the common stockholder who is voting in a corporation. The last phenomenon is to some extent counterbalanced by the people and organizations whose stock holdings in a given corporation are large enough so that they do become informed. The corporate structure is designed so that ideally these people will act as proxies for the other common stockholders rather than using their power for diverting funds to themselves.

Here, again, we have a potential scandal that almost never occurs in the United States. All corporations with a true majority stockholder or stockholding family may in fact divert things like private cars for the corporate manager, and so on, to themselves at the expense of the minority holders. The degree to which they can do this without going to jail for embezzlement, however, is limited. A judge with a much lower personal income will decide whether the expenditure was proper and ordinary. A car, trips to conventions, and some entertainment expenses are about all corporation members can safely claim.

Even officers of major corporations usually do not have this kind of option. Of course, various incentive plans are probably more generous to the management than it really deserves, but this generosity is limited. Besides, the stockholders benefit from the incentive plan because it gives managers greater motivation. Certainly, these procedures (which, under corporation law, have to be voted in by the stockholders) are usually endorsed. Presumably, the stockholders do not know anything about their particular corporation, but they do know that this technique is good.

14. Sometimes with a golden handshake.

In Europe corporate laws are different. There, cheating is common. Sometimes the people operating the corporation have succeeded in cutting out a lot of the other stockholders. The reason it does not occur in the United States is, oddly enough, because of a cartel restriction. In the days when the New York Stock Exchange had an effective monopoly, it imposed a single category of voting stock, which would be the residual legatee, on all corporations who wanted their stock listed.[15] The reason they did so was presumably to increase the attractiveness of the product. That is, they wanted to sell common stock widely because they were the principal market for it. The New York Stock Exchange has lost its monopoly status, but the effect of the rule is still strong.

Certainly, it is hard these days to sell stock that does not have such a system. When Henry Ford died, Ford Motor Company was left partly to the Ford Foundation in the form of a gigantic amount of nonvoting stock and partly in the form of a much smaller amount of voting stock to his direct heirs. Eventually, the corporation converted the nonvoting stock to voting stock to permit the Ford Foundation to sell it at a good price.

With government, the voters differ from the voters in a corporation in several ways. One is that there are no individuals with a whole pile of votes who are deeply interested in the outcome and who, therefore, may become well informed. During the period when England rose from the status of a rather backward island off the northwest coast of Europe to the world's dominant power, England did have a class of voters of this sort. The existence of the rotten-borough system meant that there were a number of men who personally sat in the House of Lords but who owned enough seats in the House of Commons so that they could strongly influence the political activities of the government. They seem to have played somewhat the same role as the large individual stockholder does in companies even where he/she owns only, say, 3 percent of a gigantic corporation. This system is generally regarded as undemocratic.

In an ordinary democracy, then, the voter is slightly better informed than the voter in the corporation. He/she suffers from not having any simple way of telling if the government is working well or badly. The politician has a way of telling whether the government is working badly in the sense that he

15. The development of warrants has to some extent made this no longer a true residual legatee arrangement. But the warrants are simply the right to buy common stock, so this makes no great difference.

counts the votes. But these votes are votes of people who have no motivation to become informed, so it is not obvious that this index is positive.

The individual voter has another problem. There is normally a conflict of interest between him and society as a whole. Let us take an old example. After Athens recovered from the defeat of the Peloponnesian war, she began construction of a second "empire."[16] The standard historical account as to why this empire failed is that the Athenian government had developed the habit of making direct payments to the voters out of surplus funds. Since the voters decided what funds were surplus, they tended to underfund the navy and overfund their own pocketbooks. They were willing to pay for the navy when Athens was actually at war, but they were not willing to keep it up in peacetime. As a result, Athens never regained its naval prominence after the Syracusan expedition.

Other more recent examples include the farm program of almost any democratic country, the Central Arizona Project, and the Tombigee Canal. A particularly striking example is the reluctance of even pacifistically inclined congressmen to close military bases in their districts.

Again, for this phenomenon to be absent in corporations, the accounting system must be more than a simple profit-and-loss account. Individual stockholders no doubt would exert similar pressure on the corporation except that, fortunately, it is illegal and almost instantaneously detectable. Unfortunately, in democratic politics things are not so simple; hence, this kind of activity is common.

But why do we have government? Clearly, it is not a terribly efficient organization. However, in my opinion, dictatorships are less efficient and less interested in the well-being of every citizen.[17] The answer is that although the market can be highly efficient in certain areas, in other areas—where there are large externalities—it is highly inefficient.

The choice is between two types of instruments: one is intermittently efficient and the other is almost always mediocre. We should choose the market where it is efficient, and where it is less efficient than the mediocre government, we should choose the government.

16. "Empire" is not a very good description of the Athenian polity. The individual city-states that fell within it were self-governing and in most cases seem to have been quite happy about the whole arrangement. Many of them remained loyal to Athens even in the last desperate days of the Peloponnesian war.

17. I have written a book on dictatorships, *Autocracy* (Dordrecht, Netherlands: Martinus Nijhoff, 1987).

I mentioned above that a traditional duty of the government is the enforcement of contracts and property rights. This task is allocated to the government. That is not because there is a great externality in that activity, but maintaining a force on hand capable of this enforcement does generate externalities. Many of our legal decisions are handled by organizations called arbitral courts. The great Roman law was developed by a group of jurisconsults who held no government position. As a final example, the modern Roman-Dutch tradition depends on essays written by law professors rather than by courts or legislatures. Indeed, our law is frequently changed by nongovernmental officials engaging in some kind of educational activity aimed at legislatures or judges.

There is no reason why we should complain about this, but also no reason why we should argue that it is ideally efficient. If a number of groups undertook the forceful act of enforcing these decisions, however, there would be problems. For example, I could hire someone to dispossess a householder whom I alleged had not kept up the payments on his mortgage, and he could hire someone else because he alleges that he has. A small war would ensue. The current conditions in Lebanon indicate what one might expect from living for a number of years with that approach. Because our desire to avoid it is understandable, we try to keep the use of force in society restricted to one agency—a so-called monopoly of force—and consider it a sensible policy.

Of course, in the United States a number of different agencies can use force because the individual citizen is subject to several different levels of government. If I did not keep up the payments on my mortgage I would be dispossessed by a county official, the sheriff; if I speed, depending on where I am, I might be arrested by either a state policeman or a municipal policeman. If worse comes to worst and public order breaks down, the military can be called in.

If our two levels, the state and the federal government, do not get into war with each other, there is no great difficulty. The obvious small size of any given low-level organization as opposed to the central organization normally prevents that from happening but, of course, we did have the Civil War. The War of the American Revolution could also be used as an example where local governments decided to fight the central government.

The general picture here is that hierarchies are rather similar, whether they are government or private. The private hierarchies have an element of efficiency that makes measurement of their performance easier, more so than in the government. Certain people—corporate raiders, for instance—can make a great deal of money by discovering that one of these hierarchies is behaving inefficiently and by taking steps to improve it. Unfortunately, this is not characteristic of the government. The internal lives of the two organizations are quite similar, however. To re-quote William Niskanen: "Sociologically, there is no difference between the federal government and the Ford Motor Company."

What we have, then, is a society in which a large number of different organizations—some of them small, some of them simply individual people—are interacting. Our goal should be a structure in which the individual organizations are motivated to behave efficiently and the interaction is efficient. Over the history of the human race, these objectives have been a preoccupation of truly great minds, but it cannot be said that they have been finally solved.

CHAPTER 9

RANDOM ALLOCATION

How do you control your subordinates? I have already discussed briefly methods of improving your control if you are striving for perfect control, and have pointed out that you must be satisfied with less than perfect effectiveness of these methods. Accordingly, I will now discuss relaxing your requirements.

In trying to get as much control as possible, we will begin with a simple structure: one man at the top of a hierarchy has as his only objective getting his desires implemented. We will assume that at each stage of the hierarchy in our structure, each person supervises three people. Thus, our man at the top supervises three immediate assistants, each of whom supervises three below that, and so on. We will also simplify matters by assuming that, at each level of the hierarchy, including the top person, individuals spend half their time determining what should be done and the other half seeing to it that their inferiors carry it out.

This last assumption is, I think, quite realistic. My experience with high officials indicates that they do make a lot of decisions on their own, an ability that is equally as important in determining their success as their ability to supervise inferiors. They frequently, of course, consider the advice of their inferiors in their decisions.

As mentioned earlier, the committees, or groups of administrators in large organizations, are the vehicles for producing new ideas and winnowing them down so that the ideas that reach the top are a favorable selection. Well-run organizations, however, do not simply accept the top recommendation of this administrative swamp. The higher official looks over several of the decisions, selecting the one that he likes best. Sometimes the individual at the top will invent his own idea rather than accepting the ones presented to him. Even in this case, however, he will usually turn to the administrative swamp for some processing of his basic idea.

For the time being, we will not regard this man as supervising the sources of information or ideas upon which he bases his decisions. He will simply divide his time equally between making up his own mind and seeing to it that his inferiors implement his desires.

This man's decisions constitute what we might call a general policy. He wants the people in the next step down to devote half of their time to making up their minds about the detailed instructions for their subordinates, which are in accord with his basic ideas, and half to supervision. The same thing is true with each lower stage. We assume realistically that the orders from on high require elaboration and adjustment to special conditions in each division, and the division head spends half of his time on that and the other half on supervision.

One thing the man at the top has to supervise, and which each supervisor down has to supervise as well, is the elaboration that is carried out during this half-time of decision-making by the lower-level officials.

To take a famous example, on the second day at Gettysburg, General Lee sent General Longstreet around his right to seize Little Round Top, which dominated the battlefield. But there was also the standing regulation in the armies of both the North and the South that troops march for fifty minutes and then take a ten-minute break.[1] Whether General Longstreet's corps should take their break exactly at the right time after precisely fifty minutes, or continue on for another few minutes to the top of the hill was clearly General Longstreet's decision. He decided to take the break. This decision was extremely important. Whether Lee would have won the battle if Longstreet had gone on is unknown, but Mead would certainly have been forced to realign his entire position.

Another aspect of this particular incident illustrates what can go wrong with a command structure. Little Round Top was saved for the Union by a quartermaster major-general who rode up to the top of the hill simply to look at the battlefield. He noticed Longstreet's forces coming up, dashed back, and succeeded in talking some local units not directly under his command into moving to the Little Round Top; thus, it was held.

When he arrived at the top, he found a signal corps observatory that was busily engaged in observing, using telescopes better than the ones he had, and sending messages somewhere by semaphore. Apparently, there had been a breakdown in the bureaucracy here or the general's intervention would not have been necessary.

We have here simply an example of the need for elaboration of orders. Had General Lee been physically present, he would have countermanded the ten-minute delay. But, again, one cannot be sure. In any event, it is necessary for each level as you go down the pyramid to decide, in some detail, what should

1. Which they did still when I was in the infantry in World War II.

be done with the orders from above. The guideline of using half the time for this activity simply makes the model easier to follow.

The problem I want to discuss here is how the supervisors allocate their time in the supervision part of their duties. They can devote only one-sixth of their time to each of the individuals under them, meaning that of necessity their supervision is imperfect.

In some cases, one-sixth is a perfectly adequate allocation of time. Until recently, military units in combat or in drill were arrayed in long, straight lines. The supervisors could easily and quickly tell how well the units were doing. Frederick the Great at Rosbach could see a large part of his army and a large part of the approaching French army. His lower-level commanders had an even better view of the particular troops under their command. Under these circumstances, an individual soldier who tried to hold back, or a regimental commander who was moving slowly, could assume that his activity was directly observed by his superior despite the large numbers of soldiers under him.

Even that was not perfectly simple. Generalship involved doing something your opponent did not anticipate, and that frequently meant that some of your troops would be out of his observation and also out of yours. Napoleon lost the Battle of Leipzig to a considerable extent because a portion of his army that he sent on a circuitous route around the flank miscarried.

Much depends, of course, on how easy the task is to supervise. The situation in the traditional army in which the soldiers stood in long, straight lines is unfortunately exceptional. As we have pointed out, at least the accounting system provides a way of telling whether people are achieving one narrow goal, making a profit. Unfortunately, it is imperfect because conditions surrounding each individual member of, say, the Safeway chain are different than all the others.

Even in Frederick the Great's army a straight line of soldiers advancing might find the land inconsistent. Part of the line might be in deep mud while the rest might be on hard earth. But such problems are easier to deal with than those involved in trying to decide whether two supermarket managers have different profit rates because of different levels of efficiency or because of purely local conditions beyond their control.

One way of dealing with this, used pretty uniformly by large organizations, is to have policies that are easy to monitor and that are allegedly efficient. For example, a number of supermarkets have a policy under which their house brands, that is, brands they have produced for themselves and that normally have a somewhat higher profit margin, are to be placed in the middle of a shelf, with the nonhouse brands, which they have to carry in order to remain competitive with other supermarkets, placed on either side. Supposedly, people are more likely to select the house brands from there than they would be if they had been placed at one end of the row. In any event, this is easy to check.

Other procedures are also easy to monitor, such as the continuous rotation of material on the shelves so that nothing exceeds its shelf life. Matters such as these are usually handled by special inspectors of a lower rank than district supervisors. Of course, district supervisors will occasionally monitor their inspectors by checking shelves whenever they are in the store.

Regulations also exist in higher-level areas. Most of the supermarket chains have policies about such things as displays, which part of the merchandise should be in what part of the store, and so on. The responsibility for these adjustments reverts to the local manager since, for instance, the floor space and layout vary at different stores.

In addition, certain Safeway stores are located in areas where the public's taste lies outside the mainstream, partly because of income level and partly because of ethnic variation. I live in Tucson, which has a very substantial Mexican population and where the non-Mexican population is attracted to Mexican food. If Safeway wants to make money, it must adjust in this direction, deviating from what we might call national standardization.

The military system of Frederick the Great is perhaps the easiest to supervise of any government organization we know. Safeway, however, is as close as we are likely to get in any large hierarchic organization. In many cases, large organizations face vastly more complex problems. Consider, for example, the management of a true conglomerate whose subdivisions are engaged in radically different types of production. One company may engage in making parts for air force planes, owning a couple of television stations or a chain of convenience stores, and perhaps participating in a dozen other diverse areas. Not only must it obtain efficiency within each of these divisions, it has to be able to supervise the divisions themselves, although they have nothing in common but the profit motive.

In government, the situation is much worse because the simple goal of making a profit is not there. In the United States, consider the president's immediate inferiors. He has a postmaster general, who engages rather ineptly in moving the mail around the country; a secretary of state, engaged in dealing with foreign nations; a secretary of the interior, who has a widely diverse collection of duties, mainly in the western part of the United States; the armed forces, one part of which (army engineers) does work similar to that of the Department of Interior in water projects; the Department of Justice which maintains prisons and acts as a lawyer for many government agencies. We could go on.

The president has no easy way to compare whether his attorney general is more or less efficient in carrying out his task than his secretary of the interior is. They do not have the same tasks. The situation is similar within other divisions. For instance, although the attorney general maintains prisons and a legal staff that does much of the government's legal work, his office also recommends judicial appointments and has half a dozen other activities which are only rather loosely related. Cabinet bureaus are similarly set up. In all of these cases, a supervisor must have some direct knowledge of a large variety of procedures and select from among them. Furthermore, if he does so, he must be certain that his judgement in the area is at least as good as that of the person he is supervising. If not, he may lower efficiency by his supervision rather than raise it. Obviously, he cannot do everything or know everything with which his subordinates deal, so he must make a selection.

The first problem confronting a supervisor, then, is what to supervise. Which aspects of his inferiors' work should he attempt to control? He does not want the inferior to be completely free to make decisions about everything except some small area that the supervisor checks regularly. He wants the inferior to do things which the supervisor would undoubtedly favor if he checked them. Because the superior will check only a small collection, this is difficult.

The method that automatically occurs to any economist considering this problem is random selection. Furthermore, an experienced supervisor's behavior does have some random components, but is not perfectly random for reasons we will discuss below. Let us, however, consider a situation in which the supervisor is literally random in his choices. Again, our procedure involves three inferiors of the man at the top, each of whom supervises three, each of whom supervises three; we will stop at that point, with twenty-seven people at the bottom actually taking action in the outside world, and the remainder being supervisors.

The superior now is devoting only one-half of his time to supervision; hence, he can devote only one seventy-second of his time to each of his thirty-six inferiors if he allocates time evenly among them. Roughly speaking, he could give one day every three months to each. If they did not know what day that would be, they would be under considerable pressure to design their activities such that no matter what day it turned out to be, they would not get into trouble.

If the supervisor does supervise each of his inferiors one day in every three months (this would be a small hierarchy), he could hardly hope to know as much about any given inferior's scope of operations as that inferior did. Thus, even granting that the superior is both more intelligent and better informed about his own preferences than the inferior, he may frequently decide that the inferior is doing something wrong when the inferior's action is actually in accordance with the real interests of the man at the top.

If the supervisor enters a store in Tucson and observes that the brands of specialized Mexican food are a little peculiar, he does not know whether this indicates that the local manager is inefficient or that the customers have unique tastes. Furthermore, granted the short period of time that he can devote to the matter, he cannot hope to become well informed. It would take him more time to determine whether the assortment of Mexican-type food in the store is appropriate for the local customer assortment than it would take the local store manager who already has a great deal of background in that area. Thus, in a way, the supervisor is relatively inefficient in applying his time in judging what the inferior is doing.

Safeway does have an accounting system, and although it is not a perfect way of judging the efficiency of managers, it is a great help. Look at the government and consider what would happen if the attorney general decided to personally supervise the part of a local district attorney's decisions on whether to prosecute or accept a plea bargain.[2] The local attorney has a good idea of what local juries are like, knows the prejudices and characteristics of the local judges, and has talked to almost everyone concerned. He has a fair idea as to whether certain people will make good witnesses. Even if the attorney general is a better attorney than the local district attorney, the local district attorney's judgement would still be better than that of the attorney general unless the latter devoted considerable amounts of time to becoming thoroughly familiar with the case.

The point of all this is to re-emphasize that it is impossible for the higher supervisors to engage in detailed regulation of the lower-level people in a complex situation. The only way of obtaining any real control at these levels

2. This actually means how stiff he will be in his plea bargaining negotiations. The actual terms are what determines whether it will go to trial.

is to simplify the command structure by giving lower-level personnel more basic, routine tasks. Even then it is necessary to loosen the control operations considerably.

Returning to the accounting system, let us assume that the simple straightforward task given to lower-level officials is to maximize profits as shown in the accounts, and for the time being we will not discuss possible defects in those accounts. To ignore all of the difficulties faced by individual Safeway store managers, and to simply promote those with the highest profits and fire those with the lowest, is clearly not a perfect method of operation. It may, however, be close to the best we can do.

In practice, Safeway probably approximates that system because its lower-level supervisors know much more about the individual store than just its profit, and the higher-level supervisors have some confidence in their lower-level supervisors. Of course, that the lower-level supervisor with a division of, say, twenty stores is somewhat better supervised by simply looking at the profit ratio than at the individual store manager would be because the law of large numbers comes to the aid of the higher-level supervisor.

In this case, also, the stock market, in simply looking at the total profit of each of a number of large diversified organizations, has an even better opportunity to make use of the law of large numbers. People who do best in the stock market have information about the companies in addition to knowing their profit ratios. Even here examination of the profit figures is not ideal, although a great many of the investors in the market use that simple system.

The situation with the government is more difficult. The old Imperial Chinese government had a great advantage in that it was essentially a supervisory organization over a vast number of farming families with only small cities that were scattered evenly across the landscape. As mentioned earlier, they depended on individual examination-selected officials who were sent out to control what was their equivalent of a county without much in the way of central supervision. The central government knew if these officials were collecting their taxes and also knew whether there had been any riots or mob attacks in the area. Based on compliance with these two criteria, the government could fire its officials.

This system is not optimal, but a better alternative is hard to find, particularly because the man at the top in this case tended to be far from an ideal executive. He had been raised in the Imperial palace under conditions that spoiled him; he had access to numerous forms of entertainment to distract his mind; and his intelligence was only average or even below average.

The officials who connected the magistrate running the county with the emperor were a chain of people who had passed the examination. Most had been county magistrates themselves at some point. Furthermore, the local governor would obviously know more about a given magistrate's performance than the emperor would, and we have mentioned before the existence of the censor system checking on officials. As we said, the censorate rarely paid much attention to magistrates and normally concentrated on higher officials.

An advantage to this system is that it did economize on control and did not make an effort to push the central control to levels of detail that were not possible. The fact that the only central government official in most counties was the magistrate and that the villages were actually self-governing was an even more striking illustration of the government's recognition of the declining marginal return on administration.

This system lasted for about two thousand years; in a way it is still retained by the Chinese communists. Their expectations have increased, however; they have more than one person in each county now, but they have retained the self-governing village though with less autonomy. They also have something roughly equivalent to censorship in the form of correspondence columns of their newspaper. People who write to the correspondence columns know that even if the paper doesn't publish their letter, someone will probably read it.

Although the system endured for a couple thousand years,[3] there were cyclical rises and falls of dynasties, catastrophic collapses of the whole government, invasions, famines, and floods. The system dealt with some issues well, others not; control over the Imperial army was always difficult, whether that army was engaged in defending the Great Wall or carrying out punitive expeditions far north of there.

Having a number of people engage in similar tasks and then providing fairly lightweight supervision over them is characteristic of many government activities. The district attorneys are often appointed by the attorney general primarily for political reasons. The central government exercises relatively little control over them. If they have a reasonable level of success in court and if there are not too many public complaints about their deviation from the straight and narrow path, they will be left in. They are similar to the

3. The examination system was actually only about a thousand years old, but various methods of selecting people for much the same characteristics were in use before that.

magistrates of the Chinese county except that they are district attorneys or specialized officials.

I mentioned earlier the impossibility of determining whether a given embassy is doing a good job, and, to give away a secret, the Department of State does not make any significant effort to find out. If all the routine steps are taken, the various reports filed at the right time, and congressmen pleasantly entertained, higher officials can expect a standard rate of promotion. In the lower ranks, improving your relations with those higher officials who fill out your efficiency report is more important than having good relations with the local government (of course, it may be necessary to have these good relationships in order to get a positive efficiency report).

Difficulties arise occasionally when something goes wrong. As ambassadors are shuffled from place to place, the secretary of state or his immediate inferiors could possibly cause a good deal of inconvenience for people at that rank, even though for political reasons they are reluctant to fire them.[4]

In this case, lower officers can be "selected out" by the personnel board. Most of them, however, are not, and most of them rise slowly to what we might call upper-middle rank with only a minority fortunate enough to go to the top. The key to promotion, as we have said earlier, is your relations to other people in the embassy, particularly your superiors—not what you are contributing to American foreign policy.

Both of these cases more or less follow the Chinese Imperial pattern in relinquishing a large part of supervision and supervising only some tasks. In the case of the old empire and in the attorney general's case, what they are supervising is the most important aspect of the behavior of these lower officials. In the case of the Department of State that is not obvious, but since I have already conceded I can think of no way of supervising it efficiently, this is not said in a critical spirit.[5]

Relinquishment of the legislative role is another aspect of most democratic governments, particularly the federal government at the moment. U.S. congressmen sometimes complain bitterly that the president is not doing enough to get a particular piece of legislation through or has not provided

4. It is possible to fire an American ambassador even if he is a career officer, though it is difficult.

5. In a way, I do criticize the Department of State—not for the way it is internally run but for its size. Granted the impossibility of controlling it better than it is now, we could get by with somewhere about 1 percent as many people overseas as we now have.

them with a basic draft for legislation. While reducing their interests in legislation,[6] however, they have sharply increased their intervention in the executive branch. If you have a complaint about any branch of the federal government, the sensible thing to do is to call your congressman, especially if you are a recent campaign contributor, and you can expect attention from a staff member.

This is similar to the old Chinese system because the individual civil servant knows that there is not much detailed supervision of him from on high, but if he does something to trouble people of low rank, they will complain to their congressman. The congressman, depending on whether he thinks these people should be subject to trouble, will take action; hence, through this indirect way the official's behavior is supervised.

On the other hand, the local district attorney is less well informed about the desires of the attorney general than the attorney general is himself. In this case, there is no real way he can find out unless the attorney general tells him, and if the government really wants to have him duplicate the attorney general's preferences, the attorney general will probably have to spend a long time in what is for him the unfamiliar activity of laying out in detail exactly what his preference function is. Most people are not able to do so verbally.

Thus, the decision here made by the attorney general as a way of evaluating the district attorney is a difficult one, and the shortcut of an accounting system simply does not exist. That he is in a worse situation than the division manager of Safeway should be obvious and not surprising.

But let us examine the actual difficulties here. The district attorney could rate his inferiors not in terms of examining one case but by attempting to develop a sort of accounting procedure for them. He might, for example, count the number of cases they bring or the percentage of cases they win. Unfortunately, these two criteria are, to a considerable extent, in conflict with each other.

The district attorney who wants to win substantially all of his cases—and the federal district attorneys do win about 90 percent—can simply not bring difficult cases. One reason for the high crime rate in Manhattan was that for a number of years its state's attorney did not like to lose cases. Therefore, his assistants did not bring cases unless they were reasonably sure they were

6. This does not mean that the total amount of legislation has been reduced. It is just that it is not read by the congressmen.

going to win. Since the defense attorneys knew this, too, it meant that if you committed a crime in Manhattan under even moderately ambiguous circumstances, you did not risk punishment. Even if the evidence against you were quite strong, your attorney could probably talk the officiating assistant state's attorney into a favorable out-of-court settlement.

The state's attorney, at the time an elected official, could point out when the election came around that his conviction rate was high, which was true if conviction rate was taken as the number of convictions for cases brought. His conviction rate was low, however, if one took number of convictions for numbers of crimes.

An attorney who brings many cases out of a given universe of possible cases will have a high prosecution rate and a low conviction rate. The one who carefully selects only strong cases will have a high conviction rate and a low prosecution rate. The accounting method would have to measure both of these factors.

Designing a genuine suitable accounting rate would require further investigation of the complexities. There is a substantial large element of randomness in what particular crimes come to a given attorney. Hence, it would be necessary to use large samples if one is using some function of trial and conviction as a measure. Furthermore, attorneys in different areas would face various difficulties of this sort. In certain parts of Harlem, a white state's attorney would have great difficulty getting convictions, even if he were far more skilled than his black compeer. This would, of course, indicate you should not appoint whites to the jobs in Harlem, but it also means that it is hard to compare the attorney in Harlem with the attorney out of Harlem.

The system of negotiating plea bargains makes this even more difficult because a state's attorney who is willing to accept relatively moderate pleas will, by that fact alone, get a higher conviction rate. A murderer who by agreement pleads guilty to breaking and entering[7] and goes up for one year counts as a conviction. If the district attorney is careful, no item will appear in the record indicating that he has been accused of murder.

All of these problems turn up with the Safeway manager although in a different structure. But for the Safeway manager, since the objective is fairly simple and straightforward and directly connected to his activities, that is, making a profit, his superiors have a way of measuring, at least to some degree of approximation, his contribution toward that objective.

7. As part of his murder.

I have chosen the case of the state's attorney as an example because we have a fairly clear idea of what we want him to do. We hope he would reduce the crime rate in his area by making committing crimes there dangerous and unpleasant, that is, by sending people who commit crimes "up the river" for long periods. If he was successful, he would be dealing with fewer cases, although in the present-day world that is not likely to occur, because he would probably not be that successful.

Other government activities indicate an even worse situation. For a lower-level official, one can tell more from a series of his accomplishments, rather than from an individual case, whether he tends to repeat the same methods as, for example, prosecuting attorneys do. But still, in many cases it is hard even to determine the outcome. The ambassador reports that he has had a successful conversation with the ministry of foreign affairs, with the result that he feels that the ministry will be more favorable to the United States in the future. It is almost impossible to tell if this is true.

Furthermore, suppose that relations between our country and another country deteriorate rapidly while under the aegis of a particular ambassador. It may reflect incompetence on the part of the ambassador, but it may also reflect his predecessor's incompetence, which is having a delayed effect; most likely, it reflects the international climate over which the ambassador has no control.[8]

In a similar group, it is frequently easier to judge the comparable abilities of higher-level officials than lower-level officials. An assistant state's attorney who is conducting trials will in the course of the year deal with only a somewhat restricted number of people. If the state's attorney office is large, however, and there are divisions in it, a division superintendent who had, say, ten state's attorneys under him, would have ten times that number in his sample. Thus, the judgement of whether he is competent in running his branch of the service is easier to make than the question of whether the individual assistant state's attorney is doing a good job.

The same thing applies to Safeway. It is harder by just looking at the books to tell whether an individual store manager is doing a good job than it is for a division manager with, say, twenty stores under his control. The larger sample of data, which to some extent is random, is important.

8. Grew, one of our best diplomats, was ambassador to Japan in the thirties. Our bad relations with them surely cannot be blamed on him. For a reverse case, our (politically appointed) ambassador in London during much of World War II was literally inarticulate. Our relations with England were nevertheless excellent.

As I mentioned previously, large profit-making companies also have individual divisions that are hard to evaluate. Suppose, for example, that our company has a corporate counsel who handles some of the cases personally and arranges for private counsel to handle others. Supervising his behavior is harder than supervising our state's attorney because of the fact the corporate counsel deals with so many different kinds of cases. He must make policy decisions about a range of issues: What shall we put on the label of a certain product? Should we produce a highly valuable and useful product cheaply that might lead to damage claims against the company at some future date? And so forth. Whether he is maximizing profits in these areas is clearly a very difficult problem, and the fact that we are now aiming at that simple objective, rather than the more complex set of objectives that we have in government, still does not make it easy.

So far, we have been talking about the supervisor allocating his time for supervision randomly but evenly across all his inferiors. There are two different methods of supervising inferiors: one involves accounting; the other, evaluating each case. The well-functioning supervisor will randomize his distribution of time between these two methods unless he is in the situation where one method dominates the other.

One technique, though not perfect, may help the supervisor to improve his supervision by giving up parts of his control. With this technique, the individual inferior has detailed policy instructions to carry out. The instructions themselves will not be optimal for all inferiors at all times, but their role in simplifying the supervision technique may more than compensate for individual nonoptimality.

In the case of Safeway, most things sold in the stores are provided through the Safeway warehouse and distribution system. Suppose that one manager discovers that, because of overbuying by the local wholesaler, he can get one type of canned goods much cheaper for this month than he could through the usual procedure. Will he be permitted to take that opportunity and advertise it locally as a bargain for shoppers? The question is not easy. Different chain stores follow different rules, but in general the manager would not be permitted to do so. The reason this profit opportunity is overlooked is because it makes supervision easier.

The point of this discussion has been to demonstrate that large organizations must be restricted. Perhaps some people will be surprised to hear this fact stated. It used to be true, and still is to some extent, that people of a socialist bent favored a planned economy—a central organization that gave everybody orders about everything except their consumption decisions.

I remember being assured by an honor student at the University of Chicago Law School that by the socialist method we could double per capita incomes. He had just left the army, so this remark seemed particularly surprising. One would think that he would have observed that even a large and well-organized structure is not planned in detail from the center.[9]

Once we realize that this tight control is not possible, we have found another argument against the traditional planned economy, and we have a higher degree of understanding of what organizations are. Indeed, adding a nail to the coffin of the planned economy is a work of supererogation in the present day. But if all of the other objections of planned economy were overcome, running a large hierarchical organization would be impossible.

In any large organization, officials control their own activities. Negotiations occur between different sub-bureaus. They even sign treaties with each other: for example, the famous "accord" under which the American government for a short period of time had a unified fiscal policy. Academic departments also frequently make deals with each other by trading, say, office space or time slots. Individual professors make deals with their department and with other professors. Profit-making institutions have a similar situation. The different subdivisions will disagree, hold formal negotiating sessions, and possibly enter into a contract with each other.

Members of any large organization always have a few tales to tell about their colleagues. One individual or one division is hard to get along with. They will also say that others are very cooperative. The fact that they are either cooperative or noncooperative, however, is a sure indication that somehow the orders coming from the top are not completely controlling things.

Those observations do not really contradict the existing literature, although in my opinion the literature puts too much emphasis on the degree to which the structure is internally coordinated and on the degree to which the orders go down from the top. But the dream once held by most proponents of the planned society is not held these days by any of the people who write on organizational theory.

This idealistic myth is sometimes still found in organization manuals or when introducing people to a particular organization. As I mentioned earlier,

9. This was right after World War II, and the anti-military prejudice of modern intellectuals was not much in evidence at that time. Most of my classmates were proud of their own service in the military and of the American military machine, although all of them had tales of bureaucratic bungle.

when I entered the Department of State I was given a tale about how the low-level people collected information; how it was winnowed and partially integrated by the next stage and passed on up to the decision-making groups or individual who gave orders which were then passed down with each level elaborating on it so that it fit the various people at the bottom; from all this, the end product was a coordinated department with policy based on the best information. This was a myth, but I would not be surprised if the same myth is still being perpetrated in the Foreign Service Institute despite the probability that no one believes it.

If we cannot have this kind of perfect coordination, we should not try to establish organizations that require it to succeed. If we look around the world, we find that such organizations are avoided. Claims of perfect coordination are sometimes made, but no one actually acts on the hypothesis that they are true. We must cut our suit to fit our cloth.

Taylor, in pioneering the efficiency engineering profession, made one of his most important single discoveries when he realized that people could do more if less were asked of them. He adjusted shovel size to the weight of whatever was being thrown, which meant that people were using smaller shovels than they had before. In heavy work, Taylor frequently had people take a compulsory rest period every fifteen minutes. Both of these reductions in the apparent size of the task actually increased daily productivity. We should do the same with our organizations.

An obvious case of reduced expectations is a corporation that is simply trying to make money and that uses an accounting system as a reasonably good way of telling whether inferiors are contributing to that goal. In addition, some direct supervision should be combined with that system.

This technique can be used only if your objective is making money. It is fortunate that our society is so organized that when a large number of people are attempting to make money, the wealth of other people will also be raised. Engineers who make minor improvements in automobiles do so in order to improve the profits of General Motors or Toyota, but I as a consumer benefit.

Unfortunately, there are many activities in which we cannot use this simple system. American cities, for example, do not provide incentives for homeowners to plant their gardens for an external coordinated appearance.

Most people are surprised at this possibility, but if they look at cases in which a large area is all owned by one organization, say, a collection of apartment buildings with lawns and gardens around them, they will realize that centralized control does provide a more attractive environment. The feeling that large organizations such as the city government would not do as well, however, is, I think, justified.

Government or charitable activities compose one large area in which we use centralized control without the use of cost accounting, since our objective is not to make profit. Some of these, like the post office, probably should be moved into the profit-making sector because competitive companies moving the mail, such as Federal Express and Purolator,[10] would do so more efficiently.

Air pollution, however, cannot apparently be dealt with in a similar way, although in that area many activities could be contracted out. The State of Arizona, for example, inspects all cars to find out whether their emissions are dangerous from the pollution standpoint. They have just entered into a contract under which a private company will do this in return for a fixed fee. The cost will be lower than having the state do it, but here the company is carrying out a small and specified act concerned with pollution, not reducing air pollution in general. A solution for pollution can hardly be contracted out in this way.[11] Thus, the simple profit and loss statement of accounts cannot be used as a final determinant in this area although it may be used as an intermediate instrumentality.

In these areas we cannot expect even as much efficiency as we have in the market. There are, however, other reasons for undertaking these activities even if they are badly handled. The point is that we will continue to do some things that we want to do even if our implementation of them is quite wasteful.

To take a clearcut, straightforward example, suppose we have a dictator who has a strong set of preferences of some sort but is aware of the difficulties of bureaucratic control. To turn back to our attrition of control pyramid, the dictator will normally be able to impose his will on many more matters if he has a large bureaucracy than he can by himself. In a way, he is willing to let the acts of his bureaucracy for, say, 80 percent of their total volume be things that he does not either know or care about if 20 percent are in accordance with his will. Hence, he has an increased impact on the environment. You may wish, as the dictator does, that the bureaucracy were more efficient than implementing only that 20 percent of the dictator's wishes, but nevertheless that is better than having them take all of their actions independently.

10. When I was a boy, Purolator was a specialized company that took care of water softeners in parts of the United States where the limestone problem was serious.

11. Research about it could be contracted out.

Napoleon, to take a good example of a dominating personality, certainly had only an approximate control of what his low-level officials were doing in various parts of Europe. Nevertheless, his will was carried out in Europe far better than it would have been had he not had this very large organization.

We can think of the matter from Napoleon's standpoint as follows. If he does not attempt to become emperor, he will be able to have almost all of his individual actions in perfect accord with his desires, but he will not have many people carrying out his instructions. If he becomes emperor and sets up a small organization with most local government decisions being determined by, say, local elected councils, he will have better control over that somewhat limited bureaucracy than he would have over a big bureaucracy. Nevertheless, the total number of actions undertaken by the governments which are in accord with his desires will be smaller than they would be if it were a single monolithic bureaucracy. However, a much higher percentage of those actions carried out by the small bureaucracy are in accord with his desires.

To use some numbers just for illustrative purposes, suppose that he establishes a small bureaucracy and is able to see that at least one-third of all actions undertaken by the lower-level members of the bureaucracy are in accordance with his desires. The total number of government actions taken in the society as a whole is 100,000, and this small bureaucracy deals with only 10,000 of them, with the others being dealt with by local bureaus. Thus, he has some 3,333 actions carried out in accord with his desires. If, on the other hand, he establishes a large all-encompassing bureaucracy, he is able to guarantee that the people at the bottom carry out his desires in only 10 percent of all the cases. But that is 10,000 cases instead of a little over 3,000.

Another technique would be to attempt to segregate government decisions so that the ones that Napoleon thought were most important were handled by a somewhat limited central bureaucracy, and those he thought less important were handled by autonomous agencies. This course of action was actually carried out by Napoleon. In France, his word was law, although he made some pretense of having democratic agencies. Outside of France, he had a series of quasi-independent governments. Some of them were headed by his close relatives, but a number were headed by the traditional kings or emperors whom he had conquered in war. In this outer area, he certainly had great influence on the government, but he made no serious effort to control all its acts.

This system, no doubt, gave him a smaller total number of orders of his own implemented in the spirit in which they were given than if he had established one gigantic bureaucracy. On the other hand, it meant that a higher percentage of those orders were carried out in areas he thought were important. Deliberate abandonment of control in a number of areas thought to be less important permitted improved control in the narrower area that he thought was most important.

As I have pointed out, this particular technique is widely used. In a way, a corporation that gives local officials a high degree of autonomy, and then simply looks at the bookkeeping results, is one example. However, since the local authorities are ordered to "make profits," it is a bit different.

If we look at the world, this kind of decentralization or compartmentalization of orders is also widespread. I have already mentioned that the Chinese Empire had a system in which the controls with respect to the gigantic local population were quite restricted, but in the areas where the emperor was concerned, he was able to get reasonably good compliance. This involved conscious delegating of power to locally elected village councils and magistrates of local counties. It also involved giving the lower-level officials a great deal of discretion. Again, control in less important areas was sacrificed in order to get better control in more important areas.

The Spanish Empire at one point was the world's and Europe's largest empire.[12] It was governed largely by local officials. A local council controlled most of the affairs of its particular part of the empire, most of which would have little or no contact with a central structure. This council was normally appointed by higher level officials—a viceroy, for example—but it was also selected in terms of local popularity and influence. It was rather like the lord lieutenants in English counties who are officially appointed by the central government but are selected from a very narrow list of people who would be acceptable to the local community.

Although the federal systems of the United States and Switzerland seem to be other examples, when I discuss actual voters' control I will show that they are quite different. The central government is able to get its orders carried out in the army because it pays little or no attention to street repair in Los Angeles. It has concentrated its orders to only part of the system and left

12. It outreached the later English empire since it included both North and South America, and extensive holdings in both Africa and Asia. To give one piece of history that is normally overlooked in American textbooks, Philip, for a period of time, was married to the Queen of England. Although he was not formally recognized as king, this probably made little or no difference, and he lived in London. The disintegration of this vast empire in the seventeenth century, rather than its power in the sixteenth century, dominates our history books.

the other parts autonomous; hence, by relinquishing its control in some areas, it attempts to control others.

The feudal systems in Europe and Japan, the only places where genuine feudalism existed, were other examples even though they were not very successful. The higher officials, the kings, the emperors, and so on, depended on the local officials, the earls, counts, and so on, almost exclusively for the provision of their armies. As we know, the provision of the army was not very well done, but the original idea of giving the local officials complete control over local affairs in return for their providing military force is not a priori foolish. Indeed, at the time that the idea was instituted by the successors of Charlemagne, it may have been the best option in a desperate situation.

To return to the somewhat more formal discussion, this particular technique involves the man at the top reducing his total bureaucracy by concentrating in areas that he thinks are most important. Most rulers have done so whether they admit it or not. A leader can have two levels of concentration of orders, or several. For example, during the early period when Lenin ruled Russia, he was trying to set up a government that literally controlled everything. His attempt was a disastrous failure, and he eventually recognized that he needed a "New Economic Policy." It is unfortunate for the poor Russians that his successors did not also realize this need as well.

Although Lenin theoretically had a centrally controlled organization, in practice, he did not attempt to deal with most activities. Local enterprises were put in control of the various people who were regarded as respectable by the communist party, and they were not given many orders from the center, simply because the center was busy with other matters. The adopted principle of central control, therefore, was not able to be practiced. The result was a set of enterprises and local governments being run largely by autonomous groups. The central government concentrated on political matters and a general policy.

One important matter was carefully controlled, however: the personal security of Lenin and his immediate followers. They had as their guard the Fourth Latvian Rifles, a special unit composed of non-Russians, the only people in the whole of Russia at that time who were being paid in gold.[13]

13. Lenin had set up a small secret treasury of diamonds which was for the purpose of providing support for the leaders of the government if it was necessary for them to flee abroad. Perhaps that could be regarded as being a real security system as well as the gold payments to the Fourth Latvian Rifles.

Clearly, then, this security was a matter of high priority. I think we can say that the system had several levels of control then, with the highest exerted over their personal security guard, the second level over political matters in connection with establishing their control, and the third level, the actual control of the individual economic enterprises, which, in theory, was the system's whole objective.

In practice, this system worked badly, but not because of this compartmentalization. I above talked about systems in which there are two levels of control: for example, with Napoleon dealing quite personally with certain areas and leaving others to lower-level government agencies. In practice, many different degrees of control can be spread across the government, with some areas subject to very close control, some with no control, and various intermediate stages for less important areas.

All this is efficient if we accept that control deteriorates as it goes down a large organization; that it deteriorates less rapidly in areas that you think are important and may not even exist in some areas is sensible. I will use another illustrative calculation—randomly fabricated—to clarify this point. Even if the numbers are not correct, the qualitative conclusions should be unchanged.

Suppose we have a society of forty people, one of whom is a fairly dominating type with a good chance of becoming the dictator of an organization. Each of these forty people in the average day performs 10 acts; these citizens, then, affect the outside world by 400 total acts each day.

One of them is the potential dictator, and under our present circumstances, 10 of the 400 acts are those he favors, and the other 390 are randomly related to his desires. Suppose that he now becomes a complete authoritarian dictator using our previous three-for-one structure: i.e., he will have three immediate inferiors, each of whom supervises three, and each of them also supervises three. With this structure, there are now twenty-seven people at the bottom having acts within the outside world, and the other thirteen are our dictator and his supervisory personnel. The net effect is that there are 270 acts relating to the outside world, whereas before there were 400.

We will assume that at each stage there is a 25 percent deterioration, therefore, of the acts performed by the top-level inferiors who are simply supervising, 75 percent will be in accordance with the real wishes of the dictator and 25 percent not, and so on down the line. In this situation, the twenty-seven people at the bottom will end up with 42.6 percent of their acts carrying out the wishes of the dictator, or a total of 113.90 acts.

On the other hand, 156.09 of their acts will not be in accordance with the dictator's preferences but will be randomly distributed.[14] Certainly, from the dictator's standpoint, having roughly 114 acts in accordance with his desires in their effect on the outside world is better than 10. He has gained; in fact this is the largest number of acts affecting the outside world that he can have.

But let us suppose that there are some things he wishes to control in which his interests are more serious or more important than others. Assume that he establishes a smaller organization for the purpose of dealing with fewer things—specifically, one organization in which he has three supervisors under his control, and they each control three people who actually affect the outside world. In other words, we drop off the bottom rank. In this case, there will be 270 acts that are not controlled, because they are performed by people who are not part of the hierarchy, 90 acts performed by the bottom nine people in the hierarchy; so, again, the total number of acts performed is less than the original 400, and not all of those bottom 90 acts are in accordance with the desires of the dictator. Using our 25 percent deterioration, we find that 56 percent of the acts at the bottom level are performed in accordance with the desires of the dictator, or 50 together. The people at the bottom also perform 39.6 acts that are not in accordance with his desires, and the total number of acts thus is therefore 309.6.

Obviously, this situation is less desirable from the standpoint of the dictator unless the 50 acts that are now subject to control are more important than the others. There is no reason why that could not be so, and, as a matter of fact, most dictators do follow this kind of a pattern or some system under which they have even less control. In other words, the dictator has reduced his total control over the environment in order to concentrate his control over some things that he finds very important.

Our final model here is one in which the dictator has not two but three levels of importance for acts. The things he thinks are important, he does himself; we will assume he uses one-third of his time and therefore gets 3.3 contacts with the outside world perfectly in accord with his preferences. There is another one-third of the acts which are dealt with through a very small bureaucracy. Since he is now devoting one-third of his time to controlling that bureaucracy, he does not get fifty contacts with the outside world in

14. In this example, I am assuming for the sake of simplicity that the act that each person has, has many different possibilities so that the prospect of an individual just accidentally doing what the dictator wants is substantially zero.

accordance with his preferences, but only twenty. The rest of the society is also organized in a gigantic hierarchy with him at the top, and he devotes only one-third of his time to supervising that, with the result that 20 of their acts are not in accordance with his preferences. For a grand total, he has 43.3 acts in accordance with his preferences.

Clearly, this situation is worse than either of the other two, but he has stratified things so that the most important acts are certainly in his control, the second level of importance are to a considerable extent under his control, and the ones that are least important are only modestly controlled. Whether this is better than the earlier systems depends on whether he has strong feelings about which policies are most important.

This fabricated structure is actually quite realistic. Supervisors, whether they are dictators or branch managers of Safeway, do make some decisions themselves for direct action to the outside world; they supervise some through a narrow hierarchy; they allow many aspects to be dealt with by a wide hierarchy. Even this system with three levels of importance is a simplification since many things are seen as not significant enough to supervise.

We began this chapter with a discussion of the difficulties of getting perfect control, and then we proceeded to a way of organizing a bureaucratic structure so that the man or group at the top abandons some part of that control in order to get more important desires fulfilled and tasks accomplished. This dictatorial model could be replaced by a democratic model with the voters at the top. In the next chapter we will look into other ways of reducing the total span of control.

CHAPTER 10

RENT SEEKING AND THE IMPORTANCE OF DISORGANIZATION

Currently, rent seeking is all the rage in economics. Since I actually invented the idea, although not the name, the reader might be surprised if I did not discuss it in this book.[1] That is not the only reason for bringing it up. One aspect of rent seeking is of great importance in the internal structure of any large organization.

A number of organizations engage in rent seeking with the intent of improving their absolute size. For example, some corporations have lobbyists in Washington to ensure that tariffs protect them from foreign competition. Farm organizations also exist whose primary purpose is raising farm prices.

Rent seeking is the activity of attempting to get some kind of special advantage from society that benefits you but actually injures other people. Organizing a monopoly would be a case in point. In the present day, it would more likely be accomplished through pressure and lobbying the government than by the mainly private methods once used by J. P. Morgan.

There are many other ways of getting these special advantages. The Central Arizona Project is not a monopoly; it is a highly wasteful system of canals and pumps that provides water to a select group of beneficiaries at a cost to the taxpayer which is vastly higher than its actual value. Nevertheless, it was obtained by rent seeking.

The man who invents something of value, patents it, and then sells it for profit has achieved a rent, but we don't call this rent seeking. He has obtained his profit by doing something that benefits society, and in a competitive market it is difficult to obtain a profit by measures that do not benefit other people. The man who has not invented anything new, but gets the government to restrict his competitors, on the other hand, is engaged in rent seeking.

1. My original article was "The Welfare Costs of Tariffs, Monopolies, and Theft," but further work has been done by all sorts of people. This has been collected in *Toward a Theory of the Rent-Seeking Society*, edited by James M. Buchanan, Robert D. Tollison, and Gordon Tullock (College Station: Texas A&M University Press, 1980), and *The Political Economy of Rent-Seeking*, edited by Charles K. Rowley, Robert D. Tollison, and Gordon Tullock (Boston: Kluwer Academic Publishers, 1988). I have done a book of my own called *Economics of Special Privilege and Rent-Seeking* (Boston: Kluwer Academic Publishers, 1989).

The market is not a zero-sum game. Some activities produce a profit and some cause a loss. The individuals who participate in the profitable activities are not regarded as rent seeking, while those getting a profit for themselves while lowering the gross national product (GNP) are rent seeking.

Most of the new work in rent seeking is an effort to deal with the additional costs caused by this activity. From the first article I wrote,[2] the main theme has been that of the higher cost to society from these activities—much higher than economists previously thought. Anne Krueger, in an important article,[3] estimated that the cost of this kind of rent seeking from one type of situation alone, foreign exchange certificates, was 7 percent of the GNP of India and 15 percent in Turkey. Those are big figures, particularly with the high number of rent-seeking activities in both countries.

Many experts on the Orient believe that the basic reason for much poverty in China and India, despite their ancient and highly developed civilizations, is the dominance of rent seeking as the principal form of economic activity by the more aggressive segments of their populations. Fortunately, the United States has not experienced this activity as intensely.

But the point of this discussion is not organization of the company in order to generate rents from dealing with the government or its customers. Although that would be efficient from the corporation's point of view, we hope that the corporation won't be efficient along those lines. That would compare to drug dealers also being efficient in their business.

What we are concerned about is rent seeking in the interior of the corporation. Let us elaborate on our previous discussion of leveraged buyouts.[4] Suppose that we have a large corporation, and there appear to be profits from taking it over and reorganizing it. The method of taking it over has changed over time. Long ago it was proxy fights, then it became the activities of corporate raiders, and now it tends to be leveraged buyouts. Let us consider the typical leveraged buyout of a mythical Behemoth Corporation.

Senior executives of Behemoth get in contact with a banker willing to bankroll them, and they offer to buy the entire common stock of the company at a price that typically is about 50 percent above the market value before

2. Tullock, "Welfare Costs."

3. Anne O. Krueger, "The Political Economy of the Rent-Seeking Society," *American Economic Review* 64 (1974): 291–303.

4. An excellent summary of recent work in this area is contained in Andrei Shleifer and Robert W. Vishny, "The Takeover Wave of the 1980s," *Science*, 17 August 1990, 745–49.

people heard about the leveraged buyout effort. Let's assume that they are successful.

The new management, which is the old management who now owns the corporation instead of being paid employees, needs to sell off a number of subsidiaries and use the money to repay part of the gigantic loans they have received. Because of the size of the loans, however, the bankers charge a somewhat higher interest rate than they would for an ordinary loan. It's rather surprising how little the premium and interest rate are in these cases, but it is positive.

The common stockholders who sold their stock have obviously made a large profit—about 50 percent of the previous value of their stock. There is no particular prediction here about the people who buy the segments the company sold off. Presumably they were sold off at a reasonable price, and the purchasers on the whole do reasonably well. If they did wonderfully well, it would imply that the new management sold the segments too cheaply.

The operation itself, however, in most cases turns out to be modestly—not immensely—successful. It now has a very much larger capital value, most of which is denominated in debt, and hence must make a larger return on its assets to pay interest on that amount and still retain a reasonable profit. Normally it is able to obtain as good returns on this enlarged "capital" as the original corporation did on the earlier "capital." It does not usually make extraordinarily high returns as a percentage of the new "capital."

The new management is subject to considerably more pressure for efficiency, because it now holds only a highly leveraged part of the corporation, and minor slippage in efficiency can wipe them out. They perhaps have an equity which is $150 million and have bonds outstanding of $1,350 million. These bonds pay a relatively high rate of interest. Before the buyout the stockholders had an equity worth $500 million, with bonds in the amount of another $500 million.

How does this new management succeed? They are the same people who were running the corporation before, but they now must be making a much larger return on the same body of physical assets. Of course, they have sold off some of these physical assets to repay part of the debt. But they now have a much higher bonded indebtedness for the assets that they retained.

The answer seems to be twofold. One is that these managers, themselves being subject to much stronger pressure, simply work harder. The other is that the only major changes we always observe in such cases is a large-scale purge of the middle management. Many people in what I've referred to as "the corporate swamp" are fired. These two changes observed in all of these corporations seem to be enough.[5]

These corporations now proceed to produce a considerably higher return on their physical assets than they did before; indeed they have to if the corporation is to remain out of bankruptcy. Why would this elimination of people who previously were voluntarily hired by substantially the same management greatly increase efficiency? That it does increase efficiency, I think, is fairly clear, because once again these companies are able to survive and pay the interest on their bonds in most cases, although their current bonded indebtedness is very much higher than the sum of the bonded indebtedness and equity was before.

To explain this, we must turn to an internal version of rent seeking. Roland MacKean, when explaining a difference between private companies and nonprofit or government agencies, used to say that in a private company, if the owner saves money he can take it home with him. In a nonprofit or a government agency, he can't.

The reason MacKean thought this was important was essentially psychological. Many unpleasant decisions must be made if you want to maximize profits. You have to fire people you personally like, you have to put pressure on your inferiors even though this clearly will mean that your relations disintegrate, you may have severe fights with, let us say, your labor union or with neighboring organizations who are competing with you, even though in the case of the nonprofit and government, the word *competition* is not always used.

Furthermore, all of these basically unpleasant decisions must normally be made rather quickly, before you have obtained enough information so that you're certain. Doctors talk about difficult decisions in medical strategy. For example, it used to be said that a doctor had to make certain strategic decisions when it came to cutting off people's legs. A doctor who was a radical and cut off many legs would cut off legs that did not need it. A doctor who was conservative and who rarely cut off legs would not have that problem, but he would have patients die who otherwise wouldn't.[6]

The same type of dilemma confronts most managers. The decision to fire someone or simply yell at him, all of which tend to reduce the pleasantness of your environment, can best be made before the evidence is completely in. If you wait until it all is in, you will find that your competitors have beaten you out. Thus, you will almost certainly make mistakes which are likely to be brought firmly to your attention—which makes life even more unpleasant.

5. It is now more highly specialized because it has sold off some of its subsidiaries.

6. This is before the antibiotics which have made these problems much easier.

For the owner of a company, the pain is compensated for by the fact that he can take the money home with him after he has made the decision, even if he chooses to take some kind of risk. It's his money he's risking, and whether this will make him be more cautious or less cautious depends on his personality. But if he is a hired employee of a company and he does something that is risky but has high profit potential, if the profit potential is achieved he will receive back only a small part of it. If, on the other hand, the company is driven into bankruptcy, he will suffer a large loss.

A relatively risk-neutral person would probably be more likely to take chances with his own corporation than with a corporation by which he is hired. I have a friend who, for a time, was a high official in one of the more powerful and older American corporations. He said one of the real functions of the committee structure in this corporation was that it permitted people to take large risks without any responsibility. You never could trace any losses back to anyone. This protection may have offset the other phenomenon.

This is the difference between the owner of a corporation and an employee of a government or nonprofit organization. Think of the higher-ranking employees of a large corporation. They face somewhat the same kind of problem, though not as extreme. They are not going to take home the entire profit of the company nor will they pay the full cost if it loses. On the other hand, they will pay the full cost in their personal relations—the need to fire people they like and admire, the need to face rumors floating around about how he fired so-and-so because the man resented his attentions to his wife, and so forth, and in addition he only gets part of the return.

Another issue important here is a little way down the pyramid rather than at the absolute top: the development of minor tradeoffs and alliances. People who saw that wonderful movie *9 to 5* will recall that there was one unsympathetic character who is listed as a "spy for the boss." She passes along to higher officials things that the lower officials don't want them to get. One understands perfectly why other people didn't like her, but from the standpoint of the efficiency of our total economy or that corporation only, she was performing a social function. When the other people succeeded in sending her off to Paris to prevent her from reporting a fairly major sin to their superiors, they were lowering efficiency.[7]

Anybody who's been in an organization knows about efforts to prevent information which would be of use to higher officials from getting to them.

7. In this particular case that was not true. Complex and indirect results of getting rid of her did indeed raise the profits of the company. This would not happen very often in the real world.

For example, I was in a rather small organization in which one of the secretaries characteristically arrived late. It did not affect her getting the work done; she was indeed very efficient. Nevertheless, the office supervisor reported her to the head of the organization. The other secretaries regarded this as a crime almost equivalent to rape.

Normally, the situation is not as clearcut as in that incident. Almost everybody around the office participates in a certain amount of relaxation, and all of them refrain from reporting it because they worry about reciprocation. There is a sort of bargain whereby you don't cause trouble with the superiors for me and I won't cause it for you. This is rent seeking that reduces not only the profits of the company but the GNP.

In addition to this kind of bargaining, over time if people are operating in the same office in close contact, many personal relations will develop—mostly friendship, but antagonism, too. Friendship also leads to people's not reporting.[8] Of course, rivalry and intense chronic infighting between colleagues occur just as commonly as covering up defects.

But even this rivalry may mean that defects are covered up. Most people who are fighting their way to the top are attempting to cultivate relations with certain superiors and develop a train of inferiors behind them. Therefore, they have strong motives to protect some people while knifing other people in the back. Again, information may not go upward.

The higher officials who live in an environment with a certain amount of ambiguity will, if they press hard, get more efficiency out of their inferiors than if they don't press, but they also have less in the way of pleasant relationships. This is because they don't take the funds home. Here is the reason for the basic improvement in efficiency with these leveraged buyouts. The higher officials can take the money home with them. Indeed, they're in a situation where if they do not improve efficiency, they might lose the money they've already put in and go through bankruptcy. Under the circumstances, their environment changes rapidly, and their behavior changes in an equally radical way. Suddenly they may begin to work harder themselves in addition to putting pressure on their inferiors and firing people in large numbers. Apparently the "corporate swamp" described earlier shrinks by about a third.

The total cost saving in firing this one-third of middle managers is not very

8. The corporation I used to work for had a rule against hiring husband and wife pairs. It was thought this kind of interrelation led to personnel difficulties.

great, although it is worth picking up. These middle managers face a change in the incentive structure when they suddenly realize that their superiors are no longer likely to be tolerant and understanding. The money these superiors can make by putting screws on a particular junior manager is now preferable to pleasant relations with him.

The people running corporations have dealt with this problem by instituting various bonus schemes. The leveraged buyout is really a large bonus scheme as well as a severe increase in pressure on the people concerned. That it pays off is fairly good evidence that a lot of administrative slack and rent seeking exists even in well-managed private corporations. Compared with what there is in nonprofits and the government, of course, it is trivial. Still, here we have a case of internal rent seeking.

Another instance can be found in governments who frequently shift military officers around. They justify it as training. The actual reason, however, is I think much more ancient. Shifting people around makes it much harder for them to develop the kind of personal relations with each other which might make the military dangerous.[9]

Obviously, the operators of a large corporation don't need to worry about this problem. A low-ranking official may indeed engage in intrigue and succeed in replacing the current chairman of the board, but he does so by attracting the favor of the stockholders and other directors and not by literally overthrowing him. He does not necessarily need the active assistance of, say, a majority of the officials, so it differs as such from a military coup.

Large corporations shift their junior managerial personnel around a great deal. Furthermore, these shifts are commonly geographical, which is a great inconvenience for most junior officials. Surely corporations have to pay these officials higher salaries than if they didn't impose these transfers on them.

This approach is clearly an effort to make the "you don't talk about me, and I won't talk about you" trades more or less impossible. Because nobody has deep personal ties with anyone else, there is less rent-seeking behavior. Furthermore, if an individual does something to irritate one of his colleagues, the cost is modest because either he or the colleague will be going

9. The English have gone at this in a somewhat different way. If you join the British Army as either an officer or an enlisted man, you join a particular regiment and you stay in that regiment until you either die, resign, or are promoted to general officer. Furthermore, the regiments are trained in such a way that they have a great deal of regimental patriotism and tend to look down on all the other regiments. Conspiracy among them is almost impossible.

somewhere else shortly. Thus this shifting, although apparently inefficient in that it prevents specialization and requires higher wages, is actually quite efficient.

Roger Congleton has pointed out that the committee itself may, in a special way, reduce rent-seeking activity.[10] Personal goals are harder to push through a committee than through an individual because of the number of people to convince. An offsetting factor is that individuals do not have as much riding on the matter and therefore may put less energy into it. Nevertheless, there surely is some truth in Congleton's position. It would indicate that the innumerable committees, which we observe in large corporations, and meetings on all sorts of subjects, actually serve the function of making rent seeking somewhat less severe.

Also, although one must keep good relations with one's colleagues, there is something to be gained by stabbing one of them in the back. Complex and devious intrigues must frequently be concealed not only from their superiors but from many of their equals and inferiors, which makes it harder for these intrigues to be implemented.

The net effect is that certain types of rent seeking are reduced by the structure. The corporate swamp, in addition to having the characteristics we have discussed before, also makes it harder to carry off various rent-seeking activities than in a simpler command structure.

This means not that individuals are pressed to be highly efficient, but that it's rather dangerous for them to engage in more rent seeking than is the norm. There may be a gradual fall in the energy with which they push the objectives of the corporation. The tendency to avoid unpleasant clashes with their colleagues, and so on, can grow. As long as it is general, it will not lead to career difficulties. The standard by which officials are judged gradually falls, with resulting inefficiency.

This is the reason that the sharp increase in pressure which we have described in the takeovers tends to be efficient. The average level of work intensity and devotion to the corporate ideals can gradually slide down in the bureaucracy, and the buyout brings it up again to a high level. It's dangerous to be lazier, more devious and plotting, and more interested in internal matters within the company than the average official in your office. It's not dangerous to stick with the average level even if it is going steadily downward.

10. Roger D. Congleton, "Committees and Rent-Seeking Effort," *Journal of Public Economics* 25 (1984): 197–209.

These are private corporations. How about government agencies? The first thing to be said is that although the military follows the rotation system I have described, as do the Department of State and the FBI, many other government agencies do not.

Although this shifting around does reduce the speed with which the net efficiency of the organization declines, it doesn't reduce it to zero. We can say that the FBI is more efficient than the Post Office, but obviously this is not strong praise.

The efficiency of the government is even further reduced by the fact that, in practice, it's very, very difficult to fire anyone. It's also difficult to demote them; even denying them routine promotion is hard. Libecap's studies show that the principal characteristic of promotion is simply seniority.[11]

Under these circumstances we would anticipate a great deal of rent seeking in which people simply don't work very hard, are not devoted to the objectives of their organization, and so on. We can also anticipate that if they are interested in some aspect of their agency—for example, expanding it—they could freely devote a lot of energy to it. We would expect the average efficiency to be lower, with no prospect of a true takeover bid dealing with it.

The absence of the takeover bid was once not that important in the United States or in other democracies. The election in part served that purpose. The bulk of the government employees could be fired at any time, and when a new government came in, it had a strong tendency to purge the existing structure. The politicians, although they did want the roads to be properly repaired, had other things they wanted the civil servants to do as well. They seem to have paid the civil servants more than the going rate while requiring them to pay the surplus in campaign contributions to the party in power. Nevertheless, there was something like the takeover bid. In those days the government was smaller, and the votes of its employees weren't especially important.

All this has changed. Civil servants today are almost guaranteed against being fired, and hence, the bulk of them do not make campaign contributions. Indeed, it's actually illegal for them to do so although there are various indirect ways to circumvent it. More important, their numbers and votes have increased greatly. As a result we now have a situation in which the politicians cannot fire the civil servants, but the civil servants, if the politicians do

11. Gary D. Libecap and Ronald N. Johnson, "Bureaucratic Rules, Supervisor Behavior, and the Effect on Salaries in the Federal Government," *Journal of Law, Economics and Organization* 5 (Spring 1989): 53–82.

something that actually annoys them, can fire the politicians. This has led to a further decline in net efficiency.

Here's a true horror story. A political appointee in the Reagan administration discovered that one of his high-ranking civil servants was never in the office. When he inquired, he learned that the man was a dipsomaniac and was home drunk. Since the appointee had some crusading fervor, he decided that the civil servant should be fired if he did not cure himself.

The lengthy procedure for getting rid of a civil servant requires that his supervisor have several interviews with him in which the defects of his work are pointed out. Since the man was almost never in the office this approach proved difficult. However, when it was finally accomplished, the man was fired. He promptly sued the government for reinstatement, and the Civil Service Commission not only reinstated him, but compelled the government to pay his lawyer's fee.

The Civil Service Commission regards as its principal activity the protection of people from their political superiors. A great deal of political clout lies behind this protection because there are so many civil servant votes. The civil servants don't have very much in the way of positive ideas when they vote, but the politician who chooses to take them on is going to find himself out of office before he gets rid of very many of them.

The net result of this is another example of the kind of rent seeking which we have been describing inside the corporation, but immensely more powerful. Friendly relations with colleagues, complicated intrigues about matters which in general are of no great importance, and rivalry with other parts of the government are all what we would expect and what we get. We observe this in local, state, and federal government, but it is much more severe in the federal government than in the other levels. This is partly because there are more civil servants in the national government, but also because of the great distance between the average civil servant and the voters.

In local governments, for example, many potential increases in funds available for government activities actually require a popular vote either for a bond issue or a tax increase. It does you little good as a civil servant to vote against the mayor of your city if his replacement is still unable to increase taxes and use the money to raise your salary. But this is unfortunately not true of the federal government.

One of the results of all this is a move to amend the constitutions of many states to require balanced budgets and to let various particular expenditures be put to popular vote. As Bennett and DiLorenzo have proved in their

Underground Government,[12] these limitations have by no means been completely successful, but they undoubtedly make the lives of various bureaucrats more difficult than they otherwise would be.

Currently there is a movement afoot in the state governments to put restrictions on the length of time that a legislator can serve. In California, it is a constitutional amendment. It makes this kind of rent seeking more difficult, thus perpetrating the present situation in which local government is more efficient.

One offsetting problem is that the individual legislators will all be less experienced in dealing with their jobs. Whether this is important is a matter left to the reader.

Let us return to the title of this chapter, "Rent Seeking and the Importance of Disorganization." When an organization gets more thoroughly acclimated to its task and develops a greater degree of specialization, two things happen. First, all its employees accumulate more knowledge of their task and hence have a greater ability to carry it out. Second, they acquire more knowledge of what they can get away with, who their true friends are—who should be protected and who will protect them—and what the best rent-seeking method is of getting promoted or getting other advantages. One of these two improves the efficiency of the corporation, and the other reduces it. The only known way of eliminating the second is to impose some kind of disorganization on the corporation that may take the form of a leveraged buyout or simply the transfer of personnel from one place to another.

Obviously we have a tradeoff here. The company or government that shifted all its personnel around every day would never get anything done. On the other hand, the company or corporation that leaves its personnel in the same positions has a group of highly skilled individuals with their skills emphasizing rent seeking and avoiding work.

The rotation of personnel is one way of laying off this tradeoff with the appropriate time in job, varying from job to job from one company and government organization to another. This system, per se, however, is not really sufficient. General corporate culture can withstand rotation, and corporate culture can lead to a gradual relaxation and lowering of standards. This means that more drastic reorganizations are necessary from time to time.

12. James T. Bennett and Thomas J. DiLorenzo, *Underground Government* (Washington, D.C.: Cato Institute, 1982).

The private market takes care of this by such things as bankruptcy, corporate reorganizations imposed by the creditors or by new stockholders, the leveraged buyout, and so on. Governments have little opportunity for doing so, particularly in the present circumstances where the bulk of their employees can't be fired almost regardless of what they do.

The standard Chinese historic theory about the rise and fall of dynasties has as one of its arguments the gradual growth and corruption of the bureaucracy. Granted that the Chinese bureaucrats were all selected by a difficult examination and were automatically moved every five years or more frequently; clearly this extends past the interoffice friendship problem. A gradual relaxation of the corporate culture is what eventually leads to a new dynasty after the old one collapses.

If we look back over history, we see that democracies have never been permanent organizations. We must work out some equivalent of the type of periodic sharp disorganization that is vital to the maintenance of the efficiency of private corporations.

This chapter has been devoted to rent seeking within large corporations and government. Keeping it under control is a problem, one which the corporations have handled much better than the government. It should be remembered that this is internal rent seeking. Corporations frequently are engaging in the other kind of rent seeking—efforts to get monopolies or special privilege out of the government—and the more efficient they are in repressing their internal rent seeking, the more likely they are to be efficient in getting these rent-seeking special privileges.

CHAPTER 11

RESTRICTED SCOPE

Chapter 9 ended with a discussion of ways in which the dictator or person in control of some area could improve his actual control of the world by reducing the number of things he attempts to control and/or by giving different levels of control to different things, depending on his perceptions of their importance. After the digression to internal rent seeking in Chapter 10, we will continue with our discussion of control in this chapter and, in fact, will become more radical.

To begin with, in Chapter 9, I pointed out the possibility of confining your direction to only a few inferiors or giving different levels of direction to different inferiors. There is another way of doing the same thing that can change the level of supervision: you give to your inferiors different degrees of intensity of supervision by subject matter. For example, the division manager of Safeway might make it a habit to visit all his stores at about the same frequency, but while in the store he might look carefully at the meat counter and ignore the detergent section.

This approach would involve a differential investment of resources, but it could also simply recognize reality. Let us suppose that it is easy to tell whether a supermarket has given the right amount of shelf space for different brands of detergent, but that determining whether the meat assortment is proper is much more difficult. The same level of control could be attained by different investments of time in these two areas.

On the other hand, there might be a difference of importance in addition to the difference in difficulty of control. Assume, for example, that to get an idea of the degree to which a meat display is done properly takes about three times as much time as for the same inspection of the detergents. If, on the other hand, you felt that the meat area was much more important, you might nevertheless give it five times as much time as the detergents. This, again, could improve efficiency.

There might be other aspects of the inspection process to which the supervisor would not need to give any conscious attention at all. The external appearance of the store and whether the aisles are clean would be matters which I presume he would not consciously consider but nevertheless would notice if something were wrong. I do not know whether this should be listed as supervision. Perhaps the inspector would spend more time walking through the store than just taking the most direct route from his entry to the place he wants to inspect in order to allow himself the opportunity to notice something like this, but more likely it would be a pure byproduct.

The combination of giving different amounts of time to different inferiors, and different amounts of time to different aspects of the inferiors' work, would be optimally efficient and, again, would mean that a number of things were done which were not in accord with the preferences of the superior, but this would be a byproduct of getting performance more in accordance with his preferences in certain areas.

Again there is the problem here of not permitting your inferiors to know too much of what you are doing. The supervisor may normally, upon entering the store, look at the meat counter very carefully and glance only briefly at the detergent shelves. It would be sensible, however, for his inferiors to know that once in a while he looked carefully at the detergent shelves. He wants his inferiors to devote more attention to the meat shelves than to the detergent shelves, but he does not want them to ignore the detergent shelves totally.

Although a random pattern is desirable, in this case the general pattern of the randomization should be known by the inferiors. They should not be able to predict when he enters the store what he will look at, but they have a weighting function that tells them the probability that he will look at different things. This gives him optimal supervision efficiency.

The main theme of this chapter is that the individual who wants to be effective must confine himself to a fairly restricted area. He must accept that his work will have limited scope simply because he has human limits.

At the time of this writing, the communist societies in Eastern Europe are in a state of at least temporary disintegration. As the disintegration proceeds, it becomes more obvious that they had not succeeded in their original goal of controlling everything. The higher level was issuing orders, but the lower levels were not obeying them. In fact, it seems likely that the Tolkach and the black market were the basic coordinating factors in their economy.

Certain orders were carried out. For example, one that guaranteed that no one could be fired no matter how inefficient he was apparently had a great deal of public support. Other orders—ones that told individuals to introduce new equipment, invent, and so on—were carried out in a restricted way. They copied foreign developments with a lag. Russia is in the process of getting into the stage that Italy had reached in, say, 1950, when traffic jams were just starting to be common; the number of cars is exceeding the capacity of the streets.

The quality of their goods is known to be poor. It is unfashionable to wear Russian clothes if you can possibly get Western clothes. New technology is confined almost exclusively to the military. Even so, for example, the atom bomb was undoubtedly stolen from the United States, although perhaps not the hydrogen bomb. In the case of the atom bomb, the permeable barriers of their separation device were made in East Germany because the Russian plants could not meet the manufacturing specification, and all this at a time when they were vigorously accusing the United States of developing a nuclear arms industry in Germany.

Two different industrial sectors apparently exist in Russia, one concerned with arms, which does a reasonable job, and the other concerned with everything else. In essence, it would appear that the higher-ranking Russians concentrated their attention strongly on things that were reflected directly in their living standard.[1]

The second priority should have been the security apparatus, but it would appear that everyone except Castro and Ceausescu felt confident enough so that they did not devote much attention to this part of the organization. Policemen, army officers, and even to some extent the special political police have turned out to be quite unreliable in Eastern Europe, and in Russia they do not seem to be playing any role in the current difficulties.[2]

A third level of priority would appear to be control over the military, which at the higher level the party certainly retained. The economy itself came in as a fourth level. Even in this fourth level, they seem to have tried to control only portions of the economy and were apparently perfectly happy to have the black market continue functioning without much concealment.

There were elaborate plans, but the plans were normally based on inadequate information, and the lower officials had strong motives to deceive. No one paid much attention to failures of those plans in anything except the most obvious way. Indeed, the plans frequently led to severe distortion.

1. At the time of this writing, the East Germans are revealing what they refer to as luxurious quarters for their higher-ups. They are decidedly not luxurious from the standpoint of Westerners. The East Germans' complaint that they were much better than what anyone else in East Germany had, however, is well justified.

2. They have just contributed a wreath to a monument to their victims, erected across Dzerinsky Square from the Lubyanka.

Under an agreement with Fiat, the old Fiat car equipment was all shipped to Russia, and a plant was set up to produce the old small Fiat while Fiat itself moved on to higher and better things. After some time, it was decided to try and export some cars to the West. This led to a number of difficulties, including the British motoring association refusing to drive the car from the dock to their test area on the grounds that it was intrinsically too dangerous.[3]

All of this is not to criticize the Russian government. Although, as I suppose the reader knows, I detested it. Under the circumstances, they were recognizing the real requirements of their job. It was not possible for them to carry out the official theory of their society. What they did, in addition to seeing that they themselves lived fairly well, was to provide a superficial appearance that a plan was being carried out while permitting various things to go on that were not in accordance with it.

The superficial appearance seems to have fooled most of Western intellectuals and, more important, a number of Russians, even the ones who themselves regularly used the black market.

The problem here, or the solution, appears to lie in Plato's distinction between the "essence" and the "accidents." Everyone believed that the essence of the Russian system was planning and so forth. But there were the accidents, the difficulties of the real world which were thought of as deviations from a great grand plan which was the essence of the system. In fact, it seems likely that the "deviations" were the essence of the system, and the grand plan was purely decorative.

Having a purely decorative plan is not at all uncommon. Many American companies occasionally have drawn up a program for the future, and since expensive executives devote some time to making them up, we must assume that they perform some function. Whatever the function is, however, it is not to control the future in any detail.

Such plans are omnipresent. My sister and brother-in-law live in a small town in Iowa, and the town has just received, courtesy of the federal taxpayer and the University of Northern Iowa, a plan for the next twelve years. It is a nice plan, and its authors, experienced in such matters, make parts of it vague enough so as not to be caught out by actual developments. But it would be mere coincidence if the city actually carried out the plan.

3. In the United States, although we do not control in this way, our cost-of-living index has to be adjusted for quality of the vehicle. For a while, we were using just that particular idiotic measure, the weight of cars, as an evidence of their quality.

The reader may recall that some time ago indicative planning of the French model was all the rage. A French economist giving a lecture on this subject referred to it as not a *plan indicatif* but a *plan decoratif.* In other words, it had no effect on the actual economy. As part of the planning process, high executives at various companies in the same industry formed committees, which may have given them an opportunity to engage in a certain amount of monopolistic plotting.

While I was at George Mason, we had a student who spoke Norwegian fluently, and we sent him off to Norway to do a doctoral dissertation on the Norwegian economic plan. We thought this would be particularly interesting because Norway has 40 percent of the economy in the foreign trade sector. He discovered that the Norwegian plan was even less effective than the French one. It was indeed printed every year, put out by a small collection of civil servants, but the relationship between it and the world was more or less random. Indeed, he found that in the period he examined, the government did more things that the plan said that they definitely would not do, than things that the plan said that they definitely would do. Perhaps this was merely a coincidence.

Aside from this digression, the main point of this discussion is a certain amount of curiosity as to why organizations bother to build up these plans. Perhaps it has something to do with morale, or perhaps the general spirit of the plan is helpful to the company. It also may be that simply thinking over the whole organization of some company or governmental unit every now and then is a worthwhile exercise, even if the "plans" are not likely to be carried out.

So far we have been talking about ways of adjusting effort to get the maximum control. I would now like to turn to a different way of increasing control: selecting the subjects to be controlled in terms of the ease of control. In a way, this contains a contradiction. An individual who would like to do A thinks A is too difficult and hence does B. It is not really clear that this increases his control. It would depend on his relative evaluation of A and B.

There is a reason to believe that people might be quite happy with the change, however. It is called "reduction of cognitive dissonance." Most people, after a decision has been made, change their preference functions so that their particular decision seems better than it did before they made it. This well-known psychological phenomenon may apply here. It used to be said of General de Gaulle, for example, that instead of doing what he liked, he liked doing what he had to do. Many of us succeed in altering our preference functions so that whatever we find ourselves doing or consuming stands higher in our preference function than it did before we began doing or consuming it. Apparently, this is another example of the widely noted ease with which human beings can be indoctrinated.

But let us now turn to other aspects of selecting what you are doing in terms of what you can control rather than in terms of what basically you would like if control problems did not exist. One example is a particular aspect of government usually brushed over in organizational studies, but which is nevertheless of immense importance and does require an organization: the law. Suppose that we have a dictator who has definite preferences about what he would like to have people do. Among those preferences is a feeling that they should refrain from theft. He announces a law against theft and sets up an enforcement apparatus to prevent theft. Such organizations are fairly easy to design.

There are two different tasks here: one is detecting the thief and the other is making decisions as to what should be done. This last decision includes winnowing out accidental or erroneous detections from genuine detections—in other words, seeing to it that whatever you do about theft, it does not happen too often to innocents who are accidentally caught by the detection apparatus.

The detection apparatus is fairly easy to control; in fact, it is not even necessary to have one. Many societies—the traditional Mohammedan society, for example—did not have any formal government structure to detect thieves. Security depended on individual citizens observing theft of their own property or accidentally finding someone who had committed theft and reporting it to the court system. Probably this detected fewer thieves than would have been detected by a formal police force, but they compensated for that by the ferocity of the punishments imposed. Although this system worked reasonably well, today we object to cutting a thief's hands off.

In countries with formal police departments, however, determining their efficiency in catching thieves is not terribly difficult. You can observe how many thefts occur simply by asking ordinary citizens whether they have had anything stolen recently, and you can observe how many thieves are presented to your court system for trial and what percentage of them the court finds guilty. If the court finds too large a percentage of people innocent, that is, it has standards of proof that make it difficult to convict thieves, then the inefficiency may lie in the court system rather than in the police system. If the punishment allotted for the guilty person is light enough so that, granted how few people are actually caught and convicted, theft becomes a paying profession, then the problem, again, lies with the courts and not the police.

It should be fairly easy for a dictator to determine whether the fault lies with the police or the court system. In the United States at the moment, we have a situation in which the court system is causing a good deal of inefficiency. The courts combine making the punishments light[4] and conviction difficult. It may be true that the dictator is convinced, say, that criminals are mentally ill and in need of treatment rather than punishment and therefore we should not punish them. If so, the whole apparatus may have very little effect on anything. We will assume that our dictator, however, is rather old-fashioned and simply thinks that punishing thieves is a good way of reducing the theft level.

We will consider mainly the courts, not the police department, because the police is an easy area to supervise by the method given above, if we look at their actual detection rate as a percentage of total crimes committed. It should be emphasized here that the court system, in the United States in any event, includes the district attorney and other legal personnel.

In recent years, the federal courts in particular have done a number of things that make it much more difficult to convict criminals. Their strategy has not led to a reduction in the conviction rate, because the district attorneys usually bring only cases that they think have a good chance of succeeding. Thus, tightening up the laws of evidence has not lowered the conviction rate which in federal courts is above 90 percent.

As a result of court rules, many people that the police have detected as criminals are null pros'ed by the district attorney who feels, for one reason or another, that the evidence is not sufficient to get through under the present rules. Further, the police may not even arrest people they know are guilty if they anticipate that the courts will free them. This is as much a failure of the court system as the actual acquittals would be, and can be blamed straightforwardly on the judges. The district attorneys and police are simply adjusting to the procedural rules.

Let us stick to only the judges in this apparatus although, as we have pointed out, it is fairly easy to supervise all levels. The judges are *very* easy to control. It is a simple system used by almost every country in the world, although in the United States many of the "judges" are the amateurs that we

4. Mainly by making the prisons expensive and not terribly unpleasant. Indeed, the combination of expensiveness and the not terrible unpleasantness means that the sentences are necessarily short (to save money) and not all that nasty.

call jurymen. Let us begin with a professional judiciary of the sort found in most of the world, and not the odd rules of the Anglo-Saxon system, and then turn to the jury later.

What is normal is a body of people who make decisions in cases and who are required by law to pay some attention to the evidence. They usually hold a formal hearing of some sort. They should also not have any personal interest in the case. Normally, failure on either of these conditions would be easy to detect, particularly in the case of theft where the judge is unlikely to have any personal interest unless he happens to be related to the defendant.[5]

This simple pair of rules provides a high level of performance of the dictator's laws for punishing theft. The requirement that the judge hold a hearing or in some way become familiar with the case, together with his absence of any motives to do anything except enforce the law,[6] means that he is likely to carry out the instructions. The likelihood can be improved by an appeals system, but let us leave that aside temporarily.

The official who does this kind of work is not necessarily a specialist in the law. Characteristic of most European-type governments, as well as the American system, formal judges are full-time specialists. Of course, the juries that make the decisions in many American cases are amateurs,[7] but this system is not by any means worldwide. In the old Chinese Empire, the British Empire outside of England,[8] and the Roman Empire the judge was simply the principal executive official of the area of concern. The magistrate in China was essentially the central government's control figure in a county, and judging cases was only one of his duties. The same was true of those Roman proconsuls who actually had cases.[9] In the British Empire, the district commissioner did everything.

5. Courts in which the judges are actually in the pay of criminal groups, as is unfortunately true in certain American cities like New York, are quite unusual in the world as a whole. There is no reason why the dictator, if he actually wants to avoid such activity, cannot prevent it. The bribable judge is a man who, of necessity, must make his being bribable known to potential defendants. Thus, he must at least to some extent advertise, and it should be possible for the police to detect his advertisement.

6. His motives for that are quite weak, but they are put against zero motives for anything else.

7. So are the assessors who participate in many European trials.

8. This system was not absolutely uniform, but general.

9. In Rome, every effort was made to have the actual cases shoved down to the self-governing municipalities rather than handled by the government. But those that were handled by the central government were handled by the ordinary officials. As in China, the emperor himself was the ultimate court of appeal.

The specialization of judges is obviously not a necessity, and any American who is willing to let his decision go to a jury must agree. What is necessary is that the decision be made by someone who has become reasonably familiar with the facts, and a formal hearing is one way of making certain that is done. But whether the whole thing could be handled by paper—that is, pleadings, transcripts of evidence, and so on—we do not know.

The only argument I know in favor of the formal hearing is that the judge and/or jury actually have some contact with the evidence. If they are permitted simply to read things in the quiet of their studies, they may decide not to bother with a good deal of the evidence. Otherwise, the use of written evidence would be much more efficient than oral hearings. The Anglo-Saxon appellate courts operate that way.

The importance of insuring that the decision maker be familiar with the facts in the case explains the almost universal aversion to having "political" intervention in the judicial process. This aversion is found as much in dictatorial regimes as elsewhere, although the dictator himself normally exempts his will from the rule against politics. On the other hand, he rarely has time or interest enough to intervene in most cases. For instance, George Bush might not necessarily be worse at making decisions about a person's guilt or innocence than a jury of twelve randomly selected individuals would, but he actually would probably make the decision on the basis of inadequate knowledge of the facts simply because it is not worth his time to devote much emphasis to the matter.

Therefore, if some dictator were to begin sending orders down to judges on individual cases, it would reduce the efficiency of the court in carrying out his laws. Dictators, in practice, rarely intervene in individual cases and normally make strong efforts to see to it that their other high officials also do not. Under these circumstances, a dictator's laws can be carried out quite efficiently.

Here, then, is an area where the dictator can get his will carried out with little in the way of supervision. If he wants more supervision than simply depending on the absence of conflict of interest on the part of the individual lower-level decision maker, it can be provided by an appellate court system. After a decision is made by the initial court, it can be appealed to a higher court composed of, say, five judges, possibly even better judges than in the regular court, and the precautions we have been describing are somewhat reinforced. The appellate court is even less likely to be directly involved in the case and can be easily prevented from having conflicts of interest. Because it takes a second view of the matter it is probably less likely to make simple mistakes. Again, an easy-to-supervise activity is available for carrying out the dictator's will.

The jury, however, is a special technique. (It is not clear, however, whether it increases or reduces the control which the people of the United States have over the population's behavior by way of law.) The jury itself is an eminently democratic organization in which the twelve people are given an opportunity to get information about a particular case. The laws of evidence mean that they do not get as much evidence as they would perhaps like, but on the basis of the information they receive, they make the ultimate decision. It seems likely that although a sample of twelve is rather small, they tend to reach the decision that the people of the United States would reach if all of them had this information.

On the other hand, there is no doubt that they pay relatively little attention to the law when it deviates from what they think is right. In a way, this is an almost extreme example of short-circuiting. The people of the United States, by way of the jury, are able to obtain what is probably a fairly good implementation of their ideas on law enforcement without any real supervision at all, but there is a tax cost. Periodically, people are compelled to serve on juries.[10]

The problem of the jury and its control raises what is almost the only real difficulty in the use of law as a control mechanism in the way of getting your will done. You have to have an agency that is either indifferent to the actual outcome or tends to agree with you. Historically, most rulers have simply attempted to select judges who are in general accord with the dictator on most matters. Although the jury is an outstanding way of selecting people in general accordance with the average man who is supposed to control in a democracy, the six-hundred-man panels that the Athenians sometimes used would be a better sample of the population.

To repeat, a jury does not mean that the written law will necessarily be carried out if there is some conflict between it and moral principles. Historically, it seems likely that the dictators, kings, and other rulers have tended to select judges who are in agreement with them. In our system the jury rarely pays too much attention to the law. On questionnaires, judges also have been found to give "justice" as either their first or second objective, and also to give "adherence to the written law" as their first or second objective. Republicans favor adherence to the written law, and Democrats favor justice, but both rank the other as second. This is, I think, an expression of the fact that the people giving the orders—the people in the United States, dictators elsewhere—are not absolutely clear in their own mind exactly what it is they want to do.

10. Granted true random jury selection, the tax of compulsory jury service is equivalent to a head tax and thus has a minimum of excess burden.

In the United States when we turn to detailed regulations, and our law has many of them, we normally depend on judges alone and not juries. The regulations are enforced by injunctions rather than by formal trials with a jury, particularly in the case of the income tax in which the Internal Revenue Service is, to put it mildly, extremely reluctant to go before a jury. Only if a wealthy man has done something obvious will they be willing to trust their case to a jury. Otherwise, they have worked out various ways of avoiding the right to a jury trial for the person alleged to have violated the code.

But this particular way of getting your will carried out without much difficulty is obviously available for only a limited set of decisions, albeit important ones. Most governments have depended on this particular technique. Something similar to it exists in private organizations as well. Normally, most companies have an elaborate set of rules for the accounting function which produces the data later used at a higher level for policy decisions. In some cases, this elaborate set of rules is established by the accounting profession itself, but in other cases there are rules for the specific company.

Most companies have an apparatus that enforces these rules in the form of an auditing bureau. This bureau acts much like a European magistrate: it goes out and looks at the subject matter carefully, talks to people, and then decides whether there have been violations. Again, the system works without much supervision because the auditors have substantially no conflicting interests. This is another case in which one's orders can be carried out without much difficulty but, again, only in a limited area.

In both the cases of judges and jury on one hand and auditors on the other, there is one area in which private interests of the decider conflict with those at the head of the organization. The judges may want to take more leisure than the ruler wants, that is, to give the cases less consideration than he thinks is desirable. The appellate procedure to some extent deals with this by providing a re-hash of the case, with the individual judge possibly being found wrong; hence, his future career is somewhat affected. Of course, if he is an American federal judge and cannot be fired, this variable is not important. Most corporations also have an arrangement under which an outside accountant firm makes an annual audit, and the firm is changed from time to time.

In both of the above cases, it is relatively easy to get exact compliance with the wishes of whoever is making the decisions without a great deal of time devoted to supervision. On the other hand, both cases apply to only a rather restricted area of the possible command structure. It seems likely, however, that the heavy dependence on the law by most states, and the very heavy dependence on accounts by most corporations, are the result of the simplicity of getting orders of the higher-ups carried out in these cases. The purpose of this chapter is to discuss areas in which one can get one's orders carried out easily; hence, the person who wants his will carried out will specialize in such areas.

In one of these cases, auditing, the approach works only if the objective of the man at the top is simply making money. We have pointed out before that people may change their objectives in the direction of what they can obtain. It may be that the dominance of the money-making part of most economies comes from the fact that in this area supervision is relatively easy.[11]

Purchasing is another area where supervision is relatively easy. If one considers companies, the question of whether to make or buy is frequently referred to as a difficult one. One of the major reasons for choosing to buy must surely be that if you have a number of competitive suppliers, your control over what you actually get is probably much easier than if you were dealing with your own manufacturing institution. Indeed there is, as we have mentioned, a whole branch of research initiated by Oliver Williamson pointing out that where a company deals with a monopoly supplier, it may be wise for the company to buy the supplier because of the impossibility of making competitive purchases.

Most people do not think when they purchase something that they are imposing their will on other people, but if you are a fairly large purchaser, it is literally true. Various producers will make efforts to guess what it is you want and provide it for you. They will also make efforts to deceive you a bit as to exactly what they are selling, but that would be true in your own organizational hierarchy as well.

We have mentioned that one way of getting your will carried out is simply to want large profits and to use the accounting system as a measure of that. This is a rather extreme example of restricting your desires to something that can be easily controlled; even there, as we have emphasized before, you will not really maximize profits if all you do is pay attention to the accounting system. Still, this is probably the best way of getting your will carried out, even if it requires changing your will.

11. This includes communist economies, although the money-making part of the economy there is frequently either illegal in the form of the black market or concealed in the form of the compensation of the higher officials.

It is possible that this simple fact is one of the reasons why purchase and sale, manufacturing, and so on, tend to dominate any economy over time. Even the former so-called planned economies of Eastern Europe required such profit-maximizing entities as the Tolkach and the black market to function. The dominance of the profit-maximizing methods is never complete, and economies can be run in which it is quite small. The subsistence agriculture economies in which most people lived until fairly recently composed such an organization, but in this case, the basic economy was raising food for yourself, and any trade was maximized by using profit-maximizing techniques.

Nevertheless, it is hard to argue that specializing in activities that are easy to control is the be-all and end-all of human society. Fortunately, a reasonably free market using this method of control will in fact achieve many other individual goals, although not everything. Nevertheless, it is an important consideration to keep in mind.

In the previous chapter, we talked about ways of improving your control over areas by simply reducing the area under control. In this chapter, we have discussed increasing your control by attempting to control only subjects that are easy to control. The two ideas are closely related but not identical. Further, the approach of the last chapter did not require any specialization of your own preferences, whereas the ideas of this chapter do. Another characteristic that both have in common is that they assume that you have some way of seeing to it that your inferiors are apt to carry out orders given to them. These incentives and what the lower officials do to prevent themselves from being completely controlled are the topics for the next chapter.

CHAPTER 12

INCENTIVES

Most individuals have preferences of their own and do not enjoy carrying out the preferences of others, even if those others are nominally their superiors. The same is true in ordinary commercial transactions. The courteous waiter in a high-quality restaurant probably does not especially care whether the customer gets his order in good condition. He provides it only because that is the way he makes a living, although what is known as pride of workmanship does exist in places.

The waiter is in a particularly clearcut situation. Supervisors in the restaurant see to it that he is reasonably busy, and a sizable part of his income comes from customer tips so that he has a strong financial motive to please them. An individual in a large bureaucracy usually has much greater ability to avoid carrying out the wishes of his superiors if he wants.

The solution to this problem is usually the carrot and the stick. Even slave labor camps make use of the carrot. The reader will recall in the first chapter of *One Day in the Life of Ivan Denisovich* that the management of the camp asks for volunteers for a particular task rather than simply giving orders. The volunteers are promised a better situation, but Ivan believes it will not be provided and therefore he refuses the opportunity.

The use of the carrot and the stick has disadvantages from the standpoint of the people at the top in that there are resources involved which they would like to use for something else. For instance, if you did not have to pay your employees, you could take more vacations on the Riviera. But, unfortunately, you do have to pay them. Indeed, the supervision time we discussed earlier is in part devoted to deciding exactly what rewards would be given to individuals. In our society, we frequently deal with employees of either the federal or local government, private companies, or nonprofit organizations. There are no actual punishments, although this fact is slightly concealed because things are sometimes listed as punishments.

It used to be said that when J. Edgar Hoover did not like an official he would send him off to the FBI offices in Butte. This was regarded as a punishment, but it really was not since the person could freely leave if he wanted. What it was really was reducing his rewards sharply. It is easy to mix up the choice between a cut in the rewards a person receives and actual punishment.

From the standpoint of the person's situation before the change is made, there is no great difference except that it is always possible for the person to refuse to accept the reduction in reward and quit. He cannot do that with a true punishment.

It is one of the characteristics of capitalism, or, for that matter, any kind of open economy, that the basic method of getting obedience is the carrot—the stick is restricted to preventing crime and things of that nature. A man given a sentence of ten years cannot just decide to quit. One of the characteristics of communism as it was, not as it was claimed to be, was that it depended heavily on the stick rather than the carrot.

Except within the party hierarchy itself and for certain favored intellectuals, there was not really a great deal of legal difference in income available. Furthermore, what difference of income that was available depended upon promotion to executive rank, and only a small part of the personnel in a factory could be promoted to that level. Consequently, only the stick was available. The various arrangements making it hard for the person to quit his job in the Soviet Union meant that, to a considerable extent, the various industries did not compete for labor.

On the other hand, certainly after the death of Stalin and more recently, officials were more reluctant to use the stick. At the time of this writing, the question is open of whether the government of the Soviet Union can change the situation so that the simple stick of firing can be used. Whether they will accept the carrot of differential wages with some of the higher returns going to people who have just been lucky—we have no way of avoiding that—is an open question.

Most American intellectuals prefer the combination of the high productivity that comes from the widespread use of different-sized carrots in a truly free economy with the security that goes with the Russian system. Obviously, the two cannot be combined. The traditional point of view of right-wing U.S. citizens is that incomes should be permitted to vary freely but that there should be a safety net into which people can fall. This means, except in criminal matters, a complete dependence on the carrot and not on the stick, but it also means that some very big carrots will be distributed to some people.

Enough of this speculation on life in communism, which now appears to be undergoing a rapid change. Let us turn to the situation of the U.S. official somewhere in the hierarchy, either government or private, and consider the ways in which he attempts to maximize his own preferences rather than the preferences of his superiors. We should keep in mind that some of his preferences probably relate to what tasks are performed by his inferiors. He has a combined problem of obtaining independence for himself and obtaining control of his subordinates. But for now we will discuss the former aspect.

What, then, are the actual desires of an inferior? First, he probably will not want to work as hard as his superior would like him to. He may just not be terribly hard-working or may be hard-working but want to work on something else. The problem is particularly acute with people who have mental work. It is almost impossible to tell by looking at a man what he is thinking. He may be thinking about the problem which has been assigned to him, or he may not be.

Judgement by result, observing whether he comes up with a solution, is a method, but unfortunately different problems have different degrees of difficulty. A supervisor who is not willing to devote as much time to a problem as the person attempting to solve it is not really in a good position to tell whether the person has reached the best solution or even whether he has been thinking about the matter continuously over a period of time. By the rather simple procedure of giving a person many problems and then applying the law of large numbers to both the quality and the quantity of solutions, this difficulty can be resolved.

Determining the quality of the solution of these problems, however, is probably impossible unless there is an objective measure. The superior would have to devote so much time to judging these solutions that he would have little time for anything else. Over a very long period of time, by drawing a random sample of a small set of these decisions, the superior could use this method without devoting too much time to it. But we do not know whether this is an efficient procedure.

Physical labor is somewhat easier, but even here, only careful study can determine how much work a person should turn out. The usual method is simply to compare different workers on similar tasks. The foreman has a good idea of how long it should take. In practice, this probably means that strong healthy people do not work as hard as they could and that smaller people who are not in terribly good health are overworked. This discrepancy comes from holding everyone to the same standard. Ways of avoiding this problem do not have general application.

The conclusion we draw from these considerations is that perfect supervision is difficult, particularly with mental labor. Nevertheless, supervisors should try to do as well as they can. In a business firm, increasing the pressure put on inferiors may mean that they quit or that they get paid a higher salary.

We are talking here about the lower-ranking official and his effort to maximize his own utility rather than that of his superiors. Whatever rewards or absence of penalty his superior can inflict or award is part of his utility, although he has others. We have already mentioned his desire normally not to work as hard as his superior would want. Again, this does not necessarily mean that he is lazy. If he is engaged in mental work, he can do idle daydreaming, worry about his personal stock portfolio, or even try to solve a scientific problem of no interest to his employer, all while he appears to be concentrating on his employer's desires.

The federal government has a particularly difficult problem of this sort. Many individual employees have developed strong ideas as to what their particular bureau or suboffice within that bureau should be doing. They may devote much energy to this pursuit rather than to the objectives of their superiors. This may be exactly what the government as a whole wants, but more often it is not. Usually it is not something that, per se, would be contrary to the public interest, although sometimes that can be true as well. But it is normally something that does not contribute, and may well be contrary, to the major drive of the organization as seen by its superiors.

In the Foreign Service, which I left a long time ago, the basic lack of coherence between the desires of the higher officials and the activity of the junior officials was primarily that junior officials were not doing very much. It was not an extremely industrious collection of people, except for individuals who were simply following various special hobbies. For example, one ambassador hated the government head of the country to which he was accredited. This head of government was not on terribly good terms with the U.S. Department of State either, but the ambassador succeeded in being much more negative in his dealings with him than would normally be the case, and his reports back to the United States were also clearly affected by his strong personal feelings.

General Taylor, the commander of the Eighth Army during my last few days in the embassy in Korea, was barely interested in what went on in his army and immensely interested in what went on in the Pentagon and in the Executive Office of the president. His efforts relating to his command were geared mostly toward seeing that nothing happened to get him bad reports at those higher levels.

But this method is merely part of the individual's way of dealing with his superiors. If the individual's activity is going to differ from what his superior wants, he must see to it that the information reaching his superior does not indicate any discrepancy. If the individual is carrying out his superior's wishes with perfection, he still wants full control of the information flow because he wants to make sure the good news is passed on.

This discussion of the way a lower-ranking official attempts to control the behavior of his superior by controlling his information repeats things said earlier in the book. The main point of saying it again is that the incentives of necessity are based on information that reaches the superior—information that may be inaccurate either because of random error or, more important, because the inferior wants it to be inaccurate.

The more intense the incentives that the superior puts on the inferior to carry out his wishes, the more the inferior is motivated to distort the information reaching the superior. There used to be a theory of the "band of brothers" in what used to be the British civil service. All promotion was by seniority; hence, there was substantially no reason why any of the people in the band of brothers should deceive any of the others. This does not mean that no such deceit existed. Various informal incentives such as saying nice things or bad things, inviting people to dinner, and so on, depend on the information that other members of the band of brothers have; therefore, there is still a modest need to deceive them on occasion.

To take the other extreme, during the 1930s, Stalin provided what can be described only as extraordinarily severe incentives for obedience to his higher officials. It is likely that this maximized their motives for attempting to control the information he received. Apparently, he dealt with this by killing people for the most trivial information and deviations from his will. Since he was insane, random killing occurred as well.

Let us now turn to incentives themselves and then later mix the information problem and the incentive problem. A strong mythological view exists in our society that positive incentives are better than negative incentives. I think this view is largely motivated by the fact that the former are nicer. Talk about rewarding virtue is more pleasant than talk about punishing vice. The same phenomenon can be seen in modern criminology where most criminologists prefer not to think about punishment as an infliction of pain. They regard it instead as an educational process that will rehabilitate. Since we can inflict pain but do not know how to rehabilitate, this attitude is self-frustrating.

The view that negative incentives will not work, especially in complex activities, is contrary to the evidence we have. Solzhenitsyn's *The First Circle*, which is a novel based firmly on fact, deals with a research laboratory maintained by the Russian secret police and was also a prison for scientists who had done something that irritated the secret police or who perhaps had been picked up in a random sweep. They were incarcerated in this prison and ordered to engage in scientific research. If they refused, they were threatened with various disciplinary measures in the prison, or sent to an ordinary concentration camp. So in the novel and in the real world, they conducted the research.

Another example of advanced work obtained by negative incentives was the German concentration camp at Dachau which contained within it a factory making high-tech buzz bombs. In spite of the sole use of negative incentives,[1] prisoners manufactured this hard-to-produce device efficiently and in large volume. Like the research facility maintained by the NKVD, this work was by no means routine. As a result of the American-British bombing offensive, supplies were intermittent and frequently delayed, resulting in occasional rapid changes in the manufacturing process. The prisoners, most of whom hated the Nazis, were compelled by negative incentive to cooperate with these changes.

Negative incentives have been used in many other operations throughout the world's history. Most southern slave plantations were so. After the liberation of the slaves, the production of cotton and other crops in the South fell sharply because the slaves were not willing to put in the long hours and devoted work in return for a positive reward that they had been willing to put in to avoid a flogging. But this does not mean that the real production of the area fell. The leisure that the slaves could now consume, which they had been prevented from consuming before, clearly was one product of the southern economy valued by the slaves more highly than they valued the cotton. Thus the net effect was really an increase in the total product. It is just that leisure is not included in the statistics.

It is also a little hard to tell the difference between a positive and a negative incentive. In the last ten years or so the Chinese countryside has undergone a gigantic increase in productivity as a result of an open market system that has permitted the Chinese peasants to obtain positive rewards for their work.[2] If, however, an American farmer were confronted with the range of income and living standard given to the Chinese farmer in return for the

1. Unless you are going to say that permitting you to stay in the camp rather than being killed is a positive incentive.

2. More accurately, an only moderately controlled market system.

same levels of work, the American would no doubt regard it as an extreme example of negative incentives.

Technically, the problem is where the zero point lies that distinguishes positive and negative incentives. Suppose a southern slave master of the Simon Legree type announces a policy of fifty lashes every Friday for all the slaves,[3] but offers positive rewards such as refraining from whipping or reducing the whipping for those who work hard. We might object that the zero point in the chain should not include the whipping (but there is no intrinsic reason why that is necessary). This is particularly true if we talk about salary levels. Humans are now living at varying salary levels in different parts of the world. What would appear to an Indian peasant as a largely improved income would be regarded as a severe punishment by an American. Indeed, most American prisons offer a higher living standard than is obtained by much of the world's free population.

If the discussion of positive and negative rewards has any meaning at all, it must start from the status quo of the person under consideration. Thus a vice-president of a large corporation who is now being paid $500,000 a year would regard a shift to $250,000 as a severe penalty. Another assistant vice-president who is now being paid $250,000 a year would regard a potential increase to $500,000 as positive. Although the change of income is exactly the same for both people, one can only declare the incentive as positive or negative by using status quo as a base. For many people in the company, an income of $250,000 would be regarded as a great positive incentive.

Really severe negative incentives are not permitted in our society. We cannot flog workers, shoot them, or send them to the Gulag. Indeed, most of the people who write in this area are academics who have jobs where they cannot be either demoted or fired.[4] Under these circumstances, the negative incentive spectrum is narrow although not zero, and the positive incentive is wide; therefore, it is probably sensible for most people to depend mainly upon the positive incentives. Under these circumstances the sensible thing to do is to set an employee's standard pay lower than you would if you had access to the full range of incentives. Doing so gives you more opportunity to have positive incentives.

Another problem is that positive incentives fairly uniformly cost the supervisor or his employer money, whereas negative incentives tend to be

3. Simon Legree, of course, was a foreman, not a master.

4. They can be harassed, and in an inflationary period, they can have pay raises denied.

cheap. Indeed, the reduction of the working capacity of the victim of the negative incentive, either through his execution or through his being unable to work hard because he has been injured severely in the course of receiving the negative incentive, is the principal cost of the negative incentive to the employer. In our society, to repeat, negative incentives are not permitted. I am certainly not complaining about that fact, but we should keep in mind that the unwillingness to use this kind of incentive system restricts its use, not that it would be ineffective.

Negative incentives do exist in our society, although they are modest. A strong reproach is frequently thought of as a negative incentive, but normally it is mainly important because it carries with it a threat of firing. Aside from firing, things such as imposing fines on employees to be deducted from their salary, lowering their salary, or transferring them to a less significant place with lower salary are all possible but rarely used. Superiors apparently feel that having someone stay around who is unhappy with his position is worse than firing the man and hiring someone else in his place. Because of this attitude, in a flexible labor market such as we have, negative incentives turn heavily in the direction of simply firing.

To repeat, it is not necessarily obvious whether you have negative or positive incentives. For example, consider an auto agency that hires salesmen at a base salary plus commission on sales, with a low base salary. It is difficult to say here whether it is offering positive incentives in the form of commissions on cars or negative incentives in the form of absence of commissions if no sales are made. If the salesmen take the job knowingly, they presumably are willing to accept this incentive system without too much effect on their morale.

If information and control were perfect, it would be sensible to use a large number of small incentives in order to completely control the behavior of the inferior. In practice, we do not have good enough information to do that with most direct employees. Thus we are usually forced to offer bonuses or pay raises or, for that matter, occasionally refrain from making pay cuts over fairly long periods of time considering quite a large bundle of behavior as a unit.

One area in our society where the rewards and punishments are handed out in small increments as a result of detailed specific decisions, however, is when the person making the decision is the residual claimant. Say that the owner-operator of a store gains every time he makes a right decision and loses every time he makes a wrong one. If the decision is an unimportant one, his gain or loss is small; hence, he has an incentive to concentrate his attention optimally on big decisions and to give less attention to small decisions. Although this approach is highly efficient, the economies of scale and differential individual talents seem to indicate that it will not work everywhere.

Beginning with economies of scale, consider a large company that is necessarily large because, say, it is the Ford Motor Company in the early twenties and is making one-third of the world's automobiles on one assembly line at great savings. In some cases, such companies actually are owned by a single person or small group, as the Ford Motor Company was, who gets the optimal incentives. Usually it is a corporation with wide ownership of the shares. In this case, the residual claimants are the shareholders, and they do not play a major role in the management.

The solution adopted for this problem in most corporations is to provide a bonus or stock warrant scheme so that higher officials, particularly the chief executive, find that their income varies according to the fluctuations, first, in the profits of the company and, second and even better, the capital value of its stock.[5] At various times, the income tax law has made it difficult to offer this kind of bonus, but at the moment bonuses can be large, as in the famous case of the broker who got $400 million in one year.

In large corporations, however, although this works for the higher officials, it is difficult to produce a similar system for the lower level—say, the division managers. The problem is that the divisions are to some extent in conflict with each other, and an incentive system might exacerbate that conflict.

Basically, there are two ways of dealing with this problem, neither of which is very good, and there are compromises among them. First, when a friend of mine was working at Ford Motor Company he discovered that the bonuses distributed to all of the senior employees regardless of where they worked were simply a function of the total profits of Ford Motor Company that year. This meant that as far as the bonuses are concerned, these employees had no reason to undercut each other. They also did not have much chance of improving their bonus by improving the profits of their division. They still could consider the possibility of promotion, but not as much as if the bonus system had been allocated to the individual.

The second case is one in which the accounting division is asked to compute, insofar as it can, the pure contribution of profit of each profit center, and then the head of that center is given a bonus based on that figure. This

5. As discussed at length in Chapter 10, apparently actual ownership by way of a leveraged buyout is a better incentive.

case embodies the opposite problem. It provides the strongest possible motives for individuals to attempt to switch profits out of other divisions into theirs by hard bargaining, noncooperation, and so on. At the same time it also gives them the highest possible motives to work hard and to maximize the profits in their division.

Most companies have some compromise between these two systems which gain advantages of each and suffer from the disadvantages.

Another incentive system, and surely the most common in our society, is used by large corporations like Ford for all except the highest-ranking officers. It is simply to have the superiors promote and demote and raise and lower salaries according to their views of what the individual contributes to the firm. Formal incentive systems exist because there is no superior at the top level. The stockholders pay little or no attention to the actual management; therefore, an automatic system such as a bonus scheme is certainly better than letting the stockholders vote on who should get what.

Of course, the subjective judgement of the superior is subject to error. If he is given the same bookkeeping data used to compute the bonuses, however, it is likely that his judgement is better than any of the automatic systems I have mentioned. The problem here is giving the person who makes the decision appropriate motives, and thus we have switched mostly to such automatic systems.

Profit-making businesses are not the only places where problems of this sort arise. The Pope, as the manager of a very large organization, has problems of who should be a monsignor, who should be bishop, and so on up. In his case, he has some fairly clearcut negative incentives since he can unfrock a priest.[6]

The government is a larger organization, and most modern democratic governments have handicapped themselves by making it impossible for the senior officials to do much in the way of either rewarding or penalizing most of the civil service employees. The people at the top, on the other hand, are rewarded or penalized by the voters who are only somewhat better informed than the average stockholder, and, unlike the average stockholder, do not have optimal incentives from the standpoint of efficiency.

Much evidence now exists on the effect of transferring the operation of various government services from the government civil service to some kind of contract provider who is a profit-making individual or corporation. The

6. In the past his negative incentives were somewhat more effective.

savings are usually large, probably because of this defect in the government's supervision process,[7] which means that this large cost-saving activity is not taken advantage of as much as one might hope. Furthermore, in many cases the private contractors were able to influence the outcome positively.

In private companies, each individual should ideally receive a bundle of small rewards and penalties, depending on exactly how he behaves on the job. An individual entrepreneur has a set of rewards like this, but no one else in the economy does.

The ultimate owner of the business, whether he is a single small man or John D. Rockefeller, may have preferences which are not solely those of maximizing the firm's profit. From the standpoint of the economy as a whole, this consideration is more or less irrelevant. The artist who, instead of producing paintings he thinks will sell well, produces ones that will sell only moderately well but that he likes is maximizing his own utility even if he is not maximizing the utility of potential purchasers. In a competitive market other people would tend to fill the gap, and, in any event, the entire cost in monetary terms would fall on that entrepreneur.

The same would be true of the owner of a large enterprise. Henry Ford refused for a number of years to replace his Model T with a more modern and convenient car. This cost him a great deal of money,[8] and its main effect on the economy was the growth of General Motors, Chrysler, Nash, and so on. Probably we were somewhat better off with the dominant control of this one monster manufacturer shrinking a bit.

It is in this sense that we can refer to the economic system as optimally efficient, although sometimes we do not want optimal efficiency. As far as I can see, the "industry" that provides cocaine, marijuana, heroin, and other drugs is run by a group of profit-seeking entrepreneurs who are extremely efficient despite the fact that some of their competitive techniques are frowned on by society. Nevertheless, in this case, most people believe that we would be better off if this industry were less efficient.[9]

Many people would say that this industry is inefficient because its customers are injured by its product. This truth can be applied in a lesser extent to many other industries that provide what the customers will pay for, not

7. A credible threat to make such a transfer sometimes results in equivalent savings within the bureaucracy itself.

8. He remained a billionaire.

9. As a typical Chicago economist, I am in favor of legalizing these drugs.

what some outside observer thinks is the ideal product. If you are the outside observer, too bad. On the other hand, if the outside observer is going to restrict *your* consumption potential, you would object.

In any event, this individual entrepreneur is not what we observe most of the time. For a variety of reasons not well understood, large enterprises seem to work better than small ones in many parts of the economy.

In part, this is simple economy of scale. Perhaps the most simple and famous example is the Alchian and Demsetz movement of a large crate. Economies of scale encompass more, because a great many large economic enterprises operate different factories in different locations producing different things. These cases probably have economies of some sort in the higher management. Perhaps, for example, high skill in merchandising—which mainly consists of guessing what people will buy—is a rare talent; therefore, it is best used at the head of a large diversified corporation.

I won't argue that this is so. In fact, I do not know exactly why many of these very large organizations such as Fairfield, LTV, and ARA exist. What we can say is that they have won in the competitive fight.[10] In any event, in these large organizations, the incentive problem is real and cries out for a feasible solution, even though it will be far from perfect.

In other organizations, the problem is much more difficult. In the government, for instance, there is no simple measure of efficiency and no group of people who have strong motives for wanting the organization to be efficient (even if like stockholders they have little motive for becoming informed about it).

Here, again, the actual mix of government units is quite disparate. Many different countries compose the world, and the boundaries of the countries are the result of past wars or, in those cases where there is an irredentist movement, will be determined by the outcome of a future war. These countries have radically different forms of government, running from Castro's Cuba on one end to Switzerland at the other, but within any given country there may be a large number of governments, depending on how thoroughly decentralized control is.

This situation is somewhat different from the market situation. There is every reason to believe that a highly competitive market among other things puts pressure on all its participants to achieve optimal scale. Whether this pressure is strong enough, and whether simple historical development does

10. LTV won its fight for a long time but is having difficulty at the moment.

not mean that things which were optimal in size and scale ten years ago are still around although there has been a technical change, is not clear. What is clear is that very little pressure of this sort exists in the government area.

Traditionally, war has been the main competitive technique for determining size of the nation-states. Unfortunately, war probably does give impetus to states which are the most efficient military machines, but there is no reason to believe they are optimally sized for other functions.

If we look at the mix of local and centralized governments, again, there does not seem to be any significant pressure for efficiency. And, again, history may have led to a division that was efficient at some point in the past and no longer is.

In theory, we have a rather good way of telling the optimal size of government for any particular activity. The smaller the government, down to and including a government that has only one citizen, the more likely it will carry out individual preferences. Suppose a particular government activity can be done at either level A or level B and that roughly half the population favors A and half B. Let us assume that total population is twenty-five, and thirteen prefer A, and twelve prefer B. Using simple majority voting if they are all in one government unit, twelve people do not get their wishes.

Assume, however, that there are five government units and the twenty-five voters are divided randomly, five to a unit. Although we cannot make exact calculations, it is obvious that the number of people who find themselves in a government following a policy of which they disapprove will be fewer than twelve because thirteen voters cannot form a three-person majority in more than four of the governments. If they do, there will be a fifth government that follows policy B, and where only one person—the one who favors policy A—is disappointed. This gives us nine disappointed people, although with random assortment we would anticipate the system would do better.[11]

This phenomenon—first noted by Pennock—is perfectly general. The more we divide the government up, the fewer the people who will find themselves in a minority. This is true even if there is no voting with the feet; that is, they all stay in a given area. With voting with the feet, the effect is stronger.

This obviously is an argument for smaller governments. Unfortunately, there is an equally strong argument pointing in the opposite direction. Various

11. See "Mosquito Abatement," in my *Private Wants, Public Means* (University Press of America, 1970), pp. 3–28. Also see Yoram Barzel, "Two Propositions on the Optimal Level of Producing Collective Goods," *Public Choice* 6 (Spring 1969), 31–37.

externalities have different geographic scope. What I do on my property affects what my next-door neighbor can do on his. Furthermore, what we do on our government's territory affects people in other governmental areas. Internalizing these externalities requires larger groups, and, in fact, there are externalities large enough so that only a world government would be able to internalize them adequately. Thus there is a strong argument for large governments. It is possible to set these two different tendencies against each other and find the optimal one,[12] thus permitting us to obtain optimal government sizes.

But even this is too simple. We are assuming that the individuals all vote and cast reasonably informed votes—an unlikely assumption, and we are also putting no cost on the time they spend in voting. Addition of these results would no doubt lead to a new optimum that is somewhat different from the one above. Nevertheless, these calculated efficient optimums have nothing to do with the government units that we observe.

History is even more likely to be the dominating characteristic in governmental units than it is in private business. For instance, both California and Nevada are optimally efficient in state sizes. Pretty clearly, it is simply the result of history.

With government incentives, the situation is even worse. I mentioned earlier the civil service which in most Western countries makes it impossible to fire people. In most countries, seniority is important for promotion, with the result that even the reward of promotion for efficiency is limited. The United States has been experimenting with direct monetary rewards administered by higher officials to lower officials, but in my opinion these tend to be routine. It is dangerous for a secretary who has been in office only a few months and who plans on leaving in a few months to allocate these rewards according to what he thinks is the merit of the officials.

Indeed, in the United States, the permanent officials with their security of tenure and their well-established communication channels, especially with the press, may be in a better position to bring pressure to bear on their nominal superior than he is to bring pressure to bear on them. The effect of this on the incentive scheme is obvious.

Nevertheless, the fact that our government is broken up and we are decentralized is clearly an advantage. The Swiss situation in which the decentralization proceeds even further and in which almost any decision by the

12. It would be necessary here to take into account externalities of one activity on another as well as the pure geographic externalities.

government can be reversed by popular vote probably provides even better incentives than ours. Certainly their government performs more efficiently than ours.

It is difficult to think of anything one could do about all of this considering that the higher part of the organization, the voters themselves, have no simple easy way of telling whether their objectives are being carried out. In most cases they probably do not know what specific objectives they would like the government to maximize. To repeat what I have said several times, as bad as this system is, the alternative forms of government seem worse.

In that part of the economy where there is strong pressure for efficiency, an approach similar to federalism is one possible solution. The widespread use of franchise operations is clearly an effort to split the entrepreneurial function into two levels.

At the top we have an organization composed of specialists who make decisions in efficient merchandising and other policy matters. At this level, the return in which small policy changes lead to almost immediate effect on the franchising organization is clear. Ray Kroc's building of McDonald's is a famous case.

The organization, however, is made much smaller and less bureaucratic by referring a large number of detailed decisions to individuals who run individual stores, or in some cases small subchains of stores, and whose rewards and penalties are handed out in small quantities, depending on how efficient they are because their costs and their returns are both directly personal.

Unfortunately, the franchise system, although it does improve the incentive scheme, is not universally applicable. It is very hard to see how Ford could have run his assembly line by this method, but something can be done experimenting that way. Several industries (I have mentioned building and the New York clothing industry) have many small businessmen engaging in sales and purchases from each other, with the result that complicated items are produced without a centralized organization.

Rumor has it that Chrysler, with the exception of its transmission train, has shed almost all its research in improved technology onto its parts suppliers. They buy components, say, brakes, and simply shop around among different possible sellers to get a good quality product, thus putting pressure on the brake manufacturers to do respectable research and to improve design. Whether this is a better method than doing it all yourself, as some other automobile manufacturers do, I do not know. Certainly the Japanese manufacturers have always depended more on specialized suppliers than American companies have.

Here we are back to the kind of puzzle we have dealt with before. Again we find that there is a wide perspective of types of organization, and it is hard to say why some companies use one kind and others use another. As we discussed in Chapter 10, one gets the impression that a radical change in structure is frequently more important simply because it is a radical change than because the new structure is an improvement over the old. Perhaps the breaking up of all the little rent-seeking conspiracies is the real function of corporate reorganizations.

Incentives are an all-important tool of management, and the organizational structure is affected by the incentives just as incentives affect the organizational structure. It would be nice if we had better information on these matters than we have, but at least we can make use of what we now know.

CHAPTER 13

SUMMING UP

By now the reader has discovered that I have more puzzles than solutions, which could reflect the present level of knowledge in this area. A large group of scholars who got their initial start from the work of Herbert Simon have studied these problems in detail. I usually call them the Williamson group because most of them are organized in a sort of feudal train behind Oliver Williamson. They have discovered a great deal of detailed information.

I have mentioned several times in this book the hypothesis that when two companies are involved in a supplier-supplied relationship and they each have some monopoly or monopsony power over the other, they are likely to merge. I emphasize the word "likely." Many times there is no merger, and other arrangements are made so that neither is able to exploit the other.

Furthermore, even though we can accept the monopsony/monopoly argument, many large corporations involve different divisions that appear unrelated. Most industries have a large collection of companies of different scale and with radically different organizations. For one example, at the time Henry Ford was producing the Model T in a completely integrated way, with Ford iron ore being carried in Ford ships to the Ford steel mill, and so on, another prosperous company in England, Singer, was producing a small number of cars per year and was purchasing almost all its components. Both companies flourished in a highly competitive industrial environment.

Other examples can be found in the retailing business, where all sorts of different-sized enterprises can be seen with all sorts of different internal structures. Some businesses have pronounced economies of scale, and the total market is small enough so that it is difficult for a large number of different organizations to operate, but this is far from typical.[1] Most companies that do not have government protection suffer from at least some competition. Indeed, the *Journal of Economic Perspectives* offers as a constant that the

1. I am personally involved in one that produces a rather specialized but very good cleaning fluid. The particular portion of our company that manufactures this product has four employees and currently fills more than 80 percent of the nation's demand. It is unlikely that anybody will be able to undercut, because almost of necessity they would have to start out on an even smaller scale.

proportion of manufacturing industries in which the four largest firms accounted for more than 50 percent of output is roughly one-third.[2]

The puzzle of exactly why we have large, highly diversified organizations, other than because of historic development, is a difficult one, particularly in the market where there are strong pressures for efficiency. In government, the pressures for efficiency are modest; hence, we would not be surprised to find organizations that are radically inefficient in size.

The best explanation for these large organizations—and one that I offer with considerable caution, partly because it did not originate with me but also because it is not a widely approved position—is that only a relatively few people have specialized talents such that higher executive positions are safely entrusted to them. The first example of this has to do with merchandising skill, whether we are thinking of selling aircraft to major airlines or movies to customers whose average mental age is fourteen. In both industries, it is important to guess whether the commodity will sell before large sums of money have been spent on design or construction.

It is probably even more important in percentage terms in retailing organizations. After all, they do not spend much on permanent capital compared with, say, an airplane industry which, if it starts work on designing a new transport plane, must devote several years and immense amounts of engineering skill to producing just the preliminary model.

Should McDonald's put considerable emphasis on Ronald McDonald? Should they have small playgrounds outside their restaurants? Should they have fixed menus or allow individual preferences for their hamburgers as Burger King does? Apparently such decisions are very difficult, and only a few people are highly skilled in making them.

If this is so, then centralization in large organizations that make use of these rare talents—talents that command high returns—is a sensible arrangement. If you can minimize the bureaucratic size of the structure while still centralizing this kind of control through a franchise system, that is also sensible. Most of the monster supermarket chains are, however, centralized from top to bottom. Many of them even manufacture some products on their own.

2. Julian L. Simon, "Great and Almost Great Magnitudes in Economics," *Journal of Economic Perspectives* 4 (Winter 1990), 149–56, esp. 154. To add a constant of my own, the proportion of manufacturing industries where one firm produces 100 percent of the output is roughly zero.

The rather mysterious talents which, when they are missing as they were in Grant's or in Montgomery Ward, lead to collapse, and when they are present as in Sears Roebuck and in J. C. Penney, lead to great expansion, are probably not only rare but also hard to detect. Perhaps many people are as good as or better than the current managers, but there is no way of finding out except to put them at the head of one of these monsters and see how well they do.

Merchandising talent is not the only specialized talent that people at the top require. That rather mysterious entity called administrative ability is also necessary. In many cases, creativity, in the sense of knowledge of what can be done by new technologies and ordering it done, is vital. Most large organizations have elaborate research facilities, but they devote more attention to implementing ideas that come from the sales force or management than to inventing ideas of their own.

All this is an effort to solve a difficult puzzle. What we actually observe is a society of many different sizes of organizations ranging from the individual at one end to the Roman Catholic Church at the other.

Since the time of Adam Smith, it has been part of our culture to make great gains for ourselves by cooperation with our fellow man. Certainly since the Old Stone Age it has been known that we can make great gains for ourselves by competition with our fellow man in a direct and destructive sense. It has also been known since before Adam Smith that competition in a constructive sense is helpful. A partial problem is to get all three aspects into their proper scope and make use of them.

The destructive type of competition we attempt to eliminate by use of police and law. It does not follow that we have succeeded, and indeed the resources put into both police forces and legal activities are considerable in the United States. This cost is borne to prevent a loss, not to make a gain.

When we turn away from the problem of preventing murder, fraud, and theft and face the more constructive part of our activity, we observe again a large number of hierarchical organizations, some big, some small, which react with each other in manners that are partially competitive and partially cooperative.

It is our custom, and one that has been followed in this book, to divide these hierarchies into the governmental hierarchies and the market hierarchies. As a matter of fact, there are many hierarchies that are neither governmental nor market—I just mentioned the Roman Catholic Church—but they have been little discussed here, mainly because I do not understand them.

There is also another immensely important organization in our society, although I do not know whether it should be called a hierarchy. This is the family. Families come in many different forms, from the narrow nuclear family of the Western tradition to the extended family of the East. At least in the United States, families are now undergoing rapid transition. That is the extent of my discussion of them in this book.

In regard to governmental and market hierarchies, I would like to repeat something I have said several times, which is that "sociologically, they are all the same." This does not mean that they are similar in other respects. In the simple market portion of society, most of the people most of the time devote most of their attention to maximizing profit. The accounts are also not a bad way of measuring the degree to which at least some of the inferiors in a large hierarchy are achieving that goal. They are thus subject to continuous pressure for efficiency.

In government hierarchies there is also some pressure for efficiency. Unfortunately, it is not nearly as strong. Indeed, from time to time we set up special committees to look at the government, and they invariably find large inefficiencies. Quite frequently, however, the specific recommendations of these commissions are also inefficient. Nobody has millions of dollars riding on making the best decision. Note here that efficiency has a narrow technical definition. The Gulag seems to have been internally efficient.

On a more prosaic level, it is rare for a company to be in a situation where its profits can be increased by somewhat deceptive advertising or by economizing on safety devices or something similar. Here we have a kind of destructive interaction that we would like to have the police and courts prevent. Unfortunately, the police and courts themselves are not very efficient in this area. Furthermore, the police and courts may inflict great cost by preventing the development of new ideas. There has been an immense reduction in the rate in which new and improved medicines are produced. This was caused partly by the U.S. Food and Drug Administration (FDA), which has imposed criteria on new medicine that, first, makes development of new medicine immensely more expensive than it was before and thus reduces potential profits from research; second, it imposes delays on the use of new medicines. Indeed, it seems quite probable that the FDA is right up with Pol Pot in the number of unnecessary deaths it has caused.

The FDA's problem is difficult. Companies are motivated to produce new drugs (leaving aside possible legal damage claims) as quickly as possible, and some of the new drugs will no doubt turn out to be dangerous. On the other hand, the delay in introducing them is dangerous. The FDA has chosen to emphasize the danger of the new drugs and ignore the danger of delay. Hence, it has produced a completely unbalanced scheme which, to repeat, has probably caused many unnecessary deaths.[3]

Another problem has been the development of tort liability for new drugs. This has literally led to bankruptcy for several drug manufacturing companies; others have decided it is just too dangerous to experiment in some areas. A new drug introduced for some disease may, after a considerable period of time, have secondary consequences that were not discoverable at the time it was introduced. Judges and juries have turned out to be extremely generous in damage payments in such cases, and, of course, the drug company is not able to go to the people who are not damaged and to collect the value of their benefit from the drug; therefore drugs that are socially desirable may not be produced because of these potential damages.

The point of my digression is that the interaction between different types of agencies, hierarchies, and individuals is frequently complex. What we want are designs of hierarchies that work well not only internally but also in their interaction with others.

To repeat the philosophy outlined earlier, we have a society in which there are many individuals who can gain a great deal from cooperation and who also gain from predation on others. They can also suffer if they are victims of predation. Furthermore, it is fairly easy to demonstrate that the predator-victim relationship injures the victim more than it benefits the predator. Thus the cooperative relationship is the one we prefer. Its form is various, but we can divide it roughly into two categories: purchase and sale, and hierarchical interrelation. Any good society will have a mix of both categories.

This book has been mainly concerned with the hierarchical structure, but I must emphasize that the hierarchies are engaged in market-type interactions that highly influence each other. Some of these hierarchies are governments rather than private companies, and in such cases, the market reaction tends to have much weaker controls. Indeed, such relationships can easily slip into the predator-victim type organization.

3. See Sam Peltzman, Review of *Innovation in the Pharmaceutical Industry* (by David Schwartzman), *Journal of Economic Literature* 16 (1978), 149–50. Also William M. Wardell, "Economic or Medical Criteria, or Both, in Policy Decisions about Medicines?" *Journal of Health Economics* 2, no. 3 (1983), 275–79.

With hierarchies, however, there are immense numbers of different organizations in the world. No doubt part of the variance results from history rather than present-day developments, particularly with governmental hierarchies. In the market, however, a hierarchy must be efficient to survive; hence, when we find a number of radically different designs of hierarchy all apparently surviving, we have a puzzle.

This situation is, of course, what we observe in the real world. To repeat an example used earlier, retailing is sometimes carried out by individual stores purchasing through wholesalers, and so on; sometimes by big centralized organizations like Safeway, sometimes by a sort of combination which we call franchising, and sometimes by the kind of thing that is represented by Ace Hardware which I have called reverse franchising. Nor is this a complete list of all the different ways these organizations can be set up.

To repeat, the existence of this vast number of different organizations presents a puzzle. The simple solution is that organizational form does not matter very much. If this is true, there are a considerable number of professors in business and public administration who should be encouraged to seek out more constructive activity. On the assumption that it is not true, there is an alternative explanation, which is that certain details of the various problems met by these organizations dictate one particular structural form as most efficient. That seems to me the most likely explanation, but as the reader has discovered, I have been unable to put my finger on those detailed reasons.

It is fairly easy to invent a story as to why any particular structure we observe is efficient. I have returned repeatedly to the explanation for General Motors buying Fisher Body, which is the monopoly/monopsony explanation. Certainly, this is a very important part of the explanation; however, we have to explain why General Motors did not buy its principal supplier of frames. The monopoly/monopsony relationship was there, too. Perhaps there is something special about bodies that does not apply to frames, but I cannot say that I have found it.

After our survey of hierarchical forms, we can say a great deal about the way to run them most efficiently. As stated in the last chapter, the use of incentives, and well-functioning incentives, is important. The basic structure, however, remains a puzzle.

Having frankly confessed that I am puzzled by this, I could put this manuscript in a drawer and hope that in another twenty years of thought I might solve it. Since I am sixty-nine, however, that does not seem feasible. The alternative is to present the problem to my readers and hope that they will solve it, preferably in less than twenty years. Ellery Queen mysteries contain a challenge to the reader. I am following that precedent. Can you produce an explanation for these manifold different organizational forms? If you can, you should become both wealthy and famous. You would also confer a great benefit on society. With all of those incentives, surely you will try.

INDEX

References to bibliographic information appear in italics.

The typeface used for the text of this book is Galliard, an old-style face designed by Matthew Carter in 1978, in the spirit of a sixteenth-century French typeface of Robert Granjon. The display type is Meta Book, a variant of Meta, designed by Erik Spiekermann in the 1990s.

This book is printed on paper that is acid-free and meets the requirements of the American National Standard for Permanence of Paper for Printed Library Materials, z39.48–1992. ♾

Book design by Richard Hendel, Chapel Hill, North Carolina
Typography by G&S Typesetters, Inc., Austin, Texas
Printed and bound by Edwards Brothers, Inc., Ann Arbor, Michigan